❖ IRISH FOLKTALES

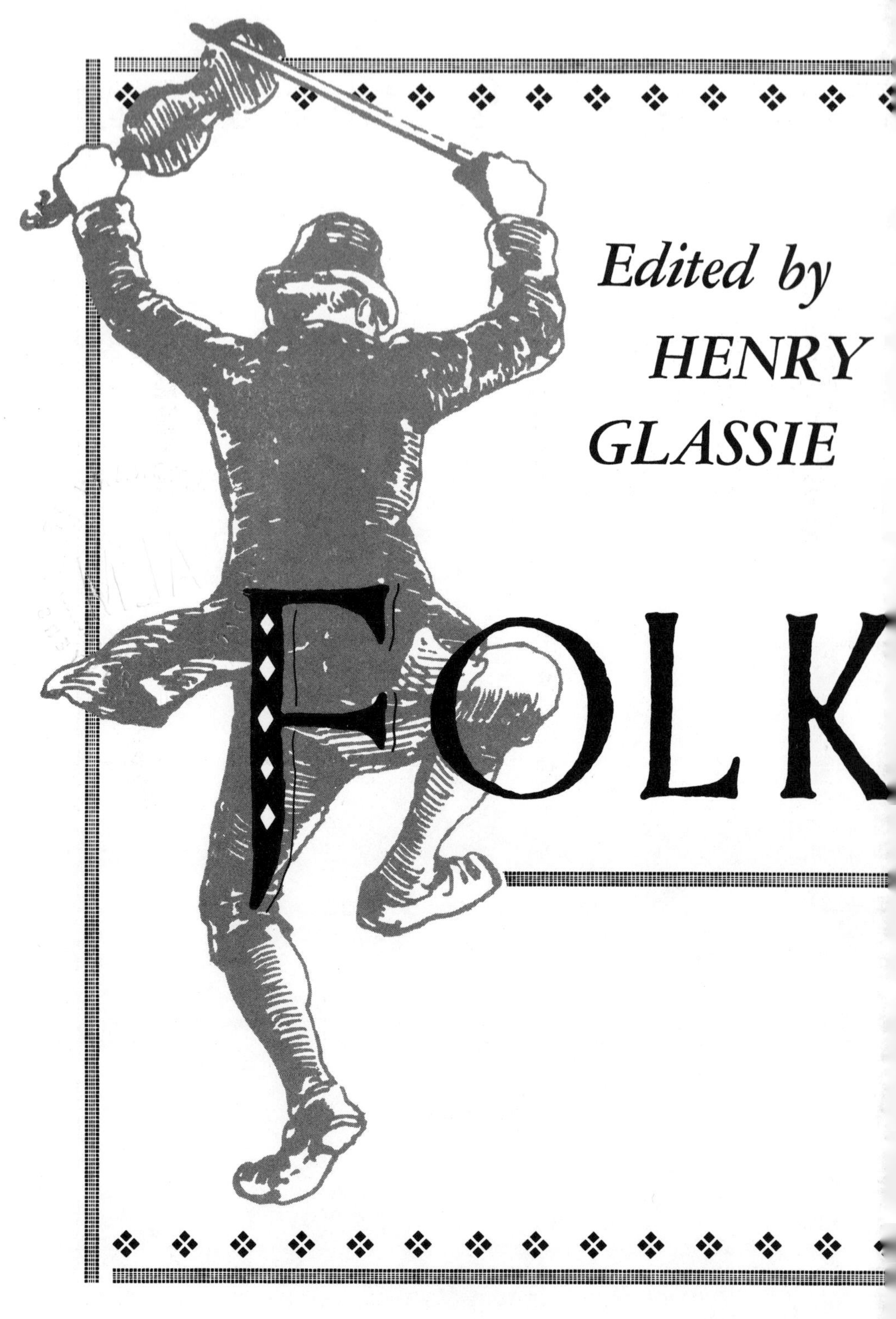

Edited by
HENRY GLASSIE

FOLK

IRISH TALES

Pantheon Books
New York

Published in the United States by Pantheon Books, a division of Random House, Inc., New York, and simultaneously in Canada by Random House of Canada Limited, Toronto.

Library of Congress Cataloging-in-Publication Data

Main entry under title:
Irish folktales.

Bibliography: p.
1. Tales—Ireland. 2. Legends—Ireland.
I. Glassie, Henry H.
GR153.3.I75 1985 398.2'09415 85-42841
ISBN 0-394-53224-4

Since this page cannot legibly accommodate all permissions acknowledgments, they appear following page 353.

Manufactured in the United States of America
First Edition

BOOK DESIGN BY FRANCINE KASS

❖ For Polly, Harry, Lydia, and Ellen Adair

❖ CONTENTS

WITS AND POETS

TALL TALES

OUTWITTING THE DEVIL

MYSTERY

DEATH AND TOKENS

GHOSTS

AWAY

ENCOUNTERS WITH FAIRIES

FAIRY TRAITS AND TREASURE

STRANGE SOUNDS AND VISIONS OF WAR

HISTORY

ANCIENT DAYS

WAR

RAPPAREES

LATER DAYS

FIRESIDE TALES

❖ PREFACE

Good Patrick of Macha stood at the end of his mission. He had built seven hundred churches and ordained three thousand priests. Ireland was a Christian land, free of stone idols, specters, and snakes. Before him stood Oisin, the last of the Fenian warriors, bent, broken, old. Saint Patrick bade him relate the ancient tales, the tales of Ireland's men and women, mountains and rivers. Brogan, Patrick's scribe, took them down in the thousands. Then Patrick recoiled from the pleasure he took in pagan things. He poured forth his worry to his guardian angels. Fear not, they told him, listen to the tales, record them in the very words of their tellers, for they will prove a delight to good people until the end of time.

Then Vikings came upon the sea, tore at Ireland's coasts, and ripped into the interior. But the monks kept to Patrick's command, teaching the faith, spreading the Good News into foreign lands, and copying the elder tales into great hide-bound books. Perhaps they were the deceptions of demons, the figments of fools, but still the pious men wrote them down as they found them and added the epics of their own heroes, of Patrick and Brigit and Columcille.

In the twelfth century, the Norman Conquest crossed the Irish Sea. But soon the invaders were speaking the sweet Gaelic, and the work of the monks went on. The Fenian warriors still raged in ink, the legends of Patrick and Columcille found their final form. And then, the long invasion reached its end. The chiefs of Ulster tasted death, the last earls flew to Europe, and new men began to crowd the North. At the beginning of the seventeenth century, Erin lay beaten. Her tradition drifted toward peril.

Beneath clouds of defeat, Irish scholars set to work. The Four Masters gathered in the North, assembled the old manuscripts, and compiled the Irish annals, filled with warfare and wonders and the misdeeds of kings. In the South, a solitary priest, banished for his denunciation of a high lady's sin, traveled the chilly lanes with precious papers rolled in his breast, seeking warm hearths where he could write. The history Geoffrey Keating wrote on the road confuses historians who want only the facts, for Keating labored to save the whole of the past, its facts and its fancy. Both, he knew, contained the tale of Ireland.

As invasion consolidated in political rule and political rule tightened, Keating's countrymen passed his manuscript along, the old people of Ireland continued to gather around their tellers of tale, and indomitable Ireland conquered her conquerors once more. Patrick, son of Britain, citizen of Rome, in his day, and Geoffrey Keating, descendant of the first English invaders, in his, had preserved the stories of Ireland. In the nineteenth century, people of the new faith, with names like Croker and Hyde, took up the old task and wrote down the Irish tale until a new nation, formed out of rebellion, could establish a commission for the preservation of the Irish tradition.

What right have I, an American folklorist, to break into this history by collecting the Irish tales recorded during the last century and a half into a new anthology? It is not because many of my ancestors abandoned Ireland, and it is certainly not because American scholars possess a special right to pillage the Irish cultural treasury. Indeed, I am embarrassed to be part of today's invasion that sends stupid films and disrespectful social scientists out of America into Ireland. My right comes of my friendship with Hugh Nolan. Mr. Nolan was the great storyteller of the community in County Fermanagh, Northern Ireland, that I have visited regularly since 1972. He and Ellen Cutler, Peter and Joseph Flanagan, Michael Boyle, Rose and Joe Murphy, Hugh Patrick Owens, and their neighbors, opened their homes to me, gave me their tales, and drew me into their lives. My littlest daughter is named for Ellen Cutler. I have published three books about them. Our friendship remains unshaken. I add a fourth.

My right to create this book, I repeat, is owed to my love for Hugh Nolan, but without the support of others in Fermanagh—Joan Trimble, Helen Hickey, Jim Nawn, P. J. O'Hare, Bryan Gallagher—I would not continue, and without help from Ireland's scholars I could not continue. In Dublin, Sean O'Sullivan and Kevin Danaher, Séamas Ó Catháin and Bo Almqvist, offered advice and aid. In Belfast, E. Estyn Evans, George Thompson, and Alan Gailey provided hospitality and direction. Fred Kniffen first introduced me to Estyn Evans when I was an undergraduate. Fred Kniffen remains my great teacher, and I am honored to call Professor Evans my master. His books attracted me to Ireland. His kind interest in my effort has restored me and kept me happily at work.

In America I have been fortunate to teach in two of my nation's major folklore programs, the Folklore Institute of Indiana University and the Department of Folklore and Folklife of the University of Pennsylvania. Both schools blessed me with generous colleagues. From my American community of scholars I have drawn constant inspiration. These must be thanked: Roger Abrahams, Robert Plant Armstrong, Ilhan Başgöz, Dan Ben-Amos, Sacvan Bercovitch, Tom Burns, Jan Brunvand, John Burrison,

Tristram Coffin, Cece Conway, Lewis Dabney, Jim Deetz, Linda Dégh, Richard M. Dorson, James Marston Fitch, Kenneth Goldstein, Bill Hansen, Lee Haring, Dell Hymes, Sandy Ives, Alan Jabbour, Chaz Joyner, Billy Lightfoot, John McGuigan, Rusty Marshall, Mick Moloney, Elliott Oring, Barry Lee Pearson, Phil Peek, Jerry Pocius, Ralph Rinzler, Warren Roberts, Peter Seitel, Brian Sutton-Smith, John Szwed, Dell Upton, John Vlach, Don Yoder, Wilbur Zelinsky, Terry Zug.

I could not have taken on this task were I not a collector of books about Ireland. This pleasant madness, which struck when I was a high school student and began with a copy of *Two Tales of Shem and Shaun,* has indebted me to antiquarian bookmen on both sides of the Atlantic. My thanks to my favorite shop, William H. Allen of Philadelphia, will stand for them all. This book would not be had I not received funds for my first trip to Ireland from the John Simon Guggenheim Memorial Foundation. Eric Montgomery and Bob Oliver engineered subsequent trips. I would not have been able to finish this book had not my friends Thomas Ehrlich and Dell Hymes of the University of Pennsylvania conspired to find me a place to write in peace.

The writing of books, like any good craft, comes as much from friendship as it does from the monster that coils within. As I worked, the friendship that I gained with Dan Cullen of Pantheon Books made the whole project worth it. And as I worked, I relied on my father and mother and on the friends gathered around me: Dell and Ginny, Kenny and Rochelle, John and Nan, Barry and Missy, Tom and Inger, Agop, George and Christobel. My love, Kathleen, always forgave me the time I burned up in this obsession. She helped keep my prose clean and lifted my heart. The children helped by distracting me from my work to my life.

At last, I am grieved for the loss of friends, for Hugh Nolan, Ellen Cutler, Michael Boyle, Paddy and Mary McBrien, James Owens, and Rose Murphy, and for Dick Dorson, Erving Goffman, and Bob Armstrong. But I give this book in happiness to the next generation, to my children, Polly, Harry, Lydia, and Ellen Adair.

❖ Irish Folktales

INTRODUCTION

DEVENISH ISLAND, LOWER LOUGH ERNE, COUNTY FERMANAGH
Mr. and Mrs. S. C. Hall, *Ireland*, 1850

AT THE END OF A SHORT WINTER'S DAY

Night falls, winds rise. The door is shut, the curtain drawn. A lamp sputters, shooting shadows up the wall, and the houses of the hills close in upon themselves, abandoning the world to darkness. Pure darkness welcomes the winds that skim off the ocean, roll over the mountains, and fall upon the hills to pound the home. Roof timbers groan and hold. The winds crash among the trees.

Low clouds cover the moon, and the road before me runs swiftly into emptiness. Beyond the black hedges there are houses I know, but they send no warming sign of habitation, no hum, no glow. Only the feel of the road, hard beneath my feet, and the quick repetition of steps assure me that I am moving correctly. The road turns under me, and I comply, it turns again familiarly and, pressed eastward by the wind, I walk, nearly run, until a pale rectangle forms by the roadside. I feel into the darkness for the latch, turn once more, and am greeted with my name as I gain my seat by the hearth. "A bad night," my host says, turning his face back into the small fire at our feet. I agree. "The worst," he says.

Night holds the corners and rises to the roof. A candle in a brass stick shapes a small circle of faint light on the table beside us. The fire low in the throat of the chimney touches with pink the faces of the men packed around it. There is Young Tom, with the collar of his coat turned up to shelter his ears, hunched beside me. Johnny huddles across the fire from the old man who makes his home in these two cold rooms. Johnny has come tonight, as Tom and I have come, walking the black lanes because winter nights are long and the man of this house, Hugh Nolan, is brilliant.

When Hugh Nolan was a child, this house, built by his grandfather's hands, was known as a ceili (kay-lee) house, a place for the neighbors to gather, and now they gather still, knowing that others will also seek a place at his hearth in hopes that his wit will help them pass the night safely. They call him eccentric, a bent old man in a long black coat who lives alone with his cats in his smoke-dark house, and they call him a saint. They have watched him pedal his bike to Mass, they speak of his plain blameless way and do not know that he sends the little money he gets to support a convent in England. They name him "historian." His memory is vast, the past is impeccably ordered within it, and he settles disputes among his neighbors over boundaries and rights of way across fields. His pleasure in youth, he says, came from listening to the old people talking, and his delight in old age, he says, is keeping the truth and telling the whole tale. In this small community, built upon damp hills in the North of Ireland, Hugh Nolan is the oldest man. He was born in 1896. For sixty-five years he served the earth, and now he works for the people who come to ceili with him. They call him a "star." He is the man who can reach into a dreary conversation, find a thread of silver, and spin it into a yarn that deadens time and enlivens the senses.

The body is beaten with work. The soul is numb. The company is the same. They have given all they have on nights long in the past. There is no worthwhile news, so Johnny tries again, repeating Hugh Nolan's words. The night is a bad one. Aye, the worst. We are in agreement. "Well, we have to take what comes," Johnny says. "We can't change it." Wearily Mr. Nolan replies, "Oh, aye." There is the trouble. They know each other too well. Three decades separate Tom and Johnny, and nearly three more separate Johnny and Hugh, but their experience has been too similar. They cut turf in the spring, dig spuds in the fall. They have followed the cows into the sloughs and gotten drunk together in the town. Conversations too quickly find the old ruts and sail too swiftly to first principles so perfectly framed in words that there is no knowing whether they erupt from the depths or ride on the surface. So the ceiliers come and they sit and they wait, crying inwardly for someone gifted with wit to build a story in the place that lies between inescapable daily realities and inescapable philosophical propositions.

Young Tom takes out a pack of cigarettes and offers them around. Johnny reaches out to light us. Mr. Nolan cracks a match and sucks its flame into the remains at the bottom of his pipe. Smoking together, we watch the fire. A turf fire does not flare and snap. It smolders, rolling into itself, providing a spectacle that is only about as engaging as a television set. For a while the mind follows the eye through the transformations of color into the red-gold heart of the fire, discovering tiny flecks of blue and green and curls of rosy smoke that rise past black iron pothooks and crooks into the soot-choked gullet of the chimney. The mind needs more, and it wanders, and when it wanders here, among farmers poor in the things of the world, they worry because, they say, if you think you will become sad, for life is short and death is long, and if sadness grips you it will drag you toward despair, a state in which you are of no use to your neighbor or yourself, in which you forget God's special love for you. In silent contemplation, in brooding, you drop toward damnation. You must, at all costs, avoid thinking. Your hard life has already taught you the truths philosophers seek, so you rise and go upon the roads, no matter the cold and the dark, and you gather someplace where others will help you keep your mind off the pains in your joints and the damned old cows and the muck and the winds and the rains and the terrors that visit in silence, someplace where you can help others remain alive to life. We watch the fire and we are not silent. It is just that the topics we try, the usual topics of the health of the neighbors and the prices of cattle and the bombs in the towns, all fail. None is collectively lifted toward entertainment. "Entertainment" is their word for good conversation, for music and dance, for food, for all that brings immediate pleasure and carries one forward.

A clock ticks out of the darkness behind us. Hugh Nolan shoves his chair back and makes his way along old routes over the clay of the floor, between the sharp edges of furniture, and returns, dropping turf on the fire and splashing it with oil. For an instant it blazes, bathing our faces in heat, then it settles again into its slow consuming of itself. Mr. Nolan tells us that the radio predicted frost, but, he reminds us, it has been a good year. The crop was bountiful, the cattle are fat. We agree.

A click of the latch announces another ceilier. "Well, men," a voice says. "How's Packie?" Hugh Nolan asks. "The best," replies Johnny's brother, squeezing between Tom and me on the wooden thing Mr. Nolan uses for a bed. He bends forward, opening his palms to the fire, and tells us that the radio predicted frost. This news raises its chorus of agreement, then the chat sinks and shreds. The clock ticks. Shoulder to shoulder, knee to knee, we crowd around the fire. The white cat is purring in my lap. Packie is whistling snatches of old reels under his breath. Outside the winds creak in the hedges and rattle the bones of the trees, while we hold to the topic of weather, not a trite topic for farming people whose well-being depends on the climate, whose work is conducted outdoors, whose houses do not allow them to forget. Inside and outside, it is cold and dark. The wind pops the tin of the roof, demanding that we speak of the weather. "There would not be weather the like of this now in America," Johnny says, asking. The question is courteously indirect. I am not made to perform, and months ago I would not have been forced, however obliquely, to entertain the company, but I am no longer a stranger, so I describe cold weather in America and am led to tell what I know of Iceland, drawn from the sagas and William Morris' diary of his travels. A little time passes, and the hearth's small flame shows Hugh Nolan to be at work in the enormity of his memory. A light gleams in the shadows beneath his cap.

The wind, rising and falling and pounding with the rhythms of the ocean, blows great winds into the mind and great winds carry tales. A shy smile breaks in the shadows, and I expect, and I imagine others expect, to hear again of John Brodison, one of the wits of Hugh's youth, who told of the night so windy that he saw a haystack with a man clinging to its side blown down the road past the chapel. Instead, he reminds us of George Armstrong. All of us know him from stories Mr. Nolan has used in the past to pass the time. Armstrong emigrated to Australia, but, while others prosper abroad and return only to mock the penury of those who remain, Armstrong returned impoverished and so shriveled from cholera that his mother kept him in a wee basket at the hearth. But this was later. George had recovered and he was living in a small house at the Church of Ireland Rectory. We know the spot, at Bellanaleck, a few miles distant. The Orange Hall stands there and an old gray church and the store where people go to buy life's little necessities. It was wet, this day in the past, and the men who had come to cut timber were driven for shelter into George's house. The picture forms in our minds. Aye, we understand.

"And it wasn't very long till the rector come in." It makes sense that the Protestant rector, escaping the storm and seeking entertainment, would join the workers in George's home, for George Armstrong was a great star. He glittered against the darkness around him. Mr. Nolan continues:

"So they joined to talk about storms and about—ye'd often hear tell of the windy night of eighteen and thirty-nine. It done a lot of damage in Ireland that night.

"So the rector says, I heared a lot about the damage that was done, the windy night, but some way or another, he says, I think that a lot of it wasn't the case. Because if a storm was traveling at the rate it was traveling, it would have swept a little country like Ireland away altogether."

The rector's bid, his witty comment, sends a little laugh around the hearth, but we know Armstrong is the star, so we do not delay but hasten Mr. Nolan with yes and aye to hear George's retort.

"Ah now, says George, wait'll I tell ye, your reverence.

"John MacManus, he says, had a pup in a barrel at the end of the house.

"And the pup was blew out of the barrel and it was blew in through a window at Lisbellaw."

Now we can laugh. Lisbellaw lies east of Bellanaleck, across the width of Lough Erne. We continue laughing, more because it feels good than because the story was good, more to join together than to take pleasure from the small farmer's victory in a match of wit. Hugh Nolan is free to laugh with us, for his story was not focused upon himself. He is a historian, the curator and donor of the wealth of the past. "Oh now," he says laughing, cracking another match. He has reminded his neighbors of the genius of a man like themselves. He puffs and chuckles, and we shift as one, smiling, while Mr. Nolan tells us that Armstrong told the rector about his sister who had emigrated to America. As the next story begins, we remove our eyes from him and return them into the ashes, leaving him alone in the vaults of his mind, and, while he shapes thoughts into words, we fill the tiny pauses that follow each line of his tale with quick, quiet encouragement—"Aye," "Man dear," "That's a sight"—urging him forward and helping him locate the proper pace of narration.

"She went to America when she was a young girl." Mr. Nolan's pipe is nested in his great fists. He is looking, as we are looking, into the fire. "Aye," some one of us says. Many have gone away to America. "Aye, indeed."

"And she kept writing to the mother continually.

"And she was always planning to come home. But she never came.

"And still the letters came from her.

"But anyhow, there was a twelve weeks' frost. And the Atlantic Ocean, it froze, the whole way over till America.

"So, she had heard tell of people coming and going on the ice.

"And she thought that she'd try it herself, and that she'd go home to see the *mother*.

"And she had a bicycle.

"And she came out on Boston Street at nine o'clock in the morning.

"And she went to get on the bicycle. And the bicycle slipped and she fell on the street.

"There come a policeman along, and he lifted the bicycle, and he came to where she was standing.

"And he threw his arm around her, and he left her sitting on the saddle.

"He says, You go on now.

"So she left Boston at nine o'clock.

"And she was at Bellanaleck Cross at half three in the evening."

Together we laugh and congratulate Hugh Nolan. The storyteller's goal is not verbal trickery but clarity, the smooth, precise, spare realization of a concept in words. He was wholly successful, the master of his gift, and the deep light burns in his eyes. "Well," he says, "George told that to the rector anyway." We imagine the rector's amusement, and it adds to our own. Hugh says, "George says to him, she was the first for to introduce a bicycle into this country." These farmers who ride black bikes through a world arranged for the convenience of automobiles get one last little laugh.

We are warm now. Hours remain before we part, moving over the lanes to our separate homes, and nothing else happens. But Mr. Nolan's story was enough. Not much, ten minutes out of six hours, but it was enough so that tomorrow, when we meet on the road and turn our backs to the wet winds for a trade of cigarettes and matches, we can call the night before a good one.

CONNECTIONS

When one old star on a bad cold night told the men gathered around him of another old star on a bad wet day who entertained the men around him by whipping the weather into a joke, he made two connections simultaneously and gracefully. One is the connection linking the teller of the tale with the source of the tale. The other is the connection linking the teller and the members of his audience. Hugh Nolan knew and admired George Armstrong, and he kept faith with the past through the accurate and artful restatement of the dead man's tale. He knew the men at his hearth, and he gave them something that would amuse them in the moment and carry them forward with a memory worth having. In preserving the artistic tradition he shared with a man of the past while communicating with the men of the present, Hugh Nolan asserted himself into time, bundling up the past to make it a gift to the future, and he positioned himself responsibly within society by pulling the people of his place into deeper association. To unify time and society—tradition and communication—in a narrative is to tell a folktale.

When an outsider, like myself, intrudes and claims a relationship to a tale by freezing the social arrangements of the instant into a text in ink, the unity that the storyteller achieves breaks apart, space opens, and problems arise. Hugh Nolan could answer the call of his personal muse and meet the obligations he owed history by repeating George Armstrong's story. His art and Armstrong's shared genre and style. But the aesthetic conventions and creative urges of the writer who retells folktales do not necessarily converge with those of the storyteller. Hugh Nolan knew his audience; their values ran toward oneness. He knew which ideas of significance would engage and aid the men around him, and he found those ideas in a story already set in his mind. But the ideas that move writers and their audiences do not necessarily mesh with the values built into the stories that writers discover and then attempt to re-create on the page. While striving to do anew what the storyteller has already done, connecting to a source and an audience while weaving a text, the writer meets and solves new problems.

Problems do not lie in the mere presence of an outsider. It is not strange to find a stranger at the hospitable hearth. The rector was an outsider at George Armstrong's. I was an outsider at Hugh Nolan's. But we did not retard, we probably encouraged, the storyteller's art. Problems arise when the tale that brought its teller, his source, and his audience together is relocated in a new literary context. Then dislocations appear as a result of the distance that opens between the writer and the storyteller, and confusions arise from the different motives that writers and storytellers have for telling their tales to others.

All printed texts of folktales are compromises between the written and the spoken word, between writers and storytellers. To understand the Irish folktales that we can read, let us consider together two relationships and the questions they entail. First is the relationship of the narrator and the source, the connection of tradition in which the question is: how do we approach and treat seriously the art of another? Second is the relationship of the narrator and the audience, the connection of communication in which the question is: why has the tale been preserved and told again?

TRADITION

At the beginning of the modern study of the Irish folktale stands a sprightly serious man, T. Crofton Croker. Descended from Elizabethan English settlers of Cork, and the son of a British army officer, Croker was born in the year of the Rising of 1798. He left Ireland at the age of twenty and in 1850 retired from his position as a senior clerk of the first class of the Admiralty in London. He was a dutiful civil servant and he was an artist, friend of the painter Maclise, husband to the daughter of the English watercolorist Francis Nicholson, and he was a writer, correspondent of Thomas Moore and Sir Walter Scott, who surrounded himself in England with authors who knew his native Ireland, the novelist Maria Edgeworth, the poet F. S. Mahony, the antiquarian Thomas Wright, the travelers Mr. and Mrs. S. C. Hall. Thomas Crofton Croker claims our attention because, as Richard Dorson writes in *The British Folklorists,* he was the first person in the English-speaking world who set out to collect and publish the texts of folktales. Croker called his pursuit a "sport." He wrote of "hunting up and bagging all the old 'grey superstitions.' "

In Croker's day it was not unusual for ladies and gentlemen to delight in antiquarian hobbies. Croker was not alone in recording the details of fallen gravestones and ruined churches, but when he was only fourteen he discovered for himself that "ancient and decaying" antiquities not only lay upon the Irish earth, they lived, if only dimly, in the minds of elderly people. From 1812 to 1815 he traveled Ireland, and later he returned from England, adventuring "in caves and out of caves, upon hill-tops, with boot-makers and broguemakers, with smugglers and coastguard-men, with magistrates and murderers, with pilgrims and pedlars" to build his monument, his admirable stack of books.

A natural gulf yawned between this Protestant gentleman and the people whose traditions called him. When he began to gather their art into his own, he possessed no ready genre, no convention to guide his effort. He tried different techniques. In his first great work, *Researches in the South of Ireland,* published in 1824, he alternates between two literary modes, the travel account and the antiquarian description. Neither of them suggested that he should present the beliefs he met upon the land as distinct texts. He plunged through the words of the people to pluck out conceptual essences. These he framed into generalizations that took historical significance from the comparisons he made between his findings and the words of the authors of olden times. In his landmark chapter, "Fairies and Supernatural Agency," he first informs his reader of the similarity of Irish and Scottish belief, and then, skirting the issue of ultimate origins, whether they lay in the East or in the North, he provides an account, running for twenty smooth pages, of the Irish fairy faith.

A century and a half later I would be told that the Iron Age raths, the "forths" that stand atop thousands of Irish hills, are fairy places, best to avoid. Croker put it succinctly in 1824:

"The circular intrenchments and barrows, known by the name of Danish forts, in Ireland, are pointed out as the abode of fairy communities, and to disturb their habitation, in other words to dig, or plough up a rath or fort, whose construction the superstitious natives ascribe to the labour and ingenuity of the 'good people,' is considered as unlucky and entailing some severe disaster on the violator and his kindred. An industrious peasant, who purchased a farm in the neighbourhood of Mallow, from a near relative of mine, commenced his improvements by building upon it a good stone house, together with a lime-kiln. Soon after, he waited on the proprietor, to state 'the trouble he was come to by reason of the old fort, the fairies not approving of his having placed the lime-kiln so near their dwelling;—he had lost his sow with nine *bonniveens* (sucking pigs), his horse fell into a quarry and was killed, and three of his sheep died, "all through the means of the fairies."' Though the lime-kiln had cost him five guineas, he declared he would never burn another stone in it, but take it down, without delay, and build one away from the fort, saying, he was wrong in putting that kiln in the way of the 'good people,' who were thus obliged to go out of their usual track. The back door of his house unfortunately also faced the same fort, but this offence was obviated by almost closing it up, leaving only a small hole at the top, to allow the good people free passage, should they require it. In these raths, fairies are represented as holding their festive meetings, and entering into all the fantastic and wanton mirth that music and glittering banquets are capable of inspiring."

Crofton Croker's topic was the whole of the land and its tradition, and it made sense for him in the sweep of his narrative to generalize from his experience and to quote sparingly. In our own day we find Irish custom and belief treated similarly in the magnificent books written by the geographer E. Estyn Evans. But as Croker worked, his focus tightened on the stories and songs of the country people. Our word "folklore" had not yet been invented, but Croker became a folklorist. He followed his first book with two series of *Fairy Legends,* 1825 and 1828, and one volume of *Popular Songs of Ireland* in 1839. Concentrating upon stories while compiling *Fairy Legends and Traditions of the South of Ireland,* Croker became obliged to present folktales as texts, ungeneralized and particular, but his own tradition offered him no genre of presentation. Though his books brought him fame and colleagues, he was nearly alone at first, and he had to invent some way to get oral stories into print. He tried two ways. Both not only survived through the successive editions of the *Fairy Legends,* both continued to be employed throughout the nineteenth century by Irish writers.

Croker developed one of his styles of folktale presentation from the literary genre of the sketch, in which a journalistic observation is shaped into a sparkling essay or amusing story. Sketching the folktale, Croker retold it in his own words, providing his reader with a piece of entertainment while establishing an artful tension between his diction and culture and those of his characters. Out of that tension a little humor arose.

The old teller of tale like Hugh Nolan brings his style and the style of his source into oneness. The writer of sketches shoves them apart, clarifying distinctions of style and class. What is most remarkable about Crofton Croker, standing there at the beginning, is that he felt no insecure need to make that distinction radical. He enjoys the ripple of his own prose, its light tone and learned allusions, but he restrains it, keeps it plain and direct, and when he quotes the country people he preserves their words without exaggerating them grotesquely. Other writers, though, pleasured in stretching the real social and cultural distance that lay between them and their subjects. Thomas Keightley, like Croker Irish and a founder of the discipline of folklore, carped that Croker had published stories that were his. Reclaiming his contribution during his global survey, *The Fairy Mythology* of 1828, Keightley gives us a tool to measure the distance between Croker and himself. Keightley begins his tale "The Leprechaun in the Garden" like this: "There's a sort o' people that every body must have met wid sumtime or another. I mane thim people that purtinds not to b'lieve in things that in their hearts they *do* b'lieve in, an' are mortially afeard o' too." Croker's "Seeing Is Believing" opens, "There's a sort of people whom every one must have met with some time or other; people that pretend to disbelieve what, in their hearts, they believe and are afraid of." The disbeliever is Felix O'Driscoll, who hears an old woman in a public house recount capturing a fairy who promises her wealth, but she turns her head for an instant and he is gone. "He slipped out o' my fingers," writes Keightley, "just as iv he was med o' fog or smoke, an' the sarra the fut he iver come nigh my garden agin." Croker's conclusion runs, "He slipped out of my hand just as if he was made of fog or smoke, and the sorrow the foot he ever came nigh my garden again."

There is an argument to be made for recording dialect, but misspelling little words serves science less than it serves the gentleman who wants to shake a cheap laugh out of his reader, and who, even more, wishes not to be confused with the people of the story.

Orthographic choices separate Croker and Keightley and likely signal differences in personality. Croker, though a gentleman, stepped toward the people. Though an exile in England, he remained connected to the Ireland of his birth and raising. Keightley denigrated Croker and Croker's folk and withdrew into erudite isolation. More deeply, however, Croker and Keightley were joined by a commitment to science. They spelled words differently but reported substantially the same text. No such commitment checked Samuel Lover. Born in Dublin a year before Croker, nine years after Keightley, Lover was an artist, a member of the Royal Hibernian Academy, who followed Croker closely with two series of *Legends and Stories of Ireland* and one book of *Songs of Ireland*. His sketches stretched into extravaganzas, their plots flung to wild extremes, their peasants set to kicking with preposterous result inside the English language.

At its most farcical limit, the sketch retains virtues. For one thing, when the gentleman elaborates upon folk belief and creates a comic fiction, he is not acting at variance with the country people who do the same thing. For another, the humorously sketched folktale was, as Samuel Lover makes clear, a popular upper-class oral genre, appropriate for after-dinner entertainment. While we may think of folktales as the sole possession of the unlettered and impecunious, all people tell stories, and the writers of sketches have preserved for us examples of the verbal art of the wealthy classes of times past. If our interest lies only in the country people and their art, then we will find the sketches containing kernels of traditional tale. Though the sketchers were tempted by demons of invention, Crofton Croker eliminated from his first edition tales of his own, and even Samuel Lover labels clearly the product of his own imagination. And in addition, while dressing stories up into sketches, the old authors sometimes provide us with information that modern folklorists have learned to cherish about the tellers, their personalities and occupations, and about the physical and social and conversational settings out of which stories emerge. So Samuel Lover does more than report a folktale he heard from one Paddy the Sport. He tells about Paddy, "a tall, loose-made, middle-aged man . . . fond of wearing an oil-skinned hat and a red waistcoat . . . , and an admirable hand at filling a game-bag or emptying a whisky-flask." Paddy was a "professed story-teller and a notorious liar" who "dealt largely in fairy tales and ghost stories," and we hear samples of his fare before Lover sets him in a gentleman's hall where his cleverness outstrips the rich people around him, winning him the right to tell a tale about a fox whose wit makes a man a fool. If Lover leaves us something, Croker bequeaths more, and the incidental detail with which he decorates his tales is as much to be treasured as the stories themselves, for it carries us into the presence of other people in other times.

Crofton Croker retold most of the stories that he included in the *Fairy Legends*, but the sketch was not his only experiment. His tale "The Crookened Back" begins with information on the teller, Peggy Barrett, who "like all experienced story-tellers, suited her tales, both in length and subject, to the audience and the occasion." A clear, uninterrupted text follows. Then "there was a pause," and Croker describes the varieties of reaction among the listeners, some who had heard the story, some who had not. That was no sketch but a model report of a folktale, and after "The Capture of Bridget Purcell," Croker notes, "This narrative was taken down verbatim from the lips of a poor cottager in the county Limerick, by Miss Maria Dickson, 22nd April, 1825."

So, there at the beginning, we find two distinct ways to get an orally delivered narrative onto the page. One was to remake it into a piece of prose in conformity with the reigning rules of literary art. The other was to record the text in the words of its own author, unaltered by the outsider, whose task was restricted to translating sounds into letters. From that time to the present, every writer of Irish folktales has had to decide whether to honor literary convention through reinvention or folk art through transcription.

In the days of Croker and Lover, one solution to the Irish writer's dilemma was devised by William Carleton. Glance over the sketches Carleton arranged into his immensely popular *Traits and Stories of the Irish Peasantry* of 1842 and you might be reminded of Samuel Lover, whose "unrivalled wit and irresistable drollery" Carleton admired, but probe more deeply and you will find his stories saturated with a strange darkness. Some seem affectionate, others mean, some funny, some somber. Carleton was not like those writers who could maintain their distance and their tone. They were born to be Protestant gentlemen, but he was born poor and Catholic, "a peasant's son" in rural Tyrone. He left the country for Dublin, converted to Protestantism, and confected out of his wide reading a literary style that enabled him to stand alongside the witty and wealthy, recomposing his memories into sketches filled with rural folk who speak and behave strangely. But Carleton's great heart ached. He protested that he had never been estranged from the people of his youth. His virtue, he wrote, was that he knew them, had danced and laughed and gotten drunk with them. His goal was serious, the defense and improvement of his people, so before he releases his readers into the *Traits and Stories*, he enjoins them to abandon their prejudices, and after his rollicking, painful tale was told, he added another book, *Tales and Stories of the Irish Peasantry*, in which he offers some of the tales again but narrated in a more straightforward manner, like Croker at his best. William Carleton provides two versions of the same tale. His solution was to construct for himself two contexts, one in which, through fiction, he answers the call of art, another in which, through essays, he answers the call of science. Nothing so neat, though, would suit William Carleton. He could not help but make the peoples' tales his own, for he and they were one in blood and earth. So he mounted the complicated literary apparatus he had mastered in Dublin and drove it into the heart of the tradition. At the end of *Tales and Stories*, Carleton, now learned, now prosperous, merges with his people once more, retelling an old folktale of a blacksmith who beats the Devil, and witnessing to the rural belief in ghosts, with all the literary might he could muster.

William Carleton is no man for easy schemes, yet his works yield three approaches to the folktale. In one, he utilizes the tale as a colorful element in a piece of his own in which the styles of the author and his characters, their diction and conduct, are set distinctly apart. The author, like Chaucer on the road to Canterbury, is an observer, amused, amazed, confused, offended. In another, Carleton takes the tale over and tells it again to suit a new audience, much as Shakespeare made old tales into new drama. The author becomes a storyteller, at one with the tradition. William Butler Yeats called William Carleton a "novelist" and a "storyteller" and a "historian," and the third of Carleton's approaches, the historian's, was to present the tale as a fact, worthy of preservation for the information it contains about people who are not the author. William Carleton, who was born in 1794 and who died in 1869, was an exact contemporary of Croker, Keightley, and Lover, and he epitomizes their period, the period of Thomas Moore, James Clarence Mangan, Gerald Griffin, and the first maturing of Irish literature in the English language. Carleton had two ways to make folklore into literature, the Chaucerian and the Shakespearean. At the same time, he was interested in folklore as it flourished in country places far removed from the drawing room and the office of the literary gazette. But Carleton was too close to the people, too bothered by his separation from them, to perfect his own solution to the problem of the relationship between the writer and the storyteller. That would wait until the nineteenth century was at an end. Then the perfection of Carleton's solution would become a fundamental principle of the movement that spun around William Butler Yeats and generated out of Ireland the greatest body of literature in the modern world.

"Folk art," wrote W. B. Yeats, closing *The Celtic Twilight*, "is, indeed, the oldest of the aristocracies of thought, and because it refuses what is passing and trivial, the merely clever and pretty, as certainly as the vulgar and insincere, and because it has gathered into itself the simplest and most unforgettable thoughts of the generations, it is the soil where all great art is rooted." So grandly did Yeats' own art flower from the tradition of his nation that when age began settling upon him, he was elected a senator of the new Irish Free State, and in the next year he was awarded the Nobel Prize for Literature. In Stockholm in 1923, addressing the Swedish Royal Academy, he said that when he received the Nobel medal, two others should have been standing beside him, "an old woman sinking into the infirmity of age, and a young man's ghost": Lady Augusta Gregory and John Millington Synge.

Together with Lady Gregory, Yeats had collected folktales. Each of them published clear texts, fresh from the lips of country people. Both built original works of art out of their experiences with the Irish tradition. But John Synge, because his life was brutally short, and because he was attracted both to science and art, provides us with the simplest case of the successful dynamic of their movement.

When Synge met Yeats in Paris in 1896, Yeats was the author of *The Wanderings of Oisin, The Countess Cathleen, The Land of Heart's Desire,* and *The Celtic Twilight.* He had edited a volume of Carleton's sketches and assembled two anthologies, *Fairy and Folk Tales of the Irish Peasantry* and *Irish Fairy Tales*, intermingling old texts from Croker, Lover, and Carleton with newly collected stories from Douglas Hyde. His career was more than begun. Synge, six years his junior, had published verse in the manner of Wordsworth, whom he admired for his clarity, but he had not yet found his voice. Still, there was much in Synge to appeal to Yeats. Like Lady Gregory he came of an old Irish Protestant family. In Irish matters, he was a nationalist. Politically, he was a socialist. He had read William Morris, who encouraged Yeats' early interest in folklore and efforts in poetry, and whom Yeats would always call "my chief of men." John Synge wandered alone in youth through the Wicklow hills, meeting the country people and becoming a serious naturalist. Contemplating Darwin in isolated terror, he denounced Christianity. In college at Trinity in Dublin, an interest in Irish antiquities led him through study of the Irish language into familiarity with ancient Irish literature. Paris may have been the place for an aspiring poet, but Synge's calling was higher than sprinkling pages with pretty words. "Give up Paris," Yeats told him. "Go to the Aran Islands. Live there as if you were one of the people themselves; express a life that has never found expression."

John Synge did not go to the Arans immediately, and when he did it cannot have been easy for him. Bedeviled by pains in his body, big but natively shy, Synge entertained his hosts with little magic tricks and set up his music stand in the kitchen to perform upon the violin, for he had trained at the Royal Irish Academy of Music. None of his four trips to the Arans was long, he drew his friends from the margins of society and spent much time lying on his back and watching the clouds go east, yet his experience there gave him his career and the book he wrote to tell of his adventure is a masterpiece.

The Aran Islands brings together Synge's interests in evolution and socialism. That mix characterized the folklore scholarship of his period, when folk culture was defined as a survival from an earlier evolutionary stage, marked by a generous and happy collective spirit. But Synge's book was not conventional folklore writing, which was one reason it took years to find its publisher. Nor was *The Aran Islands* anything like the old sketches of peasant life, though the sketching idea remained alive in hands like those of Seumas MacManus. And Synge's book was not journalism. Its prose was clear and new and beautiful. John Synge observed like a naturalist, and like others of his time who belonged to naturalists' clubs in Ireland, he was a pioneer photographer of rural life. He observed like a naturalist and wrote like a poet to invent a new genre of emotional ethnography.

While *The Aran Islands* was being rejected by a series of publishers, John Synge entered a state of white-hot creativity. In six years he wrote all of his plays, all but one influenced by his time on the Arans, two of them founded directly upon traditional narratives he heard there. Familiarity with the idea of the sketch breeds misunderstanding of Synge's achievement. He does not depict Irish life as it is or was, but like the old teller of tales, he enters and enacts the Irish consciousness. Do not think of the country people he knew as playing upon the stage but as sitting beside him in the darkened theater, laughing and crying and twitching at his restatement of their ideas.

"All art," John Synge said, "is a collaboration." No mere association between like-minded artists, the collaboration that powered his movement unified the artist with the national tradition. This is the structure of collaboration: in order to locate deep truths and to gain wide appeal, to avoid the trivializing constraints of academic endeavor, the artist roots his work in the folk culture and then accepts two responsibilities: to preserve the old tradition intact for the future; to do battle with the tradition so as to answer the needs of the self while creating new works for new worlds. In *The Aran Islands* and its companion, *In Wicklow and West Kerry*, Synge recorded the old ways as Lady Gregory said the folklorist should, with patience and reverence. All of his plays bear a relation to the tradition and two of them at least, *Riders to the Sea* and *The Playboy of the Western World*, are among the first great works of modern drama.

John Synge's oeuvre provides one pristine example of the perfection of Carleton's solution. In *The Aran Islands* he quotes Pat Dirane's folktale from which his play *In the Shadow of the Glen* was constructed. The story that inspired *The Playboy* is not presented as a text, and the rest of his plays are less specifically drawn from folk art. Scientist and artist, John Synge was an artist first, so we will relocate the center of his movement by balancing him with Douglas Hyde, who did write plays based on folktales, but who dedicated himself primarily to the collection and preservation of folklore.

Only Ireland could choose a folklorist for its first president. Douglas Hyde's election in 1937 capped a career that commenced in serious linguistic study. The son of a Protestant minister from Roscommon, Hyde studied Hebrew and Greek and Irish at Trinity. To improve his Irish, he went into the countryside, listened to the aged speakers, and wrote down their stories and songs. To preserve Irish, he founded the Gaelic League in 1893. The League extended its mission from linguistic to national revival and provided the context in which the spirit of rebellion was nurtured until it broke forth in war in 1916. While others pressed toward armed action, Hyde withdrew to protect his culture by writing his monumental *Literary History of Ireland* and by publishing, between 1889 and 1939, a sequence of volumes filled with folk texts.

Douglas Hyde, wrote William Butler Yeats, "knows the people thoroughly. . . . His work is neither humorous nor mournful; it is simply life." Accuracy was Hyde's concern. He surveyed the works that preceded his own in a kindly mood, but still found their stories manipulated, padded, and cooked. "Attempts," he wrote in *Beside the Fire*, published in 1890, "have been made from time to time during the present century to collect Irish folk-lore, but these attempts, though interesting from a literary point of view, are not always successes from a scientific one." Art and science obey different rules. Before Hyde, some writers of folktales leaned more toward art, others more toward science, but all created imperfect blends. In Hyde's day, his friends W. B. Yeats, Lady Gregory, and John Synge separated science and art and performed differently in different contexts to meet different responsibilities. After Hyde, division became complete. Some devoted themselves to art, others to science.

In 1902, W. B. Yeats and James Joyce met for the first time on a street in Dublin. Joyce told the poet that his reliance on folklore was a sign of his deterioration. Yeats constructed a long counterargument, contending that art depends on the popular tradition to prevent the pursuit of individualism from ending in sterility. The twenty-year-old Joyce replied, or so Yeats tells it, that it was a pity Yeats was too old to receive his influence. The next year Joyce met Synge, read *Riders to the Sea* and did not like it, and reviewing Lady Gregory's new *Poets and Dreamers* he described her storytellers as senile, feeble, and sleepy. Then the next year, with a little gift from Lady Gregory in his pocket, Joyce flew by the nets of home and religion to lodge in exile. Early in *Ulysses*, when the clever college boys speak of Hyde and Synge and "that old hake Gregory," they do so to divorce themselves from the dominant Irish literary movement of their day, but the adult Joyce incorporated the school of Yeats and about everything else into his unreadable masterpiece named after a folksong, *Finnegans Wake*. In it James Joyce makes the Irish land, its rivers and ancient murmurs, heroic to the modern world, and from Joyce on, profoundly in Samuel Beckett, contentiously in Patrick Kavanagh, hilariously in Flann O'Brien, sublimely in the verse of the major poetic school of our day, that of Thomas Kinsella, John Montague, Seamus Heaney, and Richard Murphy, the Irish land and its people and their art have continued to prove inspiring and worthy of defeat. But the work of preserving folklore has been taken up by others, committed first to science.

Three years after the rebels put down their guns and Ireland won a moment of peace, the Folklore of Ireland Society was founded and James Delargy, once assistant to Douglas Hyde, became editor of its journal, *Béaloideas*. Delargy argued that the preservation of folklore served more than the scientist's curiosity and did more than supply raw materials to artists. It was essential to the maintenance of a distinct national culture. He appealed for state support, and when funds were granted to establish the Irish Folklore Commission in 1935, he was named director. Delargy brought to Dublin a schoolteacher from Kerry named Sean O'Sullivan, then sent him for training to Sweden so that he could become the Commission's archivist, charged with the organization of the materials gathered by the Commission's full-time collectors. None of the collectors were university men. They came out of the country, received Ediphone recorders and instruction in verbatim transcription, and returned into the countryside. New men were in command of the Irish tradition. They were not outsiders but people of the people. I have listened to Sean O'Sullivan tell the old story of the man who had no story, and I have caroused around Dublin with Michael J. Murphy, then followed him across Ulster by reading the superb diaries that he, like the other collectors, has deposited in the archive. Michael J. Murphy returned from the place of his birth, Liverpool, to the place of his people, south Armagh, where he invented the idea of folklore for himself and composed a fine book, *At Slieve Gullion's Foot*. Immediately afterward, in 1941, Delargy invited him to become the Commission's collector for Ulster east of Donegal. Murphy is a playwright and a novelist, but he shines most brightly in his account of his adventures in the field, *Tyrone Folk Quest*, and in his book of Northern folktales, *Now You're Talking . . .*, published in 1975. Men like Murphy, working and reworking their territories, have made the Irish Folklore Commission—since 1971 the Department of Irish Folklore of the University of Dublin College at Belfield, and now headed by Bo Almqvist—the greatest repository of folklore in the world. From its million and a half pages, its archivists, Sean O'Sullivan and Séamas Ó Catháin, have extracted and published rich collections of folktale.

From Douglas Hyde to the present, from written dictation to the tape recorder, the progress of Irish folklore has been marked by steady improvement in the accuracy with which the words of the speakers of story have been preserved. Today, listening to the tale on tape over and over again, we can get all the words exactly right—and more. Listening again, while trying to capture on paper the stories I recorded during a decade in a small hilly place in County Fermanagh, in the southwestern corner of Northern Ireland, it became plain to me that transcriptions rendered as though they were prose distorted and muted the storyteller's art. Using italics and capital letters to signal loudness helped some, and reading the new scholarship on American Indian myths helped more. Dell Hymes argues convincingly that Indian narratives are structured poetically. Now, the stories I have recorded in Ireland are not poetry, but they are not prose either. So, I have struggled to jettison literary conventions and learned to follow subtle signs in the teller's presentation—repetitive words that start sections and sharp silences that close them—to produce transcriptions that not only include all the teller's words but also indicate something about the rhythms of narration. The result is a text composed of short paragraphs, often of only one sentence, that break up occasionally for dramatic effect. In the future, as we follow in the direction Douglas Hyde pointed, we will discover still better ways to get onto the page the purest representation of what the storyteller said.

We writers of folktale have decided that our basic obligation is to our sources. Our goal is to free ourselves from our own tradition so that we can approach other traditions directly. Our science exists to honor the storyteller's art.

COMMUNICATION

Once we have determined that our duty is to record folktales exactly and lovingly in the words of their narrators, the question remains of which tales to record and present to the reader. Its answer depends upon our motives, and different motives have driven scholars out of the study and into the field and guided them while they wrote. Return again to the beginning, to T. Crofton Croker.

Croker wished to amuse his readers, but sincere storytellers like Crofton

Croker and Hugh Nolan enter the act of communication with motives deeper than amusement. Introducing the complete edition of the *Fairy Legends* that he compiled out of affection for his recently deceased friend, Thomas Wright wrote that "the real importance" of Croker's stories lay in their "historical and ethnological" implications.

With amazing speed during Croker's era, scholars developed a theory encompassing history and ethnology that was to form the basis of folklore's first major scheme for research, the historic-geographic method. The method's goal is to read unwritten history out of spatial distributions. It commences in the recognition that stories told in distant places carry the same basic form. Comparison of these story types, alive in the minds of modern narrators, suggests connections between far-flung populations and leads toward the reconstruction of ancient histories.

"It is curious to observe the similarity of legends, and of ideas concerning imaginary beings, among nations that for ages have had scarcely any communication," Crofton Croker wrote, and in the notes that follow his tales, he not only connects new and old Irish stories and remarks similarities between Irish and Scottish, Welsh and English traditions, he ranges farther, finding parallels in Spain and Italy, in Germany and Denmark. At the end of one legend, in which a hill in Cork gains its name from a bottle out of which magical helpers popped, he calls attention to German and Eastern analogues and comments that "Mr. Pisani, formerly secretary to Lord Strangford and now in the embassy at Constantinople, relates a tale similar to the Legend of Bottle-hill, which was told him when a child by his nurse, who was a Greek woman." Even Samuel Lover, who counseled serious persons—"your masters of art, your explorers of science, star-gazing philosophers, and moon-struck maidens"—to lay his book aside, for laughter was his purpose, still follows his sketch in which a man saves himself from his compact with the Devil with the note that the tale "is somewhat common to the legendary lore of other countries—at least, there is a German legend built on a similar foundation." Despite his wish to amuse, Lover contributed to comparative study, and Croker was adamantly clear as to his purpose: "My aim has been to bring the twilight tales of the peasantry before the view of the philosopher."

The international nature of Croker's stories immediately attracted the brothers Grimm, whose translation of his work appeared within a year of the publication of the first edition in 1825. A French translation followed, and when in 1828 Croker's second series of Irish legends arrived, it came in company with a third volume containing Welsh legends and a lengthy essay by Wilhelm Grimm analyzing the Irish tales and setting them into a broad European context. Croker was no longer alone. He was part of a wide scholarly movement within which the international comparative perspective was dominant.

Folklore's comparative method was achieving its first mature formulation in Finland while Douglas Hyde was at work on the first scientific collections of Irish tale. In 1890, in the preface to *Beside the Fire,* Hyde grouped the stories of Ireland into two classes. One contained the wonder tales that folklorists, in homage to the Grimms, term *Märchen,* and it contained fairy legends. The other consisted of the poetic and marvelous adventures of Finn and the Fianna. The tales of the first class, Irish by adoption, deserved study for what they told about "our old Aryan heritage." The tales of the second class, the Fenian tales, were shared with Scotland as a result of ancient Irish colonization, but they were Irish distinctly and profoundly. They were important for the Gaelic language in which they were spoken and for the old culture of which they were part, the culture that was not English and could provide inspiration for the formation of a new Irish nation.

Add the idea of the Gaelic League to the idea of the historic-geographic school of folklore study, add nationalism to internationalism, and you have the twin motives that powered the great work of the Irish Folklore Commission. As the Commission's archivist, Sean O'Sullivan struggled manfully and successfully to bring the massive collection into usable order. In his guide for fieldworkers, *A Handbook of Irish Folklore,* he listed the tales of Ireland in accordance with the international index developed by Antti Aarne and Stith Thompson, and he added a typology of the Fenian tale. Then, working with Reidar Christiansen of Norway, he classified 43,000 tales into the Aarne-Thompson system, so you can find, for instance, that over 650 versions have been reported from Ireland of type 300, in which a hero slays three giants and then a sea monster to win the hand of a princess. When Sean O'Sullivan mobilized his unrivaled knowledge of the Irish folktale to pull from the archive his collection *Folktales of Ireland,* published in 1966, he emphasized the same classes of story that Hyde did: tales that connected Ireland to the world and tales in which Ireland's most ancient tradition glistens. But those are not the only tales told in Ireland, so at the end of his book O'Sullivan adds others, and in two other collections he stresses stories that are not to be found in the indexes or in the Fenian tradition, tales of kinds that claimed the attention of Hyde's friend Lady Gregory.

Lady Gregory was recently widowed and teaching herself Irish when she encountered two new books on Irish folklore, one by W. B. Yeats, the other by Douglas Hyde. Suddenly an old interest of hers took form and purpose. She invited them to her home, Coole in Galway; the collaboration that would produce the Abbey Theatre was about to begin. Yeats came first.

It was the same year in which Yeats met John Synge and sent him to the Arans. Soon after, Lady Gregory was out in the field "collecting fairy lore." In the next year, 1897, she was distracting Yeats from work he could not do by taking him from house to house to record old stories. They went together and both wore black, but their motives were not the same.

Yeats, inspired by William Morris, was full of hatred for the cheap materialistic side of the modern age, and he sought the fairy faith as part of his diverse, desperate quest for the spiritual. He called in the countryside for witnesses to the reality of the other world. Lady Gregory joined him and when her "big book of folklore," *Visions and Beliefs in the West of Ireland*, was at last published in 1920 with essays by Yeats at the back, it stood, as it continues to stand, as the greatest work produced out of the Irish interest in mystery that began in Croker's *Researches in the South of Ireland*, that embraced Oscar's parents, Sir William and Lady Wilde, in the days before Yeats, and that continues to call serious students of folklore.

W. B. Yeats desired proof of the limited vision of factual man, but when Lady Gregory heard stories, she "cared less for the evidence given in them than for the beautiful rhythmic sentences in which they were told." The words and cadences that she recorded taught her the language she would use in her own plays and in her translations of the old Irish epics. That language, praised by Yeats for being as beautiful as Morris and as true as Burns, inspired John Synge, helping him to shape his dramatic diction. Lady Gregory's fine ear provided the art of her movement with a voice and it made her one of the first great modern folklorists. On collecting trips with Yeats or with Hyde, and more often alone in her Kiltartan district of Galway, she listened closely and recorded with precision "because folk-lorists in these days are expected to be as exact as workers at any other science." Committed first to language, Lady Gregory was not confined by scholarly conventions of story type. Though she produced a collection of *Märchen* in her *Kiltartan Wonder Book*, she was receptive to new kinds of tale. Before her, the Dublin bookseller Patrick Kennedy, working to preserve the folk traditions of his native Wexford, had expanded his collections of international tale to include a few religious and historical texts. Out of each of these neglected varieties, Lady Gregory would construct a major collection. Protestant scholars tended to treat Irish faith as a pagan survival, but Lady Gregory faced the Catholicism of her people directly. In *A Book of Saints and Wonders*, published in 1906, she tells legends of the Irish saints and preserves testimony of Irish religiosity. Aristocratic scholars shied away from Irish folk history, in which an alternative view of the past, rife with hostility toward the invader and the landlord, implied a rebellious future. But gently nationalistic Lady Gregory gathered a sampling of historical legends, of "myths in the making," into her *Kiltartan History Book*, published in 1909, expanded in 1926. Later Sean O'Sullivan would feature these kinds of tale, the religious and the historical, in two major collections, one in the journal *Béaloideas*, one formed as a book, *Legends from Ireland*, published in 1977.

Attending more to what the people have to say than to academic convention, Lady Gregory and Sean O'Sullivan, she because of her ear for speech, he because of his responsibility to the Irish nation, suggest a different motive for the presentation of folktale texts. Stories not only carry ancient and unwritten history, they manifest the living culture of the people.

Discovering the culture in the story as a motive for reporting folklore had been there from the beginning. Both Crofton Croker and Samuel Lover explain stories of fairy pots of gold and demons that guard hidden treasure as exhibitions of the deep Irish ambivalence over material wealth. But the ethnographic concern was brushed aside during the excited scholarly search for international tales that led outward away from Ireland and backward away from the people who tell the tales. Interest in tales as evidence of contemporary culture became largely the province of travelers who, like Mr. and Mrs. S. C. Hall in the nineteenth century, or Sean O'Faolain and Brendan Behan in the twentieth, encountered folktales as features of the places they went and retold them as emblems of the people they met.

One special traveler was the American Jeremiah Curtin. He was the son of Irish immigrant parents, a staff member of the Smithsonian Institution's Bureau of American Ethnology, and an expert on American Indian mythology. In 1887 and again in 1892, he visited the West of Ireland to record *Märchen*, Fenian tales, and legends of ghosts and fairies. His knowledge of Irish was not deep, but guided by the principles in the new science of anthropology, Curtin, according to Douglas Hyde, "approached the fountainhead more nearly than any other."

Anthropology makes traveling into a profession and travel literature into scientific discourse. Modern Ireland has welcomed many anthropologists, most of them Americans, who have come to analyze the living culture. This they have done to suit the presuppositions of their science, and the tales in which the people bring their own culture into order have been left to folklorists like myself. But the American discipline of folklore within which I was trained springs from the same source as anthropology. So, like Douglas Hyde, I strive to record tales exactly, but what interests me is not the rare survival from times past; it is the culture of the people who share my times, my predicament. If a story interests the people I wish to understand, then I must learn to make it interest me too, whether or not it fits academic typologies, whether or not it preserves echoes of ancient thunder.

To bring you toward an understanding of Irish traditional culture, I have composed this book. Some of its stories are astoundingly old, some are found scattered widely across the globe, but I chose them for what they teach about the contours of the Irish consciousness.

The stories will guide you. I have arranged them so that they speak among themselves, each providing context for the other, all bodying forth pieces of a noble culture, a culture unlike our own, against which we must test ourselves during our effort to shape a mature and reasonable way of life.

A LAST WORD

I have brought into this anthology stories from forty different books, and from Ireland's pair of fine journals, *Béaloideas* and *Ulster Folklife*. In partial fulfillment of an old promise to provide comic and mysterious tales to complement the historical stories I published from Ballymenone, the place I know in Ulster, I have added new texts from my dear friends Michael Boyle, Ellen Cutler, Hugh Nolan, and Joseph and Peter Flanagan. Mr. Boyle died in 1974, Joe Flanagan in 1979, Mrs. Cutler in 1980, Mr. Nolan in 1981. Peter Flanagan, God bless him, is with us yet. We had some drinks together and shared some nostalgic chat in his house on the hill at Christmas in 1983 while this book was beginning to form.

The one book I did not plunder for texts is the best of them all, Sean O'Sullivan's *Folktales of Ireland*. I left it undisturbed in hopes that our collections might be read together, that mine might serve as an appendage to his. They are quite different. All of the stories in Sean O'Sullivan's book were recorded between 1930 and 1948 by trained collectors of folklore. This book gathers stories from the long stretch of Irish folktale writing, from 1825 to the present, and its authors include the people I have introduced to you, novelists and poets and playwrights, writers of sketches and travel accounts, professional folklorists. Sean O'Sullivan's stories come from only six of Ireland's thirty-two counties, none from Northern Ireland. Well over half come from Galway or Kerry, and Kerry supplies the most. Sean O'Sullivan's collection begins in his own experience. He is a Kerry man. His training and commitment lead him, as I think they should, to focus upon the Irish-speaking West. My collection begins in my experience, which has been in the North, and which has suggested kinds of stories and modes of organization and has led me to emphasize Ireland's dominant English-speaking population. What I believe to be most important for understanding Ireland are not the survivals of ancient tale that abound most beautifully in the rocky West, but the tales of all sorts through which the people of Ireland present to themselves that which is of enduring significance.

Let me tell you just what I have done to prepare the tales for you. I maintained my professional dedication to exact transcription unless it ran athwart the obligations I owe to the tales and their tellers. They have the right to communicate. So, without adding a word or shifting any out of order, I edited the opening sentences of a few of the tales that I lifted out of long runs of prose. Then, to bring the stories I found in print a little closer to those I heard, I broke some long paragraphs into shorter ones. In addition, I regularized punctuation and spelling. That sounds easy, but it was not. Writers have done wild things with spelling to capture the English spoken in Ireland. In their own place and day, they might have been successful, but their efforts have erected barriers between the storyteller and the reader and dragged their tales toward oblivion, so, even in texts of my own, I have shifted spelling toward standard literary usage. The distinctive textures of the Irish dialects of English remain in syntax and word choice. Mere spelling should not stand between you and the people who spoke the stories. Not all of the tales came with titles, so I invented some of them, a small matter because it is my experience that most folktales, unlike folksongs, do not exist in the tradition with native titles. After the title for each tale you will find a little information, first the name of a teller and a county, then the name of a writer and a date. Sometimes these few facts eluded me—a sad commentary on past practice—and sometimes I guessed a bit, but I wished to make the big story of the Irish folktale and its subplots clearer by setting each story in place and time. Still more, I wished the repetition of names to remind you that these stories do not come to us from some mystical agency called tradition. We owe them to the collaborative efforts of real people. I held my editing to a minimum to honor both the storyteller and the writer, but every change I made came because my first responsibility is to the storyteller.

It is the storyteller's culture I wish you to enter. To that end I clumped the texts into chapters, but the chapters do not follow scholastic convention. Academic categories serve academic needs, and they have tended to obscure whole classes of traditional narration. They rise from the values of scholars, but the values I wish you to understand are those of the tellers of tale, men like Hugh Nolan, women like Ellen Cutler, so my chapters represent neither old nor new schemes of classification. They are but hints to ease your entry into the Irish folk culture. Here is the course I recommend for your journey:

THE OLD STORY

Three texts review the Introduction and form a prelude to the collection. Each represents one of the classes of tale that have most engaged Irish collectors: fairy legends, Fenian tales, *Märchen*. And in sequence they teach of the progress in the recording of stories, from T. Crofton Croker's sketch of

1825, to Patrick Kennedy's mid-nineteenth-century attempt to write down a story as he heard it, to Douglas Hyde's exact translation of a tale taken down verbatim and published in the first truly modern Irish folktale collection, *Beside the Fire* of 1890.

FAITH

At the dawn of human time, in the first mythic moment, the saints arrive and put the finishing touches on the Irish land, planting it with proof of God's existence. They take control of nature, vanquish the Druids, convert the old warriors, and charge the people of the future to obey God's law of love. Some do.

WIT

Intelligence balances power. Inbuilt wit enables the lawyer to win his case against Satan, the outlaw to escape the authorities, and the peasant to outfox the outlaw. The tenant of story is the master of the landlord. The victory of the humbler brother proves that poverty and weakness tell nothing of wisdom or courage. Even the toughest enemy—boredom—falls before the person who can command the language to yield poetry, who can conquer pain in comic hyperbole.

MYSTERY

This world and the other occasionally veer near collision. The witnesses speak sincerely. They have heard death announced in the earth and felt the ghost's weight and seen the wizened changelings the fairies leave. It seems impossible, but if there are no ghosts, is there no immortal soul, no life after death? Fairies are the angels who fell with Lucifer after defeat at the War of Heaven. They seem, like cats, to have constructed an alternative social order in our midst. If fairies do not exist, then what of angels, what of Heaven? And what about people who foretell the future and cure ills with charms? The shape of reality remains at question, so serious investigators adhere to strict rules of evidence and argue earnestly over the facts, while sly people step into the space between terror and amusement to contrive little fictions.

HISTORY

The endless Irish chronicle of war, of invasion and resistance, expands and grows with detail during the long era of difficulty that begins with defeat at Kinsale in 1601, that intensifies during the seventeenth-century campaigns of Oliver Cromwell and William of Orange, that sinks with the failure of the Rising of 1798, and ends in the terrible Famine of 1846. This period of pain displays Irish courage and Irish error, and it teaches that in the worst of times God protects those who struggle to endure.

FIRESIDE TALES

Away from the serious mysteries of the world, storytellers have constructed an enchanted realm in which the heroes of a time before history wage beautiful, uproarious war and little children seek maturity. Child after child abandons the comforts of home and takes the strange road, learning to form proper alliances and act with courage in order to enter through marriage a new state of being. Now mature, they are left with their faith, which bids them to endure, and with their wit, out of which they learn to turn fear into laughter and life into a story.

These chapters are but a beginning. The stories I have set within them will disrupt and eradicate their boundaries. I do not want to slice tales up and box them apart. Instead, I want the tales to grope toward unity, so you will find tales that transform other tales, and tales that root up generic distinctions, and tales that interfere with each other, interpenetrating to raise the themes that hold power in the traditional consciousness and that have been molded into artful order by centuries of wise and brave Irish people.

❖ THE TALES

THE OLD STORY

FOLKLORIST AND STORYTELLER

Patrick Kennedy, *Legendary Fictions of the Irish Celts*, 1866

❖ THE LEGEND OF KNOCKFIERNA

CORK

T. CROFTON CROKER *1825*

It is a very good thing not to be any way in dread of the fairies, for without doubt they have then less power over a person. But to make too free with them, or to disbelieve in them altogether, is as foolish a thing as man, woman, or child can do.

It has been truly said that "good manners are no burthen," and that "civility costs nothing." But there are some people foolhardy enough to disregard doing a civil thing, which, whatever they may think, can never harm themselves or anyone else, and who at the same time will go out of their way for a bit of mischief, which never can serve them. But sooner or later they will come to know better, as you shall hear of Carroll O'Daly, a strapping young fellow up out of Connacht, whom they used to call, in his own country, "Devil Daly."

Carroll O'Daly used to go roving about from one place to another, and the fear of nothing stopped him. He would as soon pass an old churchyard, or a regular fairy ground, at any hour of the night, as go from one room into another, without ever making the sign of the cross, or saying, "Good luck attend you, gentlemen."

It so happened that he was once journeying in the County of Limerick, towards "the Baalbek of Ireland," the venerable town of Kilmallock, and just at the foot of Knockfierna he overtook a respectable-looking man jogging along upon a white pony. The night was coming on, and they rode side by side for some time, without much conversation passing between them, further than saluting each other very kindly. At last, Carroll O'Daly asked his companion how far he was going.

"Not far your way," said the farmer, for such his appearance bespoke him. "I'm only going to the top of this hill here."

"And what might take you there," said O'Daly, "at this time of the night?"

"Why then," replied the farmer, "if you want to know, 'tis the Good People."

"The fairies, you mean," said O'Daly.

"Whist! whist!" said his fellow-traveler, "or you may be sorry for it." And he turned his pony off the road they were going towards a little path which led up the side of the mountain, wishing Carroll O'Daly good night and a safe journey.

"That fellow," thought Carroll, "is about no good this blessed night, and I would have no fear of swearing wrong if I took my Bible oath, that it is something else beside the fairies, or the Good People, as he calls them, that is taking him up the mountain at this hour. The fairies!" he repeated. "Is it for a well-shaped man like him to be going after little chaps like the fairies? To be sure some say there are such things, and more say not. But I know this, that never afraid would I be of a dozen of them, aye, of two dozen, for that matter, if they are no bigger than what I hear tell of."

Carroll O'Daly, whilst these thoughts were passing in his mind, had fixed his eyes steadfastly on the mountain, behind which the full moon was rising majestically. Upon an elevated point that appeared darkly against the moon's disk, he beheld the figure of a man leading a pony, and he had no doubt it was that of the farmer with whom he had just parted company.

A sudden resolve to follow flashed across the mind of O'Daly with the speed of lightning. Both his courage and curiosity had been worked up by his cogitations to a pitch of chivalry, and muttering, "Here's after you, old boy," he dismounted from his horse, bound him to an old thorn tree, and then commenced vigorously ascending the mountain.

Following as well as he could the direction taken by the figures of the man and pony, he pursued his way, occasionally guided by their partial appearance, and after toiling nearly three hours over a rugged and sometimes swampy path, came to a green spot on the top of the mountain, where he saw the white pony at full liberty, grazing as quietly as may be. O'Daly looked around for the rider, but he was nowhere to be seen; he however soon discovered close to where the pony stood an opening in the mountain like the mouth of a pit, and he remembered having heard, when a child, many a tale about the "Poul-duve," or Black Hole, of Knockfierna; how it was the entrance to the fairy castle which was within the mountain; and how a man whose name was Ahern, a land surveyor in that part of the country, had once attempted to fathom it with a line, and had been drawn down into it and was never again heard of; with many other tales of the like nature.

"But," thought O'Daly, "these are old women's stories. And since I've come up so far I'll just knock at the castle door, and see if the fairies are at home."

No sooner said than done; for seizing a large stone as big, aye, bigger than his two hands, he flung it with all his strength down into the Poul-duve of Knockfierna. He heard it bounding and tumbling about from one rock to another with a terrible noise, and he leant his head over to try and hear if it would reach the bottom—when what should the very stone he had thrown in do but come up again with as much force as it had gone down, and gave him such a blow full in the face, that it sent him rolling down the side of Knockfierna, head over heels, tumbling from one crag to another, much faster than he came up. And in the morning Carroll O'Daly was found lying beside his horse; the bridge of his nose broken, which disfigured him for life; his head all cut and bruised, and both his eyes closed up, and as black as if Sir Daniel Donnelly had painted them for him.

Carroll O'Daly was never bold again in riding alone near the haunts of the fairies after dusk. But small blame to him for that. And if ever he happened to be benighted in a lonesome place he would make the best of his way to his journey's end, without asking questions, or turning to the right or to the left, to seek after the Good People, or any who kept company with them.

❖ FINN AND HIS MEN BEWITCHED

JEMMY REDDY ◈ *WEXFORD*
PATRICK KENNEDY *1866*

The king of Greek's daughter had a great spite to Finn MacCumhail, and Goll, one of his great heroes, and Oscar his grandson. So she came one day and appeared like a white doe before him. And bedad he chased her with his two hounds, Bran and another, till she led them away to the bottom of the black North. She vanished from them at the edge of a lake, and while they were looking about for her, a beautiful lady appeared sitting on the bank, tearing her hair, and crying.

"What ails you, lady?" says Finn.

"My ring is dropped into the water," says she, "and my father and mother will murder me if I go home without it."

"I'll get it for you," says he, and he dived three times one after another for it. The third time he felt the chill of death on him, and when he was handing the ring to her, he was a decrepid, weak, gray-haired old man.

"Now," says she, "maybe you'll remember the king of Greek's daughter, and how you killed her husband and her two sons."

"If I did," says he, "it was on the battlefield, fighting man to man." She left him there as helpless as the child two days old, and went away with herself.

There was great sorrow and trouble that night at Finn's house, and the next day all his warriors, except Oscar, set out after him. Well, they traveled and they traveled, till they were tired and hungry, and at last they entered an old fort, and what did they see but a fine table laid out, and seven stone seats around it. They were too hungry to make much ceremony, so they sat down, and ate and drank. And just as they were done, in walks the lady, and says she: "Sith ye merry, gentlemen. I hope your meal agreed with you. Finn is at the edge of that lake you see down there. If you like, you may come with me to pay him a visit."

They gave a shout of joy, but bedad, when they offered to get up they found themselves glued to their stone seats. Oh, weren't they miserable! And they could see poor Finn lying on a bank by the lake not able to stir hand or foot.

There they stayed in grief for a day and a night, and at last they saw Oscar following Bran that was after going a hundred miles in quest of him. Bran found Oscar lying asleep by the Lake of Killarney, and he barked so loud that the wolves, and deers, and foxes, and hares, run fifty miles away; the eagles, and kites, and hawks, flew five miles up in the sky, and the fishes jumped out on dry land.

Never a wake did Oscar wake, and then Bran bit his little finger to the bone. "Tattheration to you for an Oscar!" says poor Bran, and then he was so mad he seized him by the nose. Very few can stand to have any liberty taken with the handle of their face—no more did Oscar. He opened his eyes, and was going to make gibbets of the dog, but he put up his muzzle, and began to keen, and then trotted off, looking round at Oscar.

"Oh ho!" says he, "Finn or Goll is in danger," and he followed him hot-foot to the North. He came up to Finn, but could hardly hear what he was striving to tell him. So Oscar put Finn's thumb to his lips, for himself wasn't able to stir hand or foot. "And now, Finn," says he, "by the virtue of your thumb, tell me how I'm to get this pishrogue removed."

"Go," says he, in a whisper that had hardly anything between it and dead silence, "go to the fairy hill, and make the enchanter that lives there give you the drink of youth."

When he came to the hill, the thief of a fairy man sunk down seven perches into the ground, but Oscar was not to be circumvented. He dug after him till the clay and stones made a new hill, and when they came to the solid rock he pinned him, and brought him up to the light of the sun. His face was as gray as ashes, and as shriveled as a russidan apple, and very unwilling he was to give up the cup. But he was forced to do so, and it wasn't long till Oscar was by Finn's side, and spilling a little, drop by drop, down his throat. Up he sprung five yards in the air, and shouted till the rocks rung. And it wasn't long till himself, and Oscar, and Bran were in the middle of the enchanted men. Well, they were nearly ashamed of themselves pinned to their seats, but Oscar didn't leave them long in grief. He spilled some of the cup down by every man's thigh, and freed he was. But, be the laws, there wasn't hardly a drop in the cup when he came to the ounkran of a make-game, foul-mouthed, bald Conan. He could only free a part of one thigh, and at last Oscar, getting impatient, took him body and sleeves, and pulled him off the stone. What a roar he let out of him! His breeches—if it's breeches they wore in them old times—stuck to the seat, and a trifle of Conan's skin along with it. "Whisht!" says Oscar, "we'll get a sheepskin sewed on you, and you'll be as comfortable as any May-boy after it."

Well, when all were free, they gave three shouts that were heard as far as the Isle of Man. And for a week after they got home they done nothing but eating the vengeance of goats and deers, and drinking wine, and mead, and beer that the Danes learned them to make from heath. And gentle and simple might go in and out, and eat and drink, and no one was there to say, "Who asked you to visit us?"

❖ The King of Ireland's Son

JOHN CUNNINGHAM ◈ *ROSCOMMON*
DOUGLAS HYDE *1890*

There was a king's son in Ireland long ago, and he went out and took with him his gun and his dog. There was snow out. He killed a raven. The raven fell on the snow. He never saw anything whiter than the snow, or blacker than the raven's skull, or redder than its share of blood, that was a-pouring out.

He put himself under geasa and obligations of the year, that he would not eat two meals at one table, or sleep two nights in one house, until he should find a woman whose hair was as black as the raven's head, and her skin as white as the snow, and her two cheeks as red as the blood.

There was no woman in the world like that, but one woman only, and she was in the eastern world.

The day on the morrow he set out, and money was not plenty, but he took with him twenty pounds. It was not far he went until he met a funeral, and he said that it was as good for him to go three steps with the corpse.

He had not the three steps walked until there came a man and left his writ down on the corpse for five pounds. There was a law in Ireland at that time that any man who had a debt upon another person that person's people could not bury him, should he be dead, without paying his debts, or without the leave of the person to whom the dead man owed the debts. When the king of Ireland's son saw the sons and daughters of the dead crying, and they without money to give the man, he said to himself: "It's a great pity that these poor people have not the money," and he put his hand in his pocket and paid the five pounds himself for the corpse. After that, he said he would go as far as the church to see it buried. Then there came another man, and left his writ on the body for five pounds more. "As I gave the first five pounds," said the king of Erin's son to himself, "it's as good for me to give the other five, and to let the poor man go to the grave." He paid the other five pounds. He had only ten pounds then.

Not far did he go until he met a short green man, and he asked him where was he going. He said that he was going looking for a woman in the eastern world. The short green man asked him did he want a boy, and he said he did, and asked what would be the wages he would be looking for? He said: "The first kiss of his wife if he should get her." The king of Ireland's son said that he must get that.

Not far did they go until they met another man and his gun in his hand, and he a-leveling it at the blackbird that was in the eastern world, that he might have it for his dinner. The short green man said to him that it was as good for him to take that man into his service if he would go on service with him. The son of the king of Ireland asked him if he would come on service with him.

"I will," said the man, "if I get my wages."

"And what is the wages you'll be looking for?"

"The place of a house and garden."

"You'll get that if my journey succeeds with me."

The king of Ireland's son went forward with the short green man and the gunner, and it was not far they went until a man met them, and his ear left to the ground, and he listening to the grass growing.

"It's as good for you to take that man into your service," said the short green man.

The king's son asked the man whether he would come with him on service.

"I'll come if I get the place of a house and garden."

"You will get that from me if the thing I have in my head succeeds with me."

The son of the king of Ireland, the short green man, the gunman, and the earman, went forward, and it was not far they went until they met another man, and his one foot on his shoulder, and he keeping a field of hares, without letting one hare in or out of the field. There was wonder on the king's son, and he asked him "What was the sense of his having one foot on his shoulder like that."

"Oh," says he, "if I had my two feet on the ground I should be so swift that I would be out of sight."

"Will you come on service with me?" says the king's son.

"I'll come if I get the place of a house and garden."

"You'll get that if the thing I have in my head succeeds with me."

The son of the king of Ireland, the short green man, the gunman, the earman, and the footman, went forward, and it was not far they went till they came to a man and he turning round a windmill with one nostril, and his finger left on his nose shutting the other nostril.

"Why have you your finger on your nose?" said the king of Ireland's son.

"Oh," says he, "if I were to blow with the two nostrils I would sweep the mill altogether out of that up into the air."

"Will you come on hire with me?"

"I will if I get the place of a house and garden."

"You'll get that if the thing I have in my head succeeds with me."

The son of the king of Ireland, the short green man, the gunman, the earman, the footman, and the blowman went forward until they came to a man who was sitting on the side of the road and he a-breaking stones with one thigh, and he had no hammer or anything else. The king's son asked him why it was he was breaking stones with his half thigh.

"Oh," says he, "if I were to strike them with the double thigh I'd make powder of them."

"Will you hire with me?"

"I will if I get the place of a house and garden."

"You'll get that if the thing I have in my head succeeds with me."

Then they all went forward together—the son of the king of Ireland, the short green man, the gunman, the earman, the footman, the blowman, and the man that broke stones with the side of his thigh, and they would overtake the March wind that was before them, and the March wind that was behind them would not overtake them, until the evening came and the end of the day.

The king of Ireland's son looked from him, and he did not see any house in which he might be that night. The short green man looked from him, and he saw a house, and there was not the top of a quill outside of it, nor the bottom of a quill inside of it, but only one quill alone, which was keeping shelter and protection on it. The king's son said that he did not know where he should pass that night, and the short green man said that they would be in the house of the giant over there that night.

They came to the house, and the short green man drew the *coolaya-coric* —the pole of combat—and he did not leave child with woman, foal with mare, pigeen with pig, or badger in glen, that he did not turn over three times with the quantity of sound he knocked out of the *coolaya-coric*. The giant came out, and he said: "I feel the smell of the melodious lying Irishman under my little sod of country."

"I'm no melodious lying Irishman," said the short green man. "But my master is out there at the head of the avenue, and if he comes he will whip the head off you." The short green man was growing big, growing big, until at last he looked as big as the castle. There came fear on the giant, and he said: "Is your master as big as you?"

"He is," says the short green man, "and bigger."

"Put me in hiding till morning, until your master goes," said the giant.

Then he put the giant under lock and key, and went out to the king's son. Then the king of Ireland's son, the gunman, the earman, the footman, the blowman, and the man who broke stones with the side of his thigh, came into the castle, and they spent that night, a third of it a-storytelling, a third of it with Fenian tales, and a third of it in mild enjoyment of slumber and of true sleep.

When the day on the morrow arose, the short green man brought with him his master, the gunman, the earman, the footman, the blowman, and the man who broke stones with the side of his thigh, and he left them outside at the head of the avenue, and he came back himself and took the lock off the giant. He told the giant that his master sent him back for the black cap that was under the head of his bed. The giant said that he would give him a hat that he never wore himself, but that he was ashamed to give him the old cap. The short green man said that unless he gave him the cap his master would come back and strike the head off him.

"It's best for me to give it to you," said the giant. "And any time at all you will put it on your head you will see everybody and nobody will see you." He gave him the cap then, and the short green man came and gave it to the king of Ireland's son.

They were a-going then. They would overtake the March wind that was before them, and the March wind that was behind them would not overtake them, going to the eastern world. When evening and the end of the day came, the king of Ireland's son looked from him, and he did not see any house in which he might be that night. The short green man looked from him, and he saw a castle, and he said: "The giant that is in that castle is the brother of the giant with whom we were last night, and we shall be in this castle tonight."

They came to the castle, and he left the king's son and his people at the head of the avenue, and he went to the door and pulled the *coolaya-coric*, and he did not leave child with woman, foal with mare, pigeen with pig, or badger in glen, within seven miles of him, that he did not knock three turns out of them with all the sound he knocked out of the *coolaya-coric*.

The giant came out, and he said, "I feel the smell of a melodious lying Irishman under my sod of country."

"No melodious lying Irishman am I," says the short green man. "But my master is outside at the head of the avenue, and if he comes he will whip the head off you."

"I think you large of one mouthful, and I think you small of two mouthfuls," said the giant.

"You won't get me of a mouthful at all," said the short green man, and he began swelling until he was as big as the castle. There came fear on the giant, and he said:

"Is your master as big as you?"

"He is, and bigger."

"Hide me," said the giant, "till morning, until your master goes, and anything you will be wanting you must get it."

He brought the giant with him, and he put him under the mouth of a douac, a great vessel of some sort. He went out and brought in the son of the king of Ireland, the gunman, the earman, the footman, the blowman, and the man who broke stones with the side of his thigh, and they spent that night, one-third of it telling Fenian stories, one-third telling tales, and one-third in the mild enjoyment of slumber and of true sleep until morning.

In the morning, the day on the morrow, the short green man brought the king's son and his people out of the castle, and left them at the head of the avenue, and he went back himself and asked the giant for the old slippers that were left under the head of his bed.

The giant said that he would give his master a pair of boots as good as ever he wore, and what good was there in the old slippers?

The short green man said that unless he got the slippers he would go for his master to whip the head off him.

Then the giant said that he would give them to him, and he gave them.

"Any time," said he, "that you will put those slippers on you, and say 'high-over!' any place you have a mind to go to, you will be in it."

The son of the king of Ireland, the short green man, the gunman, the earman, the footman, the blowman, and the man who broke stones with the side of his thigh, went forward until evening came, and the end of the day, until the horse would be going under the shade of the docking, and the docking would not wait for him. The king's son asked the short green man where should they be that night, and the short green man said that they would be in the house of the brother of the giant with whom they spent the night before. The king's son looked from him and he saw nothing. The short green man looked from him and he saw a great castle. He left the king's son and his people there, and he went to the castle by himself, and he drew the *coolaya-coric*, and he did not leave child with woman, foal with mare, pigeen with pig, or badger in glen, but he turned them over three times with all the sound he struck out of the *coolaya-coric*. The giant came out, and he said: "I feel the smell of a melodious lying Irishman under my sod of country."

"No melodious lying Irishman am I," said the short green man. "But my master is standing at the head of the avenue, and if he comes he shall strike the head off you."

And with that the short green man began swelling until he was the size of the castle at last. There came fear on the giant, and he said: "Is your master as big as yourself?"

"He is," said the short green man, "and bigger."

"Oh! put me in hiding, put me in hiding," said the giant, "until your master goes. And anything you will be asking you must get it."

He took the giant with him, and he put him under the mouth of a douac, and a lock on him. He came back, and he brought the king of Ireland's son, the gunman, the earman, the footman, the blowman, and the man who broke stones with the side of his thigh, into the castle with him, and they spent that night merrily—a third of it with Fenian tales, a third of it with telling stories, and a third of it with the mild enjoyment of slumber and of true sleep.

In the morning, the day on the morrow, he brought the son of the king of Ireland out, and his people with him, and left them at the head of the avenue, and he came back himself and loosed out the giant, and said to him, that he must give him the rusty sword that was under the corner of his bed. The giant said that he would not give that old sword to anyone, but that he would give him the sword of the three edges that never left the leavings of a blow behind it, or if it did, it would take it with the second blow.

"I won't have that," said the short green man, "I must get the rusty sword. And if I don't get that, I must go for my master, and he shall strike the head off you."

"It is better for me to give it to you," said the giant, "and whatever place you will strike a blow with that sword, it will go to the sand though it were iron were before it." Then he gave him the rusty sword.

The son of the king of Ireland, the gunman, the earman, the footman, the blowman, and the man who broke stones with the side of his thigh, went forward after that, until evening came, and the end of the day, until the horse was going under the shade of the docking, and the docking would not wait for him. The March wind that was behind them would not overtake them, and they would overtake the wind of March that was before them, and they were that night in the eastern world, where was the lady.

The lady asked the king of Ireland's son what it was he wanted, and he said that he was looking for herself as wife.

"You must get me," said she, "if you loose my geasa off me."

He got lodging with all his servants in the castle that evening, and in the night she came and said to him: "Here is a scissors for you, and unless you have that scissors for me tomorrow morning, the head will be struck off you."

She placed a pin of slumber under his head, and he fell into his sleep, and as soon as he did, she came and took the scissors from him and left him there. She gave the scissors to the King of Poison, and she desired the king to have the scissors for her in the morning. Then she went away. When she was gone the King of Poison fell into his sleep. And when he was in his sleep the short green man came, and the old slippers on him, and the cap on his head, and the rusty sword in his hand, and wherever it was the king had left the scissors out of his hand, he found it. He gave it to the king of Ireland's son, and when she came in the morning, she asked: "Son of the king of Ireland, have you the scissors?"

"I have," said he.

There were three scores of skulls of the people that went to look for her set on spikes round about the castle, and she thought that she would have his head on a spike along with them.

On the night of the next day she came and gave him a comb, and said to him unless he had that comb for her next morning when she would come, that the head should be struck off him. She placed a pin of slumber under his head, and he fell into his sleep as he fell the night before, and she stole the comb with her. She gave the comb to the King of Poison, and said to him not to lose the comb as he lost the scissors. The short green man came with the old slippers on his feet, the old cap on his head, and the rusty sword in his hand. And the king did not see him until he came behind him and took away the comb with him.

When the king of Ireland's son rose up the next morning he began crying for the comb, which was gone from him. "Don't mind that," said the short green man; "I have it." When she came he gave her the comb, and there was wonder on her.

She came the third night, and said to the son of the king of Ireland to have for her the head of him who was combed with that comb, on the morrow morning. "Now," said she, "there was no fear of you until this night, but if you lose it this time, your head is gone."

The pin of slumber was under his head, and he fell into his sleep. She came and stole the comb from him. She gave it to the King of Poison, and she said to him that he could not lose it unless the head should be struck off himself. The King of Poison took the comb with him, and he put it into a rock of stone and three score of locks on it, and the king sat down himself outside of the locks all, at the door of the rock, guarding it. The short green man came, and the slippers and the cap on him, and the rusty sword in his hand, and he struck a stroke on the stone rock and he opened it up, and he struck the second stroke on the King of Poison, and he struck the head off him. He brought back with him then the comb to the king's son, and he found him awake, and weeping after the comb. "There is your comb for you," said he. "She will come this now, and she will ask you have you the comb, and tell her that you have, and the head that was combed with it, and throw her the skull."

When she came asking if he had the comb, he said he had, and the head that was combed with it, and he threw her the head of the King of Poison.

When she saw the head there was great anger on her, and she told him he never would get her to marry until he got a footman to travel with her runner for three bottles of the healing-balm out of the well of the western world; and if her own runner should come back more quickly than his runner, she said his head was gone.

She got an old hag—some witch—and she gave her three bottles. The short green man bade them give three bottles to the man who was keeping the field of hares, and they were given to him. The hag and the man started, and three bottles with each of them. And the runner of the king's son was coming back halfway on the road home, while the hag had only gone halfway to the well. "Sit down," said the hag to the foot-runner, when they met, "and take your rest, for the pair of them are married now, and don't be breaking your heart running." She brought over a horse's head and a slumber-pin in it, and laid it under his head, and when he laid down his head on it he fell asleep. She spilt out the water he had and she went.

The short green man thought it long until they were coming, and he said to the earman: "Lay your ear to the ground and try are they coming."

"I hear the hag a-coming," said he. "But the footman is in his sleep, and I hear him a-snoring."

"Look from you," said the short green man to the gunman, "till you see where the foot-runner is."

The gunman looked, and he said that the footman was in such and such a place, and a horse's skull under his head, and he in his sleeping.

"Lay your gun to your eye," said the short green man, "and put the skull away from under his head."

He put the gun to his eye and he swept the skull from under his head. The footman woke up, and he found that the bottles which he had were empty, and it was necessary for him to return to the well again.

The hag was coming then, and the foot-runner was not to be seen. Says the short green man to the man who was sending round the windmill with his nostril: "Rise up and try would you put back that hag." He put his finger to his nose, and when the hag was coming he put a blast of wind under her that swept her back again. She was coming again, and he did the same thing to her. Every time she used to be coming near them he would be sending her back with the wind he would blow out of his nostril. At last he blew with the two nostrils and swept the hag back to the western world again. Then the foot-runner of the king of Ireland's son came, and the day was won.

There was great anger on the woman when she saw that her own foot-runner did not arrive first, and she said to the king's son: "You won't get me now till you have walked three miles, without shoes or stockings, on steel needles." She had a road three miles long, and sharp needles of steel shaken on it as thick as the grass, and their points up. Said the short green man to the man who broke stones with the side of his thigh: "Go and blunt those." That man went on them with one thigh, and he made stumps of them. He went on them with the double thigh, and he made powder and prashuch of them. The king of Ireland's son came and walked the three miles, and then he had his wife gained.

The couple were married then, and the short green man was to have the first kiss. The short green man took the wife with him into a chamber, and he began on her. She was full up of serpents, and the king's son would have been killed with them when he went to sleep, but that the short green man picked them out of her.

He came then to the son of the king of Ireland, and he told him: "You can go with your wife now. I am the man who was in the coffin that day, for whom you paid the ten pounds. And these people who are with you, they are servants whom God has sent to you."

The short green man and his people went away then, and the king of Ireland's son never saw them again. He brought his wife home with him, and they spent a happy life with one another.

FAITH

THE SHRINE OF SAINT MOGUE
Margaret Stokes, *Early Christian Art in Ireland*, 1890

❖ The Baptism of Conor MacNessa

SEOSAMH Ó COLLA ❖ *DONEGAL*
SEAN O'SULLIVAN *1938*

Long ago people were few, and the priests used to travel about saying Mass and spending a night here and there. Some of them arrived at a house and they asked the boy to go out and cut some rushes with a sickle to make a bed. The boy went out to a clump of rushes, and a voice spoke to him from out the clump:

"Don't put me out of my dwelling."

The boy went away from the clump and told the priests in the house what had happened.

"Didn't you bring the rushes?" they asked.

"No, Father," said he to one of them. "If I told you what I have heard, you wouldn't go there either."

"Come along and show me where this was said."

They went out to the clump. The priest put on his stole and read something, and a voice spoke from the clump.

"Who are you?" asked the priest.

"I am Conor of Ulster," said the voice.

"How long have you been here?"

"Since the Savior was crucified," said the voice.

"And what put you here?" asked the priest.

"It happened this way. I was in a battle, and a piece of something entered my skull. When I heard later on that the Savior was crucified, frenzy came upon me. I went out into the woods with my sword, and the piece fell out of my skull, and I died. The Savior then put my soul into my skull until the Day of Judgment."

"I'll baptize you now, and you will go to Heaven," said the priest.

"Must I die a second time?" asked the voice.

"You must."

"Oh, Father, I'd rather stay in my skull until the Day of Judgment," said the voice.

When the priest heard these words, tears fell from his eyes down on the clump, and Conor of Ulster immediately rose up from it like an angel.

"I'm on my way to Heaven now, Father!" said he. "Your tears have baptized me!"

❖ Saint Patrick

GALWAY
LADY GREGORY *1926*

There were many great saints in Ireland, but Saint Patrick was the bush among them all. He used to be traveling and blessing all before him.

He was about seventy years when God bade him come to Ireland, and he didn't like to be put out of his way, being old, and he said he would not come.

So then God said if he would not come he would give him a bad next-door neighbor that would be fighting and quarreling and slandering him.

So when he heard that, he said it would be as good to go to Ireland.

❖ Saint Patrick on Inishmore

HUGH NOLAN ◈ *FERMANAGH*
HENRY GLASSIE *1972*

Well, the principal story that ever I heard related, it was when Saint Patrick came to Ireland.

He landed down south and he traveled on towards the north.

And you'd think for to hear about Saint Patrick that he was just a lonely missioner that landed in this country, and he had nobody *along* with him.

But he had a very big contingent.

He had tradesmen of all classes.

And there was a staff of women for to make vestments (that'd be the robes that the priest would be wearing while he would be saying the Mass), and for to make all the linens in connection with the altars. He had them.

And he had men then for making the altar vessels and everything that was a-wanting.

And then he had men for looking after the horses and keeping them shod and keeping them *right*.

But they traveled on anyway and finally they got as far as Inishmore.

They come on right up from the south of Ireland and they were traveling through Inishmore on this occasion.

And didn't the horse that he was riding upset, he slipped and he hurted his back, and of course he wasn't able to get up.

So there was some kind of an herb, or something in the grass,
and Saint Patrick lifted it up
and he rubbed it to the horse's back,
and the horse jumped up.

Well, for years and years after, there used to come people from all airts and parts where they'd get hurts, or bruises, or cuts or anything.

And there was people, they were the name of Nobles.

And they were Protestant farmers.

And it was on *their* land that this herb was.

And they were all the men that knew it or could point it out.

So they used to point it out to these people.

And they used to apply it.

So I haven't heard any word now about it this long time, because the family died out, do ye know, and whether they bequeathed this knowledge they had to anyone else, I never heard.

But they knew it, and they would point it out to you or me or any other person that was suffering.

The herb was known as dho. That was the name of it.

❖ SAINT PATRICK AND CROM DUBH

MICHAEL MACRUAIDHRI ◈ *MAYO*
DOUGLAS HYDE *1915*

Before Saint Patrick came to Ireland there lived a chieftain in the Lower Country in County Mayo, and his name was Crom Dubh. Crom Dubh lived beside the sea in a place which they now call Dún Padraig, or Downpatrick, and the name which the site of his house is called by is Dún Briste, or Broken Fort. My story will tell why it was called Dún Briste.

It was well and it was not ill, brother of my heart! Crom Dubh was one of the worst men that could be found, but as he was a chieftain over the people of that country he had everything his own way; and that was the bad way, for he was an evil-intentioned, virulent, cynical, obstinate man, with desire to be avenged on everyone who did not please him. He had two sons, Téideach and Clonnach, and there is a big hollow going in under the road at Glen Lasaire, and the name of this hollow is Poll a' Téidigh or Téideach's Hole, for it got its name from Crom Dubh's son, and the name of this hole is on the mouth of English-speaking people, though they do not know the meaning of it. Nobody knows how far this hole is going back under the glen, but it is said by the old Irish speakers that Téideach used to go every day in his little floating curragh into this hole under the glen, and that this is the reason it was called Téideach's Hole.

It was well, my dear. To continue the story, Crom Dubh's two sons were worse than himself, and that leaves them bad enough! Crom Dubh had two hounds of dogs and their names were Coinn Iotair and Saidhthe Suaraighe, and if ever there were wicked mastiffs these two dogs were they. He had them tied to the two jaws of the door, in order to loose them and set them to attack people according as they might come that way. And, to go further, he had a big fire kindled on the brink of the cliff so that anyone who might escape from the hounds he might throw into the fire. And to make a long story short, the fame of Crom Dubh and his two sons, and his two mastiffs, went far and wide, for their evil-doing. And the people were so terrified at his name, not to speak of himself, that they used to hide their faces in their bosoms when they used to hear it mentioned in their ears, and the people were so much afraid of him that if they heard the bark of a dog they would go hiding in the dwellings that they had underground, to take refuge in, to defend themselves from Crom Dubh and his mastiffs.

It is said that there was a linnaun shee or fairy sweetheart walking with Crom Dubh, and giving him knowledge according as he used to require it. In place of his inclining to what was good as he was growing in age, the way he went on was to be growing in badness every day, and the wind was not quicker than he, for he was as nimble as a March hare. When he used to go out about the country he used to send his two sons and his two mastiffs before him, and they announcing to the people according as they proceeded, that Crom Dubh was coming to collect his standing-rent, and bidding them to have it ready for him. Crom Dubh used to come after them, and his trickster along with him, and he drawing after him a sort of yoke like a wheelless sliding car, and according as he used to get his standing-rent it used to be thrown into the car, and everyone had to pay according to his ability. Anyone who would refuse, he used to be brought next day before Crom Dubh, as he sat beside the fire, and Crom used to pass judgment upon him, and after the judgment the man used to be thrown into the fire.

Many a plan and scheme were hatched against Crom Dubh to put him out of the world, but he overcame them all, for he had too much wizardry from the fairy sweetheart.

Crom Dubh was continuing his evil deeds for many years, and according as the story about him remains living and told from person to person, they say that he was a native of Hell in the skin of a biped, and through the horror that the people of the country had for him they would have given all that ever they saw if only Crom Dubh and his company could have been put an end to. But there was no help for them in that, since he and his company had the power, and they had to endure bitter persecution for years, and for many years, and every year it was getting worse. And they without any hope of relief because they had no knowledge of God or Mary or of anything else which concerned Heaven. For that reason they could not put trust in any person beyond Crom Dubh, because they thought, bad as he was, that it was he who was giving them the light of the day, the darkness of the night, and the change of seasons.

It was well, brother of my heart. During this time Saint Patrick was going throughout Ireland, working diligently and baptizing many people. On he went until he came to Fochoill or Foghill. And at that time and for long afterwards there were nothing but woods that grew in that place, but there is neither branch nor tree there now. However, to pursue the story, Saint Patrick began explaining to the pagans about the light and glory of the heavens. Some of them gave ear to him, but the most of them paid him no attention. After he had taken all those who listened to him to the place which was called the Well of the Branch to baptize them, and when he had them baptized, the people called the well Tobar Padraig, or Patrick's Well, and that is there ever since.

When these pagans got the seal of Christ on their forehead, and knowledge of the Holy Trinity, they began telling Saint Patrick about the doings of Crom Dubh and his evil ways, and they besought him if he had any power from the Almighty Father to chastise Crom Dubh, rightly or wrongly, or to give him the Christian faith if it were possible.

It was well, brother, Saint Patrick passed on over through Tráigh Leacan, up Béal Trághadh, down Craobhach, and down under the Logán, the name that was on Crom Dubh's place before Saint Patrick came. When Saint Patrick reached the Logán, which is near the present Ballycastle, he was within a quarter of a mile of Crom Dubh's house, and at the same time Crom Dubh and Téideach his son were trying a bout of wrestling with one another, while Saidhthe Suaraighe was stretched out on the ground from ear to tail. With the squeezing they were giving one another they never observed Saint Patrick making for them until Saidhthe Suaraighe put a howling bark out of her, and with that the pair looked behind them and they saw Saint Patrick and his defensive company with him, making for them. And in the twinkling of an eye the two rushed forward, clapping their hands and setting Saidhthe Suaraighe at them and encouraging her.

With that Téideach put his forefinger into his mouth and let a whistle calling for Coinn Iotair, for she was at that same time hunting with Clonnach on the top of Glen Lasaire, and Glen Lasaire is nearly two miles from Dún Padraig, but she was not as long as while you'd be saying Deo Gratias coming from Glen Lasaire when she heard the sound of the whistle. They urged the two bitches against Saint Patrick, and at the same time they did not know what sort of man Saint Patrick was or where he came from.

The two bitches made for him and coals of fire out of their mouths, and a blue venomous light burning in their eyes, with the dint of venom and wickedness, but just as they were going to seize Saint Patrick he cut a ring round about him with the crozier which he had in his hand, and before the dogs reached the verge of the ring Saint Patrick spoke as follows:

"A lock on thy claws, a lock on thy tooth,
A lock on Coinn Iotair of the fury.
A lock on the son and on the daughter of Saidhthe Suaraighe.
A lock quickly, quickly on you."

Before Saint Patrick began to utter these words there was a froth of foam round their mouths, and their hair was standing up as strong as harrow-pins with their fury, but after this as they came nearer to Saint Patrick they began to lay down their ears and wag their tails. And when Crom Dubh saw that, he had like to faint, because he knew when they laid down their ears that they would not do any hurt to him they were attacking. The moment they reached Saint Patrick they began jumping up upon him and making friendly with him. They licked both his feet from the top of his great toe to the butt of his ankle, and that affection is amongst dogs from that day to this. Saint Patrick began to stroke them with his hand and he went on making towards Crom Dubh, with the dogs walking at his heels. Crom Dubh ran until he came to the fire and he stood up beside the fire, so that he might throw Saint Patrick into it when he should come as far as it. But as Saint Patrick knew the strength of the fire beforehand he lifted a stone in his hand, signed the sign of the cross on the stone, and flung the stone so as to throw it into the middle of the flames, and on the moment the fire went down to the lowest depths of the ground, in such a way that the hole is there yet to be seen, from that day to this, and it is called Poll na Sean-tuine, the Hole of the Old Fire, and when the tide fills, the water comes into the bottom of the hole, and it would draw "deaf cows out of woods"—the noise that comes out of the hole when the tide is coming in.

It was well, company of the world. When Crom Dubh saw that the fire had departed out of sight, and that the dogs had failed him and given him no help (a thing they had never done before), he himself and Téideach struck out like a blast of March wind until they reached the house, and Saint Patrick came after them. They had not far to go, for the fire was near the house. When Saint Patrick approached it he began to talk aloud with Crom Dubh, and he did his best to change him to a good state of grace, but it failed him to put the seal of Christ on his forehead, for he would not give any ear to Saint Patrick's words.

Now there was no trick of deviltry, druidism, witchcraft, or black art in his heart, which he did not work for all he was able, trying to gain the victory over Saint Patrick, but it was all no use for him, for the words of God were more powerful than the deviltry of the fairy sweetheart.

With the dint of the fury that was on Crom Dubh and on Téideach his son, they began snapping and grinding their teeth, and so outrageous was their fury that Saint Patrick gave a blow of his crozier to the cliff under the base of the gable of the house, and he separated that much of the cliff from the cliffs on the mainland, and that is to be seen there today just as well as the first day, and that is the cliff that is called Dún Briste or Broken Fort.

To pursue the story. All that much of the cliff is a good many yards out in the sea from the cliff on the mainland, so Crom Dubh and his son had to remain there until the midges and the scaldcrows had eaten the flesh off their bones. And that is the death that Crom Dubh got, and that is the second man that midges ate, and our ancient shanachies say that the first man that midges ate was Judas after he had hanged himself. And that is the cause why the bite of the midges is so sharp as it is.

To pursue the story still further. When Clonnach saw what had happened to his father he took fright, and he was terrified of Saint Patrick, and he began burning the mountain until he had all that side of the land set on fire. So violently did the mountains take fire on each side of him that himself could not escape, and they say that he himself was burned to a lump amongst them.

Saint Patrick returned back to Fochoill and round through Baile na Pairce, the Town of the Field, and Bein Buidhe, the Yellow Ben, and back to Clochar. The people gathered in multitudes from every side doing honorable homage to Saint Patrick, and the pride of the world on them that an end had been made of Crom Dubh.

There was a well near and handy, and he brought the great multitude round about the well, and he never left mother's son or man's daughter without setting on their faces the wave of baptism and the seal of Christ on their foreheads. They washed and scoured the walls of the well, and all round about it, and they got forked branches and limbs of trees and bound white and blue ribbons on them, and set them round about the well, and every one of them bowed down on his knees saying their prayers of thankfulness to God, and as an entertainment for Saint Patrick on account of his having put an end to the sway of Crom Dubh.

After making an end of offering up their prayers every man of them drank three sups of water out of the well, and there is not a year from that out that the people used not to make a turus or pilgrimage to the well, on the anniversary of that day. And that day is the last Sunday of the seventh month, and the name the Irish-speakers call the month by in that place is the month of Lughnas, and the name of the Sunday is Crom Dubh's Sunday, but the name that the English-speakers call the Sunday by is Garland Sunday. There is never a year from that to this that there does not be a meeting in Cill Chuimin, for that is the place where the well is. They come far and near to make a pilgrimage to the well; and a number of other people go there too, to amuse themselves and drink and spend. And I believe that the most of that rakish lot go there making a mock of the Christian Irish-speakers who are offering up their prayers to their holy patron Patrick, high head of their religion.

Cuimin's Well is the name of this well, for its name was changed during the time of Saint Cuimin on account of all the miraculous things he did there, and he is buried within a perch of the well in Cill Chuimin.

There does be a gathering on the same Sunday at Dún Padraig or Downpatrick at the well which is called Tobar Brighde or Brigit's Well beside Cill Brighde, and close to Dún Briste. But, love of my heart, since the English jargon began a short time ago in that place the old Christian custom of the Christians is almost utterly gone off.

There now ye have it as I got it, and if ye don't like it add to it your complaints.

❖ SAINT BRIGIT

GALWAY
LADY GREGORY *1906*

Now as to Brigit she was born at sunrise on the first day of the spring, of a bondwoman of Connacht. And it was angels that baptized her and that gave her the name of Brigit, that is a Fiery Arrow.

She grew up to be a serving girl the same as her mother. And all the food she used was the milk of a white red-eared cow that was set apart for her by a Druid.

And everything she put her hand to used to increase, and it was she wove the first piece of cloth in Ireland, and she put the white threads in the loom that have a power of healing in them to this day. She bettered the sheep and she satisfied the birds and she fed the poor.

And when she grew to be strong and to have good courage she went to her father Dubthach's house in Munster and stopped with him there.

And one time there came some high person to the house, and food was made ready for him and for his people; and five pieces of bacon were given to Brigit, to boil them. But there came into the house a very hungry miserable hound, and she gave him out of pity a piece of the bacon.

And when the hound was not satisfied with that she gave him another piece. Then Dubthach came and he asked Brigit were the pieces of bacon ready; and she bade him count them and he counted them, and the whole of the five pieces were there, not one of them missing. But the high guest that was there and that Brigit had thought to be asleep had seen all, and he told her father all that happened.

And he and the people that were with him did not eat that meat, for they were not worthy of it, but it was given to the poor and to the wretched.

After that Brigit went to visit her mother that was in bondage to a Druid of Connacht.

And it is the way she was at that time, at a grass-farm of the mountains having on it twelve cows, and she gathering butter.

And there was sickness on her, and Brigit cared her and took charge of the whole place.

And the churning she made, she used to divide it first into twelve parts in honor of the twelve apostles of our Lord; and the thirteenth part she would make bigger than the rest, to the honor of Christ, and that part she would give to strangers and to the poor.

And the serving boy wondered to see her doing that, but it is what she used to say: "It is in the name of Christ I feed the poor; for Christ is in the body of every poor man."

When she was a poor girl she was minding her cow one time at the Curragh of Lifé, and she had no place to feed it but the side of the road. And a rich man that owned the land came by and saw her and he said: "How much land would it take to give grass to the cow?" "As much as my cloak would cover," said she. "I will give that," said the rich man.

She laid down her cloak then, and it was spreading out miles and miles on every side. But there was a silly old woman passing by and she said: "If that cloak goes on spreading, all Ireland will be free." And with that the cloak stopped and spread no more.

And Brigit held that land through her lifetime, and it never had rent on it since, but the English Government have taken it now and have put barracks upon it. It is a pity the old woman spoke at that time. She did not know Brigit to be better than any other one.

On the day of the battle of Almhuin, Brigit was seen over the men of Leinster, and Columcille was seen over the Ua Neill; and it was the men of Leinster won that battle.

And a long time after that again, when Strongbow that had brought great trouble into Ireland and that was promised the kingdom of Leinster was near his end, he cried out from his bed that he saw Brigit of the Gael, and that it was she herself was bringing him to his death.

But if Brigit belonged to the east, it is not in the west she is forgotten, and the people of Burren and of Corcomruadh and Kinvara go every year to her blessed well that is near the sea, praying and remembering her.

And in that well there is a little fish that is seen every seven years, and whoever sees that fish is cured of every disease. And there is a woman living yet that is poor and old and that saw that blessed fish, and this is the way she tells the story:

"I had a pearl in my eye one time, and I went to Saint Brigit's well on the cliffs. Scores of people there were in it, looking for cures, and some got them and some did not get them.

And I went down the four steps to the well and I was looking into it, and I saw a little fish no longer than your finger coming from a stone under the water. Three spots it had on the one side and three on the other side, red spots and a little green with the red, and it was very civil coming hither to me and very pleasant wagging its tail. And it stopped and looked up at me and gave three wags of its back, and walked off again and went in under the stone.

"And I said to a woman that was near me that I saw the little fish, and she began to call out and to say there were many coming with cars and with horses for a month past and none of them saw it at all.

And she proved me, asking had it spots, and I said it had, three on the one side and three on the other side. "That is it," she said.

And within three days I had the sight of my eye again. It was surely Saint Brigit I saw that time; who else would it be? And you would know by the look of it that it was no common fish. Very civil it was, and nice and loughy, and no one else saw it at all. Did I say more prayers than the rest? Not a prayer. I was young in those days. I suppose she took a liking to me, maybe because of my name being Brigit the same as her own."

❖ Saint Columcille

HUGH NOLAN ◈ *FERMANAGH*
HENRY GLASSIE *1977*

Columcille.

Well, do ye see, he was a native of Donegal.

There's a place in Donegal they call Glencolumcille, and I think maybe that's where he's from.

You see,
he had to leave this country
over a book.

I don't know what's this man's name was, but he wrote this religious book.

(I'm just not well up on this story.)

And I think that Saint Columcille got the book for to read.

And he took a copy of the book, do ye see.

So when he was giving back the book, as far as I can remember, he wanted to keep the copy, do ye see, that he had wrote.

So the man that owned the book, he wouldn't agree to that.

And they wrangled and wrangled and wrangled for a long time about this.

So finally the case was referred to the high king.

There was a king in this country at that time.

So the way he decided it was:
that
to every cow belongs her *calf*,
and
to every book belongs its *copy*.

So he give judgment in favor of this man that owned the book.

So then Saint Columcille, of course, naturally enough, he was vexed.

And any man would be vexed
about being deprived of his own writings
and what he considered to be his own.

So anyway, he decided that he would put it to a battle,
and whoever would win the battle that
this copy of this book would be his.

So anyway, both men prepared for the battle.

And there was a day appointed.

And a battle took place.

And Saint Columcille's men won the battle.

And he had to get a copy of the book.

So whenever it was *over,* he got sorry for what he done, for putting it to that fellow.

And he went to some holy *man* to get his advice on it.

And what this man told him was that he'd have to do a little penance for the loss of what life was in the battle, that he'd have to try and convert as many as was killed in this battle.

So anyway, his sentence was
that he'd have to leave Ireland
for all time
for to never return,
and that he'd have to go to some pagan land
and convert as many to Christianity
as was killed in the battle
that was over the book.

So anyway, he started.

And it was in Scotland he landed.

And he wrought in Scotland till he died in preaching and converting.

All the time that ever he came back to Ireland was—and he had to come back blindfolded because the penance that was left on him was that he'd never see Ireland more and that he'd have to *leave it.*

So he came back blindfolded on an errand.

And the errand was:

There was at a *time* and there was a section of the Irish people used to go about in bands: they were the bards.

There was an instrument, there are instruments to this day yet in places in Ireland: the harp.

These ones played on harps and others sang and they went round from one town to another, and noted places like Arney and Derrylin and Enniskillen, and put in nights and amused the *people.*

So there was some kind of a law that these people were all going to be banished out of the country.

So Saint Columcille was informed about it in Scotland that that was coming to pass in Ireland.

So he came back to Ireland blindfolded.

And he made an appeal to the authorities for not to banish these because he was a lover of music and stuff like that.

So that was all the time he got back to Ireland from he had to leave it.

So he died in Scotland at a very big age.

He was a great, a great man, and wonderful for bringing people to the knowledge of God and Christianity.

And then he had his own troubles too.

❖ Columcille's coffin

PÁDRAIG Mac an LUAIN ◈ *DONEGAL*
SÉAMAS Ó CATHÁIN *1972*

After Colm was sentenced to exile, he sailed away from Derry for Scotland. He wasn't even allowed to look back as he went. He came to Iona and spent his life converting pagans over there.

Colm had a lovely big white horse of which he was very fond and when Colm grew old and lay on his deathbed, the horse came into the house and over to the bed where he lay. It sniffed and nosed all around him and then went out again. Colm died that night. But before he died, he asked that his name be put on his coffin and that the coffin should be cast out into the sea. And so it was done.

Down at the lower end of Inishowen, there was a man who had a lot of cattle and he had a boy hired to herd them. The boy used to take them down to the shore every day to graze. But there was one cow which never ate any grass and was forever down on the sands licking at something or other.

The boy never paid much attention to her, but the farmer noticed that this particular cow was beginning to give more and more milk, far more than the rest of them, so much so, in fact, that there weren't enough vessels about the place to hold it all.

"What's that cow eating more than any of the rest of them?" asked the farmer.

"She's not eating anything at all," said the boy. "But she's always down on the sands licking at something or other."

Down they went to see what the cow was licking and, sure enough, there was Columcille's coffin sticking up out of the sand on the shore with his name on the lid and orders for him to be buried in Downpatrick. And so it was done.

❖ ❖ ❖

❖ SAINT KEVIN

MR. WYNDER ◈ *WICKLOW*
MR. AND MRS. S. C. HALL *1841*

One day in spring before the blossoms were on the trees, a young man grievously afflicted with the falling sickness fancied that an apple would cure him, and the dickens an apple tree at all at all was about the place. But what mattered that to the Saint! He ordered a score of fine yellow pippins to grow upon a willow, and the boy gathered and ate and was cured.

The Saint was one day going up Derrybawn, and he meets a woman that carried five loaves in her apron.

"What have ye there, good woman?" says the Saint.

"I have five stones," says she.

"If they are stones," says he, "I pray that they may be bread. And if they are bread," says he, "I pray that they may be stones."

So, with that, the woman lets them fall, and sure enough, stones they were, and are to this day.

The Saint managed to get from King O'Toole a grant of the land upon which he built his churches.

The king was old and weak in himself, and took a mightly liking to a goose, a live goose. And in course of time the goose was like the master, old and weak.

So O'Toole sent for his Holiness. And his Holiness went to see what would the pagan—for King O'Toole was a heathen—want with him.

"God save ye," says the Saint.

"God save ye kindly," says the king.

"A better answer than I expected," says the Saint.

"Will ye make my goose young?" says the king.

"What'll ye give me?" says the Saint.

"What'll ye ask?" says the king.

"All I'll ask will be as much of the valley as he'll fly over," says the Saint.

"Done," says the king.

So with that Saint Kevin stoops down, takes up the goose, and flings him up, and away he goes over the lake and all round the Glen, which in course was the Saint's hereditary property from that day out.

❖ Saint Finbar

DONNCHA Ó CRÓINÍN ◈ *CORK*
SEAN O'SULLIVAN *1937*

Long long ago, before Saint Finbar came to Gougane, the little lake was between the mountains, and on a calm day you would like to be looking at it, the water was so still. At that time there was a small house there and a widow and her son lived in it. They had one cow, and every day the son would mind the cow while his mother was busy around the house.

One day when he went down to the lake, what did he see, instead of the water, but an ugly serpent that was almost as big as one of the hills around. The boy was terrified and he ran home. They didn't know from where the serpent had come or why she came, so there was great excitement around the place. The serpent remained there and came out every day and swept off anything she met. At last the people of the district were ruined, and were afraid to go outside their doors.

Saint Finbar came to the district and the people begged him to do something for them. They had no great faith in the saint for the parish priest had spent his time trying to banish the serpent. That was good and it wasn't bad.

One night when the great world was asleep, and the serpent along with them, Saint Finbar went out with two of his friars. He never halted until he reached the lake. He walked around it three times, praying. When he reached the mouth of the lake the third time, he stopped, took out a small bottle of holy water that he had, and sprinkled it three times on the serpent. The serpent shook herself and let out a roar that shook the hills round about. Then she moved from where she was and tore and devoured the land until she came to where Lough Loo is today. She made a bed there for herself. Next morning she moved on again and never stopped till she reached Cork Harbor. There she entered the sea.

Water has filled the track she left behind her, and that's the River Lee today. The people of the place were so grateful to Saint Finbar that they drew stones and earth and made a small island in the middle of the lake. There he built a monastery.

❖ JAMES MURRAY AND SAINT MARTIN

TIMOTHY SHEAHY ◈ *KERRY*
JEREMIAH CURTIN *1892*

There was a small farmer named James Murray, who lived between this and Slieve Mish. He had the grass of seven cows, but though he had the land, he hadn't stock to put on it; he had but the one cow. Being a poor man, he went to Cork with four firkins of butter for a neighbor. He never thought what day of the month it was until he had the butter sold in the city, and it was Saint Martin's Eve at the time. Himself and his father before him and his grandfather had always killed something to honor Saint Martin, and when he was in Cork on Saint Martin's Eve he felt heartsore and could not eat. He walked around and muttered to himself: "I wish to the Almighty God I was at home. My house will be disgraced forever."

The words weren't out of his mouth when a fine-looking gentleman stood before him and asked: "What trouble is on you, good man?"

James Murray told the gentleman.

"Well, my poor man, you would like to be at home tonight?"

"Indeed, then, I would, and but for I forgot the day of the month, it isn't here I'd be now, poor as I am."

"Where do you live?"

"Near the foot of Slieve Mish, in Kerry."

"Bring out your horse and creels, and you will be at home."

"What is the use in talking? 'Tis too far for such a journey."

"Never mind. Bring out your horse."

James Murray led out the horse, mounted, and rode away. He thought he wasn't two hours on the road when he was going in at his own door. Sure, his wife was astonished and didn't believe that he could be home from Cork in that time. It was only when he showed the money they paid him for the other man's butter that she believed.

"Well, this is Saint Martin's Eve!"

"It is," said she. "What are we to do? I don't know, for we have nothing to kill."

Out went James and drove in the cow.

"What are you going to do?" asked the wife.

"To kill the cow in honor of Saint Martin."

"Indeed, then, you will not."

"I will, indeed," and he killed her. He skinned the cow and cooked some of her flesh, but the woman was down in the room at the other end of the house lamenting.

"Come up now and eat your supper," said the husband.

But she would not eat, and was only complaining and crying. After supper the whole family went to bed. Murray rose at daybreak next morning, went to the door, and saw seven gray cows, and they feeding in the field.

"Whose cows are those eating my grass?" cried he, and ran out to drive them away. Then he saw that they were not like other cattle in the district, and they were fat and bursting with milk.

"I'll have the milk at least, to pay for the grass they've eaten," said James Murray. So his wife milked the gray cows and he drove them back to the field. The cows were contented in themselves and didn't wish to go away. Next day he published the cows, but no one ever came to claim them.

"It was the Almighty God and Saint Martin who sent these cows," said he, and he kept them. In the summer all the cows had heifer calves, and every year for seven years they had heifer calves, and the calves were all gray, like the cows. James Murray got very rich, and his crops were the best in the county. He bought new land and had a deal of money put away. But it happened on the eighth year one of the cows had a bull calf. What did Murray do but kill the calf. That minute the seven old cows began to bellow and run away, and the calves bellowed and followed them, all ran and never stopped till they went into the sea and disappeared under the waves. They were never seen after that, but, as Murray used to give away a heifer calf sometimes during the seven years, there are cows of that breed around Slieve Mish and Dingle to this day, and every one is as good as two cows.

THE BEST ROAD TO HEAVEN

MARY GLYN ◈ *GALWAY*
LADY GREGORY *1903*

There was a woman I knew was very charitable to the poor; and she'd give them the full of her apron of bread, or of potatoes or anything she had. And she was only lately married. And one day, a poor woman came to the door with her children and she brought them to the fire, and warmed them, and gave them a drink of milk; and she sent out to the barn for a bag of potatoes for them.

And the husband came in, and he said: "Kitty, if you go on this way, you won't leave much for ourselves."

And she said: "He that gave us what we have, can give us more."

And the next day when they went out to the barn, it was full of potatoes —more than were ever in it before.

And when she was dying, and her children about her, the priest said to her: "Mrs. Gallagher, it's in Heaven you'll be at twelve o'clock tomorrow.

THE MAN FROM KILMACOLIVER

MICK McCARTHY ◈ *TIPPERARY*
ROSE SPRINGFIELD *1955*

Now the Cross at Ahenny is in the graveyard, and a man from Kilmacoliver was passing by one day (and he was so mean that his soul was as narrow as a knitting needle, and if you had a cold in the head he would grudge it to you)—well, when he saw the cross he said to himself: "That would make a grand hone for my scythe, if I sawed off an arm of it."

He went home and got his saw, and he began to saw it off, and he looked up and saw his house on the opposite hill at Kilmacoliver was on fire, and he dropped his saw and ran to save his house, and when he got there it was no fire, only the setting sun shining on the windows.

Still and all, he would not be warned, and he called his son, who was a young lad, to go back with him. And the young lad was to carry back the arm of the Cross when it was sawed off. And they went back, and he picked up the saw, and began to saw again in the same notch, and as he sawed, drops of blood fell from the notch he had made and fell on him, and he gave one mighty skirl that was heard as far as Mullinahone, and the echo of it as far as Grangemockler and Toor, and even to Kilcash, and he fell down with the falling sickness, and the young lad ran off for help. And when the people came, he was wriggling like an eel, but no matter how he twisted, the blood drops still fell on him, and each place they dropped on was burned through to the bone, and in the latter end he died. And it was as well.

❖ THE PIOUS MAN

KATE AHERN ◈ *LIMERICK*
KEVIN DANAHER *1967*

There was a man there long ago, and he had a great name of being very holy. He was the first up the chapel on Sunday, and there was never a pattern or a mission that he wasn't at, praying all around him. And he was being held up as a good example to the sinners as a very holy man that never missed his duty.

Well, he said to himself that it would be a good thing for him to count all the times he was at Mass, so he got a big timber box and he made a hole in the cover of it, and he locked the box so that no one could interfere with it in any way, and he hid the key where no one could possibly find it.

And every time he went to Mass he picked up a small pebble of a stone on his way home and dropped it in through the hole in the cover of the box.

And he was not satisfied with going to Mass on Sunday, and he started to go every single weekday as well, and sometimes he'd be at second Mass as well as at first Mass on the Sunday, and all the time he was putting the stone into the box every time he came home from Mass.

Well, the years were going on and, like all the rest of us, he was getting old, and he was saying to himself that there must be a great heap of stones inside in the box, and that maybe he would have to get a new box, that the old one must be nearly full.

He called in the servant boy. "Pull out that box for me, boy, until I open it. And mind yourself, because it must be very heavy."

The boy handled it. "It is not a bit heavy, sir, but as light as you like," says the boy.

He opened it and there were only five stones inside in it. He couldn't understand it, and off with him to the parish priest with his complaint—after all his Masses was he only going to get credit for five of them, or was it how someone was bad enough to steal the stones out of his box, but how could they do that, and it locked and the key hidden, and no sign that it was ever meddled with?

Well, this parish priest had great wisdom. "It is like this, my good man," says he. "It was not about the Mass you were thinking, and it was not for your neighbors that you were praying all the times that you were at Mass, but all the time thinking how pious you were and how everyone should have great respect for you. And that is a sign to you from Heaven that you heard only five of the Masses properly, and that is the only five you will get credit for. And remember that, now, the next time you go to the church."

I tell you that it is not the one that is first to the chapel that is the highest in the sight of God.

❖ An Actual Saint

SEÁN MURPHY ◈ *KERRY*
LAWRENCE MILLMAN *1975*

I used to always go to an old person for to get a few histories. 'Twas an old man that in nineteen twenty-eight told me this: he said that there was a wonderful man living just beyond here, a sheepherder for a Protestant landlord years ago, and this man had no knowledge of anything but his sheep and his lands. He was away up in the mountain beyond minding sheep, and he never seen a chapel, he was miles away from a chapel.

There was a priest crossing one time, and the priest began to talk to this man, and he says, "Do you go to Mass?" "What is that?" says he. The priest asked him his age, and he told him, a man well gone in years, a white bawneen he was wearing. "Next Sunday," says the priest, "you'll see the people going to Mass, and follow them. Follow them down the mountain." "All right," says he.

Sure enough, the next Sunday he followed them down the mountain and into the chapel. The day was very warm, and after walking, and when he was coming inside, he started to pour sweat. There was a sunbeam coming in from the window, and he thought it was a rope, and he took off his white bawneen and threw it up upon it, and faith, believe it or believe it not, the coat caught up on the sunbeam and the sunbeam kept the coat. Then the priest, seeing the coat hanging there, said to the congregation, "Thanks be to God, there's a saint at Mass today."

After Mass, the priest came up to the old man and told him he needn't come any more. Why? Because he was a true Christian, a living saint, Because if he continued coming to that chapel, could happen next Sunday, he could fall into sin and the sunbeam wouldn't hold up the coat. He might look at a handsome lassie, that's all the marks you need ever pass, that's a sin for you. So he stayed away for the rest of his life.

You see, that man was an actual saint. He was in the mountains all his life, out there on his own, and there was more religion in him than there could ever be if he went looking for it, at the chapel. I don't think the sunbeam would have held up that priest's coat.

That happened for a fact. But they're very few saints left in it today, of that you can be even more sure. No, not many saints at all and altogether too many priests, at least that's what I think.

❖ Old Thorns and Old Priests

ARMAGH

MICHAEL J. MURPHY *1975*

Old thorns and old priests should be left alone: there's power in the pair of them if they want to use it. You may not believe it, but there was a time in Ireland when everyone believed it and maybe right they were. It's better be sure than sorry.

Anyhow, there was this fellow one time and he was very fond of the drink. Worse still he had a wife and a family, and the way he was drinking himself out of house and habitation they were living on the clippings of tin, licking the stones. She was sick, sore, and tired scolding him and asking him to have sense, so in the latter end she went to the old parish priest about him.

The parish priest listened to her story and said he would see what he could do. So this day there was a market or something in the village and the priest knew your man would be there and wouldn't leave the public house till he lowered every cent in his pocket down the red lane, and maybe rise more on the slate if his name was good.

So the priest was in the village and he seen your man heading for the public house. He called him over.

"I forbid you to go in there this day," says he.

"Only one drink, Father," says he, "and then I'm going home to my wife and childer."

"One drink," says the priest, "will lead to another drink and another and another till you go home with the two legs plaiting under you. Now listen here," says the priest, "I don't want to use my power, but if you go inside that public house today or let drink wet your lips, I'll turn you into a mouse by twelve o'clock tonight."

At that the priest turned and walked away home, and your man turned and walked home too. He didn't want to draw the anger of the priest on him and he believed he had the power when he wanted.

He wasn't far outside the village on his way home and who does he meet but an old pal who'd been years in England or America and was just home. Well, you know how it is. Handshakes and great talk and what not. And before your man knew where he was, he was back with this pal in the pub in the village and didn't leave it till he couldn't see a hole in a ladder.

It was dark, down night when he got as far as his own house and his wife, Mary, was sitting lamenting to herself at the fire. He staggered in and looked at the mantelpiece and he could see the clock all right but he was that cross-eyed with drink he couldn't tell what time it was.

"Mary," says he, "what time is it?"

"What time do you think?" says she. "It's a few minutes off midnight."

"Mary," says he, "if you see me getting wee and hairy . . . put out that bloody cat."

❖ PRIESTS AND FARMING MEN

PETER FLANAGAN ◈ *FERMANAGH*
HENRY GLASSIE *1972*

There was a man out here, he was the name of Tom Nabby.

And the priest engaged him this day to clean up the cemetery.

So, he started to work and was working a considerable length of time.

He was fond of a drink, like meself, and he was expecting one too. And the priest came into the graveyard where he was working. And he had a half-pint in his hand.

"Now," he says, "Tom," he says, "I'm going to treat you."

"I'm very thankful to ye, Father," he says, "surely."

"I'm sure you'd like it."

"Oh indeed I would," he says, "like it surely. I was always used to a half-one."

So the priest handed him the half-one, or the glass, whatever it contained.

"And now," says the priest to him, he says, "do you know Tom, I'm not against you drinking," he says, "but *every* one of them that you drink," he says, "is a nail in your coffin."

So Tom took and he put it on his head and he drunk it *down.*

"Well," he says, "please, Father, while you're at it," he says, "just drive another nail into me coffin."

Aye.

There was another man like meself: he was a fiddler, and he lived up at Derrylin.

And of course, I think the fiddlers longgo, they hadn't too much money, and any drink they got, they drunk it.

This man, well, whether he had drink in him or not, he appeared to be drunk nearly every day. He was drunk in the priest's eye every day.

He lived near the parochial house, and every time the priest went out, he met him nearly, and this day, "Och, Tom," he says:

"Drunk the day again," says he to Tom.

"Aye," and says Tom back to him:

"So am I."

❖ Saved by the Priest

ANNIE O'HAGAN ◈ *TYRONE*
SÉAMAS Ó CATHÁIN *1980*

I remember hearing Brian telling this story—somebody told it to him. It was some church anyway, but there was a funeral. And there was this wee man—a Catholic man—and he went to the wake. And at that time, away years ago, the morning of the funeral, the man of the house, he'd have two or three men go round with a bottle of whiskey and a glass to treat every man that went to the funeral.

So this wee man got enough, he got a wee drop too much anyway and he went to the church and when the service was over, didn't he fall asleep with the drink from the night before and all. Nobody in the church seen him—he was in the seat but he fell down and he was sleeping.

It was very late on that night when he wakened and come till himself and realized where he was.

So he couldn't get out—it seems they locked up and he had no way of getting out.

So the only thing he could think of was to ring the bell. So he started to ring the bell in the Protestant church the same night as the night of the funeral. And, of course, the neighbors heard it and the minister heard it and they come and they took fear and they wouldn't go in. The minister wouldn't venture in, do you see, for the bell had been tingling and ringing, and neither would the men.

So it gathered up before all was over that there was a right crowd of people gathered to know what had happened. So they decided anyway that they would go for the parish priest.

The parish priest landed anyway, got up out of his bed and landed, and he had a—now, whether he had a car, now, or a side-car—but he had a big rug with him and whether he put it around his shoulders or what, they were that excited they never noticed.

So the priest opened the church door and he went in. He walked in and seen his man and knowed him so well and he had a wee chat with him inside. The man told him the whole story: "I was at the wake," says he, "last night and I got a lot of drink. I got more this morning," he says, "and when I went into the church I fell asleep."

"Well," says the priest, "just keep quiet and we'll make a good thing out of this."

So he got this big hairy rug. "Now," says the priest, "I want you to walk bent over like this and I'm putting this rug over your head, right over your head. Now, you do what I bid you and walk in the front and I'll go behind you. And I'll go out now and I'll tell the boys that he's here all right!" That was the Devil—but it was only a Catholic man.

He went out and he says to the minister, "I'll tell you what you'll do. Go on every side, make a path in the middle, you men, now. Keep on each side," he says, "I'm taking him out now—I'm putting him out."

In he goes and he warned him to be sure and bend down and walk very low, just bend and crawl along and the rug was right out over his head. And he got behind him and your man walked out of the church door and up the path.

Well, he said that they fainted in all directions. Some of them fainted and some of them run. They run in all directions when they seen what was coming out of the church. They thought it was the Devil and instead of that it was a Catholic man the worse of drink!

❖ THE DOOM

GALWAY

LADY WILDE *1887*

There was a young man of Innismore, named James Lynan, noted through all the island for his beauty and strength. Never a one could beat him at hunting or wrestling, and he was, besides, the best dancer in the whole townland. But he was bold and reckless, and ever foremost in all the wild wicked doings of the young fellows of the place.

One day he happened to be in chapel after one of these mad freaks, and the priest denounced him by name from the altar.

"James Lynan," he said, "remember my words. You will come to an ill end. The vengeance of God will fall on you for your wicked life. And by the power that is in me I denounce you as an evil liver and a limb of Satan, and accursed of all good men."

The young man turned pale, and fell on his knees before all the people, crying out bitterly, "Have mercy, have mercy; I repent, I repent," and he wept like a woman.

"Go now in peace," said the priest, "and strive to lead a new life, and I'll pray to God to save your soul."

From that day forth James Lynan changed his ways. He gave up drinking, and never a drop of spirits crossed his lips. And he began to attend to his farm and his business, in place of being at all the mad revels and dances and fairs and wakes in the island. Soon after he married a nice girl, a rich farmer's daughter, from the mainland, and they had four fine children, and all things prospered with him.

But the priest's words never left his mind, and he would suddenly turn pale and a shivering would come over him when the memory of the curse came upon him. Still he prospered, and his life was a model of sobriety and order.

One day he and his wife and their children were asked to the wedding of a friend about four miles off. And James Lynan rode to the place, the family going on their own car. At the wedding he was the life of the party as he always was. But never a drop of drink touched his lips. When evening came on, the family set out for the return home just as they had set out; the wife and children on the car, James Lynan riding his own horse. But when the wife arrived at home, she found her husband's horse standing at the gate riderless and quite still. They thought he might have fallen in a faint, and went back to search, when he was found down in a hollow not five perches from his own gate, lying quite insensible and his features distorted frightfully, as if seized while looking on some horrible vision.

They carried him in, but he never spoke. A doctor was sent for, who opened a vein, but no blood came. There he lay like a log, speechless as one dead. Amongst the crowd that gathered round was an old woman accounted very wise by the people.

"Send for the fairy doctor," she said. "He is struck."

So they sent off a boy on the fastest horse for the fairy man. He could not come himself, but he filled a bottle with a potion. Then he said:

"Ride for your life. Give him some of this to drink and sprinkle his face and hands also with it. But take care as you pass the lone bush on the round hill near the hollow, for the fairies are there and will hinder you if they can, and strive to break the bottle."

Then the fairy man blew into the mouth and the eyes and the nostrils of the horse, and turned him round three times on the road and rubbed the dust off his hoofs.

"Now go," he said to the boy. "Go and never look behind you, no matter what you hear."

So the boy went like the wind, having placed the bottle safely in his pocket. And when he came to the lone bush the horse started and gave such a jump that the bottle nearly fell, but the boy caught it in time and held it safe and rode on. Then he heard a cluttering of feet behind him, as of men in pursuit. But he never turned or looked, for he knew it was the fairies who were after him. And shrill voices cried to him, "Ride fast, ride fast, for the spell is cast!" Still he never turned round, but rode on, and never let go his hold of the fairy draught till he stopped at his master's door, and handed the potion to the poor sorrowing wife. And she gave of it to the sick man to drink, and sprinkled his face and hands, after which he fell into a deep sleep. But when he woke up, though he knew everyone around him, the power of speech was gone from him. And from that time to his death, which happened soon after, he never uttered word more.

So the doom of the priest was fulfilled—evil was his youth and evil was his fate, and sorrow and death found him at last, for the doom of the priest is as the word of God.

The Right Cure

MALACHI HORAN ◈ *DUBLIN*
GEORGE A. LITTLE *1943*

But let me tell you this: there is many a cure that comes from God. Sorra the saint that was ever in the country but left his cure behind him in a well. That was to put you in mind of the goodness and of the power of his Master. Look at Lacken Well! It has cured thousands. It is for the rheumatism, particularly when it catches the hip. You say the Rosary at the well and drink the water. Bring the water home, then, and drink it again and rub the hip. If there is a cure for you, you will be cured.

Tobar Moling cures dry retching and stomach troubles. It cured me forever. And Saint Ann's Well, here, on Killenarden, nigh to Martin's cottage, they say is as good as Moling's Well.

Aye, and there is Our Lady's Well at the De Selby quarry. It cures wounds. Lady de Selby built a shrine there. Troth, she did. It was in thanks to the Holy Mother for curing workmen hurted in the quarry. I will bring you there some time. The day the well is visited is the fifteenth of August.

The worst of it is that there are fools who think they can buy a miraculous cure like they would a twist of tobacco. That's not the way of it at all. A man must earn his cure. He must try everything that's to his hand first. What is a man in the world for but to work? Bread and salvation, them are the masters for which a man must labor. But when he has done his best and failed, then the saints will step in and, by the mercy of God, play the good neighbor. That's fair play; is it not?

I remember the chief knuckle of my hand getting a touch from a reaping-hook. Cut to the bone it was. It festered fast, and my arm swelled to the girth of my thigh. The pain near drove me frantic. I went down to Tallaght to the doctor that used be in it. He told me I would have to go to the hospital. But I told him how could I and I with oats down and the rain coming. But he just kept saying I would have to go. The man had no sense at all. The next day I went over to Blessington, and the man there told me the same thing. As if a man could turn his back on his crop and the rain coming!

That night I was sitting here twisting in mortal agony, when a neighbor man came in to find out what way was I. When he seen how it was, he told me the cure was frog-spawn.

"Well," says I, "I may as well try it, for this pain will douse me anyway." So I did it. That night I slept. The next day I was well enough to stook. But, boys, oh boys, by night it was worse than ever. Till the crack of day it never stopped bealing and throbbing till I thought it must burst. "I'm fairly knackered this time," I thought. I did not know what way to turn or what to do, when I suddenly thought of Father Larkin, the Dominican, beyond in Tallaght. If ever there was a saint on this earth, that man was him. God be good to him forever! Amen, I say, and amen again.

What-a-way I got to Tallaght I do not know; but Father Larkin came to me to the door and brought me in. I told him my trouble. He was not for doing anything. He told me it was not his business to attend on the sick. I must go to hospital, he said, like the doctors told me. But I held his sleeve and would not let him go. I got to my knees and pled with him not to turn me out in the trouble that was on me. I was near crying.

"It lies with God," says he. "We will ask Saint Dominic to put in a word for us." He brought a statue of Saint Dominic and set it before me to put me in mind of him. Then I knelt, and he read over me a long office from out of his book. He advised me to go to confession then; and I did it. As I was going away he told me to pray hard and ask Saint Dominic to put in a word, and to take the old rags off my arm and throw them at the butt of a bush. I done all he told me, and the next day I was cured forever. Cured forever, may God be thanked, and thank him too. Aye, the Man up there is the *right* doctor. If you suffer enough and do your best, He has the pity and He has the cure.

Aye, sir, there is a power in prayer. It gets into a thing and stays in a thing. It is like the tempering of a plow-shoe. The share looks the same after it's treated as before, but the nature of it is changed.

❖ HELL AND HEAVEN

AN OLD ARMY MAN ◈ *GALWAY*
WILLIAM BUTLER YEATS *1902*

I have seen Hell myself. I had a sight of it one time in a vision. It had a very high wall around it, all of metal, and an archway, and a straight walk into it, just like what 'ud be leading into a gentleman's orchard, but the edges were not trimmed with box, but with red-hot metal. And inside the wall there were cross-walks, and I'm not sure what there was to the right, but to the left there were five great furnaces, and they full of souls kept there with great chains. So I turned short and went away, and in turning I looked again at the wall, and I could see no end to it.

And another time I saw Purgatory. It seemed to be in a level place, and no walls around it, but it all one bright blaze, and the souls standing in it. And they suffer near as much as in Hell, only there are no devils with them there, and they have the hope of Heaven.

And I heard a call to me from there, "Help me to come out o' this!" And when I looked it was a man I used to know in the army, an Irishman, and from this county, and I believe him to be a descendant of King O'Connor of Athenry.

So I stretched out my hand first, but then I called out, "I'd be burned in the flames before I could get within three yards of you." So then he said, "Well, help me with your prayers," and so I do.

And Father Connellan says the same thing, to help the dead with your prayers, and he's a very clever man to make a sermon, and has a great deal of cures made with the Holy Water he brought back from Lourdes.

❖ THE WOLF'S PROPHECY

GALWAY
LADY GREGORY *1907*

It chanced one day not long after the coming of the Gall from England into Ireland, there was a priest making his way through a wood of Meath. And there came a man fornenst him and bade him for the love of God to come with him to confess his wife that was lying sick near that place.

So the priest turned with him and it was not long before he heard groaning and complaining as would be heard from a woman, but when he came where she was lying it was a wolf he saw before him on the ground. The priest was afeared when he saw that and he turned away; but the man and the wolf spoke with him and bade him not to be afeared but to turn and to confess her. Then the priest took heart and blessed him and sat down beside her.

And the wolf spoke to him and made her confession to the priest and he anointed her. And when they had that done, the priest began to think in himself that she that had that mislikeness upon her and had grace to speak, might likely have grace and the gift of knowledge in other things; and he asked her about the strangers that were come into Ireland, and what way it would be with them.

And it is what the wolf said: "It was through the sin of the people of this country Almighty God was displeased with them and sent that race to bring them into bondage, and so they must be until the Gall themselves will be encumbered with sin. And at that time the people of Ireland will have power to put on them the same wretchedness for their sins."

WIT

THE FOX AND THE RANGER, etching by Samuel Lover
Samuel Lover, *Legends and Stories of Ireland*, 1834

❖ The Three Questions

MICHAEL MURPHY ◈ *ARMAGH*
MICHAEL J. MURPHY *1975*

It was this codger and he was hired as a herdsboy to a bishop. Things were bad in Ireland at the time: the enemy had come and conquered the country and took the land and was killing all before them, priest and people.

So this evening the herdsboy come home and he seen the bishop walking up and down and looking very down-in-the-mouth.

"My Lord Bishop," says the herdsboy, "what ails you? You look very downhearted?"

"I'm to die in the morning," says the bishop.

"How is that?" says the herdsboy.

"I'm to lose me head," says the bishop. "The chief that took over this country," he says, "sent for me this morning and give me three questions to answer by the morra morning and if I'm not fit he's to take the head off me."

"What's the three questions, my lord?" says the herdsboy. "I might be fit to help."

"You could not," says the bishop. "You might only lose your own head as well."

Anyway he got the bishop to tell him, and the herdsboy said that he would go in place of the bishop next morning and to leave all to him.

"You'll only lose your head, too," says the bishop.

Morning come and the herdsboy set off and meets this big fellow and stands before him.

"Who are you?" says he.

"I'm herdsboy to the Lord Bishop," says he.

"Why didn't he come himself?" says he.

"The Lord Bishop didn't think it worth his while," says he, "to come himself to answer three simple questions."

"Then if you're not fit to answer them you'll lose your head," says this big fellow.

"Fair enough," says the herdsboy.

"Here's my first question then," says the big fellow. "What's the first thing I think of in the morning when I rise?"

"What you'll eat," says the herdsboy.

"That's right," says he. "Now here's me second question: How many loads of sand are there round the shores of Ireland?"

"One," says the herdsboy, "if you had a cart big enough to hold it."

"Right," says the big fellow. "And now here's my third and last question: How much am I worth?"

"Twenty-nine pieces of silver," says the herdsboy.

"How do you make that out?"

"Well, our Lord God Himself was sold for thirty pieces," says the herdsboy, "and you can't be as good as Him."

And he got him and the bishop off.

❖ The Farmer's Answers

A FARMER-LIKE MAN ◈ *GALWAY*
LADY GREGORY *1902*

There was a poor man one time—Jack Murphy his name was; and rent day came, and he hadn't enough to pay his rent. And he went to the landlord, and asked would he give him time. And the landlord asked when would he pay him; and he said he didn't know that. And the landlord said: "Well, if you can answer three questions I'll put to you, I'll let you off the rent altogether. But if you don't answer them, you will have to pay it at once, or to leave your farm. And the three questions are these: How much does the moon weigh? How many stars are there in the sky? What is it I am thinking?" And he said he would give him till the next day to think of the answers.

And Jack was walking along, very downhearted; and he met with a friend of his, one Tim Daly; and he asked what was on him. And he told him how he must answer the landlord's three questions on tomorrow, or to lose his farm. "And I see no use in going to him tomorrow," says he, "for I'm sure I will not be able to answer his questions right." "Let me go in your place," says Tim Daly, "for the landlord will not know one of us from the other, and I'm a good hand at answering questions, and I'll engage I'll get you through."

So he agreed to that. And the next day Tim Daly went in to the landlord, and says he: "I'm come now to answer your three questions."

Well, the first question the landlord put was: "What does the moon weigh?" And Tim Daly says: "It weighs four quarters."

Then the landlord asked: "How many stars are in the sky?" "Nine thousand nine hundred and ninety-nine," says Tim. "How do you know that?" says the landlord. "Well," says Tim, "if you don't believe me, go out yourself tonight and count them."

Then the landlord asked him the third question: "What am I thinking now?"

"You are thinking it's to Jack Murphy you're talking, and it is not, but to Tim Daly."

So the landlord gave in then. And Jack had the farm free from that out.

Half a Blanket

JAMES LOUGHRAN ◈ *LOUTH*
MICHAEL J. MURPHY *1963*

This son was married and he had a young son himself in the cradle, and the old grandfather, the son's father, was knocking about, not much good then for anything only eating and smoking. So the son of the old fellow said the old man would have to go; leave—that was the word: take the broad road for it.

Well, his own son, the child was in the cradle. And the wife was pleading with her husband for to give the old man a chance but he wouldn't listen. So she pleaded with her husband to give the old fellow a blanket when he was ready to go.

"Give him a whole blanket," says she.

The son was for giving him half a blanket but he says: "All right. I'll give a whole blanket."

"Do no such'n a thing," says the child in the cradle. "Give him only half a blanket and keep the other half safely by. For I'll need it when I have to give it to you when it's my turn to put you out to the world."

That was from the child that couldn't talk. So the old fellow was let stay, he wouldn't get leave then to go at all, when the son heard what his own child had in store for himself.

❖ The Shadow of the Glen

PAT DIRANE ◈ *GALWAY*
JOHN MILLINGTON SYNGE *1898*

One day I was traveling on foot from Galway to Dublin, and the darkness came on me and I ten miles from the town I was wanting to pass the night in. Then a hard rain began to fall and I was tired walking, so when I saw a sort of a house with no roof on it up against the road, I got in the way the walls would give me shelter.

As I was looking round I saw a light in some trees two perches off, and thinking any sort of a house would be better than where I was, I got over a wall and went up to the house to look in at the window.

I saw a dead man laid on a table, and candles lighted, and a woman watching him. I was frightened when I saw him, but it was raining hard, and I said to myself, if he was dead he couldn't hurt me. Then I knocked on the door and the woman came and opened it.

"Good evening, ma'am," says I.

"Good evening kindly, stranger," says she. "Come in out of the rain."

Then she took me in and told me her husband was after dying on her, and she was watching him that night.

"But it's thirsty you'll be, stranger," says she. "Come into the parlor."

Then she took me into the parlor—and it was a fine clean house—and she put a cup, with a saucer under it, on the table before me with fine sugar and bread.

When I'd had a cup of tea I went back into the kitchen where the dead man was lying, and she gave me a fine new pipe off the table with a drop of spirits.

"Stranger," says she, "would you be afeard to be alone with himself?"

"Not a bit in the world, ma'am," says I; "he that's dead can do no hurt."

Then she said she wanted to go over and tell the neighbors the way her husband was after dying on her, and she went out and locked the door behind her.

I smoked one pipe, and I leaned out and took another off the table. I was smoking it with my hand on the back of my chair—the way you are yourself this minute, God bless you—and I looking on the dead man, when he opened his eyes as wide as myself and looked at me.

"Don't be afraid, stranger," said the dead man; "I'm not dead at all in the world. Come here and help me up and I'll tell you all about it."

Well, I went up and took the sheet off of him, and I saw that he had a fine clean shirt on his body, and fine flannel drawers.

He sat up then, and says he—

"I've got a bad wife, stranger, and I let on to be dead the way I'd catch her goings on."

Then he got two fine sticks he had to keep down his wife, and he put them at each side of his body, and he laid himself out again as if he was dead.

In half an hour his wife came back and a young man along with her. Well, she gave him his tea, and she told him he was tired, and he would do right to go and lie down in the bedroom.

The young man went in and the woman sat down to watch by the dead man. A while after she got up and "Stranger," says she, "I'm going in to get the candle out of the room; I'm thinking the young man will be asleep by this time." She went into the bedroom, but the divil a bit of her came back.

Then the dead man got up, and he took one stick, and he gave the other to myself. We went in and saw them lying together with her head on his arm.

The dead man hit him a blow with the stick so that the blood out of him leapt up and hit the gallery.

That is my story.

❖ A HUNGRY HIRED BOY

MICHAEL ROONEY ◈ *CAVAN*
MICHAEL J. MURPHY *1973*

This old man, he was getting very old, and he had a young wife; and she used to say to him every day:

"John," she would say, "you should get some man to help you to do a spot of work, because you're getting old."

And they had no family.

"I might, I might; some day I might go into the village of a fair day and hire a boy if I could get a man."

So he went into the fair anyway, and he searched through the whole fair, and he could see nobody suitable in the whole fair. So he was just about on his way home and he went in to this public house for a bottle of Guinness. And he seen a likely-looking young fellow standing about a couple of yards down the bar.

"Well," he says, "that's a fine young fellow."

And he moved down and he says:

"There'd be no chance," he says, "that you'd be a young man looking for work?"

"Well," says he, "I'm in the fair all day and no man asked me would you hire me. I'll definitely hire with you surely. I'm short of a few quid and I'll definitely hire with you."

They made a bargain there and then.

"We'll have another couple of bottles of stout."

So, he had a horse and trap. So they filed off and home. And when he came home—aw, sure, the wife was all delighted, all lit up.

"Well, that's a great job, John. You brought a young man to do a bit of work, a spot of work for you. You're getting old, and sure you're not able to do it yourself. Well, I'm delighted that you have a young man."

Well, there was cattle, there was cows to be foddered and cows to be milked. The young fellow and him went out and they foddered the cattle and they done the whole work, out in the farmyard. When they came back in again she had two big blue duck eggs for John and for the young fellow. And she had a big fadge cake in the press and she took it out, sawed it up, and had a great big heap of bread on the table.

So, John went out to do something else, to give a calf a drink or something.

"Now," she says to the young fellow, she says, "we have no family. And only one bed. And if you wouldn't mind you could share the bed with me and John."

"Wouldn't I sleep in an old chair there at the fire; it'll do me rightly for the night."

"Throt you'll not sleep at the fire; if you don't mind you'll share the bed with me and John."

"I don't mind where I sleep for the night."

"All right."

John came back in, when he had the calf fed, or whatever he was doing. So when ten o'clock came they all filed into bed. The young fellow fellow went in at the wall, and John in the center, and her ladyship out at the stalk. And sometime in the middle of the night a cow give a big loo in the byre.

"Go down, John, quick," she says, "for there's a cow or something—there's something wrong. There's a cow going to calve."

"Will I bring the young fellow?"

"Let the poor fellow alone; he might be tired. Leave him where he is. If there's anything wrong you can come back for him."

So John put on his trousers, threw a coat on him, and went down to the byre; there was a cow sick a-calving. And he hadn't the latch gone off the door when she tipped the young fellow.

"John is gone down to the byre to see a cow."

"Will I go down with him?"

"Stay where you are. You're all right, stay where you are."

"John . . . Would John be long away in the byre?"

"He . . . he'll be long enough; the byre's a good bit from the house."

"Would he be ten minutes?"

"He'll be long enough."

"Do you think . . . would he be fifteen minutes?"

"Won't he be long enough?"

"God, I'm going to do something . . ."

"Ah, well do it quick," she says, "whatever you're going to do."

"Bejasus I'll go down to the kitchen for another slice of thon old cake. I'm starving with hunger."

❖ THE FIRST MIRROR

MICHAEL McCANNY ◈ *TYRONE*
SÉAMAS Ó CATHÁIN *1976*

Well, before it leaves my head now, I'll tell you something about a pair that lived up thonder. You know in them days, everybody, every man, especially, was out, well, out, any day he could stay out—and some days he couldn't—he was out digging. Naturally enough, some people's hands was harder than others and the harder the hand the worse it was, for it cracked up, you know, hacked, bleeding. So mirrors was never used then, they were hardly known, you know, and you were above the ordinary if you had a mirror in the house.

But then this Vaseline box came out then to the relief of the country—Vaseline they got for sore hands. So these old pair got a box and Paddy used to put it on when his hands would be sore. So he come in this day and there were one of his hands bleeding and he says: "Where's that Vaseline?" So Rosie got him the Vaseline and she says: "All's in it, take it with you, and if your hands be sore, put it on. They're not much in it now anyway."

So Paddy took it with him to the field and after a while he got it and from the first time when he was born, he seen himself in this wee mirror—there was a wee mirror in the lid of the box. I'm sure you seen one of them.

So, this was his father! After all these years he was dead—and that was him! So every now and again when he was smoking, he admired this, admired himself and he thought it was his father in this little mirror.

But Rosie called him in to his tea and he was interested in this and she thought she would see what he was looking at. So that night—she forgot all about it then—they were going to bed. Paddy was away to bed anyway, he was tired and she was ready to go to bed. There were very few nightgowns at that time, you know. But she minded about this, and she went to Paddy's purse and she got the Vaseline box.

She was like Paddy—she seen herself for the first time ever. So she left it down and she reached for the tongs and she till Paddy in the bed. She says: "If that's the sort of an old dame you're interested in, in soul I'm long enough here!"

So Paddy parleyed with her and said everything would be all right, and he says: "We'll see in the morning what we're going to do about it."

So she got up in the morning and made breakfast and she produced the Vaseline lid. "I think in God's name," she says, "we'll put it in the fire and be done with it."

"Oh," he says, "that wouldn't be right at all, that's my father."

"It's not a bit odds," she says, "I never seen your father," says she, "and I suppose I never will. But I'm sure," she says, "he never had hair and diddies like what I seen on that old dame last night."

And, naturally enough, when the glass got the heat, it sparked out. "Now," she says, "didn't I tell you! Thanks be to God," she says, "there it is. I told you it was bad from the start."

❖ ROBIN'S ESCAPE

AN OLD MAN ◈ *GALWAY*
LADY GREGORY *1902*

There was a man one time went to the market to sell a cow. And he sold her, and he took a drop of drink after. And instead of going home, he went into a sort of a barn where there was straw stored, and he fell asleep there.

And in the night some men came in, and he heard them talking. And they had a lot of silver plate with them, they were after stealing from some house in the town, and they were hiding it in the straw till they would come and bring it away again.

And he said nothing, and kept quiet till morning. And then he went out; and the people in the town were talking of nothing else but the great robbery of silver plate in the night. And no one knew who had done it. And the man came forward, and told them where the silver plate was, and who the men were that stole it. And the things were found, and the men convicted. But he did not let on how he had come to know it, or that he had slept in the barn.

So he got a great name. And when he went home, his landlord heard of it; and he sent for him, and he said: "I am missing things this good while, and the last thing I lost was a diamond ring. Tell me who was it stole that," he said. "I can't tell you," said the man. "Well," said the landlord, "I will lock you up in a room for three days. And if you can't tell me by the end of that time who stole the ring, I'll put you to death."

So he was locked up. And in the evening the butler brought him in his supper. And when he saw evening was come, he said: "There's one of them," meaning there was one of the three days gone.

But the butler went downstairs in a great fright; for he was one of the servants that had stolen the ring, and he said to the others: "He knew me, and he said, 'There's one of them.' And I won't go near him again," he said, "but let one of you go."

So the next evening the cook went up with the supper, and when she came in, he said the same way as before: "There's two of them," meaning there was another day gone. And the cook went down like the butler had gone, making sure he knew that she had a share in the robbery.

The next day the third of the servants—that was the housemaid—brought him his supper. And he gave a great sigh, and said: "There's the third of them." So she went down and told the others. And they agreed it was best to make a confession to him. And they went and told him of their robberies. And they brought him the diamond ring; and they asked him to try and screen them some way. So he said he would do his best for them, and he said: "I see a big turkey-gobbler out in the yard, and what you had best do is to open his mouth," he said, "and to force the ring down it."

So they did that. And then the landlord came up and asked could he tell him where the thief was to be found. "Kill that turkey-gobbler in the yard," he said, "and see what can you find in him." So they killed the turkey-gobbler, and cut him open, and there they found the diamond ring.

Then the landlord gave him great rewards, and everyone in the country heard of him.

And a neighboring gentleman that heard of him said to the landlord: "I'll make a bet with you that if you bring him to dinner at my house, he won't be able to tell what is under a cover on the table." So the landlord brought him; and when he was brought in, they asked him what was in the dish with the cover. And he thought he was done for, and he said: "The fox is caught at last." And what was under the cover but a fox! So whatever name he had before, he got a three times greater name now.

But another gentleman made the same bet with the landlord. And when they came in to the dinner, there was a dish with a cover, and the man had no notion what was under it; and he said: "Robin's done this time"—his own name being Robin. And what was there under the cover but a robin! So he got great rewards after that, and he settled down and lived happy ever after.

❖ JONATHAN SWIFT, DEAN OF SAINT PATRICK'S CATHEDRAL

GALWAY
LADY GREGORY *1926*

Dean Swift was a great man; very sharp-tongued he was, and fond of women terribly.

Himself and his man Jack went riding to some place and they went for shelter into a public house. There was a fire on the hearth and there were two men sitting beside it and they made no offer to move aside, where the Dean and Jack wore very simple clothes, knee breeches as the gentlemen used to do.

So the Dean says to Jack, "Did you put up the horses?"

"I did," says Jack.

"What did you give them for a feed?" says the Dean. "I gave them a feed of oysters," says Jack.

So when the two men heard that they went out for to look at the great wonder, the horses to be eating oysters. And when they came in, the Dean and Jack had their two places taken by the fire.

The Dean was eating his dinner one time and he gave Jack but the bone with very little left on it. "It is the sweetest bit that is next the bone," says he.

Well, a while after they were on the road, and he bade Jack to tie up his horse where he'd have a feed of grass. So Jack brought him to a big stone and tied his head to it.

"Why did you tie him in that place?" says the Dean.

"Sure you told me yourself," says Jack, "the sweetest of the grass is next the stone!"

Some eggs Jack brought him one time, in his hand, just as you might be bringing them to a man out on a bog. "Let you put a plate under everything you will bring from this out," says the Dean.

So the next morning when Jack brought up his boots, he had put a plate under them.

The Dean sent Jack for a woman one night, and it was a black woman Jack brought up to the hotel, and the Dean never saw her till morning, and when he did he thought it was the devil. He sacked Jack that time.

"What were you sacked for?" says Jack's mother.

"It is that he sent me for a pullet and I brought back a hen," says Jack.

"That's no great fault," says the mother and she went to the Dean and said he had a right to take Jack back again, and so he did.

❖ Daniel O'Connell

OWEN A-SLAIVIN ◈ *DONEGAL*
SEUMAS MACMANUS *1899*

Och, the likes of Dan—the heavens be his bed!—never was known afore, nor will his likes ever be seen again as long as there's a bill on a crow. He was the long-headedest man—glory be to God!—ever stepped in shoe-leather.

There was once and there was a poor boy up for murder—he fell foul of a friend in a scrimmage, and he cracked his brain-box for him without intending it, and the poor man died. And the short and the long of it was this poor boy was taken up for the murder of his friend with no chance whatsomever for escape, because the evidence was straight and square that it was him, and none other, give him the dying blow. And that meant hanging, the poor boy knew well; for in them days they'd string ye up for a dickens sight smaller matter.

Well, lo and behold ye, it was the morning of the trial, and the poor boy, Heaven knows, was downhearted enough, and his friends all crying round him, trying to get him to keep up his spirits, though they knew, too, that it was a hopeless case. All at once it struck one of his friends, and says he:

"It's a bad case, no doubt, but what harm to consult Counselor O'Connell?"

Faith, the poor boy leaped at it.

"Consult the Counselor," says he, "for the Lord's sake! It's small's the chance; but still and all, if there's a ghost of a chance he'll see it."

No sooner said than done. They had Dan on the spot in three hops of a sparrow, and explaining the whole case to him. When Dan heared the outs and ins of it, he shook his head.

"It's a pretty straight case," says Dan.

"Is there no chance at all, at all, Counselor?" says they.

"The queen's son," says he, "couldn't be saved on the evidence. In spite of all the counselors in the country, and if ye had Saint Patrick himself to plead for ye, ye'd be sentenced," says he.

This was the last blow for the poor prisoner, and ill he took it.

But all of a sudden, Dan looks him pretty hard in the face:

"If I don't mistake me much," says Dan, says he, "ye're a pretty bold, fearsomeless fellow?"

"Och," says the poor fellow, says he, "the day was and I was all that, but I'm thinking that day will never come again."

"Well," says Dan, says he, "I have considered the whole question over, and if ye're a right bold fellow, and act right bold, out of nine hundred and ninety-nine chances you have just one half chance for your life."

"What is it?" says the poor fellow, jumping at it.

"It's this I'm going to tell ye," says Dan. "When your case is heard, the jury without leaving the box will return a verdict of 'Guilty, me lord!' and his Lordship will then mount the black cap for the purpose of condemning ye. You're at that instant to have all the wee nerve ye can about ye, and having your brogue loose upon your foot, ye're to stoop down and get a good grip of it in your fist, and the minute ye see his Lordship open his mouth to sentence ye, take good sudden aim, and with all the veins of your heart give him the brogue fair atween the two eyes—then leave the rest to Providence."

True enough, it was a queer advice, and maybe the poor lad didn't think so—but then it was Dan O'Connell's advice, and that put another face on matters. When Dan said it, it was worth trying. So he observed it to the letter. And when the jury was bringing in their verdict of "Guilty, me lord!" he was getting his brogue loose on his foot. And when the judge got on the black cap, he got a good grip of the brogue, and gathered all his nerves, and the very next minute, as the judge opened his mouth to give him sentence, he ups with the brogue, and with all the powers of his arm and the veins of his heart, let him have the full weight of the brogue fair atween the two eyes, and knocks him over flat. An astore! astore! Up was the judge again in an instant, and him purple in the face, and he gulders out:

"My verdict is that the scoundrel be burned, beheaded, and hung!"

"Easy, easy, I beg your pardon, me lord," says Dan O'Connell, jumping up in his place in the court. "I beg your Lordship's pardon," says he, "but I think ye have transgressed your rights," and he handed up to the judge the book of the law that he might see for himself. "Ye can't," says he, "according to English law as printed in that book in black and white, sentence a man to be both burned, beheaded, and hung. Prisoner," says Dan, then says he, turning to the dock, "prisoner, you're at liberty to go free." And the sorra his mouth could the dumbfounded judge open, as the prisoner stepped out of the dock a free man, for he saw Dan had him squarely.

Well, there was again, and there was a poor man, who had got some ha'pence, and he speculated on a drove of cattle, and started up to Dublin with them to sell them, and make profit on them. As me brave man was driving the cattle down Dublin street, out comes a man that kept a tobaccy shop, a clever lad, and he saw his chance, and says he to the man who owned the cattle:

"How much," says he, "will ye take for the best and worst of them cattle of yours?"

Well, the poor man looked at the best beast in the drove, and at the worst beast, and he prices the two of them in his own mind, and:

"I'll take so much," says he, mentioning it.

"All right," says the other, "I'll give ye your asking." And into his yard he had the whole drove driven. It was no use whatsomever for the poor man to object, for the other said he bought the best and the worst of the cattle, which was all of the cattle, and he had witnesses to prove it.

Away the poor man, in spite of himself, had to go with the price of barely two beasts in his pocket in payment for his whole drove, and away he went lamenting, and not knowing how he'd face back to his family again, with their wee trifle of money as good as gone. That night he put up in a public house, and the woman of the house coming to learn the poor fellow's lament asked him why he didn't go to the Counselor, and have his advice on it. If it did him no good, she said, it couldn't anyhow do him no harm, and if there was one way in a thousand out of it Dan would soon find that way.

Right enough, the very next morning to the Counselor the poor man set out, and laid a full program of his case afore Dan, and asked him could anything be done. No answer Dan give him, till first he took three turns up and down the parlor. And then:

"Yes," says Dan, "something can be done. There's one way you can get back your cattle, and only one."

"What's that?" says the man.

"You'll," says Dan, says he, "have to cut off the small toe off your left foot, and go and bury it on Spek Island, and when you've done that come back to me."

As he was directed, he done with no loss of time, and back to Dan he comes for further directions.

"Now," says Dan, "come along with me."

And off both of them started and never halted till they were in the tobacconist's shop. And och, it was welcome Dan was with the lad behind the counter, who was bowing and scraping to him, and thanking him for the honor he done him coming into his shop.

"Can ye serve me," says Dan, says he, "with a little piece of good tobaccy?"

"I can," says the lad, "serve your honor with as good tobaccy as ever ye put until a pipe-head."

"And have ye much of it?" says Dan.

"More nor you'd care to buy," says the lad.

"Now what," says Dan, says he, "would ye be after charging me for a sizable piece—say as much as would reach from me friend's nose to the small toe of his left foot?"

The lad laughed at the quality of the order, but he knew Dan's odd ways. So, he sized the man up and says he:

"I'll take so much," mentioning some few shillings.

"It's a bargain," says Dan.

But lo and behold ye! When the lad went to measure it he finds the toe gone.

"There's no toe here!" says he.

"I know there isn't," says Dan. "Me friend buried it in Spek Island a few days back. Ye'll have to carry on the tobaccy till ye get there."

The lad laughed heartily at this, as being one of Dan's best jokes.

But Dan didn't laugh at all, at all.

But, "Troth, and," says he, "I hope ye'll be laughing when ye've finished measuring me out me bargain."

"Och, Counselor, your honor," says the lad, says he, "but sure ye don't really mean it? Isn't it joking ye are?"

"I tell ye what it is, me good man," says Dan back to him, "you measure me out me bargain, and be very quick about it, too; or, if ye don't," says he, "be all the books in Christendom, I won't leave a slate on your roof, or a stick or stave on your premises I won't sell out till I have paid meself the sum of five thousand pound for breach of contract," says he, "and here's me witness."

"It's ruinated I am entirely, out and out," says the lad.

"It's ruinated ye deserve to be," says Dan. "Ye thought little of ruinating this poor stranger here beside me, when he come up to Dublin with his little grain of cattle, striving to make a support for the wife and childer. It's ruinated ye ought to be, ye low-lifed hang-dog ye! Turn the decent man out his cattle this instant, in as good condition as you got them, and moreover nor that, leave with him the price of the two beasts which ye paid him, as a slight compensation for the mental trouble you have caused the poor fellow. Then I'll forgive ye your bargain, on condition that, as long as ye live in Dublin, ye'll never again try to take in the poor and the stranger, and bring a bad name on the town."

And with a light heart, and a heavy pocket, that poor man went home to his wife and childer after all. And all by reason of Dan's cuteness.

That was Dan for ye!

May the soft bed, and the sweet one, in Paradise be his that never forsook the poor and the distressed. God Almighty rest him. And Amen! Amen!

❖ Owen Roe O'Sullivan

MR. BUCKLEY, THE TAILOR ◈ *CORK*
ERIC CROSS *1942*

Owen Roe O'Sullivan was one of the greatest poets that ever was. It's no use for anyone to be talking. They were all poets in those days, every bloody man.

But that was not all about Owen Roe. He was an auctioneer as well, and he was middling good as a doctor as well. He was good enough at every trade. He spent a part of his time in the navy, and was at the battle of Waterloo. But do you know what was his best trade, after poetry? It was making small lads.

He was one of the most frolicsome men that ever was. It was said of him that if he threw a copper over a fence it would, like as not, fall on the head of one of his own. He must have been as good as King Solomon almost.

One day a young gossoon met him on the road, and Owen spoke to him for a while, and then he gave him a penny, telling him that the next time that he saw him he would give him a shilling. Well, by the mockstick of war, what did the young lad do? He hopped over the fence and ran over a couple of fields and was there on the road before Owen Roe again.

"You said that you would give me a shilling the next time that you saw me," said he.

"True for you," answered Owen. "Here is the shilling, and another for your intelligence. You must be one of my own."

Owen and the priests did not get on any too well together. Many is the time they had a battle, and Owen did not always get the worst of it, for he was a powerful and a barbarous man with his tongue. All true poets are. It's a gift they have. They see things as they are, and have the power over words to describe things as they are.

Though Owen did not get on well with the priests, he got on very well with the women. I told you that he was a frolicsome class of a man, and the women were clean daft about him wherever he went. It was over a woman that he had one of his famous battles with a priest.

He was staying in the town of Mallow at the time, and he had committed himself with a woman of that town.

On Sunday, after Mass, the priest asked, "Is Owen Roe here?"

Owen stood up and showed himself, and said that he was.

"Very well," said the priest. "I command you to leave this parish."

"Whyfor that?" asked Owen, knowing well the reason the priest had against him.

"Because of what you have done with a woman of this place," replied the priest.

Owen thought for a moment, and then he spoke up.

"Good enough!" said he, "but before I go I would first say this. Remember that it was on account of a woman that our first parents were cast out of the Garden of Eden; that it was over a woman that Samson lost his strength and the Philistines were defeated; that it was over a woman that the fierce wars of the Seven Branch Knights were fought; that it was over a woman that Troy was besieged and the long Trojan wars were waged; that it was over a woman that the misfortune came to King Lir; that it was over a woman that Caesar and Antony fell; that it was over a woman, Devorgilla, that the English first came to Ireland; that it was over a woman that England was lost to Rome; and that it is over a woman that I, Owen Roe, am forbidden the town of Mallow."

"Hold!" said the priest to him then. "We'll say no more about it. Mallow has misfortunes enough already. You'd better stay where you are, and let the women look after themselves, and you come and have the dinner with me."

That was one battle out of many that he had and that he won. On another day he was passing a priest's house with a companion, and there was a grand smell of salmon cooking coming out of the house. The two of them were middling hungry, and the companion said to Owen Roe, " 'Tis a shame that we are starving and that the priest should have more than enough."

"I'll bet you for a wager," said Owen, who was always ready for a bit of sport, "that I will both eat the dinner with the priest and put him to shame."

"Done," said the companion, and Owen set about the business. He knocked at the door of the priest's house and asked if he could see the priest.

"You cannot," said the housekeeper, after she had looked him up and down, "his reverence is just sitting down to his dinner, and he said that he was not to be disturbed."

"But it is a very important matter," said Owen then. "Go up to him and tell him that I have a troubled mind, and that I want to know what should a man do if he has money found."

The housekeeper went up and told the priest, and came back and asked Owen inside.

"The priest says that, if you wait until he has his dinner finished, he will answer your question, and he told me to give you this herring," said she, putting a sprateen of a herring before him.

Owen looked at the herring for a minute, and then he took it up on the fork, and he whispered to it, and then he put its mouth to his ear and listened. He had some sort of witchappery of talk. The housekeeper watched him, and then she went up to the priest again, and she told him of Owen's queer antics.

"Go down to him," said the priest, "and ask him what he is doing, and why is he doing it."

Down went the housekeeper again, and she asked Owen.

"Oh!" said Owen, "I had a brother who traveled to foreign parts years ago, and I was just asking the herring if he had any news of him."

When the housekeeper told this to the priest, he thought that he had a simple fool to deal with, and would soon be able to settle the business of the found money.

"Send him up to me," he told the housekeeper.

When Owen arrived in the dining room, the priest told him what the housekeeper had told him.

"You say that you can understand the language of fishes," he said.

"Yes," answered Owen.

"Well," said the priest, "I had a brother, too, who traveled abroad. Could you get news of him for me from your friend the herring?"

"You had better ask that of the salmon before you," answered Owen. "He is a much bigger and stronger fish, and more used to priests and their kin than the common herring."

"You are a deal smarter man than I took you to be," said the priest, thinking at the same time that he would have more trouble in settling the business of the found money than he thought at first. "You'd better sit down and eat the salmon with me," he said then, thinking that they might be able to come to some agreement over the money.

They ate the salmon away together, and then he asked Owen to drink the punch with him, which Owen did. When the dinner was finished, and they had their bellies full, the priest turned to Owen.

"You sent up word that you had a troubled mind about found money," he said then.

"That is true, I did," replied Owen.

"Now how much money would it be that you found?" asked the priest.

"The divil a copper," said Owen. "I was only wondering what would be the case if I did find money."

He had the priest beaten, and put to shame, and had his wager won. I tell you he was the smart man, and the man who would beat him would be the divil of a man entirely.

❖ Robert Burns

PETER FLANAGAN ◈ *FERMANAGH*
HENRY GLASSIE *1972*

Bobby Burns. He was a sharp man.

This attorney or solicitor died, and the remains were a-carrying to the burying place, wherever he was a-burying.

And Bobby was standing carelessly at the corner and there was a few boys along with him. Dumfries in Scotland, that's where he lived.

And says one of the boys to him, "Now Bobby," he says, "there's a solicitor there, his remains going out," he says, "could you make a bit of a poem on it?"

"Aw," says Bobby, "I think I could."

There was four solicitors carrying him.

So Bobby *started off*:

"One *rogue*," says he, "above,
Four in under.
His *body's* to *earth.*
His *soul's* on its *journey.*
And the *Devil's at law*
And he wants *an attorney*."

He was a rogue, and the four that was carrying him was rogues: "One rogue above," says he, "four in under. His body's to earth; his soul's on its journey. And the Devil's at law and he wants an attorney."

Well, he went to see this man, Bobby Burns, and he seen that he was in great pain, and that he was of a huge size, you see.

And he came to the conclusion he had led a bad life, and well, he pretended that the Devil was coming for him, you see.

It was the Devil was coming for him.

But the Devil wouldn't take him, he was such a burden, you see. He was such a burden; he was that weighty.

When the Devil entered the room where Richard was in his last stage, says Bobby, he says:

"When he entered the room where poor Richard was moaning,
And saw the four bedposts with its burden a-groaning,
He vowed to himself that he'd take to the road
Before he would carry such a damnable load."

He was Richard Lawton, this man; Lawton was his name. And Bobby made out that he had died from the effects of cutting his corns, you see.

Bobby went to the grave and looked round and he says:

"Here lie the bones," says he, "of Richard Lawton.
Alas, his death was strangely brought on.
One day when trying his corns to mow off,
The razor slipped and cut his toe off.
The toe from that to which it grew
To inflammation quickly flew.
Then it turned to mortifying,
And that was the cause of Richard dying."

It turned to mortifying, you see: gangrened the flesh. It's a very dangerous disease.

And there was another one. Aye. He was a wee small man, and he was cranky with Bobby one day.

Well, Bobby went in for a drink. And he says to Bobby, "I'm as good a poet as you."

"Go on ahead," says Bobby.

So, I don't know now really the verse that he made. But then Bobby in revenge took a notion he'd make little of him. Andrew Horn was his name. So he started off:

"In eighteen hundred and seventy-*nine*," says he,
The Devil thought of making *swine*.
Next again," said he, "he changed his plan,
And made it something like a man,
And called it Andrew Horn."

"Then," says he, "Andrew, would you beat me?" says he.

The Devil made swine and he turned the swine into a man called Andrew Horn.

I think he was convinced he couldn't make anything better than Bobby anyway.

Well, I could listen to yarns like that. I could sit for a whole night.

❖ TERRY THE GRUNTER

SLIGO
SÉAMAS Ó CATHÁIN *1931*

There was, at one time, an old tramp called Terry the Grunter who used to wander round these parts often times. He lived principally on his wits and he composed satires about people who did not please him. He happened to be in Sligo when a certain solicitor died and he asked some of this man's brother solicitors for help. They refused him. When the funeral was starting, four solicitors carried the coffin part of the way to the cemetery. Terry the Grunter gave the following description of the affair:

There's a knave overhead and four underneath,
The body is dead and the soul on a journey,
The Devil is at law and he wants an attorney.

When the Protestant church at Riverstown was being built, the bishop of Elphin came to consecrate it. He met our hero who, as usual, was on the lookout for money. The bishop refused him and the tramp wrote the following:

An English bishop came from Elphin,
To consecrate the church at Cooper Hill;
But if the Devil himself came up from Hell,
He would do it fully as well!

❖ THOMAS MOORE AND THE TRAMP

PETER FLANAGAN ◈ *FERMANAGH*
HENRY GLASSIE *1972*

Thomas Moore was lying looking, him and this other, his companion, looking at the Meeting of the Waters and bragging: it was such beautiful scenery, *gorgeous*, never saw anything like it.

And this poor tramp came up.

And badly dressed, in rags, and bad boots on him with his toes sticking out through his shoes.

And he asked help of Thomas Moore.

And Thomas didn't recognize him atall; he ignored him asking for help. And he stood for a few minutes and he started his wee poem as follows:

"If Moore was a man without place of abode,
Without clothes on his back, and him walking the road,
Without bit in his belly or shoes on his feet,
He wouldn't give a damn where the bright waters meet."

This Moore told him, "Repeat that," he says, "again."

So the tramp repeated it again.

And he put his hand in his pocket, and he gave him half a sovereign. He says, "That's as good as I ever heard," he says, "I couldn't do it better meself."

That was that.

It was a great piece of composition. It was me father told me that one; it was him that I heard at it. Surely.

JOHN BRODISON AND THE POLICEMAN

MICHAEL BOYLE ◈ *FERMANAGH*
HENRY GLASSIE *1972*

There was a famous character in our country. He lived at Bellanaleck, he was the name of John Brodison.

He was a famous liar.

Aye, he was a famous liar. I knew him. I was often talking to him. He was a kind of a smart old boy, you know: quick-witted.

He was coming out of Enniskillen one night with the ass and cart. And the law was: ye had to have a light after a certain time on a cart, do you see, when it was dark. Ye had to have a light.

So the policeman was standing at Bellanaleck Cross, and Brodison knew that the police would be *there* at the time.

So he got out of the cart.

And he took the donkey out of the cart, and he tied it *behind*.

And he got into the shafts, and he started to pull the cart, and the donkey walking behind him anyway.

And when he came to the Cross, the policeman says, "Brodison," he says, "Ye have no light."

"*Where's your light,* Brodison?"
"*Ask the driver,*" he says.
Aye. "Ask the driver."
Well, that was the sort of a boy he was.
Ah, he had great bids in him.

A BIG POTATO

HUGH NOLAN ◈ *FERMANAGH*
HENRY GLASSIE *1972*

John Brodison tells this story that one season, some years ago, he had a field of potatoes convenient to the Sligo and Leitrim Railway Line.

And it was a very steep hill that he had the potatoes planted in.

And they done remarkably well, and when it came to the time for to dig them, they turned out a powerful fine crop of potatoes.

And he was digging, he tells us, one day, and he came to a spot on the ridge and he found out that there was a potato from one broo to the other.

So, he got behind, as he thought, this potato for to roll it out.

But he found out that it had grew across the furrow in through a ridge on both sides of the ridge that it was planted on.

So he had to go to both these ridges and dig all the mold that was around the potato.

So *then* when he had it properly uncovered, he found out that it was a very deep distance in the ground.

And he had to start for to rise it with a spade out of the ground.

And he was a very long time a-digging the mold from round it, for to get it, to get the spade in under it.

But finally the mold all cleared and he started with the spade, rising it up,
and rising it up,
and rising it up,
till finally he got it to the top of the ground.

And it joined to roll.

So, he was that much fatigued and tired after the job that he had it; he never bothered looking where it went to.

And he started again, and he heared a cart coming along the road from the direction of Enniskillen. And the next thing he heard was a terrible *bang.*

So he looked round, and he seen where this cart had tumbled.

So he stuck the spade. He run down to it. He found that the pratie had rolled onto the road, and in trying to get by it, the man hadn't enough room between the pratie and the other hedge for to get by clear, and the wheel of the cart went up onto the potato, and it tumbled.

So there it was: there was nothing only sacks of meal and sacks of flour lying here and in all directions. And the horse was lying on its side in the road.

But *then*, in them days there was a lot of people traveling on horses' carts and donkeys' carts, and it wasn't very long till there came a go of men making for home.

So, them all got down and they got the horse released from the *cart*. And they got the horse up on his feet again.

So, they had to take and they had to move every sack that was lying along the hedge away from about the cart still they got the cart back on its wheels again and got it pulled alongside the *potato*.

So then they had to help this man again put on his load again.

So, it was getting very near night, and he tells us that he didn't like for to leave it on the road all night for fear of more capsizers or more accidents.

So he went home.

And he had a talk with the wife.

So they came to the conclusion—they had a new crosscut—so they came to the conclusion that they'd put the donkey in the cart, and that they'd start away with the crosscut, and that they'd cut it into shares and draw it to the house.

So they started anyway, and at a very late hour they had it all cut at the house.

So, that was a terrible hard night, he said, one of the hardest nights of his life, between the way he had to labor for to get the potato *up* out of the *earth*, and then the hardship that he had that *night*, him and the wife after.

Oh, John used to tell that story.

Oh, many a good story John told.

❖ THE FOX AND THE RANGER

PADDY THE SPORT ◈ *WICKLOW*
SAMUEL LOVER *1831*

The fox is the cunningest beast in the world, barring the wren.

All birds build their nest with one hole to it only, excepting the wren. But the wren builds two holes to the nest, and so that if any enemy comes to disturb it upon one door, it can go out on the other. But the fox is cute to that degree, that there's many a mortal a fool to him—and, by dad, the fox could buy and sell many a Christian, as you'll soon see by and by, when I tell you what happened to a wood ranger that I knew once, and a decent man he was, and wouldn't say the thing in a lie.

Well, you see, he came home one night, mighty tired—for he was out with a party in the domain, cock-shooting that day. And when he got back to his lodge, he threw a few logs of wood on the fire to make himself comfortable, and he took whatever little matter he had for his supper. And, after that, he felt himself so tired that he went to bed. But you're to understand that, though he went to bed, it was more for to rest himself like, than to sleep, for it was early. And so he just went into bed, and there he diverted himself looking at the fire, that was blazing as merry as a bonfire on the hearth.

Well, as he was lying that-a-way, just thinking of nothing at all, what should come into the place but a fox. But I must tell you, what I forgot to tell you before, that the ranger's was on the borders of the wood, and he had no one to live with him but himself, barring the dogs that he had the care of, that was his only companions, and he had a hole cut on the door, with a swinging board to it, that the dogs might go in or out according as it pleased them. And, by dad, the fox came in, as I told you, through the hole in the door, as bold as a ram, and walked over to the fire, and sat down forenenst it.

Now, it was mighty provoking that all the dogs was out—they were roving about the wood, you see, looking for to catch rabbits to eat, or some other mischief, and so it happened that there wasn't as much as one individual dog in the place. And, by gor, I'll go bail the fox knew that right well, before he put his nose inside the ranger's lodge.

Well, the ranger was in hopes some of the dogs would come home and catch the chap, and he was loath to stir hand or foot himself, afeared of frightening away the fox. But, by gor, he could hardly keep his temper at all at all, when he seen the fox take his pipe off of the hob, where he left it afore he went to bed, and putting the bowl of the pipe into the fire to kindle it (it's as true as I'm here), he began to smoke forenenst the fire, as natural as any other man you ever seen.

"Musha, bad luck to your impudence, you long-tailed blackguard," says the ranger, "and is it smoking my pipe you are? Oh, then, by this and by that, if I had my gun convenient to me, it's fire and smoke of another sort, and what you wouldn't bargain for, I'd give you," says he. But still he was loath to stir, hoping the dogs would come home. And, "By gor, my fine fellow," says he to the fox, "if one of the dogs comes home, saltpeter wouldn't save you, and that's a strong pickle."

So, with that, he watched until the fox wasn't minding him, but was busy shaking the cinders out of the pipe, when he was done with it, and so the ranger thought he was going to go immediately after getting an air of the fire and a shough of the pipe. And so, says he, "Faix, my lad, I won't let you go so easy as all that, as cunning as you think yourself."

And with that he made a dart out of bed, and run over to the door, and got between it and the fox. And, "Now," says he, "your bread's baked, my buck, and maybe my lord won't have a fine run out of you, and the dogs at your brush every yard, you marauding thief, and the Divil pity you," says he, "for your impudence—for sure, if you hadn't the impudence of a highwayman's horse, it's not into my very house, under my nose, you'd dare for to come."

And with that, he began to whistle for the dogs. And the fox, that stood eyeing him all the time while he was speaking, began to think it was time to be jogging when he heard the whistle—and says the fox to himself, "Troth, indeed, you think yourself a mighty great ranger now," says he, "and you think you're very cute, but upon my tail, and that's a big oath, I'd be long sorry to let such a mallet-headed bog-trotter as yourself take a dirty advantage of me, and I'll engage," says the fox, "I'll make you leave the door soon and sudden."

And with that, he turned to where the ranger's brogues was lying hard by beside the fire, and, what would you think, but the fox took up one of the brogues, and went over to the fire and threw it into it.

"I think that'll make you start," says the fox.

"Divil receive the start," says the ranger. "That won't do, my buck," says he. "The brogue may burn to cinders," says he, "but out of this I won't stir." And then, putting his fingers into his mouth, he gave a blast of a whistle you'd hear a mile off, and shouted for the dogs.

"So that won't do," says the fox. "Well, I must try another offer," says he. And, with that, he took up the other brogue, and threw *it* into the fire too.

"There, now," says he, "you may keep the other company," says he. "And there's a pair of ye now, as the Divil said to his knee-buckles."

"Oh, you thieving varmint," says the ranger. "You won't leave me a tack to my feet. But no matter," says he, "your head's worth more nor a pair of brogues to me, any day. And, by the Piper of Blessingtown, you're money in my pocket this minute," says he.

And with that, the fingers was in his mouth again, and he was going to whistle, when, what would you think, but up sits the fox on his hunkers, and puts his two forepaws into his mouth, making game of the ranger. (Bad luck to the lie I tell you.)

Well, the ranger, and no wonder, although in a rage he was, couldn't help laughing at the thought of the fox mocking him, and, by dad, he took such a fit of laughing, that he couldn't whistle, and that was the cuteness of the fox to gain time. But when his first laugh was over, the ranger recovered himself, and gave another whistle. And so says the fox, "By my soul," says he, "I think it wouldn't be good for my health to stay here much longer, and I mustn't be trifling with that blackguard ranger any more," says he, "and I must make him sensible that it is time to let me go. And though he hasn't understanding to be sorry for his brogues, I'll go bail I'll make him leave that," says he, "before he'd say *sparables*."

And, with that, what do you think the fox done? By all that's good—and the ranger himself told me out of his own mouth, and said he would never have believed it, only he seen it—the fox took a lighted piece of a log out of the blazing fire, and run over with it to the ranger's bed, and was going to throw it into the straw, and burn him out of house and home. So when the ranger seen that, he gave a shout out of him:

"Hilloo! hilloo! you murdering villain," says he. "You're worse nor Captain Rock. Is it going to burn me out you are, you red rogue of a Ribbonman?" And he made a dart between him and the bed, to save the house from being burned. But, my jewel, that was all the fox wanted. And as soon as the ranger quitted the hole in the door that he was standing forenenst, the fox let go the blazing faggot, and made one jump through the door, and escaped.

But before he went, the ranger gave me his oath, that the fox turned round and gave him the most contemptible look he ever got in his life, and showed every tooth in his head with laughing. And at last he put out his tongue at him, as much as to say, "You've missed me, like your mammy's blessing," and off with him!—like a flash of lightning.

❖ THE HORSE'S LAST DRUNK

MR. BUCKLEY, THE TAILOR ◈ *CORK*
ERIC CROSS *1942*

Do you know that the jennet is the most willing animal in the world? Man alive, a jennet never knows when he is done. Years ago, I saw a jennet drawing a load up Patrick's Hill in Cork, and that's like the side of a mountain. The load was too much for it, and for all its trying the jennet could go no farther.

But do you know what happened? With the height of willingness and the power of pulling, its eyes came out of its head before it, for they were the only part of it free and not tackled to the cart. That was willingness for you!

The man who owned that jennet was carrying from Cork to Kenmare. It was in the days before there were any motorcars and before their like had been thought about at all.

He was coming one day with the divil of a load of wheat, maybe it could be about a ton weight, and he saw that his horse was failing. He wondered if he had overfed her or what could ail her. He wanted to get into the town of Macroom that night at least.

Well, he had a bottle of poteen with him, and he put it back into the horse, and she was as lively as could be for another piece of the road. But just when he was to the east of Macroom, didn't the horse lie down on the road, under the load, and the divil a stir from her.

They thought that she was dead. There wasn't a move out of her, no matter what they did. One of the men with him said that they had as well make the best of it, and if they skinned her they would be able to sell the skin in Macroom.

So they set to, and they skinned her, and when they had that done she moved. She wasn't dead at all, but only dead drunk with the poteen she had taken, and the cold had put a stir into her when the skin was off.

They were in the devil of a fix, for the skin was after stiffening. One of them had an idea. There were sheep grazing in a field near by, and he hopped over the wall, and killed four of the sheep and skinnd them, and they sewed the warm skins on to the horse, and she got up after her debauch, and pulled away as good as ever.

Ever after that he used to shear her twice a year—and you should have seen the grand fleece she had on her. She lived for fourteen years after that with two shearings a year.

❖ HARE AND HOUND

DAN ROONEY ◈ *DOWN*
MICHAEL J. MURPHY *1960*

John McLoughlin that lived out the Point Road had this hound. There never was the beating of her. She pupped in a teapot.

One time she was carrying the pups, and a hare riz and she made after it and ripped the belly out of herself on this ditch, on wire or something; and the pups, the greyhound pups, spilled out of her. And one of them up like hell, and after the hare and stuck till her till he caught and killed her.

And when the greyhound died, John McLoughlin had her skinned and he put a back in a waistcoat with her skin. And one day he was out over the water hunting and this hare started up; and begod, he said, the back of the waistcoat on him barked!

❖ SLEEPY PENDOODLE

MICHAEL BOYLE ◈ *FERMANAGH*
HENRY GLASSIE *1972*

Ah, this Hughie McGiveney, he was a great character.

He used to keep a couple of cats.

And he used to have funny names on them. There was one cat he called Yibbity Gay, Yibbity *Gay*. And there was another cat he called Willy the Wisp. Aye.

Well then, he used to tell a great yarn; he used to tell about—he had a wee Irish terrier bitch, a wee bitch, you know.

And she used to have pups every year. This wee Granny—he called the wee bitch Granny—she used to have pups every year. Supplied the whole—there wasn't a wee lad in the country wasn't running after one of her pups.

And Granny was going to have pups this time, and didn't she die.

So he was in terrible grief about her.

And he buried her with honors of war. "I buried her," says he, "with honors of war."

And he put down a stick at the grave.

And he used to go every day and stand at the grave.

And this day, he used to tell the yarn, he was standing at the grave, and he heard a squealing, you know, a mumbling down in the grave.

And he got a spade and he opened the grave.

And there was two pups shut up in the grave. Two pups.

There was one pup dead. The other was living. So he brought it home.

And he got a supping bottle; you know, that's what young childer used to be fed on longgo, a supping bottle. See, a big long tube down into the bottle, and a wee dummy, a wee tit in their mouth.

Well, he got one of them, and he reared the pup. Sat up at night with it, and reared it anyway.

It grew up to be a great big fat lump of a thing.

And it was a month old, and its eyes never opened. Its eyes still kept *closed.*

And there he was, and he was in a terrible way about the pup, that his eyes wouldn't open.

So. He was in town this day, in Enniskillen. And he went into a public house the name of Herbert's for to get a pint of porter, and he was on his way home.

And there was a big swank of a fellow in it, and he had a big red dog with him.

So Hughie and him joined to chat about the *dog*, do you see. He was explaining to Hughie McGiveney the qualities of the dog and the breeding of him and everything, and didn't Hughie start to tell him about his *pup*, about his *pup*, and that his eyes didn't open.

So he had listened to him for a while. "Well now," he says, "I'm glad you mentioned *that*, because," he says, "I can be of great *help* to ye."

"Ah," he says, "are you in a hurry?" he says.

"Aw, not atall," says Hughie.

"Well, wait a minute now," he says, "here."

And he went away anyway. He says to the barman, "Give him a pint there," he says, "till I come back."

The barman put up the pint for him, and Hughie was drinking the pint, and the lad came back anyway, and he had a wee piece of white paper in his hand.

And he says to McGiveney, "Now," he says, "have you good memory?"

"I have," says Hugh, "the best."

"Well, you'll have to be able to mind this, that I'm going to tell ye. Because," he says, "if I write it down on a piece of paper, it'll be no good; it'll take the charm away. You'll have to be fit for to mind it in your head."

So now anyway, he says, "When you go home," he says, "get the pup on your knee and sleek it down the head," he says. "There's a wee powder in that paper, and don't tell anybody this till you go home, or don't show the paper to anybody, or tell no one about it. There's a powder in that paper," he says, "and when you go home, get the pup up on your knee, and with your right hand sleek it down the back, and say, three times after the other:

"Open your eyes, Sleepy Pendoodle.
Open your eyes, Sleepy Pendoodle.
Open your eyes, Sleepy Pendoodle.

And the pup will be all right."

So McGiveney drunk his pint, and he out, up the streets of Enniskillen shouting:

"Pendoodle, Pendoodle, Pendoodle, Pendoodle, Pendoodle."

And on he came running—he run the whole road home, and the paper in his hand, the wee piece of paper in his hand.

And damn it anyway, there was a man lived on the roadside beside that old school; the house is nearly down now. He was a man named Keenan, Frank Keenan, Francis Keenan, and he seen Hughie coming.

And he was standing on the road.

And Hughie came on running.

And he says, "Anything wrong, Hughie?"

"Oh, not a damned haet wrong," he says, "not a damned haet wrong. Pendoodle, Pendoodle, Pendoodle, Pendoodle," he says.

"My God," says Francis, "he's gone mad. He's gone straight for a madman."

So anyway, he went on anyway, and he was going by another house.

That house was Nolan's. Hugh Nolan's father was living at the time, and he was in the road.

"Well, Hughie," says he, "any news in town the day?"

"Ah, news be damned," he says. "Pendoodle, Pendoodle, Pendoodle, Pendoodle, Pendoodle."

So when he went home, the old wife was sitting in the corner, and she joined to grumble: "What the devil kept you so long, and, troth, you may go to the Bottom for the cows"—a hundred and fifty orders in the one—an old grumbling creature.

"Ah, cows be hanged," he says. "Where's the pup?"

"PUP! Well, bad manners to the pup. And, troth, if I'd've been able to walk to the lough, the pup would've been in the lough."

"He'll not be in the lough," he says.

Well, damn it, he got the pup on his knee, and got the powder out anyway, stroked it three times down the head:

"Open your eyes, Sleepy Pendoodle.
Open your eyes, Sleepy Pendoodle.
Open your eyes, Sleepy Pendoodle."

And the third time, the pup opened his eyes, and looked up into his face, and wagged his tail.

So he christened the pup Pendoodle.

Aye, and Pendoodle grew up to be a big strong red dog.

Pendoodle he called the pup.

He *used to tell that yarn.*

He made it all up. He made it all up, surely. He was a terrible clever man.

Ah, I mind Hughie well.

❖ A MEDICAL EXPERT FROM LISNASKEA

NED NOBLE ◈ *FERMANAGH*
PADDY TUNNEY *1979*

I mind the time I was over in the cancer hospital in Manchester getting the spot cut off my lip. In them times they were not that well up in science and indeed it's many's the consultation they held with myself when their experts were clean beat.

This day, anyway, weren't they operating on a man and they had his stomach out on the table scraping it when the bell rang for dinnertime. Away my bully surgeons went and forgot to close and lock the operating theater door.

There was this big buck-cat that kept us awake half the night chasing and catterwailing with she-cats. He was very fond of titbits and didn't he steal into the theater and eat the poor man's stomach. When the doctors came back at two o'clock and they found the stomach gone, they were in a bit of a quandary. They sent for me. "What would you suggest, Paddy?"—they always called me Paddy.

"Well now, boys," I told them, "I'm no surgeon but the sensible thing to do would be to go round to the slaughterhouse and get the stomach of a young heifer or bullock and stick it into him. If you do so, it's my candid opinion the old worn-out one you spent all morning scraping at will never be missed." Away goes the head surgeon and picks a nice tender young stomach, comes back and grafts it into the patient.

All went well until he was able to take food again. They put him on milk foods first and eventually he got beef and broth and whatever was going. No matter how much food he ate the pangs of hunger never left him.

It's a holy sight surely, with all their learning and the number of men and women they had knifed, that they had to come again to Ned for a solution. "Well now," I told them, "but I could be wrong, I don't think you are giving him the right diet." There was a boyo out in the grounds with a lawn-mower, cutting away for all he was worth.

"Now," says I, "wouldn't it be a good thing if some of you men went out and brought him in an armful of grass to see if he'd be satisfied." Arrah man! the armful of grass was not at his head until he was munching away with great relish and he didn't leave a cuinneog of the grass!

When I left the hospital he was lying there in the bed chewing his cud contentedly. Can you beat that?

❖ GEORGE ARMSTRONG'S RETURN

HUGH NOLAN ◈ *FERMANAGH*
HENRY GLASSIE *1977*

George Armstrong used to tell about: when he was a young man, he took a notion of traveling.

And he went to Australia.

And he was doing rightly in it. But the cholera broke out in it.

And the most of the whole continent was ailing from it, and a good deal of the people died. But he took it anyway, and he failed terribly.

Finally he mended. But he knew be the way he felt that he might go back to Ireland, for he would never be able for to do anything to earn a living in Australia, wouldn't be able to work. He was too far gone.

So *anyway*, he started for home.

And he landed at Enniskillen. There was a railroad station in them days at Enniskillen. It's way above where the present mart is. So he got out of the train and he went over and he sat down.

And he rested himself.

And he took a notion that he'd try and make his way home.

So anyway, he started.

He had no money to get any refreshment in the town. He started out walking, hoping that he'd reach Bellanaleck some time or another.

So there was a railroad crossing on this Derrylin Road in them days that was below Lisgoole. And when he came that length, the gates was closed, the train was coming.

So he took a notion he'd count his money.

And he had thruppence.

That's all he had back out of Australia.

And he had weighed on the journey somewhere.

And he was three pound weight.

So anyway, he trudged on, trudged on.

When the train passed, the gates was open, and he trudged on, trudged on.

Finally he landed at Bellanaleck Cross.

Turned up for Arney, and made his way along till he came to the turn that would take you to where the mother lived.

So, he made his way up to the house.

But there was *no noise off his step.*

He was that light.

So anyway, the mother was doing chores through the house, and she didn't find him coming atall, till he spoke at the *door*.

So she knew his voice and she run towards him.

And *aye*, he was hardly able for to lift his hand to shake hands with *her*.

So *anyway*. She got hold of him and she lifted him and she brought him and she left him standing on the hearthstone.

And there was a wee basket that she had from the childer was small.

And it was hanging up on the wall.

And she took down the basket, and she put him into the basket.

And she put a white cover over him and left him at the fireside.

So *anyway*. The rumor was out that George Armstrong was home out of Australia. So the people used to come for to see him, have a talk with him, and when they'd come in, there'd be no sign of anyone in the house, only the mother, and after some time they'd say:

"Well, I heard George was at home, and I just come over to see him."

"Oh, here he is, he's here," she'd say, and run up to the basket and she'd lift the white cloth.

"There, he's in there."

Aye.

It was pants like that that used to keep the community telling, and every day you'd nearly hear a fresh one. And you'd like to come across them, do ye know, when you'd go down in that locality.

Oh now, it was surely one of the trials of this life, mind you, when things turned out that way.

But he made a joke out of it.

❖ ❖ ❖

❖ The Lawyer and the Devil

MICHAEL E. MORRIS ◈ *TYRONE*
MICHAEL J. MURPHY *1950*

There was this man in it one time and he had three sons and he wanted to make something of them but hadn't the money. So he sells himself to the Divil to rise money to school the three boys, and he did. He made one a priest, the other a doctor and the third one was a lawyer. The Divil give him the money to pay for their education.

But anyway, at the end of seven years the Divil showed up to claim the old man and his soul and take him and it down to Hell. He had his three sons there, or one at a time in with him. So when the Divil come the priest began to pray and beg and appeal for sparings for his father, and in the heel of the hunt he got a few years more off the Divil for his father.

When that was up and the Divil come again the doctor was there and he appealed for sparings for his father and got them. And when the Divil come a third time to claim the old fellow the lawyer was there. The lawyer says to the Divil:

"You've given sparings to my father twice already and I know you can't be expected to do it again. But," says he, "as a last request, will you give him sparings while that butt of a candle is there?"

The candle was burning on the table.

The Divil said he would; it was only a butt of a candle and wouldn't be long in it.

At that the lawyer picks up the butt of a candle and blows it out and puts it in his pocket. And that was that! The Divil had to keep to his bargain and go without the old man, for the lawyer held on to the butt of a candle. Trust the lawyer to beat the Divil.

❖ Coals on the Devil's Hearth

HUGH NOLAN ◈ *FERMANAGH*
HENRY GLASSIE *1979*

This man, he was very poor, and he was getting it very tight to live, with a wife and family.

And he sold himself to the Devil.

But the bargain was, that he'd have to go with him at the end of a number of years.

But anyway, he got very rich.

And he got his family reared.

And the way it was: when him and the Devil made the bargain, the Devil gave him a *drum*, and a pair of drumsticks.

And he told him that every time that he'd want money, for to go out and give a roll on the drum, when he wanted anything done, and he'd do it for him.

So anyway, he went be the orders of the Devil. But in the long run, he joined to get very nervous and got afraid of the journey that he had to *go.*

So he joined to fret terribly.

And the wife remarked him terribly failed, and in bad form.

He never let on to her how they came to have the *money* or anything like *that.* And she knew nothing about this bargain that he had made off the Devil.

So anyway, he wouldn't tell her what the cause of it was. But she *still* was at him for to tell her what was troubling him.

So in the long run he told her.

So, she says, "There's a plan to get rid of him."

"Well, *what is it?*" says the man. *And he got terrible excited.*

"Well," she says, "you told me there that you had a drum, that you notified him when you wanted anything."

"Aye, I have it," he says.

"Well," says she, "take out the drum now, and give a roll on it, and when he comes, tell him that you want churches and chapels built. *At once!*"

So he went out and gave a roll on the drum and the Devil came along.

Your man says to him, "Well," he says, "I want you to do a thing, but whether you'll do it or not, I don't know. Would you put up churches and chapels here and there through the country?"

"Ah, I will, of course," says the Devil.

So anyway there was churches and chapels erected be night that the people couldn't understand atall.

So, when him and the Devil was parting, the Devil says to him, "Let that be the last thing now that ever you'll ask me *to do*."

So he was in as bad fettle as ever when he came back to the wife.

But the buildings went *up*.

So, aw, he was getting that she didn't know what was going to happen.

Says she, "There's one plan yet, that ye'll get shut of him forever."

She says, "Get out the drum, and give a *roll* on it, a good *loud* one. When he comes, tell him that you want him to do the last thing that ever you'll ask him to do.

"And when he asks you what it is, tell him that you want him to make all lawyers honest men."

He out with the drum.

And he gave a rattle.

No time till the boyo appeared.

"*Well,*" he says, "*what do you want* me to do the *day*? *You told me the last time that we were talking that you'd never ask me to do more* for you."

"Well," he says, "this is going to be the last."

"Well, what is it?" says the Devil.

"I want you," he says, "for to make all lawyers honest men."

"*Ah,*" says the Devil.

"Give me that drum," he says.

"There's women at the back of this. If I done what you want, there's times that I wouldn't have a coal on me hearth."

MYSTERY

THE BANSHEE
T. Crofton Croker, *Fairy Legends and Traditions of the South of Ireland*, 1862

❖ NO MAN GOES BEYOND HIS DAY

TOMÁS Ó CRITHIN ◈ *KERRY*
ROBIN FLOWER *1945*

A fisherman must follow the sea, and how can a man escape the day of his death? There is such and such a time marked out for a man on this earth, and, when his day is come, if he went into an ant's hole, death would find him there. We have only our time, and, young or old, a man must go when he is called.

There was a boat going out to Inis Tuaisceart once to fish from the rocks, and when they were halfway out they found that they had left the mast behind them. So they went back for the mast.

And there was a man on the slip who was the best man on the Island at fishing from the rocks, for at every craft there is one man is better than all others, if it were only at driving nails with a hammer. They set out again, taking this man with them, and, when they came to Inis Tuaisceart, they went about the island putting one man out on a rock here and another there, till at last they were all in their places fishing.

After they had been thus for a time, the day began to rise on them, and the boat went again to pick up the men. But when they came to the rock where they had put this man out, he was not to be found.

A wave had come up out of the sea, they said, and taken him, for death wanted him and his day was come, and when they went back at the beginning of the day it was not for the mast they went, as they thought, but for the man. No man goes beyond his day.

❖ A LIGHT TOKENS THE DEATH OF MR. CORRIGAN

HUGH NOLAN ◈ *FERMANAGH*
HENRY GLASSIE *1972*

Well, I was coming along the road convenient to Drumbargy Lane.

And I seen this light.

And it seemed for to start—I couldn't just say whether it started from Francy's or whether it come past it. But it was a little below Francy's when I seen it first.

And it was a powerful light and what struck me was that: wasn't it a wonder that it wasn't *blacked out*, do you see, for the way it was at that time it was only the underpart of a bicycle light that you'd see; the upper part of the glass had to be either blackened or there had to be a black cloth over it. It was during the war, do you see.

But this was a *full light*.

And it came on very, very, very, very quick.

And it was just coming forward to where the turn is on the road when it disappeared.

So I was on this side of Drumbargy Lane at that time. And the thought that struck me was that they either got a burst or a puncture or something had happened to the bicycle.

So I came on anyway, expecting for to come across some man in difficulty, or some person, man or woman.

But there was nobody on the road.

So I took from that, that it was some kind of token.

John O'Prey was working here with Francy's father at the time.

And he was coming home one night.

And *this light* came along, as he thought, *meeting* him.

But it went out *before* they met.

And there was nobody on the road.

I just don't know how long it was before I seen it that John O'Prey seen it. But Francy's father died about in a week or a fortnight, a short time after.

❖ A CLOCK TOKEN

A CONNEMARA WOMAN ◈ *GALWAY*
LADY GREGORY *1920*

One night the clock in my room struck six and it had not struck for years, and two nights after—on Christmas night—it struck six again, and afterwards I heard that my sister in America had died just at that hour. So now I have taken the weights off the clock, that I wouldn't hear it again.

❖ THE BANSHEE CRIES FOR THE O'BRIENS

MRS. O'BRIEN ◈ *GALWAY*
LADY GREGORY *1920*

The Banshee always cries for the O'Briens. And Anthony O'Brien was a fine man when I married him, and handsome, and I could have had great marriages if I didn't choose him, and many wondered at me.

And when he was took ill and in the bed, Johnny Rafferty came in one day, and says he, "Is Anthony living?" and I said he was. "For," says he, "as I was passing, I heard crying, crying, from the hill where the forths are, and I thought it must be for Anthony, and that he was gone." And then Ellen, the little girl, came running in, and she says, "I heard the mournfullest crying that ever you heard just behind the house."

And I said, "It must be the Banshee."

And Anthony heard me say that where he was lying in the bed, and he called out, "If it's the Banshee it's for me, and I must die today or tomorrow." And in the middle of the next day, he died.

❖ The Banshee Cries for the Boyles

ARMAGH
T. G. F. PATERSON *1945*

I saw the Banshee when old Boyle's mother died. I was coming home in the dusk with a load of sods, and the old gray horse and me mother with me.

And says she till me, "Some poor woman has lost her man or maybe a son."

And the thing wore a shroud as if had come from a coffin, and its hair was streaming in the wind. We both saw it.

And me mother, she said a prayer or maybe two. "That's the Banshee," says she.

Aye, it cried for many an old family here, and some say it's one that has gone before. Be that as it may, no human heart could utter such grief, so, mind ye, I doubt it.

❖ Experience of the Banshee

JOSEPH AND PETER FLANAGAN ◈ *FERMANAGH*
HENRY GLASSIE *1977*

JOSEPH I heard the Banshee twice.
I might have heard it three times.

PETER Well, tell us one experience of it anyway.

JOSEPH Well, I was coming down one night. It was at one o'clock in the night.

And the house was over about John Carson's. It would be about a quarter of a mile from where I was.

And *there* the crying started.

I stood.

And there it went on.

It would cease for a minute. Then it'd start again.

So I began to think then that it must have been the Banshee.

Then I had a long bit to go home. And a lonesome journey. I had to go up a place they call the Church Avenue and by a graveyard.

So then, they say when the Banshee cries that it's always some person belonging to the family dead or dying or going to die.

So in a day or two after, we heared there was one of them dying. It was way up in Cork. He wasn't living here, but he was one of the family; he lived up in Cork.

PETER Aye, I heard it once too.

It started in a house just down below Carson's.

And I came on up there, and I came just to that hill. And I was out there just on the head of that brae. You know it. First brae as you turn the road.

It *started to cry*. And the cries of it! And the river is very near there, it comes very close to the road.

And the crying was most terrific.

And it cried and it cried, as I thought along the river.

And then I had to turn up at the end of Stony Road, turn up toward Swanlinbar, across from old Drumane Bridge.

And says I to meself, says I, "It'll get out. What'll I do?" Says I, "I'll be in an awful state. I'll have to turn back and go back."

So I came as far as Drumane Bridge, and it seemed to be a bit in on the field, about a hundred or two hundred yards from me.

I went on up the road, and when I was passing by that house just above Drumane Bridge, John Rooney's (he's dead now since you were here), the rooster slapped his wings. That's a sign that there's something very near, some evil thing near you when the rooster does that way. That was supposed in this country, you know.

And he started to crow and crow,
and crow and crow,
till I was frightened,
the life was frightened out of me.

And the Banshee came on.

He still kept nearer and nearer.

He drew nearer.

He was just right beside the road.

And with that, the next flash he gave, he took a cut, and he landed away about two or three hundred yards from me. With the result, he went away back from me. "Well, God bless us," says I, "what'll I do if he comes out? And he'll cross me path." I had to turn right, and he was on the left-hand side. Says I, "What'll I do," says I, "if he happens to get in front of me?"

And I had a long journey to go then.

But, lucky enough, when I turned right, the cry started to fade out. There was a pretty rough wind, and with the rattle of the bushes and all, it just died out just as it started.

And the next day there was a person died just right beside it.

Well, it sounded really just like a young child there crying, middling strong, we'll say two year old. You often heard a two-year-old child there with a middling good strong rough cry, like that. And to die out like the same as you heard a thing there of a windy night or a windy day, and it would just fade away, the same as a car just revving up and dying out like that. It went like that.

And it died out and I got more content as it died out and passed away.

I got home and that was that. But this person died, and that made me believe surely that it was really the Banshee.

It cried from that wee house there, you know Andy Boyle's. It cried on out that stretch of road, and then when I turned for Swanlinbar, it cried up *along* the road and landed up at Derryhowlaght Hill.

You know where Derryhowlaght is: that first hill as you cross Drumane Bridge. It cried that length.

Well, if it was another—if it was cats, you know, I'd know a cat there. You know cats yourself. A cat's cry is quite different.

This was really a Banshee.

That was the only time ever I heard that I could just certify that it was a Banshee. But I heard a person saying—a very sensible woman; she was Hewitt; she was from Belturbet, and she was married to a man the name of Crawford in Kinawley—and she said the Banshee cried for her—I'm not really sure, but it was some of her parents anyway. And she said it came onto the windowsill.

And it sat on the windowsill.

And it cried the whole *night*.

And she was a very very nice woman, a very quiet person. And she told me the Banshee cried and cried. Well, she said it appeared very very much like an old woman of ninety or a hundred years; it was just faded out, you know, past recognition.

The Banshee was of that type. Well, in her explanation, or what it appeared to her.

JOSEPH There was one man telling me:

Them all kneeled down to say their prayers one night by the fire. And there was a back door. And they were about in the middle of the prayer. The crying started outside the back door.

There was a cry outside the back door.

Ah, they went up and looked, and wondered terribly at it. But they knew what it *was*.

It went on, cried on.

They kneeled down and finished their prayers. They were in this house belonging to another man. So the boss came down the next day, and this man was telling him about this, about the cry outside the door, the cry that riz when they were kneeling saying their prayers.

"Well," he says, "no matter where they are in this world, there's some of the Keenans dead," he says.

So in a few days after they got word out of America: there was one of them had died and was buried.

Now wasn't that the Banshee?

❖ GRANDFATHER'S GHOST

JAMES SMALL ◈ *DOWN*
RONALD H. BUCHANAN *1956*

I can remember me sister and meself sitting on two creepies in front of the open fire; there was a hen with a flock of birds in the hole at the side of the brace. There was nobody in the house but our two selves. Ye know where the room door was yonder on the left-hand side? Well I looks up and there was a man standing at it with a long-tartled coat and a beard and a hard hat on him. He was a big man, just the full of the door; and he was a sort of bent over, standing leaning on two sticks. He looked at the pair of us, and turned on his heel and walked into the room again.

Well, me mother was out in the yard, and I called her and she came running in and we told her what we'd seen. And she went and got me aunt and they both went down the room together, but they could see nothing. When me father came home that night he tacked me with what I seen, so I told him what the old man looked like, and he just shook his head. "It was your grandfather," says he. And mind ye, he was dead afore I was born.

❖ TERRIBLE GHOSTS

PETER FLANAGAN ◈ *FERMANAGH*
HENRY GLASSIE *1972*

This man, he started work one morning. And when bedtime came, he was showed his room.

He went into the room, lovely bed, very comfortable-looking.

The room was all furnished. It was one thing that he just remarked very much: that a bedroom was furnished so highly.

He knelt down and he said his prayers, and he got into bed.

And, of course, owing to it being a strange room, he didn't sleep so quick after he got into bed, you know, as anyone will do. Well, it would apply to me for one, anyway, that went into a strange room, into a strange bed, I wouldn't sleep for maybe half the night, till I'd get overpowered with sleep and I suppose then I'd sleep.

But anyway, he found the furniture a-moving, a-moving all through the room.

The rest of the occupants of the house was all fast asleep. And this went on. You'd think that the room was going to come down on top of him.

And on top of that: the weight went in on top of him into the bed.

And there he was in an awful condition; he thought there was tons and tons of weight on top of him.

And he was trembling.

And he started to sweat.

And he got into that great a temperature that the sweat boiled out through the clothes.

And out of that, he just went away in a swoon and remained that way till daylight in the morning.

He woke up the same as if he was in a fever. He wasn't hardly fit to leave the bed.

He managed to get out of the bed, and get up and put on his clothes. Came down to the kitchen. Went out to his work.

So, there was another man hired, engaged in it. And says the man to him, he says, "Jimmy," he says, "how did you get on last night, how did you sleep?"

"Oh," he says, "I got on very badly," he says. "I put in a terrible night." Says, "I was nearly killed."

He says, "I am very, very lucky to be *alive*." He says, "There must be a terrible ghost in that room."

"Ah," says the fellow to him, "you're only joking." He says, "What happened?"

So he explained to him what I'm after explaining to you, what really did happen.

"Ah," he says, "you only imagined it."

He says, "I did not," he says, "I'm going to put in the day and look for me clothes and get away."

So, when they had the farmyard work done, they went out to the field to start to work, and he still kept at the fellow all the time—he was an old employee in the business—still asked him, "Is there a ghost in that room?"

He'd say, "Is there a ghost, now tell me the truth, for it doesn't make a bit difference to me?" he says. "*Ghost* or no ghost, I'm not going to put another night in it," he says. "I put in a shocking night. I never thought that I'd have to undergo such a punishment," he says, "as I underwent last night."

"Aw," says the fellow to him finally, "there is a ghost all right," he says, "and they shouldn't have done it. There's a ghost stationed in that room, stationed," he says, "for all time in it. And I wonder," he says, "that they put you into it."

The fellow told me he wasn't the same for six months after, and in fact, he said, for six years after. He suffered that much.

That bid to be a bad ghost. And I was talking to the man. That's out of the man's lips. It was a man the name of Jimmy Williamson. He emigrated to England some years ago.

The house was just below the town there, a few miles out of the town, out of Enniskillen.

And another man was telling me about another ghost.

I'll tell a ghost story.

The three of them was famous card players. And they were playing cards in this house until some late hour in the night, one or two or maybe three o'clock.

And on their journey home—it was walking they were in them days—and they came to a bridge.

And this man—there was three of them, and he was walking in the center—and he looked across his shoulder. "God bless us," he says, "look at what is coming after us."

"What," says the other two men to him, they says, "what's coming after us?"

"Well, Lord," he says. "Look at that."

They could see nothing.

And at THAT he was whipped clean from between the two of them. And they were two men just as big as you and I'd say they were six stone weightier, each man.

And this man was whipped clean
off his feet.

And there was a high hedge and he was lifted clean out of the position that he was walking in, out from between the two of them, and he was landed in on top of the hedge.

Wasn't that terrible?

And *they, they run* to the hedge, and each of them caught an arm, and they had then—they were very very strong men—they had to pull. And pull. And pull.

And very tight they got with very ferocious pulling that they pulled him back onto the road.

And he wasn't fit to get his legs in under him. They got him straightened up. And they held him there.

And they said some prayers; they were three of me own persuasion.

And they got him straightened up, and they had a mile to bring him.

And they got him on to where he was employed.

And brought him in and he fell on the floor.

And they had to waken the occupants of the house, and got him down, and they got him on to bed.

He lay down in bed.

And he lay for a few minutes, and he never, he never mended up; he passed away.

He died of it.

He died of it.

That was just at Kinawley there. I could show you where this took place.

The other men never saw it, and they were two powerful good men. One of them was Lunny, and the other was Owens. They were two of as strong men as there was in Kinawley Parish. And they got it very very hard to get him pulled off the hedge.

When they had him off the hedge, that was the most embarrassing thing: his legs was that way that they couldn't get them straight in under him; they had to carry him, partly carry him.

And he never recovered. He passed away.

You wouldn't believe the like of that would happen.

We heard the man telling it himself, and he wasn't a man that'd tell lies, because it was a most terrifying story; it would be very bad to tell it, I mean, on anybody.

It was really genuine.

He did describe it to them. It wasn't an earthly thing anyway. He said he had flames out of his mouth. Bid to be a desperate—it was the most terrifying thing that I heard in my time anyway. I didn't like to hear it. Honestly, I thought it a most terrifying story.

We heard tell of a lot of ghost stories, and people seeing ghosts, and all that sort of thing, but I never heard as terrifying a story, I think, as that one was. Surely.

And the man that told it now, he wouldn't tell lies. I know that rightly. I know that perfectly well.

The thing was genuine.

Aye.

❖ ❖ ❖

❖ The Soldier in the Haunted House

PATRICK SHEARLOCK ◈ *CLARE*
JAMES DELARGY *1930*

Well, there was a soldier one time in it, and he was a very good soldier, and he had a lot of service done.

So this time in his quarterly accounts, when he looked it up, he was wronged fourpence ha'penny, and being wronged this fourpence ha'penny he said he'd soldier no more if he couldn't get it.

He went to the paymaster and explained his story to him. "All right," says the paymaster, "you'll get it in the next account."

"Well, it's now I want it," says the soldier.

So that was all the satisfaction the paymaster gave him about it.

The following morning he demanded for to see his company officer. He was brought in front of his company officer to make his complaint. He told his company officer that he was wronged fourpence ha'penny in his accounts. The company officer told him that it'd be all right, that he'd get it in the next account. He said that wouldn't do him, that he wanted it now. So he got no more satisfaction from his company officer. He went to his commanding officer and he explained his story to him. The same reply he got from his commanding officer. He said he'd go to the brigadier general. He went to the brigadier general, and he explained his story to the brigadier general. So the brigadier general told him that it'd be all right, that it'd run in to his next accounts. So the soldier said that that wouldn't do him. He said he'd desert or leave the army. He went to this lord's place. There was the chief general of the whole British Army. He explained his story there to him. He told him that if he'd sleep in this building tonight that he'd get him back his fourpence ha'penny in his accounts.

"Yes, I will," says the soldier.

He brought him into this building, and put down a big fire, left the soldier sitting by the side of it, gave him plenty to eat and to drink and plenty tobacco to smoke.

So the soldier was sitting down that night by the fire, and he heard all sorts of music and dancing upstairs, and he says: "Ye're keeping it very quietly to yerselves, wouldn't ye come down in the kitchen and let me see, and we won't feel the night passing by?"

That was all right till the cock crew in the morning, and he couldn't hear no more of it. He went up to the lord.

"Now, sir, can I get back and get my fourpence ha'penny?"

"Will you sleep tonight in that big building?" says the lord.

"Yes, I will," says the soldier.

The soldier went down that night, and he stood by the fire. What noise he heard the first night was nothing to what he heard the second night, till the cock crew in the morning, till he could hear no more about it. He went up to the lord and said to know could he go back for to get his fourpence ha'penny. The lord asked him to know would he sleep the third night in the house, and he said, "Yes."

So the third night he was sitting by the fire when he heard any amount of noise and dancing again around the room. After a short time what came down the stairs but a bull, and this bull had two big horns, and a coffin laid on the top of them, came down to the fireside, stooped down on her knees and left the coffin down by the soldier's side. The soldier took the lid off of it to see who was in it, and an old man stuck his head up through it.

"Come up out of that!" says the soldier. "What business have you there, and sit up alongside me by the fire!"

The old man that was in the coffin, he only started to grin and sneer at the soldier.

"Maybe," says the soldier, says he, "you'd have a smoke?"

He pulled out a clay pipe and filled it with tobacco, and handed it to the old man to take a smoke of it. The old man took the pipe in his hand and dashed it against the ground.

"If you do that again," says the soldier, "I'll knock the head off of you, but of course it's I'm worse for to give it to you!"

So he went to fill another to hand it over to the old man, and when he turned around to hand him the pipe, the coffin and the old man was disappeared.

So that morning before the cock crew a young man walked down the stairs to him and told him: "You're one of the best men that ever slept before in this big house, for I'm the man that created all the noise and disturbance around it. And you must have a great heart. An old soldier always had a good heart. So if you were to remain in this house for twenty years you would not hear a mouse in it. So here's a letter for you, and give it to my father. As soon as my father'll see this he'll know you were speaking to me, and you can tell my father there's three crocks of gold in such a room in this house. One of them is to be given to you, another for himself, and one to say Masses for me."

The soldier went up and he handed the lord the letter, and when he read it he knew that the soldier was speaking to his son, for he knew his son's handwriting. The lord turned around, and he went to the room, and he got the three crocks of gold. He did not keep one for himself, but he gave the soldier two; kept one to get Masses said for his son.

"Go back now," says the lord, "and you can soldier on, and I'll make an officer of you."

"It's not for that I came here," says the soldier, "but can you tell me am I going to get my fourpence ha'penny?"

"Yes, you are," says the lord.

The soldier went back to the barracks, and they went to make a prisoner of him when the lord came there. Instead of he being a private he made a commanding officer of him. There was a sergeant in his room that always had a downfall and a set upon him. He reduced that sergeant to the ranks, and other officers. He made corporals and sergeants of a lot of his own pals. After a short time he got a chance at his own commanding officer for being drunk, tried him by court-martial, and got him stripped and reduced to the ranks as a private.

So that's the finishing of my story!

❖ DANIEL CROWLEY AND THE GHOSTS

MR. GARVEY ◈ *KERRY*
JEREMIAH CURTIN *1892*

There lived a man in Cork whose name was Daniel Crowley. He was a coffinmaker by trade, and had a deal of coffins laid by, so that his apprentice might sell them when himself was not at home.

A messenger came to Daniel Crowley's shop one day and told him that there was a man dead at the end of the town, and to send up a coffin for him, or to make one.

Daniel Crowley took down a coffin, put it on a donkey cart, drove to the wake-house, went in, and told the people of the house that the coffin was there for them. The corpse was laid out on a table in a room next to the kitchen. Five or six women were keeping watch around it; many people were in the kitchen. Daniel Crowley was asked to sit down and commence to shorten the night: that is, to tell stories, amuse himself and others. A tumbler of punch was brought, and he promised to do the best he could.

He began to tell stories and shorten the night. A second glass of punch was brought to him, and he went on telling tales. There was a man at the wake who sang a song. After him another was found, and then another. Then the people asked Daniel Crowley to sing, and he did. The song that he sang was of another nation. He sang about the Good People, the fairies. The song pleased the company, they desired him to sing again, and he did not refuse.

Daniel Crowley pleased the company so much with his two songs that a woman who had three daughters wanted to make a match for one of them, and get Daniel Crowley as a husband for her. Crowley was a bachelor, well on in years, and had never thought of marrying.

The mother spoke of the match to a woman sitting next to her. The woman shook her head, but the mother said:

"If he takes one of my daughters I'll be glad, for he has money laid by. Do you go and speak to him, but say nothing of me at first."

The woman went to Daniel Crowley then, and told him that she had a fine, beautiful girl in view, and that now was his time to get a good wife; he'd never have such a chance again.

Crowley rose up in great anger. "There isn't a woman wearing clothes that I'd marry," said he. "There isn't a woman born that could bring me to make two halves of my loaf for her."

The mother was insulted now and forgot herself. She began to abuse Crowley.

"Bad luck to you, you hairy little scoundrel," said she, "you might be a grandfather to my child. You are not fit to clean the shoes on her feet. You have only dead people for company day and night; 'tis by them you make your living."

"Oh, then," said Daniel Crowley, "I'd prefer the dead to the living any day if all the living were like you. Besides, I have nothing against the dead. I am getting employment by them and not by the living, for 'tis the dead that want coffins."

"Bad luck to you, 'tis with the dead you ought to be and not with the living. 'Twould be fitter for you to go out of this altogether and go to your dead people."

"I'd go if I knew how to go to them," said Crowley.

"Why not invite them to supper?" retorted the woman.

He rose up then, went out, and called:

"Men, women, children, soldiers, sailors, all people that I have ever made coffins for, I invite you tonight to my house, and I'll spend what is needed in giving a feast."

The people who were watching the dead man on the table saw him smile when he heard the invitation. They ran out of the room in a fright and out of the kitchen, and Daniel Crowley hurried away to his shop as fast as ever his donkey could carry him. On the way he came to a public house and, going in, bought a pint bottle of whiskey, put it in his pocket, and drove on.

The workshop was locked and the shutters down when he left that evening but when he came near he saw that all the windows were shining with light, and he was in dread that the building was burning or that robbers were in it. When right there Crowley slipped into a corner of the building opposite, to know could he see what was happening, and soon he saw crowds of men, women, and children walking toward his shop and going in, but none coming out. He was hiding some time when a man tapped him on the shoulder and asked, "Is it here you are, and we waiting for you? 'Tis a shame to treat company this way. Come now."

Crowley went with the man to the shop, and as he passed the threshold he saw a great gathering of people. Some were neighbors, people he had known in the past. All were dancing ,singing, amusing themselves. He was not long looking on when a man came up to him and said:

"You seem not to know me, Daniel Crowley."

"I don't know you," said Crowley. "How could I?"

"You might then, and you ought to know me, for I am the first man you made a coffin for, and 'twas I gave you the first start in business."

Soon another came up, a lame man: "Do you know me, Daniel Crowley?"

"I do not."

"I am your cousin, and it isn't long since I died."

"Oh, now I know you well, for you are lame. In God's name," said Crowley to the cousin, "how am I to get these people out of this? What time is it?"

" 'Tis early yet, it's hardly eleven o'clock, man."

Crowley wondered that it was so early.

"Receive them kindly," said the cousin. "Be good to them, make merriment as you can."

"I have no money with me to get food or drink for them. 'Tis night now, and all places are closed," answered Crowley.

"Well, do the best you can," said the cousin.

The fun and dancing went on, and while Daniel Crowley was looking around, examining everything, he saw a woman in the far-off corner. She took no part in the amusement, but seemed very shy in herself.

"Why is that woman so shy—she seems to be afraid?" asked he of the cousin. "And why doesn't she dance and make merry like others?"

"Oh, 'tis not long since she died, and you gave the coffin, as she had no means of paying for it. She is in dread you'll ask her for the money, or let the company know that she didn't pay," said the cousin.

The best dancer they had was a piper by the name of John Reardon from the city of Cork. The fiddler was one John Healy. Healy brought no fiddle with him, but he made one, and the way he made it was to take off what flesh he had on his body. He rubbed up and down on his own ribs, each rib having a different note, and he made the loveliest music that Daniel Crowley had ever heard. After that the whole company followed his example. All threw off what flesh they had on them and began to dance jigs and hornpipes in their bare bones. When by chance they struck against one another in dancing, you'd think it was Brandon Mountain that was striking Mount Eagle, with the noise that was in it.

Daniel Crowley plucked up all his courage to know, could he live through the night, but still he thought daylight would never come. There was one man, John Sullivan, that he noticed especially. This man had married twice in his life, and with him came the two women. Crowley saw him taking out the second wife to dance a breakdown, and the two danced so well that the company were delighted, and all the skeletons had their mouths open, laughing. He danced and knocked so much merriment out of them all that his first wife, who was at the end of the house, became jealous and very mad altogether. She ran down to where he was and told him she had a better right to dance with him than the second wife.

"That's not the truth for you," said the second wife. "I have a better right than you. When he married me you were a dead woman and he was free, and, besides, I'm a better dancer than what you are, and I will dance with him whether you like it or not."

"Hold your tongue!" screamed the first wife. "Sure, you couldn't come to this feast tonight at all but for the loan of another woman's shinbones."

Sullivan looked a his two wives, and asked the second one:

"Isn't it your own shinbones you have?"

"No, they are borrowed. I borrowed a neighboring woman's shins from her, and 'tis those I have with me tonight."

"Who is the owner of the shinbones you have under you?" asked the husband.

"They belong to one Catherine Murray. She hadn't a very good name in life."

"But why didn't you come on your own feet?"

"Oh, I wasn't good myself in life, and I was put under a penalty, and the penalty is that whenever there is a feast or a ball I cannot go to it unless I am able to borrow a pair of shins."

Sullivan was raging when he found that the shinbones he had been dancing with belonged to a third woman, and she not the best, and he gave a sharp slap to the wife that sent her spinning into a corner.

The woman had relations among the skeletons present, and they were angry when they saw the man strike their friend. "We'll never let that go with him," said they. "We must knock satisfaction out of Sullivan!"

The woman's friends rose up, and, as there were no clubs or weapons, they pulled off their left arms and began to slash and strike with them in terrible fashion. There was an awful battle in one minute.

While this was going on Daniel Crowley was standing below at the end of the room, cold and hungry, not knowing but he'd be killed. As Sullivan was trying to dodge the blows sent against him he got as far as Daniel Crowley, and stepped on his toe without knowing it. Crowley got vexed and gave Sullivan a blow with his fist that drove the head from him, and sent it flying to the opposite corner.

When Sullivan saw his head flying off from the blow he ran, and, catching it, aimed a blow at Daniel Crowley with the head, and aimed so truly that he knocked him under the bench; then, having him at a disadvantage, Sullivan hurried to the bench and began to strangle him. He squeezed his throat and held him so firmly between the bench and the door that the man lost his senses, and couldn't remember a thing more.

When Daniel Crowley came to himself in the morning his apprentice found him stretched under the bench with an empty bottle under his arm. He was bruised and pounded. His throat was sore where Sullivan had squeezed it. He didn't know how the company broke up, nor when his guests went away.

❖ Ghosts along the Arney

HUGH NOLAN ◈ *FERMANAGH*
HENRY GLASSIE *1972*

In days gone by, ghost stories was very common, only that the tellers of these tales, they're gone, dead and gone now.

Well, it used to be very interesting for some. And then there was others and they used to get terribly afraid. There was people and when they'd hear ghost stories told—if it was on a kind of a dark day—they wouldn't go out, do you know. Oh aye.

When I was a little fellow, there was an old man, he lived here in this townland and was—oh, he was a powerful man for telling ghost stories. He was a powerful composer.

He was Maguire, James Maguire.

The house that he lived in, it's the other way now. You went up past the milkstand there, and there was a lane brought you up the hill, and his house was at the head of the first hill. Aye, indeed.

Aw, he was a great star. He had terrible experiences of ghosts, do you know. Oh *aye.* He *let on* that he had, but there was nothing about the business.

Well, I often seen him coming along here of a wet day, you know. A wet day every place is dark. When I'd hear him for about an hour or so, I wouldn't go into this room here.

Well, that was the way with a lot of the young people.

Well then, do you see, there was others then that enjoyed these stories, but they knew rightly that there was nothing at all about them.

There was one night this man was ceiliing down here where Johnny Boyle lives, down in the Hollow.

And there was a man after dying in this land and he was coming along here between this house and the head of the brae. He met that man going down in the direction of the Lake.

Aye indeed.

Aye, he was coming through the fields one night, he said, and he came to a stile.

And just as he went across the stile, he seen this man on the far side of the stile. And the man had been buried some time before it.

So anyway, he got up
    the steps
    to the head of the *stile.*

And the man wasn't seeming to *move.*

So he says to him, "*Leave me the road till I get across.*"

The man paid no attention.

He says, "I just riz," he says, "and I just leapt on top of him. And after that, there wasn't a sight of him to be seen," he says.

"I came on home."

It was alarming tales like that, do you know, that you would hear.

Well then, there was a tale told about a ghost at Arney.

Well, it's very hard to know as far as that's concerned because the man that told that, he wasn't a teller of ghost tales, do you know.

Well, I'll tell you:

There was a mansion convenient to Arney in days gone by.

It was known as Nixon Hall.

The owners of it owned all the townlands around the chapel and around the parochial house. In fact, they owned the whole townland of Mullinamesker.

And they were wealthy people. The most of them all had high-up army positions at the time.

But anyway, there was a whole lot of laborers about this place. There was a lot of horses and there was a lot of cattle. In them days, there was no water mains, nor there wasn't many places for animals to drink, especially in the summer when *ponds* would dry up.

So there was some fellow working at Nixon Hall, and he wasn't—as the men used to say—he wasn't a good article. And it was him used to bring the horses to that little brook beside Tommy Gilleece's public house for them to drink.

So there was another man in the locality, and they were deadly enemies.

So this night he had brought the horses to Arney for to drink them, and he was coming *back*.

And the way that he used to come: he used to come *out* there through a *gate* at the graveyard, next to Arney, below the chapel, between the chapel and Arney. There was a road in them days that led to this *mansion* over in the fields.

So anyway, this man and him had it *hot* some time before it. And didn't they meet on the road this night.

And of course, the feud was there and the row started again between them.

So anyway, this man he had a blade of a scythe, or some edged weapon, and didn't he take him on the neck.

And I think he partly cut the head off him anyway.

Oh, he died. Whether he got home or not, or whether he got as far as the mansion or not before he died—but he died anyway: be the hacks of it.

So that's supposed to be his ghost that be's seen.

Well, it's very seldom that it has been seen, but it has been seen a couple of times: a man without a head, between Peter McKevitt's and the chapel.

Well, Hugh Pat Owens' father seen it. And the way he told the story was: that he started for home and that this headless man started along with him, and that he put out his hand to get him by the arm as he thought.

But there was nothing to be found.

So then he invoked the Blessed Trinity and the man disappeared.

Well then, there was another man coming on the same road. And he had some experience like that.

And whether he seen this man or whether he didn't, I couldn't say. But they weren't the type of this man, Maguire, that I'm telling you about, you know; they wouldn't tell ghost stories for amusement.

And that thing, it's common about Arney, all the time.

And then, do you see, a person that's not in the habit of telling these ghost stories, do you see, there'd be something to what you hear from them in the line of seeing things from the other world, but them men like this man that I'm telling you about that could compose, do you see, that's where the value was: to make others afraid.

Well then, there's a lot of people and they imagine that they see ghosts. And if it was investigated it's just something ordinary that takes their eye, and that they be under the impression there's a ghost.

You could see a thing that looks like a ghost, and then if it was investigated, it's no ghost atall.

Now I was coming from a house away over there on the Back Road.

And I was coming through Drumbargy.

And I was walking along the pad road.

And I looked to me right.

And I seen

what I took to be

a very stout little man

standing

a distance away.

So I come on for a wee piece and says I, to meself:

"It's a pity to go home without finding out is it really a man or who would it be."

So I turned back.

And I went on down to where this figure was.

And I found out what it was.

There had been a sally runt—that's one of these plants in this country that there grows big long wattles out of, do you know. There used to be in days gone by, the old men used to be very anxious for to come across some of them; they were great for making creels, do you know—big, strong wattles.

Well, there had been some of them growing on this.

And that day they had been cut, do you know.

And the wattles was cut off this,

at the distance,

and in the darkness,

it was terrible like the shape of a wee stout man.

So.

That's what I found out when I investigated.

❖ THE GRAVE OF HIS FATHERS

PEIG SAYERS ◈ *KERRY*
ROBIN FLOWER *1945*

I have not seen a ghost, but I have known people who have, and there are many tales of them, and of strange things that happen upside down with the things of this world.

There was a lad in Ventry parish once and he could not make a living in the place where he was, so he said to himself that he would travel to the North of Ireland, and that maybe he would find something to do there that would bring a bite of food to his mouth.

And he set out with a friend from the same parish, and they walked Ireland till they came to the North and there they took service with a farmer, and were doing well for a time. But after a time this lad fell sick, and he called his friend to him, and said, "I know that I am going to die."

"Don't say that," said his friend.

"I do say that, for, young or old, when the day comes, we must go. But I always thought, when I came to die, to be buried in my own churchyard among my kindred, and now I am dying a long way from home. But promise me this much, that when I am dead you will cut the head off me, and take that and bury it in my own churchyard." His friend was unwilling at first, but at the last he gave the promise, and the lad died happy, for he knew that some part of him would rest in his own churchyard.

So, when he died, his friend was true to his word, and he cut the head from him and started throughout Ireland with the head wrapped in a cloth.

And at last he came to Ventry parish, weary with walking, and he turned into the house of his friend, and put the cloth with the head in it on the table, and told them that it was their son's head, that he had died in the North, and that he had wished that his head should be buried in his own churchyard, since his body could not rest there.

And they got in a coffin, and a barrel of porter and some tobacco pipes, and had a wake on the head.

And the next day they started for Ventry churchyard with the head in the coffin. You know that Ventry churchyard is in a place where two roads meet.

Now, as they came down their road they saw another funeral coming down the other road.

Now it is the custom, when two funerals are coming to the same churchyard at the same time, for them to race together so that the one that wins will be the first to bury its dead.

So they made all speed down their road, and the other funeral hastened down the other road. And they came together in the same moment to the wall of the churchyard, and as they touched the wall, the other funeral, the coffin and the bearers and all, vanished as though the earth had swallowed it. They wondered at this, but they said that they had come to bury the head, and that they would bury the head.

So they lifted the coffin over the wall, and came to the place where the grave was open, and there they buried the head as the young lad had asked when he was dying.

So it was for a time. But after some months another man of the family died, and they opened the grave again, and what should they find there but two coffins, and in one coffin was the head and in the other the body, so that in the end the lad had his wish, and rested, head and body and all, in the grave of his fathers.

❖ THE COFFIN

JOHN HERBERT ◈ *LIMERICK*
KEVIN DANAHER *1967*

A long time ago, when I was a young lad, I was in a farmer's house below near Monagea one evening and I saw a very strange thing there. It was what looked like a coffin without any cover on it, standing up against the wall, and it had shelves across it like a small cupboard, and there were tins and things in it, the same as you would find on the shelves of a dresser. Well, the old man of the house noticed how curious I was, and he told me about it.

It seems that one night, when he was a young married man, they were sitting around the fire in the kitchen, himself and the wife, and the old people and a few of the neighboring boys, when the door opened and four men came in with a coffin between them, and they laid it down in the middle of the floor without saying a single word, and then they turned and walked out again. They were strangers to the people in the house.

Well, what was in the house of them had not a word to say with the fright; they were staring at the coffin, and they petrified.

Well, after a while, the young man of the house plucked up his courage. "Here, in the name of God," says he, "it would be better to see what is inside in it, and to be ready to send for the priest or for the peelers, according to what is there."

The cover was loose on top of it, and he lifted it up, and the rest of them came around and looked at what was inside in it. It was a young girl, and she lying back the same as if she was asleep. "She is not dead, with that color on her," says the old woman, the young man's mother, "and let ye lift her out of it, and put her down in the bed in the room below." They did it, and she was breathing away, just the same as if she was asleep. They all stood around the bed, watching her, and in about a half an hour she woke up, the same as anyone would wake up out of their sleep. And she was greatly puzzled and very much in dread of them, for she did not know where she was or who all the strangers might be.

Well, the old woman and the young woman hunted the men up into the kitchen, and they started to comfort the poor girl and to tell her that they were respectable people, and that she need not be in dread, that nothing would happen her. And they gave her a drink of hot milk and the like of that to bring back her courage, until finally she told them that she was from near Newtown in County Kerry, and that she was after going to bed, the same as always, at home, and that the next thing she knew was to wake up in this house.

The next day she was a lot better, and they tackled the side-car and started off for Newtown; it was a journey of about fifteen miles to her own place.

And when they arrived at her people's place, they found that the whole place was very upset, for when the people of the house were after getting up in the morning three or four days before, they found their daughter, or what they thought was their daughter, dead in her sleep, and they were after waking and burying her.

And when she had them persuaded that she was their real daughter, didn't they send a few men to the churchyard to open the grave, and, God between us and all harm, wasn't the coffin in the grave empty.

❖ THE CAPTURE OF BRIDGET PURCELL

KATE PURCELL ◈ *LIMERICK*
T. CROFTON CROKER *1825*

Biddy Purcell was as clean and as clever a girl as you would see in any of the seven parishes. She was just eighteen when she was whipped away from us, as some say. And I'll tell you how it was.

Biddy Purcell and myself, that's her sister, and more girls with us, went one day, 'twas Sunday too, after hearing Mass, to pick rushes in the bog that's under the old castle.

Well, just as we were coming through Carrig gate, a small child, just like one of them little creatures you see out there, came behind her, and gave her a little bit of a tip with a kippen between the two shoulders. Just then she got a pain in the small of her back, and out through her heart, as if she was struck. We only made game of her, and began to laugh; for sure that much wouldn't hurt a fly, let alone a Christian.

Well, when we got to the bog, some went here, and more there, everywhere, up and down, for 'twas a good big place, and Biddy was in one corner, with not one along with her, or near her—only just herself. She had picked a good bundle of rushes, and while she was tying them in her apron, up came an old woman to her, and a very curious old woman she was. Not one of the neighbors could tell who she was from poor Biddy's account, nor ever saw or heard tell of the likes of her before or since.

So she looks at the rushes, and, "Biddy Purcell," says she, "give me some of them rushes."

Biddy was afeared of her life. But for all that she told her the bog was big enough, and there was plenty more rushes, and to go pick for herself, and not be bothering other people. The word wasn't out of her mouth, when the old woman got as mad as fire, and gave her such a slash across the knees and feet with a little whip that was in her hand, that Biddy was almost killed with the pain.

That night Biddy took sick, and what with pains in her heart and out through her knees, she wasn't able to sit nor lie, and had to be kept up standing on the floor, and you'd hear the screeching and bawling of her as far, aye, and farther than Mungret.

Well, our heart was broke with her, and we didn't know what in the wide world to do, for she was always telling us, that if we had all the money belonging to the master, and to lose it by her, 'twould not do—she knew all along what ailed her. But she wasn't let tell till a couple of hours before she died, and then she told us she saw a whole heap of fairies, and they riding upon horses under Carrig, and every one of them had girls behind them all to one, and he told her he was waiting for her, and would come for her at such a day, and such an hour, and sure enough 'twas at that day and hour she died. She was just five days sick, and, as I said before, our heart was fairly broke to see the poor creature, she was so bad.

Well, we hear tell of a man that was good to bring back people (so they said), and we went to him. He gave us a bottle full of green herbs, and desired us to boil them on the fire, and if they kept green she was our own, but if they turned yellow, she was gone—the Good People had her from us. He bid us to give her the water they were boiled in to drink. When we came home we boiled the herbs, and they turned as yellow as gold in the pot before our eyes. We gave her the water to drink, and five minutes after she took it she died, or whatsomever thing we had in her place died. Anyhow 'twas just like herself, and talked to us just the same as if 'twas our own sister we had there before us.

People says she's down along with them in the old fort. Some says she'll come back, and more says she won't, and indeed, faix, there's no knowing for certain which to believe, or which way it is.

❖ TAKEN

TOMÁS Ó CRITHIN ◈ *KERRY*
ROBIN FLOWER *1945*

It is not so long ago that a woman of my mother's kin, the O'Sheas, was taken, and when I was young I knew people who had seen her. She was a beautiful girl, and she hadn't been married a year when she fell sick, and she said that she was going to die, and that if she must die she would rather be in the home in which she had spent her life than in a strange house where she had been less than a year. So she went back to her mother's house, and very soon she died and was buried. She hadn't been buried more than a year when her husband married again, and he had two children by his second wife. But one day there came a letter to her people, a letter with a seal on it.

It was from a farmer who lived in the neighborhood of Fermoy. He said that now for some months, when the family would go to bed at night in his farm, if any food were left out they would find it gone in the morning. And at last he said to himself that he would find out what it was that came at night and took the food.

So he sat up in a corner of the kitchen one night, and in the middle of the night the door opened and a woman came in, the most beautiful woman he had ever seen with his eyes, and she came up the kitchen and lifted the bowl of milk they had left out, and drank of it. He came between her and the door, and she turned to him and said that this was what she had wanted.

So he asked her who she was, and she said that she came from the liss at the corner of his farm, where the fairies kept her prisoner. They had carried her off from a place in Ventry parish, and left a changeling in her place, and the changeling had died and been buried in her stead.

She said that the farmer must write to her people and say that she was in the liss with the fairies, and that she had eaten none of the food of the fairies, for if once she ate of their food she must remain with them forever till she died; and when she came near to death they would carry her through the air and put her in the place of another young woman, and carry the young woman back to be in the liss with them, in her stead. And when he wrote to her people, he must ask her mother if she remembered one night when her daughter lay sick, and the mother was sitting by the fire, and, thinking so, she had forgotten everything else, and the edge of her skirt had caught fire and was burning for some time before she noticed it. If she remembered that night it would be a token for her, for on that night her daughter had been carried off, and the fire in her mother's skirt was the last thing she remembered of her life on earth. And when she had said this she went out through the door, and the farmer saw her no more.

So the next day he wrote the letter as she had told him. But her people did nothing, for they feared that if they brought her back there would be trouble because of the new wife and her two children.

And she came again and again to the farmer, and he wrote seven letters with seals, and the neighbors all said it was a shame to them to leave her with the fairies in the liss. And the husband said it was a great wrong to leave his wife in the liss, and, whatever trouble it would bring, they should go and fetch her out of the liss.

So they set out, her own people and her husband, and when they had gone as far as Dingle, they said they would go and ask the advice of the priest.

So they went to the priest that was there that time, and they told him the story from the beginning to the end. And when he had heard the story, he said that it was a hard case, and against the law of the church. And the husband said that, when they had brought the woman out of the liss, he would not bring her back with him to make scandal in the countryside, but would send her to America, and would live with his second wife and her children. But the priest said that even if a man's wife were in America, she was still his wife, and it was against the law of the Pope that a man should have two wives; and, though it was a hard thing, they must leave her in the liss with the fairies, for it was a less evil that she should eat the fairy bread and be always with the fairies in the liss than that God's law should be broken and a man have two wives living in this world.

They found nothing to say against the priest, and they went back home sorrowing. And when the woman heard this from the farmer she went back with the fairies to the liss, and ate their bread and remained with them.

❖ How the Shoemaker Saved His Wife

PEADAR Ó BEIRN ◈ *DONEGAL*
SEÁN Ó HEOCHAIDH *1954*

When I was a boy about thirty years ago I was hired in a townland called Rualach in the parish of Kilcar. Here is a little story I heard the woman of the house tell one night:

A good many years ago there was a couple living at Gortalia. The wife was expecting the birth of a child and the husband was sent on horseback to Kilcar to fetch the midwife. While she was dressing herself he went about the town doing some errands, and he had a small drink. He was a shoemaker, and he decided he might as well buy a couple of pounds of shoe-nails while he was in the town.

Well and good. When he had got all he needed he returned for the midwife who was ready and waiting for him. He put her up behind him on the horse, and off with the two of them on their way to the sick woman. When he mounted the horse he had the nails in one hand and he held the reins in the other. They rode away with the horse going at full gallop. It was a cloudy moonlit night and as they were going through a place called Ált an Tairbh he heard a sound as if a flock of birds was coming towards them in the air. It came directly in their way and as it was passing overhead he threw the paperful of nails up in the air. He was full of anger and spoke out from his heart:

"May the Devil take you with him!"

No sooner were the words out of his mouth than he heard the sound of something falling at the horse's feet. He turned around and dismounted, and when he looked at the thing that had fallen what did he find but a woman! He looked sharply at her and who did he find her to be but his own wife whom he had left lying at home. He took her up and put her on the horse with the midwife, who held her while he led the horse home by its head.

Well. As they were approaching the house there was a hullabaloo there that they were too late, that his wife had died since he left, and there was great crying and clamor. The man led the two women he had with him into the stable with the horse and asked them to stay there until he returned. He himself went into the house, as if nothing had happened, and went over to the bed where the supposed corpse was lying. Everyone was astonished that he was not crying nor the least distraught as men usually are when their wives die. He turned on his heel and out with him and in again in a moment with the pitchfork from the byre. He went up to the bed and made a swipe at the thing that was lying there, but, well for her, when she saw him drawing at her she rose and went out of the window like a flash of lightning.

He went out then and brought in his wife and the midwife. Everything went well then and in due time the child was born. He and his wife spent a long life after that at Gortalia and neither the wee folk nor the big people gave them any more trouble!

❖ The Mountain Elf

PETER FLANAGAN ◈ *FERMANAGH*
HENRY GLASSIE *1972*

Well, in days gone by, they assembled every night from one house to another. I went to your house, and you went to my house, and we sat down and we told fairy tales.

And it seems to me it was definitely true, for I have heard tell of several children being taken away and sickly elves left in their place. There was often a substitute child *left.*

I saw one meself. I'll tell you about it.

Well. We were on a mumming expedition. And it was up here on the mountain. I'll not mention the names of the people, you know. But we went into this house.

After doing our mumming transaction, you know, going through the whole performance, I saw this wee boy in the corner.

And he had wee, thin long hands, similar there to a monkey.

And he had feet on him, I'd say really they were nine or ten inches long. His legs were not thicker than the leg of the tongs.

And he had a pile of wee straws. He was nipping it in the corner, breaking them all to pieces.

There was only two old men in the house. And I didn't really remember seeing him when I went in, you know. And then I looked, and he had a very thin worn face on him; you'd think that he was a thousand years of age. A very faded-out-looking figure.

I didn't ask the boys atall anything about him, but a certain length of time after I asked, and there was a lot of people didn't know anything about him, but there was one fellow told me he was supposed to be left be the fairies.

The normal child was taken away a considerable number of years before that.

And this boy could do anything. He could go out and he could
fly from one house to another,
rise up and fly
as far as he liked.

Could be he would come back again in a few minutes, and he might be away for the whole day.

He was seen here, and he was seen there, miles and miles away.

He could be on the street at the very same time when a meal would be ready, no matter how *far* he was away.

Then there was wee tales, yarns like that told about him.

And he lived on for years, years. He stayed there in fact for years and years, until one morning the two old men was looking for him and he was gone. Completely.

And he never returned again.

He never seemed to grow older. He kept the one, he was the same. He was put in the cradle where the normal child was until he had them just harried out.

He got up and he walked through the floor, and he could jump here and jump there, and he could light, and they didn't know what to do with him.

The doctor was acquainted, but he give no decision on him or anything. He stayed in the house till they were fed up with him. They were a pair of nice quiet old men.

And finally this is what took place: he just riz up, and cleared away, Christmas morning, and was gone.

That was the end of it.

❖ INISHKEEN'S ON FIRE

ELLEN CUTLER ◈ *FERMANAGH*
HENRY GLASSIE *1972*

There was a woman and she had a wee baby boy in a cradle. Them days there was no such thing as a pram.

So this boy come in, and the child was taken out of the cradle, and this funny boy got into it.

The child was never seen, and the funny boy was in the cradle all the time.

And a man come in, a neighbor man come in, and the boy in the cradle says, "GIMME A LIGHT FOR ME PIPE.

"GIMME A COAL THERE OUTTA THE FIRE."

So the boyo got the coal and he smoked.

And then there was another man going to a blacksmith. He was going to get a loy fixed. It wasn't a spade now; it was a loy.

So. The man was going away to get the loy fixed with the blacksmith. He looked into the cradle. And he knew it was no child.

He knew it was no baby.

And the boy in the cradle put up his head. "WOULD YOU GIVE ME A LIGHT FOR ME PIPE," he says.

So the man that went in, he went out to the street, and he let a big curse out of him:

"Inishkeen's on fire.
"Inishkeen's on fire."

The boyo got up
    and hopped out of the cradle
        and away
            and he never was seen after.

He was frightened, you see, when he heard about the fire in Inishkeen. That's where they lived, you see.

I often heard me husband telling it.

The man says, "Inishkeen's on fire."

So he disappeared.

I often heard him telling me that.

THE BLOOD OF ADAM

KATE AHERN ◈ *LIMERICK*
KEVIN DANAHER *1967*

There was a priest in this parish long ago, and the old people used to tell us a lot of stories about him. He was a fine singer, they said, and he could play the fiddle finely and he was very fond of music. He was a noted horseman, too, although it was a horse that killed him in the end—it was how he was out one night on a sick call, and it was late and very dark when he was coming home, and the horse stumbled and threw him, and they found him in the morning and his neck broken. It was behind on the Gort a' Ghleanna road it happened, just at the bridge halfways down the hill.

Well, what I'm telling you happened a good while before that, on another night when he was out riding late, when he was back on the lower road, near the county bounds.

It was a bright moonlight night and he was walking the horse along when he heard this sweet music coming from the bank of the river, and he stopped to listen to it. After a while he put the horse at the ditch of the road and cleared it into the field and down to the river.

And there was this very big crowd of small people, men and women about as big as a twelve-years-old child, and they all gathered around listening to a lot of them that were playing every kind of a musical instrument.

And the priest was sitting on his horse, enjoying the music, when some of them saw him. " 'Tis a priest," they said and the music stopped.

And they all gathered around the horse. And one of them, the head man of them, maybe, spoke up. "Such a question, Father, and will you answer it?" says he.

"I will, and welcome, if I have the answer," says the priest.

"What we want to know is this, will we go to Heaven?" says the little man.

"I do not know," says the priest, "but I can tell you this much: if you have any drop of Adam's blood in your veins, you have as good a chance of Heaven as any man, but if you have not, then you have no right to Heaven."

"Ochón Ó!" says the little man. And they all went off along the river-bank, all crying and wailing so that it would break your heart to listen to them.

❖ WE HAD ONE OF THEM IN THE HOUSE FOR A WHILE

MR. AND MRS. KELLEHER ◈ *WICKLOW*
LADY GREGORY *1920*

MR. KELLEHER I often saw them when I had my eyesight. One time they came about me, shouting and laughing and there were spouts of water all around me. And I thought that I was coming home, but I was not on the right path and couldn't find it and went wandering about, but at last one of them said, "Good evening, Kelleher," and they went away, and then in a moment I saw where I was by the stile. They were very small, like little boys and girls, and had red caps.

I always saw them like that, but they were bigger at the butt of the river; they go along the course of the rivers. Another time they came about me playing music and I didn't know where I was going, and at last one of them said the same way, "Good evening, Kelleher," and I knew that I was at the gate of the College; it is the sweetest music and the best that can be heard, like melodeons and fifes and whistles and every sort.

MRS. KELLEHER I often heard that music too, I hear them playing drums.

MR. KELLEHER We had one of them in the house for a while, it was when I was living up at Ticnock, and it was just after I married that woman there that was a nice slip of a girl at that time. It was in the winter and there was snow on the ground, and I saw one of them outside, and I brought him in and put him on the dresser, and he stopped in the house for a while, for about a week.

MRS. KELLEHER It was more than that, it was two or three weeks.

MR. KELLEHER Ah! maybe it was—I'm not sure. He was about fifteen inches high. He was very friendly. It is likely he slept on the dresser at night. When the boys at the public house were full of porter, they used to come to the house to look at him, and they would laugh to see him but I never let them hurt him. They said I would be made up, that he would bring me some riches, but I never got them. We had a cage here, I wish I had put him in it, I might have kept him till I was made up.

MRS. KELLEHER It was a cage we had for a thrush. We thought of putting him into it, but he would not have been able to stand in it.

MR. KELLEHER I'm sorry I didn't keep him—I thought sometimes to bring him into Dublin to sell him.

MRS. KELLEHER You wouldn't have got him there.

MR. KELLEHER One day I saw another of the kind not far from the house, but more like a girl and the clothes grayer than his clothes, that were red. And that evening when I was sitting beside the fire with the Missus I told her about it, and the little lad that was sitting on the dresser called out, "That's Geoffrey-a-wee that's coming for me," and he jumped down and went out of the door and I never saw him again. I thought it was a girl I saw, but Geoffrey wouldn't be the name of a girl, would it?

He had never spoken before that time. Somehow I think that he liked me better than the Missus. I used to feed him with bread and milk.

MRS. KELLEHER I was afraid of him—I was afraid to go near him, I thought he might scratch my eyes out—I used to leave bread and milk for him but I would go away while he was eating it.

MR. KELLEHER I used to feed him with a spoon, I would put the spoon to his mouth.

MRS. KELLEHER He was fresh-looking at the first, but after a while he got an old look, a sort of wrinkled look.

MR. KELLEHER He was fresh-looking enough, he had a hardy look.

MRS. KELLEHER He was wearing a red cap and a little red cloth skirt.

MR. KELLEHER Just for the world like a Highlander.

MRS. KELLEHER He had a little short coat above that; it was checked and trousers under the skirt and long stockings all red. And as to his shoes, they were tanned, and you could hardly see the soles of them, the sole of his foot was like a baby's.

MR. KELLEHER The time I lost my sight, it was a Thursday evening, and I was walking through the fields. I went to bed that night, and when I rose up in the morning, the sight was gone. The boys said it was likely I had walked on one of their paths. Those small little paths you see through the fields are made by *them.*

They are very often in the quarries; they have great fun up there, and about Peacock Well. The Peacock Well was blessed by a saint, and another well near, that cures the headache.

I saw one time a big gray bird about the cowhouse, and I went to a comrade-boy and asked him to come and to help me to catch it, but when we came back it was gone. It was very strange-looking and I thought that it had a head like a man.

❖ FAIRY PROPERTY

MICHAEL QUINN ◈ *GALWAY*
ROBERT GIBBINGS *1945*

Well, I can tell you what was told to me by a parish priest, and it happened to a man he knew, so it must be true. It was not far from Doonlaun near Shrule, and it was to a man of the name of Tom Monahan that it happened.

Tom was one of the finest hurlers in the district, and one bright moonlight night he was on his way home, and he had to pass by a field that sloped down from a wood, in the face of the moon. What was his surprise to see two teams of men playing hurley. Well, he watched, and he watched, and after a while it came to him that they were the Good People. And they were playing wonderful, and he stood for a long while admiring their play, until in the latter end, with the dint of delight that he had in a great stroke, he let out a shout from him. Then they all knew he was there, and him a mortal.

"Would you like to join in?" asked one of them, as nice as you please.

"I would, indeed," said Tom, "but is there a place for me?"

"There is surely," said they, "for there's a gap in one side."

"Have you a hurley?" asked Tom.

"Here's the best," said they, handing one to him. A lovely stick it was.

So Tom played, and he played as never before, and his side won the match.

"I'll tell you who we are now," said the Good People, for they were very friendly with Tom. "We are from the churchyard beyond. But," they added, "we are in a great fix, for we have to play our old rivals from Knockma on this night week, and they've got a mortal, the red-headed Paddy, Paddy Ruadh, to play for them, and he is the best hurler in Mayo. Could you help us?" said they.

"I could," said Tom, "but could I have the same hurley?"

"You can," said they.

So a week from that night Tom crept out, telling no one where he was going, and he reached the same field, and there were the two teams, and his hurley was waiting for him. And they played and they played, and in the finish Tom's team won, and there was great joy in his team.

"What would you like now, and we'll give it to you?" they said. "Anything you'd like at all?"

"I'd like that hurley," said Tom. " 'Tis the finest hurley I ever played with," he said, "for I never missed a ball, high or low, with it."

"That's true enough," they said. "You never missed a ball, high or low, but you've asked the one thing we can't do. 'Tis fairy property and we couldn't give it away."

Tom was kind of hurt at this and he was an obstinate sort of a fellow.

"I must have it," he says.

"You can't," they said.

"I must," said Tom.

With that there was a great altercation, and, in the end, Tom walked off, taking the hurley with him.

Well, Tom was hardly home before he began to sicken. His mother could do nothing for him, and the doctor could do nothing for him.

"Is there anything at all that you'd wish?" said his mother to him one day.

"There's a hurley up in the rafters," said he. "Will you bring it down and put it on the end of the bed so I can see it?" he said.

And all the time he grew worse and worse. And when they seen that he was going to die, "Have you any last wish at all?" they said.

"Promise me one thing," he said.

"We will," they said.

"Promise me," he said, "to put that hurley in the coffin alongside of me."

Sure enough they did it. So maybe he's still winning matches for Doonlaun.

❖ THE BLACKSMITH OF BEDLAM AND THE FAIRY HOST

PEADAR Ó DÓNAILL ◈ *DONEGAL*
SEÁN Ó HEOCHAIDH *1954*

Long ago there was a blacksmith living here at Bedlam, where O'Donnell's forge is now, who was known by the nickname of Yellow Billy. He and his wife had a small house west of the bridge on the right-hand side of the road, and there was no one else in their household.

It used to be said that there was no night of the year that the wee folk did not come in to yarn and chat with Billy. They had become so familiar with him that they used to throw things into the room to him. His wife noticed nothing odd as she could see nothing, but there was none of their tricks that Billy could not see.

At that time there was no road in the district except for a narrow path which went up to the head of the glen, and when people were bringing up sea-wrack this was a very difficult way. There was a sharp rock thrust out into the path which used to catch the panniers and people had to drive very carefully to get past it and often their loads were overturned. Many times they implored Billy to break this rock, since he had the only sledge hammer in the district, but Billy would not as much as lay a finger on it. He always used to say the rock was gentle and it might be better to leave it than to interfere with it.

Well and good. One night they made Billy drunk and then they dared him to break the rock. They enraged him so that he took his sledge hammer with him and made splinters of the rock.

The next night he did not get a wink of sleep. The wee folk came and filled his house with filth and dung. On the third night Billy went to the priest and told him how things were.

"Well," said the priest, "I will be going to Gweedore on Sunday to say Mass and on my way home I will banish them, and if it is your wish I will put them in a place where they will never be able to harm a living person any more, but you must be of one mind with me."

Billy went home and he was a very short time indoors before a little old man came in to speak with him.

"Billy," he said, "you are bringing adversity on us after all we have done for you."

"Well, you yourselves are to blame," said Billy. "If you had behaved yourselves it would be long before I would interfere with you, but since I could get no peace, I had to do something."

"Well, it is not right to bring adversity on us all because of a couple of rogues amongst us. It was a couple of our young lads who caused you all the trouble, and if you let us off this time maybe you will be the better for it and not one bit the worse."

"I have nothing against you," said Billy, "and if you let me off I won't go further in the matter."

"Well," said the little old man, "there is a chest of gold buried out on the Yellow Sandbank and there is a man down there at Bun an Inbheara who has a boat. He will take you out and when he is over the sandbank, all he has to do is to put the gaff over the side of the boat, and as soon as it reaches the bottom it will hook the chest of gold."

"I am afraid," said Billy, "that when you had me out there you would drown me."

"Don't be the least afraid," said the old man. "Take a bottle of holy water with you in the boat and nothing will come near you."

"I won't go," said Billy.

"Well," said the little old man, "there is a man up here at Caiseal whose foot is festering, and an herb growing in his own garden would cure it. If you go up, one of us will go with you and show you the herb, and all you will have to do is to rub the wound with it. That will cure him and from that on there is nothing you ask that he won't do for you."

"I won't go there on any acount," said Billy. "The way there is very lonely."

"Well, Billy," said the old man, "I can do no more for you. I know of nothing else about here that would help you unless it is some gold, a little or a lot, over there on the far side of the river and if you like, go over and take it. It is not worth much, but all the same, if you want it, take it."

That same night Billy took a pickaxe across and began to dig at the place where the old man told him the gold was. He went on digging, but if he had been digging ever since, he could not have found the gold. When he had been digging for some time a little man came to the bank of the river opposite him and shouted to him to dig on the other side of the high ground in such and such a place and there he would find the gold. He did so, and soon he came on gold coins as large as five-shilling pieces. He took them home. A little while later he sold them to a pedlar who came the way for sixpence apiece.

Well and good. Sunday came and when Billy thought it was time for the priest to be returning from Gweedore, he was waiting for him and when he came he spoke to him.

"Priest," said he, "I think I will not interfere at all with the wee gentry."

"Perhaps," said the priest, "it is better so. See what they have done to me. They threw a fiery dart at me when I was coming through Gleann Thualla!"

So they were left undisturbed and from that day to the day he died they gave no trouble to Billy nor to anyone belonging to him.

❖ Fairy Forths

PETER FLANAGAN ◈ *FERMANAGH*
HENRY GLASSIE *1972*

It was a fairy tale told that if you could get ahold of a fairy, that he would tell you where there was a crock of gold.

Supposed to be gold buried here in Ireland at all these forths.

They're on the top of every hill.

They were supposed to be made at the invasion of the Danes.

The Danes invaded Ireland, you see—away back—well, a thousand years ago. I can't give you the particular date.

And these are fortifications built.

The Danes are the first stranger invaded Ireland—used to come in canoes, and it was for plunder they came, the Danish people.

And the Irish had to *all* collect, *on* the hilltops, and build these fortifications round, round as an *O*, or as round as that ovenlid there. And all get inside of it and they were all on the watch out.

I was here on this hillside in my fortifications, and if they saw the Danes coming, they'd blow their bugles, and it passed on from one to the other, from one end of Ireland to another, whenever the Danes invaded.

So there was a king. He was Brian Boru. He raged war against them, and 'twas ten hundred and fourteen, that's the date he banished the last of the Danes. In ten hundred and fourteen, at Clontarf, here in the south of Ireland. And that ended them. So.

And there's supposed to be money buried at these forths, and that's where the fairies are supposed to *be*.

There was witch*craft* in Ireland *too*, in them days.

And these witches were supposed to say to the people, "*If* you shoot me, I'll watch this crock of gold till the Day of Judgment, till the end of time."

And they're supposed to be watching, and the Good People knows where these crocks of gold is, and if you could catch one of these fairies—some calls them leprechauns, that's another name—well, they'd tell you where the crock of gold was.

But.

A man made a great effort up here to catch one of them. He walked out of this clump of bushes, and he spoke up to him, and he told him that he was going to tell him where the crock of gold was.

He wanted to do him a favor,
but the man couldn't understand him,
so he made a grab at the fairy.

And the fairy just leaped up above him, and lit just on a branch.

And that was that.

He couldn't get him.

It was the nearest fairy tale that ever I heard. And I saw the man.

I saw the man. Yes.

He spoke calmly to the fairy. He says, "Wait," he says, "till I catch you." So he went to make a grab at him like that, on the ground.

But he had wings on him and he went up in the branches.

And that was that.

And if he had of taken him calmly, the fairy said that he'd tell him where the crock of gold was.

But then, he scared the fairy, the way the fairy disappeared into thin air.

That was that.

He was an old beardy man. I saw him. He's not so very long dead now. That's that.

❖ GORTDONAGHY FORTH

ELLEN CUTLER ◈ *FERMANAGH*
HENRY GLASSIE *1972*

Well, a forth: it's round as a ring. And there's trees growing all around the edge of it. And the grass grows inside.

And you're not allowed to take anything out of a forth. Because it belongs to the Good People.

And I remember me husband one time,
he had killed *pigs*
for the market.

And he went out to this forth to get a piece of a skiver to put in the *pig*.

And he got the piece of a stick, or rod, and he went out the next morning, the best pig he had, his two hams were broken. Because he cut that out of there.

I said for him to not go out *there*, so he went on. Went out the next morning to get the two pigs for market, their hams were broken.

They were broken that they were past using, you see.

He brought the pig to the market, and he didn't get half-price for it.

There was another time, a man went out into a forth with an axe. He was after buying the new axe.

And they had no firing.

And he says to the mother, "I'll go up to the forth and get a fire out of the windfalls," out of the whitethorns that was down.

So, he went up with the new axe,
and he hit the whitethorn,
and the hatchet went in pieces,
and blood flew out of the tree.

So he was very glad to leave it there.

And so would I.

So he went back. The mother says, "I told you not to go near it."

And then where me mother's uncle built the house. It was away down near Derrygonnelly.

And he had it well on to be built.

And he was told not to build it.

And he says, "Why?" And he wouldn't be told.

And he was told a second time to not build it. And the man said then, "You're building it on the fairies' pass."

He paid no heed. He built away, and he finished the house, completed it.

The next morning when he went out, the house was down, every stone of it, every stone of it, not one touching another one, no indeed, not one.

So then, the neighbor man says, "You were told to not, you were told to not build it."

He knew it was on their pass, you see.

Funny, there was no forth beside it. Do you see, it was like the time me husband saw the fairies.

Of course, there's people now would laugh at you, but sure, when you see the thing.

He saw the light coming across that hill at the end of the house there.

And he watched the lights. He watched the lights, and he could hear them singing, and they went on round, and down through the other field, across in under the house, and they were playing *lovely* music, and *lovely* lights.

And they just crossed below the house and went into the forth, just at the end of the house there.

Oh, me husband seen them, and he come into the house here and he says, "Terry, come out till you hear this lovely music. And there's a whole pile of lights," he says. So Terry went out, and when Terry went out, he could see nothing.

So, me husband was told after: If he had of touched Terry, just touched him, like give him a pull to follow him like, he'd have seen them.

But when he told Terry, Terry seen nothing.

Shouldn't have spoke, you see.

He was told after.

THE FAIRIES RIDE FROM GORTDONAGHY TO DRUMANE

HUGH NOLAN ◈ *FERMANAGH*
HENRY GLASSIE *1972*

There was people used to tell fairy tales.

I heard a story about two old men that was coming from a wake.

And the wake was in that lane that you go to Mrs. Cutler's, to go to the house where this man was *dead.*

So, these two old men left at some time in the middle of the night.

And one of them had to come here to Derryinch, that's where he lived, and the other man lived a wee piece up there off the road. It's a house above John Moore's; it's James Monaghan that lives in it now.

So *after they come out to the main road*, they parted. And this Derryinch man took the fields, and the other man came along the road.

And when he was coming at Phil McHugh's—it's that small slated house on the roadside—he heard the loveliest music ever you seen. In Gortdonaghy. That would be at the back of Phil McHugh's.

And the next thing he heared was a troop of horses starting out of Gortdonaghy.

And they galloped on into Drumane and away up the hill to where there's a forth on the top of the hill.

So anyway, they started then a dance at the forth.

And, ah, there was the loveliest music ever you heared and the wonderfullest dancing, the wonderfullest carousing.

There was lumps of turf in a field along the roadside.

And he got in and he fixed himself up against one of these lumps of turf just for to listen to the music.

So the music went on anyway till it started to break day, and then it quit.

So he got up and prepared for home, and when he come to the other side of the lump, this companion of his was at it. He had heared the music and he had came back.

And the two had met together again, and they come out to the road, and he went home, and this other man went home to Derryinch.

So then the next *day*, he went to the owner of this land *round* the forth.

And he *told him* what he had heared the night afore. There seemed to be that many horses that the *whole* field round the forth would be all tracks.

So this man went and he examined, and there wasn't the least track of a horse.

So. Of course, that might never have happened, you know. It could be all fiction, do you know.

But it used to be great pastime listening to tales like that.

❖ LANTY'S NEW HOUSE

TYRONE
WILLIAM CARLETON *1846*

Lanty M'Cluskey had married a wife, and, of course, it was necessary to have a house in which to keep her. Now, Lanty had taken a bit of a farm, about six acres; but as there was no house on it, he resolved to build one; and that it might be as comfortable as possible, he selected for the site of it one of those beautiful green circles that are supposed to be the playground of the fairies.

Lanty was warned against this. But as he was a headstrong man, and not much given to fear, he said he would not change such a pleasant situation for his house, to oblige all the fairies in Europe. He accordingly proceeded with the building, which he finished off very neatly. And, as it is usual on these occasions to give one's neighbors and friends a housewarming, so, in compliance with this good and pleasant old custom, Lanty, having brought home the wife in the course of the day, got a fiddler, and a lot of whiskey, and gave those who had come to see him a dance in the evening.

This was all very well, and the fun and hilarity were proceeding briskly, when a noise was heard after night had set in, like a crushing and straining of ribs and rafters on the top of the house. The folks assembled all listened, and without doubt there was nothing heard but crushing, and heaving, and pushing, and groaning, and panting, as if a thousand little men were engaged in pulling down the roof.

"Come," said a voice, which spoke in a tone of command, "work hard: you know we must have Lanty's house down before midnight."

This was an unwelcome piece of intelligence to Lanty, who, finding that his enemies were such as he could not cope with, walked out, and addressed them as follows:

"Gentlemen, I humbly ask your pardon for building on any place belonging to you, but if you'll have the civilitude to let me alone this night, I'll begin to pull down and remove the house tomorrow morning."

This was followed by a noise like the slapping of a thousand tiny little hands, and a shout of "Bravo, Lanty! Build halfway between the two whitethorns above the boreen." And after another hearty little shout of exultation, there was a brisk rushing noise, and they were heard no more.

The story, however, does not end here, for Lanty, when digging the foundation of his new house, found the full of a kam of gold, so that in leaving to the fairies their playground, he became a richer man than ever he otherwise would have been, had he never come in contact with them at all.

JACK AND THE CLURICAUNE

A COMFORTABLE FARMER ◈ *WEXFORD*
MR. AND MRS. S. C. HALL *1841*

A man by the name of Jack Cassidy was the only one I ever knew, who, out and out, had a hold of a Cluricaune. And this was the way of it:

Jack was a frolicsome, gay sort of fellow, full of spirit and fun and diversion of all kinds, a gay boy entirely, and one that had no more care for the world than the world for him. And Jack had been making fierce love to a very pretty slip of a girl, with a good penny of money, but Peggy's father wouldn't listen to any reason that wasn't set to the tune of "guinea gold." And this almost drove Jack beside himself.

And he had often heard tell of a Cluricaune that used to be below the battered farmhouse of Eddyconner. And, bedad, Jack let his uncle's plowing and sowing take care of itself, and set to watch the little old chap day and night, hearing him, sometimes in one corner, and sometimes in another, until after creeping, creeping along the hedge, he fixes his eye on him, and he sitting as sly as murder, hammering away at the old brogue.

Well, in course he knew that as long as ever he kept his eye on the little rogue he couldn't stir. And the cute nagur turns round, and says, "Good morrow, Jack."

"Good evening to you, kindly," answers Jack.

"Evening and morning is the same to a lazy man," says the Cluricaune.

"Who said you was lazy?" answers Jack. And he catches up the little brogue-mender in his fist. "Take it easy," says the chap, "and give me my hammer."

"Do ye see any dust in my eye?" says Jack, who knew every trick the likes of them are up to, to get off with themselves.

"The dickens a grain," says the Cluricaune, "and no wonder the pretty Peggy's so taken with them fine eyes of yours. It's a pity her father doesn't see their beauty as well as the daughter."

"Never fear, my jewel," replies Jack, "he'll discern a wonderful improvement in my features when you find me the crock of gold."

"Well, you're a fine sporting fellow," answers the Cluricaune, "and if you'll carry me fair and easy, without pinching my toes off as if I was a bird, into the middle of the nine-acre field, I'll show you something worth looking for."

Well, to get at the nine-acre at all, Jack had to cross as deep and as dirty a bit of bog as was on the countryside, and he had on his Sunday clothes, so that he had no fancy at all for tramping through a slob. But this was not all. He had just got into the very middle of it, when a sudden blast of wind whirled off his brand-new hat. Still he was up to the tricks of his prisoner, for he kept his eyes steady upon old Devilskin.

"I'm sorry for your loss, Jack," grins the lying imp, as fair and smooth as if it was the truth he told.

"Thank ye for nothing," says the poor fellow, "but ye'll not get off for either sorrow or sympathy. I'm quite up to your tricks. Sure if I'd gone the way over the bog *you* told me, it's drowned I'd be in it long ago."

"Look ye, Jack Cassidy," croaks out the little scamp, though it was the truth he told then anyhow, "if you kept your thoughts as steadily fixed on your work as you have kept your eyes on me, you'd have money enough without hunting for Cluricaunes. But keep on to that bouchlawn there, in the very middle of the nine-acre. Bedad, you put me in mind of the girl who set one eye to watch her father and the other to watch her sweetheart, for you see everything without looking."

"Ah!" laughs Jack, "I'd go blindfold through the country."

"A bad sign," observed the old fellow, shaking his daushy head. "A roving blade gathers no more gold than a rolling stone does moss." And Jack had the sense to think to himself that, even if he got no money out of the Cluricaune, he got good advice.

"Now let me go, Jack," shouts the little fellow. "Dig up that bouchlawn, and you'll find a pot of gold." "Dig it for me yourself this instant," shouts Jack, shaking him almost into smithereens.

"Sorra a spade I have," answers the other, "or I would with all the veins."

"If you don't, I'll strangle you," exclaimed Jack again.

"Oh, Jack! save me, save me!" cries Peggy's voice at his elbow.

Poor Jack turned. There was no Peggy, and the Cluricaune was gone, with a laugh and a shout that made the bog shake again.

Well, Jack took off his garter, and tied it three times round the bouchlawn, and cut a slip of witch-hazel off a tree that grew convenient, and making a ring of it, dropped on his knees, saying an *Ave* over it, and then let it fall over the bouchlawn, so that he might preserve it from harm, and then went home. And by break of day he was back again at the nine-acre, and as true as that you are standing there, there were above nine hundred bouchlawns sprung up in the night, with nine hundred garters tied to them, and in the midst of as many hazel rings!

His heart was splitting into halves, and he sat down in the beams of the rising sun, and cried just like a babby that had lost its mother. And all of a sudden the words of the Cluricaune came into his head—"If you kept your thoughts as steadily fixed on your work as you have kept your eyes on me, you'd have money enough without hunting for Cluricaunes." From that day out Jack was a new man. He took the little brogue-maker's hint, and in five years told down two guineas for Peggy's one, all through the fortune. And maybe they haven't thirteen to the dozen of children this blessed day.

❖ BRIDGET AND THE LURIKEEN

KILDARE

PATRICK KENNEDY *1866*

A young girl that lived in sight of Castle Carberry, near Edenderry, was going for a pitcher of water to the neighboring well one summer morning, when who should she see sitting in a sheltery nook under an old thorn, but the Lurikeen, working like vengeance at a little old brogue only fit for the foot of a fairy like himself.

There he was, boring his holes, and jerking his waxed ends, with his little three-cornered hat with gold lace, his knee breeches, his jug of beer by his side, and his pipe in his mouth. He was so busy at his work, and so taken up with an old ballad he was singing in Irish, that he did not mind Breedheen till she had him by the scruff of the neck, as if he was in a vise.

"Ah, what are you doing?" says he, turning his head round as well as he could. "Dear, dear! to think of such a pretty colleen catching a body, as if he was after robbing a hen roost. What did I do to be treated in such a undecent manner? The very vulgarest young ruffin in the townland could do no worse. Come, come, Miss Bridget, take your hands off, sit down, and let us have a chat, like two respectable people."

"Ah, Mr. Lurikeen, I don't care a wisp of borrach for your politeness. It's your money I want, and I won't take hand or eye from you till you put me in possession of a fine lob of it."

"Money, indeed! Ah! where would a poor cobbler like me get it? Anyhow there's no money hereabouts, and if you'll only let go my arms, I'll turn my pockets inside out, and open the drawer of my seat, and give you leave to keep every halfpenny you'll find."

"That won't do. My eyes'll keep going through you like darning needles till I have the gold. Begonies, if you don't make haste, I'll carry you, head and pluck, into the village, and there you'll have thirty pair of eyes on you instead of one."

"Well, well, was ever a poor cobbler so circumvented. And if it was an ignorant, ugly bosthoon that done it, I would not wonder. But a decent, comely girl, that can read her 'Poor Man's Manual' at the chapel, and—"

"You may throw your compliments on the stream there. They won't do for me, I tell you. The gold, the gold, the gold! Don't take up my time with your blarney."

"Well, if there's any to be got, it's under the old castle it is. We must have a walk for it. Just put me down, and we'll get on."

"Put you down indeed! I know a trick worth two of that. I'll carry you."

"Well, how suspicious we are! Do you see the castle from this?" Bridget was about turning her eyes from the little man to where she knew the castle stood, but she bethought herself in time.

They went up a little hillside, and the Lurikeen was quite reconciled, and laughed and joked. But just as they got to the brow, he looked up over the ditch, gave a great screech, and shouted just as if a bugle horn was blew at her ears: "Oh, murder! Castle Carberry is afire." Poor Biddy gave a great start, and looked up towards the castle. The same moment she missed the weight of the Lurikeen, and when her eyes fell where he was a moment before, there was no more sign of him than if everything that passed was a dream.

❖ FAIRY TALES

PETER FLANAGAN ◈ *FERMANAGH*
HENRY GLASSIE *1977*

Well, I think all the fairy tales has been rehearsed over and over again. I don't think there's any sacred fairy tales at the moment. I'd have that belief.

I heard that many fairy tales from me father and from other people, and I got a kind of disgusted with them.

The fairy tales were a matter of entertainment. And I think again it was really to scare young people. Naturally enough, a young person would like to get out. The same as your daughter—and she was living here, she'd like to get out at night, you know. Nature takes its course. That's the way it is.

And I think it was principally told on that account—to take fear and to keep them in, and to keep them under the safekeeping of their parents. I have that imagination.

Fairy tales were handed down from one to the other who really believed it, really believed it. Then the world advanced. I mind in my day when I was about the age of your daughter there, I used to be afraid to go out, and I used to bring a lamp with me—what they called a hand lamp, the same as the battery lamp now; it was a candle used in them days—and maybe I wouldn't have the second match with me, and maybe the wind blows me lamp out, and there I was in the dark and I was in an awful mess.

I remember coming across what they called a footstick; that would be a wee plank across a drain.

And I seen the two eyes shining at me on the other side. And it was the reflection of the lamp shining in the dog's eyes.

And man, I nearly fainted.

He let a bark.

And I let a shout.

And I nearly collapsed into a drain. And from *that night* to this I never was one bit afraid.

That fright was the best thing ever happened. It came to make me nerves strong and staunch that I wasn't afraid of anything. And I never carried a lamp after that. I just walked away, and if I found a noise or a rattle or a flicker of the leaves, I never was one bit afraid.

And that was the way.

So *that* cut out the whole fairy tales. Me father was great for fairy tales; he'd tell you about seeing the fairies.

The only thing ever I heard him saying was that he seen a last that a man run and got of the fairy when he was making a wee shoe. That was above Swanlinbar.

He saw him making a wee shoe, and he run and he got it, and the last—did you ever see a foot-last?—he got the last and the last was in the house right beside where I was born. I never saw it meself, but it was there during his time.

And I'm *not* saying me father was a liar, and I wouldn't excuse him any more than any other, but the old people had that way of going on in them days. And he maintained that it was there.

There was some house, but I don't remember the name of it *now*. It was in it for years and years and years: the fairy last.

I heard another man saying he seen one of the fairies too. And he's not all that long dead.

He said he was walking this day and the fairy just stepped out. He even said that he caught him.

He told me that: that he was only a very small little mite of a wee urchin of a thing.

And he said he caught him; he lifted him up in his hand.

And the fairy told him, he says, "If you let me out, I'll tell you," he says, "where there's a good crock of gold."

"Well," he says, "you'll have to tell me," he says, "before I'll let you go." He says, "No, I'll not let you go," he says, "till you tell me."

"I cannot," he says. The fairy spoke, as he maintained, in proper English language. "I cannot tell you, until you let me go," he says.

"Release me."

So he let him go, just like that. Left him on the ground just beside him, and he disappeared out of sight, and that was that.

Well, I didn't believe him. But he was a very old man. He was eighty years of age.

Well, another man told me—I had been working in the place, and he says, "Do you see that spot there?"

"I do," says I, "see it, surely."

"And what," he says, "do you remark about it?"

"Well," says I, "I remark there's no grass on it."

And the rest of the field was fully fledged in grass. Says I, "There's no grass on it." And he said, "Do you know the reason why?"

"Ah, no," says I. I was only young at the time.

"Well," he says, "that was a boy that was taken away," he says, "about a hundred and fifty years ago," he says, "from the house I live in and that you sleep in."

"Taken away by who?" says I.

He says, "Taken away by the fairies." The Good People they called them sometimes.

And he says, "He came to the window this night, and he tapped at the window and the people inside answered the call or the tap at the window."

And so he mentioned who he was.

"And what's wrong with ye?"

"I can't," he says, "come back. I'm with the fairies," he says. "But I'm coming by on such a night"—mentioning the night, let it be Tuesday, Wednesday, Thursday, or some night in the week. He says, "At the hour of two o'clock, I'll be coming by then, coming by the house, and I'll get released," he says, "if yous are fit to take me off the horse. I'll be the second man on the second horse."

He says, "I'll be riding the second horse, and if yous are fit to pull me off with iron or anything steel, or throw a hoop around me," he says, "like a barrel hoop, or anything like that, I'll get released."

So they certified to him that they'd do their best.

Well, the time came and they heard the click click of the horses coming, and there was a person selected to throw the hoop round.

"But," he says, "if yous miss me, well, I'm done." He says, "I'll never get back."

So they made the attempt, but it wasn't successful.

And they made the attempt with this steel circle or hoop, just in this spot where he was going through a gap.

And they missed him, and he just fell like that off the horse and disappeared.

And where he fell down,
    the shape of him is on the ground,
        all the time.

And that was the last of him.

Never was seen or heard of from that day to this one.

And he says, "There never grew a grain of grass on that spot," he says. "You see the tracks of his arms," he says, "there's his head." He made an offer to form out the shape of a human being on the ground. There was no grass on it, right enough.

The whole track of him just marked the ground like. Well, I saw it. I saw that. But I couldn't certify that it was due to him falling.

If you were to take and remove the grass and make a spot on the ground, can you stop God's work of the grass growing?

Well, that's the point that I seen in it.

I had a slight belief about that.

As time rolled on, I did believe. But I never went back to the spot.

❖ The Fairy Shilling

CATHAL Ó BAOILL ◈ *DONEGAL*
SEÁN Ó HEOCHAIDH *1954*

There was a man named Paddy Ó Gadhra living beyond in Malin Glen long ago. One evening he had gone west to Caiseal in Glencolumcille and when his business was finished he faced towards home. It was a fine moonlit night, and as he was going west by Dún Ált at Screig Mhór there was a woman standing at the side of the road with a basket beside her. He greeted her and she greeted him. She bent down and lifted the basket and walked in step with him along the road. He made out from the way she was changing the basket from hand to hand that it must be very heavy.

"Give me that basket, please," he said, "and I will carry it a bit for you."

She thanked him and handed the basket to him. When he took it he was very much surprised because it had no weight at all and he thought it must be empty. They walked on, but neither of them said who he or she was nor asked the other's name. When they reached the crossroads at Malinmore Paddy said he was going to Malin Glen and maybe that was not the way she was going.

"Oh, it is!" said she, "I am going east to Jimi Jeck's house and I will be staying there till morning."

She walked step by step with Paddy. The house she was making for was the next house to Paddy's own on the east. He went as far as it with her and bade her farewell then. When he handed the basket to her, she asked him if he drank.

"Well," said he, "when I am at a fair or market to be sure I will drink a glass."

She put her hand in her pocket and handed a shilling to him.

"Now," she said, "the next time you are in a tavern, drink my health!"

Then she bade him farewell. Paddy went to his own house and she went towards Jimi Jeck's house and he saw her no more.

Next morning when Paddy rose he thought he would find out who the unknown woman was, and so he went up to Jimi Jeck's and asked them who was this woman who had come to them last night.

"Blast you!" said Jimi, "I saw no woman at all!"

"Well, that is very strange," said Paddy, telling him what I have told you about the woman who had been all the way from Glencolumcille with him and who had told him she was going to stop there overnight.

Well and good. Between then and nightfall Paddy needed an ounce of tobacco and went west to a shop in Malinmore and asked for the tobacco.

The man of the shop gave it to him and he threw over the shilling and got the change out of it. Going the road home from the west he put his hand in his pocket and looked at his money and saw that he had the change and the shilling as well.

He went on like that for a long time. No matter what shop or tavern he would go into he would get change for anything he would buy and when he put his hand in his pocket the shilling would be back in it. He kept it in that way for a couple of years, but at last be began to fear it. He feared that it might lead him some time to drink too much and to some unknown calamity —that that was maybe why it had been put in his way.

He went to the priest in Glencolumcille and told what had happened. The priest put his stole around his neck and made the sign of the cross on the shilling and it vanished as a drop of water. That was the end of Paddy Ó Gadhra's fairy shilling.

❖ THE BREAKING OF THE FORTH

ARMAGH

T. G. F. PATERSON *1945*

It was fifty years ago or more, and be the same token there's them alive the day who were at the digging. The old people were forever talking of the gold and treasure that was hid be the king of Navan, when he left without packing as it were. And some said as how it wasn't in the lake at all but in the old fort itself, and that he who would find it might eat with a silver spoon for the rest of his life.

So one fine night some brave young lads bethought themselves that they would have a try for it. And they provided themselves with spades and lanterns and quietly made off to the forth, for indeed if their fathers had knowed it they wouldn't have slept in their beds that night at all, at all, with the dread of it.

Howandsoever they started off cheerful enough like. But they were less happy before they got nearer. And the nearer they got, the less happy they were. And at last they reached the forth and the quietness of it was like till choke them, but they were together and none had the courage till say, "Leave it alone and come home with ye"—although that's what they all wanted to do, for it was them had a fear upon them right enough.

So round in a bundle they stood. And with the first spadeful dug, a cock crowed something fierce. And the more they dug the more the cocks crowed, and the hens too, all over the countryside, but that didn't stop them until the dogs started howling. Then the fear gripped them hard, for the noises began to close in on them, and them right on the top of the forth. And they remembered the dragon in the lough below and they were sure it was on its way too.

So off they fled by the side farthest from the lake. And they left their spades behind them though they had sense till hold on be the lanterns. And the spades were never seen no more, though the marks of the digging be there till this very day. And nothing happened till any of them, maybe because they were young and foolish. For the destroying of a forth is a serious thing, but they all lived till die natural deaths except them that's living still, and that's the true way of it.

❖ Dreams of Gold

JOHN PHELAN ◈ *GALWAY*
LADY GREGORY *1920*

There was a man in Gort, Anthony Hynes, he and two others dreamed of finding treasure within the church of Kilmacdaugh. But when they got there at night to dig, something kept them back, for there's always something watching over where treasure is buried. I often heard that long ago in the nursery at Coole, at the cross, a man that was digging found a pot of gold. But just as he had the cover took off, he saw old Richard Gregory coming, and he covered it up, and was never able again to find the spot where it was.

But there's dreams and dreams. I heard of a man from Mayo went to Limerick, and walked two or three times across the bridge there. And a cobbler that was sitting on the bridge took notice of him, and knew by the look of him and by the clothes he wore that he was from Mayo, and asked him what was he looking for. And he said he had a dream that under the bridge of Limerick he'd find treasure. "Well," says the cobbler, "I had a dream myself about finding treasure, but in another sort of a place than this." And he described the place where he dreamed it was, and where was that, but in the Mayo man's own garden. So he went home again, and sure enough, there he found a pot of gold with no end of riches in it. But I never heard that the cobbler found anything under the bridge at Limerick.

❖ The castle's treasure

PADDY WELSH ◈ *ROSCOMMON*
SIR WILLIAM WILDE *1852*

I dreamed one night that I was walking about in the bawn, when I looked into the old tower that's in the left-hand corner, after you pass the gate, and there I saw, sure enough, a little crock, about the bigness of the bottom of a pitcher, and it full up of all kinds of money, gold, silver, and brass.

When I woke next morning, I said nothing about it, but in a few nights after I had the same dream over again, only I thought I was looking down from the top of the tower, and that all the floors were taken away. Peggy knew be me that I had a dream, for I wasn't quite easy in myself. So I ups and tells her the whole of it, when the childer had gone out.

"Well, Paddy," says she, "who knows but it would come true, and be the making of us yet. But you must wait till the dream comes afore you the third time, and then, sure, it can do no harm to try, anyways."

It wasn't long till I had the third dream, and as the moon was in the last quarter, and the nights mighty dark, Peggy put down the grisset, and made a lock of candles. And so, throwing the loy over my shoulder, and giving Michauleen the shovel, we set out about twelve o'clock, and when we got to the castle, it was as dark that you wouldn't see your hand before you. And there wasn't a stir in the old place, barring the owls that were snoring in the chimley.

To work we went just in the middle of the floor, and cleared away the stones and the rubbish, for nearly the course of an hour, with the candles stuck in potatoes, resting on some of the big stones on one side of us. Of course, sorra word we said all the while, but dug and shoveled away as hard as hatters, and a mighty tough job it was to lift the floor of the same building.

Well, at last the loy struck on a big flag, and my heart riz within me, for I often heard tell that the crock was always covered with a flag, and so I pulled away for the bare life, and at last I got it cleared, and was just lifting the edge of it, when—

Oh, what's the use in telling you anything about it. Sure, I know by your eye you don't believe a word I am saying. The dickens a goat was sitting on the flag. But when both of us were trying to lift the stone, my foot slipped, and the clay and rubbish began to give way under us. "Lord between us and harm," says the gossoon. And then, in the clapping of your hand, there was a wonderful wind rushed in through the doorway, and quinched the lights, and pitched us both down into the hole. And of all the noises you ever heard, it was about us in a minute. *M'anum san Deowl!* But I thought it was all over with us, and sorra one of me ever thought of as much as crossing myself. But I made out as fast as I could, and the gossoon after me, and we never stopped running till we stumbled over the wall of the big entrance, and it was well we didn't go clean into the moat. Troth, you wouldn't give three ha'pence for me when I was standing in the road—the bouchal itself was stouter—with the weakness that came over me. *Och, millia murdher!* I wasn't the same man for many a long day. But that was nothing to the tormenting I got from everybody about finding the gold, for the shovel that we left after us was discovered, and there used to be dealers and gentlemen from Dublin—antiquarians, I think they call them—coming to the house continually, and asking Peggy for some of the coins we found in the old castle.

There now, you have the whole of it.

THE AIR IS FULL OF THEM

JAMES HILL ◈ *GALWAY*
LADY GREGORY *1920*

One night since I lived here I found late at night that a black jennet I had at that time had strayed away. So I took a lantern and went to look for him, and found him near Doherty's house at the bay. And when I took him by the halter, I put the light out and led him home. But surely as I walked there was a footstep behind me all the way home.

I never rightly believed in them till I met a priest about two years ago coming out from the town that asked his way to Mrs. Canan's, the time she was given over, and he told me that one time his horse stopped and wouldn't pass the road, and the man that was driving said, "I can't make him pass." And the priest said, "It will be the worse for you, if I have to come down into the road." For he knew some bad thing was there. And he told me the air is full of them. But Father Dolan wouldn't talk of such things, very proud he is, and he coming of no great stock.

One night I was driving outside Coole gate—close to where the Ballinamantane farm begins. And the mare stopped, and I got off the car to lead her, but she wouldn't go on. Two or three times I made her start and she'd stop again. Something she must have seen that I didn't see.

Beasts will sometimes see more than a man will. There were three young chaps I knew went up by the river to hunt coneens one evening, and they threw the dog over the wall. And when he was in the field he gave a yelp and drew back as if something frightened him.

Another time my father was going early to some place, and my mother had a noggin of turnips boiled for him that night before, to give him something to eat before he'd start. So they got up very early and she lighted the fire and put the oven hanging over it for to warm the turnips, and then she went back to bed again. And my father was in a hurry and he went out and brought in a sheaf of wheaten straw to put under the oven, the way it would make a quick blaze. And when he came in, the oven had been taken off the hook, and was put standing in the hearth, and no mortal had been there. So he was afraid to stop, and he went back to the bed, and till daybreak they could hear something that was knocking against the pot. And the servant girl that was in the house, she woke and heard quick steps walking to the stable, and the door of it giving a screech as if it was being opened. But in the morning there was no sign there or of any harm being done to the pot.

Then the girl remembered that she had washed her feet the night before, and had never thought to throw out the water. And it's well known to wash the feet and not to throw the water out, brings some harm—except you throw fire into the vessel it stands in.

❖ THE FEET WATER

MICHAEL DAWSON ◈ *LIMERICK*
KEVIN DANAHER *1967*

In every house in the country long ago the people of the house would wash their feet, the same as they do now, and when you had your feet washed you should always throw out the water, because dirty water should never be kept inside in the house during the night. The old people always said that a bad thing might come into the house if the feet water was kept inside and not thrown out, and they always said, too, that when you were throwing the water out you should say *"Seachain!"* for fear that any poor soul or spirit might be in the way. But that is not here nor there, and I must be getting on with my story.

There was a widow woman living a long time ago in the east of County Limerick in a lonely sort of a place, and one night when she and her daughter were going to bed, didn't they forget to throw out the feet water. They weren't long in bed when the knock came to the door, and the voice outside said: "Key, let us in!"

Well, the widow woman said nothing, and the daughter held her tongue as well.

"Key, let us in," came the call again, and, faith! this time the key spoke up: "I can't let you in, and I here tied to the post of the old woman's bed."

"Feet water, let us in!" says the voice, and with that, the tub of feet water split and the water flowed around the kitchen, and the door opened and in came three men with bags of wool and three women with spinning wheels, and they sat down around the fire, and the men were taking tons of wool out of the bags, and the little women were spinning it into thread, and the men putting the thread back into the bags.

And this went on for a couple of hours and the widow woman and the girl were nearly out of their minds with the fright. But the girl kept a splink of sense about her, and she remembered that there was a wise woman living not too far away, and down with her from the room to the kitchen, and she catches up a bucket. "Ye'll be having a sup of tea, after all the work," says she, as bold as brass, and out the door with her.

They didn't help or hinder her.

Off with her to the wise woman, and out with her story. " 'Tis a bad case, and 'tis lucky you came to me," says the wise woman, "for you might travel far before you'd find one that would save you from them. They are not of this world, but I know where they are from. And this is what you must do," and she told her what to do.

Back with the girl and filled her bucket at the well, and back with her to the house. And just as she coming over the stile, she flung down the bucket with a bang, and shouted out at the top of her voice: "There is Sliabh na mBan all on fire!"

And the minute they heard it, out with the strange men and women running east in the direction of the mountain.

And in with the girl, and she made short work of throwing out the broken tub and putting the bolt and the bar on the door. And herself and her mother went back to bed for themselves.

It was not long until they heard the footsteps in the yard once more, and the voice outside calling out: "Key, let us in!" And the key answered back: "I can't let you in. Amn't I after telling you that I'm tied to the post of the old woman's bed?" "Feet water, let us in!" says the voice.

"How can I?" says the feet water, "and I here on the ground under your feet!"

They had every shout and every yell out of them with the dint of the rage, and they not able to get in to the house. But it was idle for them. They had no power to get in when the feet water was thrown out.

And I tell you it was a long time again before the widow woman or her daughter forgot to throw out the feet water and tidy the house properly before they went to bed for themselves.

THE FAIRY RABBIT AND THE BLESSED EARTH OF TORY

JIMÍ DIXON ◈ *DONEGAL*
SEÁN Ó hEOCHAIDH *1954*

My grandfather, Donnchadh Ó Duibhir, was a great fisherman, and as well as being a good seaman he was a wonderful swimmer. He was a very strong man too. He used to go out fishing with a man from the east of the island. It was in Port an Dúin he kept his curragh and it was on the north side of the island he did most of his fishing.

One fine summer evening he went east to meet his comrade and the two of them went to Port an Dúin. They took all the boat-gear and the curragh down to the edge of the strand and set out for the northern shore.

There is a place on the east of the island near the Dún called Poll an Rutáin. It is a cavern open at both ends and it is a good short-cut compared with having to go round the nose of Tor Mór. It was through Poll an Rutáin they were going that evening. There was not a breath of wind and the sea was as smooth as a board.

They saw a rabbit sitting up on the height overhead and it seemed to them it was very bold. My grandfather drew in his paddles and began to beat them against the edge of the curragh, but not a hair did they move of the rabbit which did not stir from where it sat. The curragh was out on the water by then and both men began to shout and roar, but it seems there was no hunting it away.

"Donnchadh, that is no natural rabbit!" said the man in the stern of the curragh to my grandfather.

With that they saw a great wave coming upon them.

"God save us!" they cried. The wave swept the curragh halfway over its crest. With that they saw another wave much worse than the first one. It struck the curragh amidship and capsized it, and before they had time to offer their souls to God and Mary another wave of the same kind broke over them, but they did not let go their hold of the curragh. My grandfather shouted to the other man to keep a good grip, and he himself began to swim and draw the curragh after him with one hand. He was not able to bring the curragh to land where he was, and he had to draw the curragh and the man hanging on it a long way.

Well and good. He struggled on until he got the curragh in beside a flat rock and succeeded in landing his comrade. When they had come to themselves a little they turned the curragh but the two paddles were still afloat. Donnchadh went out swimming again and brought in the paddles. They both went out then and rescued the line-frames and other gear they had lost. They returned to Port an Dúin sodden wet, bruised, and exhausted.

As long as they lived both men held, and I heard my grandfather speak of it a score of times, that it was a fairy rabbit they had seen on the height above them and that it was trying to drown them. They had a grain of the earth of Tory in the curragh, and that surely is why it did not succeed.

❖ THE CATS' JUDGMENT

AN OLD MAN ◈ *GALWAY*
ROBERT GIBBINGS *1945*

My father was herdsman to the manor house, and one of his jobs was to boil up a good pot of mangolds and turnips every evening for the cattle. He was a very particular kind of man, and so that the roots should brew thoroughly he not only put the iron lid on the pot, but put a stone on the top of the lid to keep it firm. But night after night, to his surprise in the morning, the stone was knocked off the pot and the lid lifted.

One night he said to himself, "I'll watch," he said; and he sat up watching the pot, and the lamp had gone down and the room was dark only for the firelight. And what did he see but a big cat come in and push away the stone and lift the lid off the pot, and dip his paw into the mash just as if it was cream.

No sooner did he see the cat than he hits it a welt of a stick, and as it leaps through the door he puts his two dogs after it. But the dogs were back in no time, and they shivering, as if with the fright. So he shuts the door and goes to bed.

Well, he is hardly under the sheets when the door opens and in comes the cat that he was after hitting. And following her, in come a dozen others, one after the other.

And they all sat down in a circle and they began to talk in the cat language.

And my father in the bed was frightened out of his life to say a word for fear the cats would go for him.

And they all sat there mumbling and talking to each other, when in comes the king of the cats, a great big tomcat, he was. He walks right in, and he sits down in the middle of them all.

Then the cat that had been at the mash limps up to him, for he was lame with the welt he was after getting, and you'd think he was a lawyer in court the way he spoke to the king and the others.

And my father was near dead with the fright.

And the king of the cats considered for a long while, as if he was thinking over the evidence, and then he rose up and tapping the one that got the welt as much as to say "Not guilty, come on," he went out of the door.

And they all followed him, and when they'd all gone out, the door closed after them.

❖ NEVER ASK A CAT A QUESTION

MALACHI HORAN ◈ *DUBLIN*
GEORGE A. LITTLE *1943*

Aye, it's nature breaks through the eyes of a cat, sure enough. Someways they would put a dread on you. What company do they keep? When the moon is riding high and the wind tearing the trees, and the shadows black with cold, who is it calls them from the hearth? Tell me that? And obey they must, and obey they do.

Some do be saying that it's a meeting they do hold, and at it choose their king; and there is reason in that.

Phil Tierney was a Cavan man who owned the farm that is now Boothman's. He gave me a black cat—the largest buck-cat ever seen in this country. Quiet he was, but he had the dark evil in his eyes. Troth, you would think he knew all the Devil's work in the world and was glad to sit thinking of it.

One evening and I sitting here, it was mortal cold, and the cat was curled sleeping and he on the fireflag. The wind was tearing at the thatch, and never a sound was in it if it was not the cry of the wild geese and them crossing the moon. Of a sudden he was on his feet, every hair on him standing stiff as a hackle, his back arched, his tail like a jug-handle. He stood listening. Then, with a hiss and a snarl, he was out of the door like running water. The wind died on the moment, and not one thing stirred, bar the clock—the ticks of it would deafen you, like as if you had your ear to an anvil. Then the wind blew again, and a turf-sod shifted in the fire.

The next morning, with me mother and father—may God save them!—in the cart, I was driving to Mass, for it was a Sunday. We got as far as Spooner's below, when I seen something on the road that stopped me. The whole place was one living mass of cats. In the middle was a great buck-cat, lying with his paws drawn up under him, and him looking straight in front as if there was not a living thing near him. Around him stood others and they never lifting an eye off of him. Some on the fence, and in the ditch lay more, but they were looking away from him. Here and there a small one sneaked from one lot to another, as if they were servants and they looking for orders.

"Go on," says my father, "or we will be late for Mass. They are only choosing their king." I had to drive in the ditchside to pass. The buck-cat never moved. I was glad when I passed. I was glad to turn the corner and lose the sight of them.

And we coming back from Mass the cats were still there, but they had taken to the ditches. I saw no sign of the head buck-cat.

But that night they came back. Red Jack had the drink on him. He drove his cart through them. What he saw I never heard; or what he felt and him with them blazing eyes glaring hate at him, he never told. Or what he thought, with the whole night of them screaming and they near in the cart, no man knows. But this I know, that there were four wheelbarrows and them loaded with dead cats taken off Killenarden Road that Monday after.

Red Jack slept in a loft; leastways he did sleep, but never a wink he got for weeks from that Sunday. Wherever he turned there were cats. In his bed, on his table, under the chair, they would be watching, watching. He knew they waited for him to sleep; then they would be at his throat. All through the hours of dark he could see nothing but their watching eyes.

At last Red Jack could stand it no longer. He took what he had in the toe of the stocking, and with it bought a brace of terriers. Troth, then was the ructions. It was like devils coursing demons. But at the heel of the hunt there was not a cat to be found in the country.

Aye, cats is queer. Did you ever hear tell that cats that have killed more than their share of rats get sick of them and will hunt no more? When this happens, the rats grow that strong that they *laugh* in the face of their enemies. The cats then waste and die. No cat can own a master; they must have their self-respect.

And remember this: never ask a cat a question. She might answer back. And, troth, if she did, it is seven years of cruel luck you will have brought on your shoulders. Aye, indeed.

❖ Cats are queer articles

MR. BUCKLEY, THE TAILOR ◈ *CORK*
ERIC CROSS *1942*

I tell you, cats are the queer articles. You never know where you are with them. They seem to be different to every other class of animals. In the old days there were some foreign peoples who worshipped them, and it is not to be greatly wondered at, when you think of the intelligence of cats.

I had a strange thing happened to myself years ago with cats. It was many, many years ago now. I had a calf to sell, and it was the time of the November fair in Macroom. I'd borrowed the loan of a crib and horse from a neighbor, and was ready to set off for the fair about one o'clock in the morning.

Well, it came to one o'clock and I got up. I opened the door, and the night was so black that you would scarcely know which foot you were putting before you. I stirred up the fire and put some sticks under the kettle to make a cup of tea, and while it was boiling I went out to tackle up the horse. There was a mist coming down, so that I was wet enough already by the time that I had that job done.

I made the tea, and while I was drinking it I thought what a foolish thing it was for me to be getting out of a warm bed and going into the cold, wet night and traveling for twenty-four miles through the night. But it had to be done, so I buttoned up a grand frieze coat I had, and off we set. The horse was as unwilling as myself for the road, and the two of us were ashamed to look each other in the face, knowing the class of fools we were. We traveled for hours and hours, and not much of the first hour had gone before I was wet through and through.

As we drew nearer to the town I could see the lights in the farms by the roadside, where the people were getting up for the fair who had not to lose a night's sleep to get there. There was a regular procession now on the road of calves and cattle being driven into the fair, but it was still dark and the daylight was only just coming.

Well, I took my place in the fair, and no one came to me and made me an offer for a long time. I thought that things were not going too well with me. Then a few asked me, but were offering only a poor price. I saw other cattle being driven away, and men I knew told me to sell, for it was a bad fair and prices were low. So at last I did sell, for the heart had gone out of me with the loss of sleep, and the long journey and the cold and the long waiting.

I tell you that I was a miserable man, standing there with ne'er a bite to eat and wet to the skin, and with the prospect of the long journey home again, and the poor pay I had for my suffering. When I got the money I had something to eat and made a few purchases, and then I thought that if any man ever earned a drink it was me. So I met some friends and we had a few drinks together, and then parted and went our different ways.

I let the horse go on at her own pace, with the reins hanging loose. The rain came down again, and the power of the drink soon wore off, and I wrapped myself up in my misery. With the sound and the swing of the crib and the creaking of the wheels and the darkness coming down again I fell asleep, as many a man does on the long way home from a winter's fair.

Now and again someone passed me on the road, but I scarcely heard them at all. For miles and miles I went; now asleep, now awake, with all manner of queer notions running in my head, as does happen to a man when he is exhausted.

As I was passing the graveyard of Inchigeela a cat put his head through the railings and said to me, "Tell Balgeary that Balgury is dead." I paid little heed to that, for my head was full of strange notions. I continued on my way. At last I reached home again, and untackled the horse and watered it and fed it, and then went into the house to change out of my wet clothes.

Herself started on me straightaway. 'Tis wonderful the energy that does be in a woman's tongue and the blindness that can be in her eyes, for I was in no mood for talk.

"Well," she said, "what sort of a fair was it?"

"Ah! the same as all fairs," said I.

"Did you get a good price?"

"I did not," said I.

"Were there many at the fair?" she asked then.

"The usual number, I suppose. Did you expect me to count them?"

"Did ye hear any news while ye were in the town?"

There was no end to her questions.

"Hold your tongue," I said, "and give me the tea."

I drank the tea and had a bite to eat and began to feel better. Still she kept on asking me questions.

"Glory me! Fancy going in all that way and hearing nothing at all," she said, when I had no news for her. "You might as well have stayed at home for all the good that you get out of a fair."

I got up from the table and sat by the fire and lit my pipe, but still she plagued me and pestered me with her questions. Had I seen this one? Was I speaking with that one? Was there any news of the other one?

I suppose that the tea and the fire and the tobacco softened me. News and gossip are almost life to a woman, and she bore the hardness of our life as well, and I had brought her nothing home. Then I remembered the cat.

"The only thing that happened to me today," I said, "that has not happened on all fair days, was that when I was passing the graveyard of Inchigeela a cat stuck his head out of the railings."

"Wisha! there is nothing strange in that," she took me up.

"As I passed it called up to me, 'Tell Balgeary that Balgury is dead.'"

At that, the cat, sitting before the fire, whipped round on me. "The Devil fire you!" said he, "why didn't you tell me before? I'll be late for the funeral." And with that and no more, he leapt over the half-door, and was gone like the wind, and from that day to this we have seen no sign of him.

TOM MOORE AND THE SEAL WOMAN

KERRY
JEREMIAH CURTIN *1892*

In the village of Kilshanig, two miles northeast of Castlegregory, there lived at one time a fine, brave young man named Tom Moore, a good dancer and singer. 'Tis often he was heard singing among the cliffs and in the fields of a night.

Tom's father and mother died and he was alone in the house and in need of a wife. One morning early, when he was at work near the strand, he saw the finest woman ever seen in that part of the kingdom, sitting on a rock, fast asleep. The tide was gone from the rocks then, and Tom was curious to know who was she or what brought her, so he walked toward the rock.

"Wake up!" cried Tom to the woman. "If the tide comes 'twill drown you."

She raised her head and only laughed. Tom left her there, but as he was going he turned every minute to look at the woman. When he came back he caught the spade, but couldn't work. He had to look at the beautiful woman on the rock. At last the tide swept over the rock. He threw the spade down and away to the strand with him, but she slipped into the sea and he saw no more of her that time.

Tom spent the day cursing himself for not taking the woman from the rock when it was God that sent her to him. He couldn't work out the day. He went home.

Tom could not sleep a wink all that night. He was up early next morning and went to the rock. The woman was there. He called to her.

No answer. He went up to the rock. "You may as well come home with me now," said Tom. Not a word from the woman. Tom took the hood from her head and said: "I'll have this!"

The moment he did that she cried: "Give back my hood, Tom Moore!"

"Indeed I will not, for 'twas God sent you to me, and now that you have speech I'm well satisfied." And taking her by the arm he led her to the house. The woman cooked breakfast, and they sat down together to eat it.

"Now," said Tom, "in the name of God you and I'll go to the priest and get married, for the neighbors around here are very watchful. They'd be talking." So after breakfast they went to the priest, and Tom asked him to marry them.

"Where did you get the wife?" asked the priest.

Tom told the whole story. When the priest saw Tom was so anxious to marry he charged five pounds, and Tom paid the money. He took the wife home with him, and she was good a woman as ever went into a man's house. She lived with Tom seven years, and had three sons and two daughters.

One day Tom was plowing, and some part of the plow rigging broke. He thought there were bolts on the loft at home, so he climbed up to get them. He threw down bags and ropes while he was looking for the bolts, and what should he throw down but the hood which he took from the wife seven years before. She saw it the moment it fell, picked it up, and hid it. At that time people heard a great seal roaring out in the sea.

"Ah," said Tom's wife, "that's my brother looking for me."

Some men who were hunting killed three seals that day. All the women of the village ran down to the strand to look at the seals, and Tom's wife with others. She began to moan, and going up to the dead seals she spoke some words to each and then cried out: "Oh, the murder!"

When they saw her crying the men said: "We'll have nothing more to do with these seals." So they dug a great hole, and the three seals were put into it and covered. But some thought in the night: " 'Tis a great shame to bury those seals, after all the trouble in taking them." Those men went with shovels and dug up the earth, but found no trace of the seals.

All this time the big seal in the sea was roaring. Next day when Tom was at work his wife swept the house, put everything in order, washed the children and combed their hair. Then, taking them one by one, she kissed each. She went next to the rock, and, putting the hood on her head, gave a plunge. That moment the big seal rose and roared so that people ten miles away could hear him.

Tom's wife went away with the seal swimming in the sea. All the five children that she left had webs between their fingers and toes, halfway to the tips.

The descendants of Tom Moore and the seal woman are living near Castlegregory to this day, and the webs are not gone yet from between their fingers and toes, though decreasing with each generation.

❖ THE SWINE OF THE GODS

SLIGO

WILLIAM BUTLER YEATS *1902*

A few years ago a friend of mine told me of something that happened to him when he was a young man and out drilling with some Connacht Fenians. They were but a car-full, and drove along a hillside until they came to a quiet place. They left the car and went further up the hill with their rifles, and drilled for a while. As they were coming down again they saw a very thin, long-legged pig of the old Irish sort, and the pig began to follow them. One of them cried out as a joke that it was a fairy pig, and they all began to run to keep up the joke. The pig ran too, and presently, how nobody knew, this mock terror became real terror, and they ran as for their lives. When they got to the car they made the horse gallop as fast as possible, but the pig still followed. Then one of them put up his rifle to fire, but when he looked along the barrel he could see nothing. Presently they turned a corner and came to a village. They told the people of the village what had happened, and the people of the village took pitchforks and spades and the like, and went along the road with them to drive the pig away. When they turned the corner they could not find anything.

❖ A PIG ON THE ROAD FROM GORT

MR. STEPHENS ◈ *GALWAY*
LADY GREGORY *1920*

There was a man coming along the road from Gort to Garryland one night, and he had a drop taken, and before him on the road he saw a pig walking. And having a drop in, he gave a shout and made a kick at it and bid it get out of that.

And from the time he got home, his arm had swelled from the shoulder to be as big as a bag, and he couldn't use his hand with the pain in it. And his wife brought him after a few days to a woman that used to do cures at Rahasane.

And on the road all she could do would hardly keep him from lying down to sleep on the grass. And when they got to the woman, she knew all that happened, and says she: "It's well for you that your wife didn't let you fall asleep on the grass, for if you had done that but for an instant, you'd be a gone man."

❖ THE CROOKENED BACK

PEGGY BARRETT ◈ *CORK*
T. CROFTON CROKER *1825*

It was of all days in the year, the day before May Day, that I went out to the garden to weed the potatoes. I would not have gone out that day, but I was dull in myself, and sorrowful, and wanted to be alone. All the boys and girls were laughing and joking in the house, making goaling-balls and dressing out ribbons for the mummers next day. I couldn't bear it. 'Twas only at the Easter that was then past (and that's ten years last Easter—I won't forget the time) that I buried my poor man. And I thought how gay and joyful I was, many a long year before that, at the May Eve before our wedding, when with Robin by my side I sat cutting and sewing the ribbons for the goaling-ball I was to give the boys on the next day, proud to be preferred above all the other girls of the banks of the Blackwater by the handsomest boy and the best hurler in the village. So I left the house and went to the garden.

I stayed there all the day, and didn't come home to dinner. I don't know how it was, but somehow I continued on, weeding, and thinking sorrowfully enough, and singing over some of the old songs that I sung many and many a time in the days that are gone, and for them that never will come back to me to hear them.

The truth is, I hated to go and sit silent and mournful among the people in the house, that were merry and young, and had the best of their days before them.

'Twas late before I thought of returning home, and I did not leave the garden till some time after sunset. The moon was up. But though there wasn't a cloud to be seen, and though a star was winking here and there in the sky, the day wasn't long enough gone to have it clear moonlight; still, it shone enough to make everything on one side of the heavens look pale and silvery-like. And the thin white mist was just beginning to creep along the fields. On the other side, near where the sun was set, there was more of daylight, and the sky looked angry, red, and fiery through the trees, like as if it was lighted up by a great town burning below. Everything was as silent as a churchyard, only now and then one could hear far off a dog barking, or a cow lowing after being milked. There wasn't a creature to be seen on the road or in the fields. I wondered at this first, but then I remembered it was May Eve, and that many a thing, both good and bad, would be wandering about that night, and that I ought to shun danger as well as others.

So I walked on as quick as I could, and soon came to the end of the demesne wall, where the trees rise high and thick at each side of the road, and almost meet at the top. My heart misgave me when I got under the shade. There was so much light let down from the opening above, that I could see about a stone throw before me.

All of a sudden I heard a rustling among the branches, on the right side of the road, and saw something like a small black goat, only with long wide horns turned out instead of being bent backwards, standing upon its hind legs upon the top of the wall, and looking down on me. My breath was stopped, and I couldn't move for near a minute. I couldn't help, somehow, keeping my eyes fixed on it. And it never stirred, but kept looking in the same fixed way down at me.

At last I made a rush, and went on. But I didn't go ten steps when I saw the very same sight on the wall to the left of me, standing in exactly the same manner, but three or four times as high, and almost as tall as the tallest man. The horns looked frightful: it gazed upon me as before. My legs shook, and my teeth chattered, and I thought I would drop down dead every moment.

At last I felt as if I was obliged to go on—and on I went, but it was without feeling how I moved, or whether my legs carried me. Just as I passed the spot where this frightful thing was standing, I heard a noise as if something sprung from the wall, and felt like as if a heavy animal plumped down upon me, and held with the forefeet clinging to my shoulder, and the hind ones fixed in my gown, that was folded and pinned up behind me.

'Tis the wonder of my life ever since how I bore the shock. But so it was, I neither fell, nor even staggered with the weight, but walked on as if I had the strength of ten men, though I felt as if I couldn't help moving, and couldn't stand still if I wished it. Though I gasped with fear, I knew as well as I do now what I was doing. I tried to cry out, but couldn't. I tried to run, but wasn't able. I tried to look back, but my head and neck were as if they were screwed in a vise. I could barely roll my eyes on each side, and then I could see, clearly and plainly as if it was the broad light of the blessed sun, a black and cloven foot planted upon each of my shoulders. I heard a low breathing in my ear. I felt, at every stop I took, my leg strike back against the feet of the creature that was on my back. Still I could do nothing but walk straight on.

At last I came within sight of the house, and a welcome sight it was to me, for I thought I would be released when I reached it. I soon came close to the door, but it was shut. I looked at the little window, but it was shut too, for they were more cautious about May Eve than I was. I saw the light inside, through the chinks of the door. I heard talking and laughing within. I felt myself at three yards distance from them that would die to save me— and may the Lord save me from ever again feeling what I did that night, when I found myself held by what couldn't be good nor friendly, but without the power to help myself, or to call my friends, or to put out my hand to knock, or even to lift my leg to strike the door, and let them know that I was outside it! 'Twas as if my hands grew to my sides, and my feet were glued to the ground, or had the weight of a rock fixed to them.

At last I thought of blessing myself; and my right hand, that would do nothing else, did that for me. Still the weight remained on my back, and all was as before. I blessed myself again; 'twas still all the same. I then gave myself up for lost. But I blessed myself a third time, and my hand no sooner finished the sign, than all at once I felt the burthen spring off of my back. The door flew open as if a clap of thunder burst it, and I was pitched forward on my forehead in upon the middle of the floor. When I got up my back was crookened, and I never stood straight from that night to this blessed hour.

❖ Maurice Griffin the Fairy Doctor

JOHN MALONE ◈ *KERRY*
JEREMIAH CURTIN *1892*

There was a man at Dun Lean named Maurice Griffin. He was in service as a herder minding cows, and one morning while out with the cattle he saw something come down through the air in the form of a white cloud and drop on a hillock. It settled to be a lump of white foam, and a great heat rose out of it then. One of the cows went to the hillock and licked the foam till she swallowed every bit of it.

When he went in to breakfast Maurice told the man of the house about the cloud, and that it was a wonder to see the cow licking up what had settled on the hillock. "And it was white as any linen," said he.

When the man of the house sent the servant girl to milk the cow that evening he told her not to spill any drop of the milk till she had it brought to himself.

Maurice Griffin went with the girl, caught the cow, and held her. The vessel the girl was milking in did not hold half the milk. She did not like to leave the cow partly milked.

"Drink some of this," said she, "and let me finish, for it would spoil the cow to leave part of the milk with her."

Maurice Griffin emptied the vessel three times, drank all there was in it. The girl filled it the fourth time and went home with the milk. The master asked, "Was any of the milk spilled or used?" She told him truly, "This is the same vessel that I use always in milking, and that cow never filled it before till tonight. I didn't like to leave any milk with her, so I gave some to Maurice."

"It was his luck gave him all; 'twas promised to him, not to me," said the master. He was fonder of Maurice Griffin than ever, and Maurice began to foretell right away and cure people. The report went out through the country that all he foretold came to pass, and all he undertook to cure he cured. The priest, hearing this, didn't want to have the like of him in the parish, and spoke of him from the altar, but Griffin gave no answer. One morning the priest went to where Griffin was, saluted him, and was saluted in turn. "I hear that you are curing and foretelling," said the priest. "Where did you get the knowledge to foretell and to cure?"

"I foretell and I cure many persons, I serve people," said Griffin. "And my business is as good as yours. Some say that you have power, your reverence, but if you have, you are not foretelling or curing."

"Well," said the priest, "I'll know can you foretell or not. Answer me a question, and if you can I'll believe you."

"I'll answer you any question you'll put to me," said Griffin.

"What time or minute of the day did the last new moon appear?"

"I will tell you that," said Griffin. "Do you remember that when you were passing Travug your horse stooped to drink and his right leg was first in the river? Under your neck you wear a stone which the Pope gave you. This stone always sweats three drops at the new moon. The stone sweated three drops when the horse's right foot touched the water, and that was the time of the new moon."

"Oh," said the priest, "what is rumored of you is true. Follow your hand, I'll not meddle with you from this out."

Griffin came home then and told the conversation. The master grew very fond of him after that, and having an only daughter he gave her to Maurice, and Griffin lived with his father-in-law till the old man died and left all he had to his son-in-law.

The people thought a deal of Maurice Griffin when he got the property, and they came for counsel and cure to him.

Griffin had two sons. In course of time he grew old and at last was very weak, and his first son, Dyeermud, managed the property. In those days everything was carried to Cork on horseback. Griffin called Dyeermud one day to him and said, "I am in dread that I am going to die. I don't want you to go to Cork to be absent so long."

"The company is going, and I'd like to go, too," said Dyeermud. "My brother is here: he will care for you and attend to everything while I am gone."

"I want you here," said the father, "for it's to you I will do all the good."

Dyeermud had a great wish to visit Cork.

"Go," said the father, "but you'll be the loser, and you'll remember my words."

Dyeermud went to Cork, and during his absence the father became very sick. Once, when the younger son was sitting at his bedside, the old man said, "I am in dread your brother will not be at home."

"What you were to leave him, leave me," said the son.

"I cannot. I'll give you the gift of curing, but foretelling I could not give you if I wished."

"How can you give the gift of curing?"

"I'll give it to you," said the father. "Go out tonight, kill a sheep and dress it, pick the right shoulder as clean as any bone could be cleaned from flesh, and in the night look over that bone, and the third time you look you'll see everyone that you knew who is dead. Keep that bone with you always and sleep with it, and what you want to know to cure any disease will come to you from the bone. When a person is to be cured from a fairy stroke, look over the bone and a messenger will come from the fairies, and you will be able to cure those who come to you."

"As you will not give me the knowledge of foretelling, I will not take the curing. I will live honestly."

"I have no power to give you the knowledge," said the father, "but since you will not take the curing, I will give it to your mother. The knowledge I can give to no one but your elder brother."

Griffin gave the curing to the wife. The knowledge he could give to no one but the elder son, and to him only if present.

Maurice Griffin died and was buried before Dyeermud came from Cork.

Dyeermud was astonished when he came and didn't find the father.

"You did badly not to stay," said the younger brother.

"Didn't I leave you?"

"You did, but he could leave the knowledge only to you."

"Why didn't he give you the curing?"

"He offered it to me, but I thought it too much trouble. I would use it if I had it. I let it go to our mother. She is old; let her have it. As he did not give me the knowledge I didn't want the curing. Maybe in after years when I have children, it's on them the diseases I cured would come."

It was rumored that the curing was with the mother, and the people were coming to her.

Once her godson got a fairy stroke in the leg, and she was vexed because his parents did not bring him quickly, for next day she would not be able to cure him at all. At last they came, and she was angry that they were so slow.

"You might have made bacon of him if you waited till morning," cried she. She cured him, and he was a very strong boy after that.

The parish priest had a sick horse left out to die. The clerk was very sorry, the horse was such a fine beast. "Wouldn't it be better to go to Mrs. Griffin?" asked he.

"Oh, how could she cure the horse?" asked the priest.

"I'll go to her," said the clerk.

"If you go to her," said the priest, "I give you no leave."

The clerk went, told Mrs. Griffin that he had come in spite of the priest, and to cure the horse if she could.

"It was the priest himself that injured the horse," said Mrs. Griffin. "He gave him water while hot from driving, and because the priest is fond of the horse he patted him and muttered something without saying God bless you. Go now, spit three times into the horse's ears, and say God bless you."

The clerk went and did this. The horse rose up as well and sound as ever, and the clerk brought him to the stable. The priest was astonished, and said, "They have a gift in the family. I'll not trouble them any turn again."

Mrs. Griffin was not able to give her gift to anyone. The bone was buried with her.

❖ Biddy Early

MRS. LOCKE ◈ *GALWAY*
LADY GREGORY *1920*

It was my son was thatching Heniff's house when he got the touch, and he came back with a pain in his back and in his shoulders, and took to the bed.

And a few nights after that I was asleep, and the little girl came and woke me and said, "There's none of us can sleep with all the cars and carriages rattling round the house." But though I woke and heard her say that, I fell into a sound sleep again and never woke till morning. And one night there came two taps at the window, one after another, and we all heard it and no one there.

And at last I sent the eldest boy to Biddy Early and he found her in the house. She was then married to her fourth man. And she said he came a day too soon and would do nothing for him. And he had to walk away in the rain. And the next day he went back and she said, "Three days later and you'd have been too late." And she gave him two bottles, the one he was to bring to a boundary water and to fill it up, and that was to be rubbed to the back, and the other was to drink. And the minute he got them he began to get well, and he left the bed and he could walk, but he was always delicate. When we rubbed his back we saw a black mark, like the bite of a dog, and as to his face, it was as white as a sheet.

I have the bottle here yet, though it's thirty years ago I got it. She bid the boy to bring whatever was left of it to a river, and to pour it away with the running water. But when he got well I did nothing with it, and said nothing about it—and here it is now for you to see.

I never let on to Father Folan that I went to her, but one time the Bishop came, MacInerny. I knew he was a rough man, and I went to him and made my confession, and I said, "Do what you like with me, but I'd walk the world for my son when he was sick." And all he said was, "It would have been no wonder if the two feet had been cut off from the messenger." And he said no more and put nothing on me.

❖ ❖ ❖

There was a boy I saw went to Biddy Early, and she gave him a bottle and told him to mind he did not lose it in the crossing of some road. And when he came to the place it was broke.

Often I heard of Biddy Early, and I knew of a little girl was sick and the brother went to Biddy Early to ask would she get well. And she said, "They have a place ready for her, room for her they have." So he knew she would die, and so she did.

The priests can do things too, the same way as she could, for there was one Mr. Lyne was dying, a Protestant, and the priest went in and baptized him a Catholic before he died, and he said to the people after, "He's all right now, in another world." And it was more than the baptizing made him sure of that.

Mrs. Brennan, in the house beyond, went one time to Biddy Early, where the old man was losing his health. And all she told him was to bid him give over drinking so much whiskey. So after she said that, he used only to be drinking gin.

There was a boy went to Biddy Early for his father, and she said, "It's not any of my business that's on him, but it's good for yourself that you came to me. Weren't you sowing potatoes in such a field one day and didn't you find a bottle of whiskey, and bring it away and drink what was in it?"

And that was true and it must have been a bottle *they* brought out of some cellar and dropped there, for they can bring everything away, and put in its place what will look like it.

There was a boy near Feakle got the touch in three places, and he got a great desire to go out night-walking, and he got sick. And they asked Biddy Early and she said, "Watch the hens when they come in to roost at night, and catch a hold of the last one that comes." So the mother caught it, and then she thought she'd like to see what would Biddy Early do with it. So she brought it up to her house and laid it on the floor, and it began to rustle its wings, and it lay over and died.

It was from her brother Biddy Early got the cure. He was sick a long time, and there was a whitethorn tree out in the field, and he'd go and lie under it for shade from the sun. And after he died, every day for a year she'd go to the whitethorn tree, and it is there she'd cry her fill. And then he brought her under and gave her the cure.

It was after that she was in service beyond Kinvara. She did her first cure on a boy, after the doctors giving him up.

❖ THE BLACK ART

HUGH NOLAN ◈ *FERMANAGH*
HENRY GLASSIE *1972*

It was supposed there was people and they had what they called the black art.

And I don't know how the black art run, but it was something in the line of witchery, that they could take the milk of cows there. It was supposed that they used to go out before day in the morning with something *white* in the shape of a *rope* and trail it along the grass.

And that when the cows would go in to be milked, they'd give no milk atall.

It was a common topic in days gone by. And whether it was genuine or not, you wouldn't *know*, because cows could loss their milk for the want of grass. They want water and many a thing, do ye see. That's what they used to say was the cause of it. Aye, that it was the black art.

And these people with the black art, if they had cows, their cows would have the milk that ever was lost.

It was supposed that it was the charm, that the dragging of the rope was only—ah, it was just an accompaniment, but that they had the charm of words that took the milk.

Well, there was a man told me about that place where Mrs. Cutler lives.

In days gone by, I think, there was ten cows kept on it.

And there was another man lived beside them,
    and he had only a small farm,
        three cows in place.

It's all in Cutlers' now; Cutlers' ones, they got that farm after he left.

But this man told me that while he was in the country that he used to supply more milk to the creamery off his three cows than the McMullens (they were McMullens that lived where Mrs. Cutler's living), that he had more milk than they had off *ten* cows.

So it was supposed that he had this black art.

That was the way while he was in the country.

Well, this man told me that anyway.

It was a known fact that the McMullens' milk went down altogether from he came to the country and that his *increased*.

There used to be a story about persons that used to change into the shapes of animals for to take the milk from cows.

There was a story told about the same person and the supply of milk that the cows was giving was getting *very* small.

So they took a notion that they'd watch the fields at *night* for to see was there anyone coming milking the cows because it was a thing was often done: people that'd have no milk of their own, they used to go out and milk *neighbors'* cows.

But this night anyway there was a couple of men watching
and one of them had a gun anyway
and there come something in the shape of a *hare* along
and she started sucking a cow.

So of course, he wouldn't fire at her when she was in that vicinity because he could shoot the cow, you see.

But anyway, when she moved away, or when the cow moved away from her, he fired, and he *struck* her.

And she made off anyway.

But in the next day or so, there was some lady going about with a gunshot wound in the locality.

That was told anyway. But I wouldn't credit it.

❖ MAGICAL THEFT

PÁDRAIG MAC AN LUAIN ◈ *DONEGAL*
SÉAMAS Ó CATHÁIN *1972*

Well, these women were just ordinary country women like you still see around except that they were able to work this magic, whatever way they did it. If you had cows, they could take the "profit" of them from you. The milk you got from the cows would be useless, insipid and lifeless, and they would have the butter for themselves.

There was a man living near here one time and he had eight cows. Day in day out, he used to see this hare running about, in and out among the cows in his fields. He didn't know what the hare was doing there, but he did notice that he was making nothing from the milk his cows were giving —it was just like water.

He had a dog, a pure black hound, and they say that a hound without a speck of white in it that has a rod of the rowan tree tied around its neck is the only animal that can catch a hare like that. So one day when he saw the hare among the cows, he loosed the hound after her. Hound and hare coursed the fields back and forward and finally the hare made to jump over a high stone wall and the hound caught her by the leg and broke it. The man knew that the hound had caught the hare, and when he came up to where they were what did he find there only an old hag who lived in the locality sitting by the wall with the blood pouring out of her.

The hag was brought home and some time after that she died and the man went to the wake. They were going round with the whiskey at the hag's wake and he was offered a glass too. "Here, drink a glass for the old woman," they said.

"Indeed, I won't," said he, "for I got my fill of her."

May morning was a terrible time for working charms of all kinds but especially for stealing the "profit" of your milk.

One May morning this man was coming up through Altnapaste and he saw this hag, back and forward through a field, pulling an iron chain after her and this is what she was saying: "Come all to me, come all to me." The man was riding on horseback on the road and watching all this and he shouts: "The half of it for me."

That was all there was to that but when he got home he noticed that his cows had an awful lot of milk. All the vessels he had about the house were filled to overflowing with milk. He told the priest about it and eventually things were put right again. He had got half of what the old hag had been asking for herself.

❖ PAUDYEEN O'KELLY AND THE WEASEL

LYNCH BLAKE ◈ *MAYO*
DOUGLAS HYDE *1890*

A long time ago there was once a man of the name of Paudyeen O'Kelly, living near Tuam, in the County Galway. He rose up one morning early, and he did not know what time of day it was, for there was fine light coming from the moon. He wanted to go to the fair of Cauher-na-mart to sell a sturk of an ass that he had.

He had not gone more than three miles of the road when a great darkness came on, and a shower began falling. He saw a large house among trees about five hundred yards in from the road, and he said to himself that he would go to that house till the shower would be over. When he got to the house he found the door open before him, and in with him. He saw a large room to his left, and a fine fire in the grate. He sat down on a stool that was beside the wall, and began falling asleep, when he saw a big weasel coming to the fire with something yellow in its mouth, which it dropped on the hearthstone, and then it went away. She soon came back again with the same thing in her mouth, and he saw that it was a guinea she had. She dropped it on the hearthstone, and went away again. She was coming and going, until there was a great heap of guineas on the hearth. But at last, when he got her gone, Paudyeen rose up, thrust all the gold she had gathered into his pockets, and out with him.

He was not gone far till he heard the weasel coming after him, and she screeching as loud as bagpipes. She went before Paudyeen and got on the road, and she was twisting herself back and forwards, and trying to get a hold of his throat. Paudyeen had a good oak stick, and he kept her from him, until two men came up who were going to the same fair, and one of them had a good dog, and it routed the weasel into a hole in the wall.

Paudyeen went to the fair, and instead of coming home with the money he got for his old ass, as he thought would be the way with him in the morning, he went and bought a horse with some of the money he took from the weasel, and he came home and he riding. When he came to the place where the dog had routed the weasel into the hole in the wall, she came out before him, gave a leap up, and caught the horse by the throat. The horse made off, and Paudyeen could not stop him, till at last he gave a leap into a big drain that was full up of water and black mud, and he was drowning and choking as fast as he could, until men who were coming from Galway came up and banished the weasel.

Paudyeen brought the horse home with him, and put him into the cows' byre and fell asleep.

Next morning, the day on the morrow, Paudyeen rose up early and went out to give his horse hay and oats. When he got to the door he saw the weasel coming out of the byre and she covered with blood. "My seven thousand curses on you," said Paudyeen, "but I'm afraid you've harm done." He went in and found the horse, a pair of milch cows, and two calves dead. He came out and set a dog he had after the weasel. The dog got a hold of her, and she got a hold of the dog. The dog was a good one, but he was forced to loose his hold of her before Paudyeen could come up. He kept his eye on her, however, all through, until he saw her creeping into a little hovel that was on the brink of a lake. Paudyeen came running, and when he got to the little hut he gave the dog a shake to rouse him up and put anger on him, and then he sent him in before himself. When the dog went in he began barking. Paudyeen went in after him, and saw an old hag in the corner. He asked her if she saw a weasel coming in there.

"I did not," said she. "I'm all destroyed with a plague of sickness, and if you don't go out quick you'll catch it from me."

While Paudyeen and the hag were talking, the dog kept moving in all the time, till at last he gave a leap up and caught the hag by the throat. She screeched, and said: "Paddy Kelly, take off your dog, and I'll make you a rich man."

Paudyeen made the dog loose his hold, and said: "Tell me who are you, or why did you kill my horse and my cows?"

"And why did you bring away my gold that I was for five hundred years gathering throughout the hills and hollows of the world?"

"I thought you were a weasel," said Paudyeen, "or I wouldn't touch your gold; and another thing," says he, "if you're for five hundred years in this world, it's time for you to go to rest now."

"I committed a great crime in my youth," said the hag, "and now I am to be released from my sufferings if you can pay twenty pounds for a hundred and three-score Masses for me."

"Where's the money?" says Paudyeen.

"Go and dig under a bush that's over a little well in the corner of that field there without, and you'll get a pot filled with gold. Pay the twenty pounds for the Masses, and yourself shall have the rest. When you'll lift the flag off the pot, you'll see a big black dog coming out; but don't be afraid before him; he is a son of mine. When you get the gold, buy the house in which you saw me at first. You'll get it cheap, for it has the name of there being a ghost in it. My son will be down in the cellar. He'll do you no harm, but he'll be a good friend to you. I shall be dead a month from this day, and when you get me dead put a coal under this little hut and burn it. Don't tell a living soul anything about me—and the luck will be on you."

"What is your name?" said Paudyeen.

"Maurya Ni Keerwaun," said the hag.

Paudyeen went home, and when the darkness of the night came on he took with him a loy, and went to the bush that was in the corner of the field, and began digging. It was not long till he found the pot, and when he took the flag off it a big black dog leaped out, and off and away with him, and Paudyeen's dog after him.

Paudyeen brought home the gold, and hid it in the cowhouse. About a month after that he went to the fair of Galway, and bought a pair of cows, a horse, and a dozen sheep. The neighbors did not know where he was getting all the money; they said that he had a share with the Good People.

One day Paudyeen dressed himself and went to the gentleman who owned the large house where he first saw the weasel and asked to buy the house of him, and the land that was round about.

"You can have the house without paying any rent at all; but there is a ghost in it, and I wouldn't like you to go to live in it without my telling you, but I couldn't part with the land without getting a hundred pounds more than you have to offer me."

"Perhaps I have as much as you have yourself," said Paudyeen. "I'll be here tomorrow with the money, if you're ready to give me possession."

"I'll be ready," said the gentleman.

Paudyeen went home and told his wife that he had bought a large house and a holding of land.

"Where did you get the money?" says the wife.

"Isn't it all one to you where I got it?" says Paudyeen.

The day on the morrow Paudyeen went to the gentleman, gave him the money, and got possession of the house and land. And the gentleman left him the furniture and everything that was in the house, in with the bargain.

Paudyeen remained in the house that night, and when darkness came he went down to the cellar, and he saw a little man with his two legs spread on a barrel.

"God save you, honest man," says he to Paudyeen.

"The same to you," says Paudyeen.

"Don't be afraid of me at all," says the little man. I'll be a friend to you, if you are able to keep a secret."

"I am able, indeed; I kept your mother's secret, and I'll keep yours as well."

"Maybe you're thirsty?" says the little man.

"I'm not free from it," said Paudyeen.

The little man put a hand in his bosom and drew out a gold goblet. He gave it to Paudyeen, and said: "Draw wine out of that barrel under me."

Paudyeen drew the full up of the goblet, and handed it to the little man. "Drink yourself first," says he. Paudyeen drank, drew another goblet, and handed it to the little man, and he drank it.

"Fill up and drink again," said the little man. "I have a mind to be merry tonight."

The pair of them sat there drinking until they were half drunk. Then the little man gave a leap down to the floor, and said to Paudyeen:

"Don't you like music?"

"I do, surely," says Paudyeen, "and I'm a good dancer, too."

"Lift up the big flag over there in the corner, and you'll get my pipes under it."

Paudyeen lifted the flag, got the pipes, and gave them to the little man. He squeezed the pipes on him, and began playing melodious music. Paudyeen began dancing till he was tired. Then they had another drink, and the little man said:

"Do as my mother told you, and I'll show you great riches. You can bring your wife in here, but don't tell her that I'm here, and she won't see me. Any time at all that ale or wine are wanting, come here and draw. Farewell now. Go to sleep, and come again to me tomorrow night."

Paudyeen went to bed, and it wasn't long till he fell asleep.

On the morning of the day on the morrow, Paudyeen went home, and brought his wife and children to the big house, and they were comfortable. That night Paudyeen went down to the cellar; the little man welcomed him and asked him did he wish to dance.

"Not till I get a drink," said Paudyeen.

"Drink your 'nough," said the little man. "That barrel will never be empty as long as you live."

Paudyeen drank the full of the goblet, and gave a drink to the little man. Then the little man said to him:

"I am going to Doon-na-shee tonight, to play music for the Good People, and if you come with me you'll see fine fun. I'll give you a horse that you never saw the like of him before."

"I'll go with you, and welcome," said Paudyeen. "But what excuse will I make to my wife?"

"I'll bring you away from her side without her knowing it, when you are both asleep together, and I'll bring you back to her the same way," said the little man.

"I'm obedient," says Paudyeen. "We'll have another drink before I leave you."

He drank drink after drink, till he was half drunk, and he went to bed with his wife.

When he awoke he found himself riding on a besom near Doon-na-shee, and the little man riding on another besom by his side. When they came as far as the green hill of the Doon, the little man said a couple of words that Paudyeen did not understand. The green hill opened, and the pair went into a fine chamber.

Paudyeen never saw before a gathering like that which was in the Doon. The whole place was full up of little people, men and women, young and old. They all welcomed little Donal—that was the name of the piper—and Paudyeen O'Kelly. The king and queen of the fairies came up to them, and said:

"We are all going on a visit tonight to Cnoc Matha, to the high king and queen of our people."

They all rose up then and went out. There were horses ready for each one of them and the *coash-t'ya bower* for the king and the queen. The king and queen got into the coach, each man leaped on his own horse, and be certain that Paudyeen was not behind. The piper went out before them and began playing them music, and then off and away with them. It was not long till they came to Cnoc Matha. The hill opened and the king of the fairy host passed in.

Finvara and Nuala were there, the arch-king and queen of the fairy host of Connacht, and thousands of little persons. Finvara came up and said:

"We are going to play a hurling match tonight against the fairy host of Munster, and unless we beat them our face is gone forever. The match is to be fought out on Moytura, under Slieve Belgadaun.

The Connacht host cried out: "We are all ready, and we have no doubt but we'll beat them."

"Out with ye all," cried the high king. "The men of the Hill of Nephin will be on the ground before us."

They all went out, and little Donal and twelve pipers more before them, playing melodious music. When they came to Moytura, the fairy host of Munster and the fairy men of the Hill of Nephin were there before them. Now, it is necessary for the fairy host to have two live men beside them when they are fighting or at a hurling match, and that was the reason that little Donal took Paddy O'Kelly with him. There was a man they called the "Yellow Stongirya," with the fairy host of Munster, from Ennis, in the County Clare.

It was not long till the two hosts took sides; the ball was thrown up between them, and the fun began in earnest. They were hurling away, and the pipers playing music, until Paudyeen O'Kelly saw the host of Munster getting the strong hand, and he began helping the fairy host of Connacht. The Stongirya came up and he made at Paudyeen O'Kelly, but Paudyeen turned him head over heels. From hurling the two hosts began at fighting, but it was not long until the host of Connacht beat the other host. Then the host of Munster made flying beetles of themselves, and they began eating every green thing that they came up to. They were destroying the country before them until they came as far as Cong. Then there rose up thousands of doves out of the hole, and they swallowed down the beetles. That hole has no other name until this day but Pull-na-gullam, the Doves' Hole.

When the fairy host of Connacht won their battle, they came back to Cnoc Matha joyous enough, and the king Finvara gave Paudyeen O'Kelly a purse of gold, and the little piper brought him home, and put him into bed beside his wife, and left him sleeping there.

A month went by after that without anything worth mentioning, until one night Paudyeen went down to the cellar, and the little man said to him: "My mother is dead; burn the house over her."

"It is true for you," said Paudyeen. "She told me that she hadn't but a month to be on the world, and the month was up yesterday."

On the morning of the next day Paudyeen went to the hut and he found the hag dead. He put a coal under the hut and burned it. He came home and told the little man that the hut was burnt. The little man gave him a purse and said to him: "This purse will never be empty as long as you are alive. Now, you will never see me more; but have a loving remembrance of the weasel. She was the beginning and the prime cause of your riches." Then he went away and Paudyeen never saw him again.

Paudyeen O'Kelly and his wife lived for years after this in the large house, and when he died he left great wealth behind him, and a large family to spend it.

There now is the story for you, from the first word to the last, as I heard it from my grandmother.

❖ One queer experience

CAPTAIN SHERIDAN ◈ *MAYO*
CLIFTON JOHNSON *1901*

A good many believe that the fairies will spirit away children. They will carry off a healthy child and leave instead a weazened little dwarf. One day they played that trick on a tailor, and he kept the dwarf several years and it didn't grow any, and was just the same shriveled little thing it was in the beginning. Finally, the tailor made up his mind what the matter was.

So he heated his goose red-hot and held it over the dwarf, and said, "Now, get out of here—I know you!"

But the dwarf never let on it noticed him; and the tailor lowered the goose little by little till it almost touched the dwarf's face. Then the dwarf spoke and said, "Well, I'll leave, but first you go to the door and look round the corner."

The man knew if he did that the dwarf would get the best of him, and he said he would not. Then the dwarf saw 'twas no use, and it sprang out of the cradle and went roaring and cackling up the chimney, and a good child lay there in its place.

I had one queer experience myself. It was the time of the Fenian troubles. I was sitting up late—I suppose it must have been after midnight—but I hadn't taken anything, and was as sober as I am this minute.

Well, it got to be very late, as I said, and by and by I heard strange noises in the hall. It was like men tramping past, and they kept going and going, hundreds of them, and they were dragging dead bodies and all that. I could hear their breathing, and I could hear their clothing rub along against the walls. Then the ceiling and the sides of the room I was in began to wave. I took a candle and went out in the hall, and there was nothing there, doors all fastened, everything all right.

Now, what do you make out of that? I never have been able to account for it myself.

❖ MANY A ONE SAW WHAT WE SAW

MALACHI HORAN ◈ *DUBLIN*
GEORGE A. LITTLE *1943*

Aye, God sakes, the things that do be happening! It takes a wise man to understand what he sees and it takes a fool to doubt his own eyes.

Brian Leavy used to be working for me here and he only a lad. One night after his supper he made his bid to go home. But, troth, he did not get far! He only reached the bawn gate when back he came a-running.

"What ails ye, man?" says I. "You are as pale as a ghost!"

"And it is them I am after seeing," says he, sitting down and trembling on the chair there. Then he told me that he had seen men in the sky and them fighting. I saw he was near losing his life with the fright. I was going to keep him for the night, but it came to my mind that his mother was a widow and alone, so would be wanting him home.

"Take a hold on yourself, now, and a drink of this water and I will see you home myself," I said.

We were hardly clear of the place here when, troth, I began to feel not so comfortable myself. It was the quietness. It would have put you in mind of the room when the clock stops ticking. The sun was setting behind banks of cloud piled mountains on each other, like it was in Wicklow. Not a leaf stirred nor a bird. Over the shoulder of one of these clouds I saw an army marching. They were a great way off when I first saw them. On the opposite slope I saw another troop coming to meet them and they blacks. The Zulu War was on at the time, and I knew it was them—eighteen seventy-eight, was it? Well, no matter. On they came on each other, getting nearer and nearer, bigger and bigger. I could see now horsemen and footmen on the one side, and on the other great blacks with shields and pikes in their hands. Then, all of a sudden, they were at it. I could hear the cries and the men cursing; I could hear the roar of the galloping horses; I could hear the clank and crash of accoutrements. Bugles blowing, there was, and the rattle of arms. Rifles barked; then men falling, and screaming as they fell. And blood—it gushed from them and drenched the cloud.

The lad beside me was whimpering like a dog closed out in the rain. I think he would have fallen but for my hand on him. Nor did I blame him.

At last, someway I got Brian Leavy home; bedad, and he took his door like a rabbit its burrow.

Putting on the best face I could muster I turned for home. As I walked I tried closing my eyes; I went over a prayer; I tried turning my back on it. But I could not shut it out. The battle roared nearer to me than ever, till I thought they must leave their dead on the slopes of Cruachan. I felt demented with the noise. So close now were the soldiers I could see their uniforms. They were the Scots Greys, I think. I faced them then, for it does be doing a man harm to turn his back to what is frightening him.

At last, sometime, some way, I made my own door. I went into the kitchen where my sister was cleaning up after the supper.

"Let you go out," I told her, "and tell me what you see in the sky." She went to the corner of the haggard, and I heard her running as she returned. She slammed the door after her and barred it too.

Troth, we said our prayers better that night than ever before—or perhaps since.

I heard after that that many a one saw what we saw. There is many an old person still about this country who minds it well. They will not forget it till the day they die.

HISTORY

STAFFORDSHIRE FIGURE OF KING WILLIAM III,
by Robert Gregory
Lady Gregory, *Kiltartan History Book*, 1909

❖ THE OLD TIMES IN IRELAND

GALWAY
LADY GREGORY *1926*

The first man ever lived in Ireland was Partholan, and he is buried and his greyhound along with him at some place in Kerry. The Nemidians came after that and stopped for a while and then they all died of some disease. And then the Firbolgs came, the best men that ever were in Ireland, and they had no law but love, and there was never such peace and plenty in Ireland. What religion had they? None at all. And there was a low-sized race came that worked the land of Ireland a long time. They had their time like the others.

Tommy Niland was sitting beside me one time the same as yourself, and the day warm as this day, and he said, "In the old times you could buy a cow for one and sixpence, and a horse for two shillings. And if you had lived in those days, Padraic, you'd have your cow and your horse." For there was a man in those times bought a cow for one and sixpence, and when he was driving her home he sat down by the roadside crying, for fear he had given too little. And the man that sold him as he was going home he sat down by the roadside crying, for fear he had taken too much. For the people were very innocent at that time and very kind. But Columcille laid it down in his prophecy that every generation would be getting smaller and more liary; and that was true enough.

And in the old days if there was a pig killed, it would never be sent to the saltery but everyone that came in would get a bit of it. But now, a pig to be killed, the door of the house would be closed, and no one to get a bit of it at all.

In the old times the people had no envy, and they would be writing down the stories and the songs for one another. But they are too venomous now to do that. And as to the people in the towns, they don't care for such things now, they are too corrupted with drink.

❖ The Bath of the White Cows

MRS. K. ◈ *WEXFORD*
PATRICK KENNEDY *1866*

A great many years ago, when this county was so thick with woods that a very light person might walk on the tops of trees from Kilmeashal to the Lady's Island, a little king, or a great chief, had a fortification on the hillside, from the Duffrey gate in Enniscorthy, down to near the old abbey—but I don't know if there were any abbeys at the time.

This chief had three beautiful daughters, and all were married, and themselves and their husbands lived inside of the fort, for the young families in old times were not fond of removing far away from the old stock.

One fine morning in harvest, the watchman on the big ditch that ran round the fort struck his shield, for down below was the river covered with curraghs, all full of foreigners, and all with spears, swords, shields, and helmets, ready to spring out and attack the dun.

But my brave chief, and his son, and his son-in-laws had no notion of waiting an attack within their ditches and palisades. Out themselves and their kith, kin, and following, rushed, and attacked the Welshmen, or Woodmen, as they were called. And a bloody fight went on till the sun was near going behind the White Mountain.

At last the captain of the strangers blew a great blast on his bugle-horn, and asked the Irish chief to lay aside the fight till next morning. He consented, and both sides separated, one party moving up to the great rath, and the other down to the boats that brought them up from the Bay of Wexford, that was called Lough Garman in old times.

Well, just as they separated, a flight of arrows came from the hill on the far bank, and struck several of the Wexford men. No matter how small a scratch was made, the flesh around it began to itch, and smart, and turn purple, and burn, till the man dropped, crying out for water, and twisting himself in the greatest agony. Those that were untouched hung their shields behind their backs, and carried all that were not yet dead inside the gates.

The three son-in-laws were dead before they could cross the drawbridges, and in the chief's family there was nothing but lamentation. One of the married daughters fell on the dead body of her husband in a faint, after striving to pull out an arrowhead that had pierced into his side. But the beard of the arrow scratched her nice white wrist, and she was soon roused from her faint with the purple spreading round the mark, and the pain going to her very heart.

Well, they were bad enough before, but now they didn't know which way to turn. The poor father and the mother and brothers and sisters looking on, and no one able to do a single thing. While they were expecting every moment to be her last, three strangers walked in—an old and a young warrior, and a Druid. The young man came at once to the side of the dying princess, took hold of her arm, and fastened his lips to the wound. The Druid cried out to bring a large vessel, and fill it with the milk of a white cow and water from the Slaney; and to get all the milk from all the white cows they could lay hands on, fill vessels with it and Slaney water, and dip every wounded man that still had a breath of life in him. The young man sucked away until the bath was ready, and she was hardly lain in it till the pain left her, and in half an hour she was out of danger. All the still living men recovered just the same. And after a great deal of bustle and trouble, things got a little quieter, and it's a wonder if they weren't grateful to the strangers.

Just as the armies were parting in the evening, these men crossed the river about where the island is now. They left a hundred men at the other side. And when they all sat down in the rath to their supper, you may be sure there was *cead mile failthe* for these three.

The chief and his people were eager enough to know something about their welcome visitors, but were too well-bred to ask any questions till supper was over. Then the old man began without asking, and told all that were within hearing that himself and his son, and all their people, were descendants of a tribe that was once driven out of Ireland by enchanters and pirates, and sailed away to Greece, where their own ancestors once ruled. They were badly treated by their relations, and made to carry clay in leather bags to the tops of hills. "And even my own daughter," said he, "was carried away from her home by the wicked young prince while I was away fighting for his father. My son, at the head of some of our people, overtook and killed him. And when word was brought to me I quitted the army at once. We seized some ships and sailed away, searching for the old island where our forefathers once dwelt. My daughter fell sick on the voyage. But our wise Druid foretold that a draught of water from the Slaney would bring her to health, and that on our reaching its banks we should save hundreds of lives."

Well, there was not much sleep in the rath that night. The friendly strangers on the other bank where the chief's sick daughter still stayed were provided with everything they wanted. Other things were looked to, and a little after sunrise the men of the rath were pouring out of their gates, and the men of the woods landing from their curraghs, and forming their battle ranks.

Before they met, a shower of darts flew from the woody hill down on the

Irish, but pits were ready, lined with yellow clay, and filled with milk and Slaney water, and the moment a man found himself struck he made to the bath.

The ranks were on the point of engaging, when a great shout was heard from the hill, and the Woodmen were seen running down to the bank, pursued by the strange young chief and his men, that were slaughtering them like sheep. They were nearly all killed before they could get to the boats. And into these boats leaped the friendly strangers and rowed across.

So between themselves and the men of the fort rushing down hill, the Woodmen were killed to a man. No quarter was given to the people that were so wicked as to use poisoned arms, and no keen was made, and no cairn piled over them, and no inscription cut on an upright stone to tell their names or how they perished. Their bodies were burned, and the ashes flung into the river. And the next night, though there was some lamentation in the fort, there was much rejoicing along with it.

The Druid did not allow his people to remain long there. He said that Scotland was to be their resting-place. Some of them stayed all this time in a little harbor near the place now called River Chapel, and there they set sail again. But the young chief and two friends would not leave without the three widowed princesses, and the only return he made was to leave his sick sister, that was now as well as ever she was, with the son of the chief of Enniscorthy. The lady whose life he saved was not hard to be persuaded to marry him after he risked his life for her, and her sisters did not like to let her go alone among strange people. Maybe that's the reason that the Irish and the Highlanders like one another still, and can understand one another when they meet and begin a conversation.

❖ THE BATTLE OF THE FORD OF BISCUITS

HUGH NOLAN ◈ *FERMANAGH*
HENRY GLASSIE *1972*

Well.

I have heard a gooddeal about the Ford of Biscuits battle.

Do ye see: at that time there was no town in Enniskillen. There was only a fort.

Do you know, when you'd stand there in Henry Street, and look across the lough, you see two things like round towers. Well, that was a fort on the edge of the lake, in the middle of the sixteenth century; that'd be somewhere in the fifteen-hundreds. Aye.

Well, there was an English garrison.

Do you see, the Plantation of Ulster, it took place in the early part of the seventeenth century. That would be very early, about sixteen hundred and nine.

It 'twas after the Flight of the Earls. They were Irish gentry that had position and owned the property, the land like, in this country. So then they lost in the wars with the British, and they had to leave Ireland.

And then, James the First was the king at that time. And he brought over a very large contingent. And he gave them the lands that these *earls* owned, do you know. So that was what they called the Plantation of Ulster.

Well then, there was a garrison here at Enniskillen in days before that, while the O'Neills and the O'Donnells was in prominence.

There was an English garrison here on the island of Enniskillen.

So this garrison was attacked be Red Hugh O'Donnell; he was a Donegal chief.

They were attacked.

And nothing could get in or out because there was an army surrounded the castle.

So finally, in the long run, there was a soldier got out.

And he got into a boat.

And he rowed the boat from Enniskillen to Belturbet up Lough Erne.

Well, do ye see, the way it was at that time, the southern part of the country was in English hands, but the North wasn't, because these earls that I have told you about, they held Ulster.

And it was only an odd place that the English could get in—like getting in on this island in Lough Erne, *Enniskillen.*

So he got to Belturbet anyway, and he got word sent to Dublin about this attack on Enniskillen *castle.*

And it was ten weeks from the castle was attacked till the chief secretary got the word about it in Dublin.

So anyway, when he heard the news, he formed a powerful great army, all over the other three *provinces.*

There was Irish men on it too from Ulster, that started marching for Enniskillen.

So then O'Donnell then, he raised an army in the *North* here for to intercept the Lord Lieutenant's army.

So they came on out through this country, O'Donnell's army.

And they took up their positions
along the *banks* of the Arney River,
from Drumane *all* up to Arney.

So they waited there for the arrival of their opponents.
And there went a man on a horse on as far up as Belturbet
for to see was there any sign of the Lord Lieutenant's army coming.
And he came back,
and there was a song about it,
and his answer was put in *verse.*
He told O'Donnell—there was a general the name of Duke, and he was leading the Lord Lieutenant's forces, do ye see—so he told him:

"I saw the plumes of Duke's dragoons,
south of Belturbet town."

So anyway, they remained here through this country, and all along the banks of the Arney River.
And finally the Lord Lieutenant's army arrived on the *other side.*
That would be from Derryhowlaght down to Clontymullan, and all along there.
And they wanted to get across the Arney River and get on to Enniskillen.
So the other ones gave them battle there.
And the battle, it was a running fight, along the banks of both sides.
The English forces couldn't get across the river because it was all fords; there was no bridges, do ye see, in them days.
It was *all fords.*
Every ford that they came to, they were guarded, do ye see, and they couldn't get *across.*
So there was one ford there in particular. It'd be a wee piece up from Drumane Bridge. According to tradition, the battle finished up there.
It's called the Biscuit Ford.
The English had all sorts of food with them, do ye know, including a terrible go of biscuits.
So the battle finished up there.
And the English was beaten back.
And a lot of the provisions that they had with them went into the river.
So that's known to this day as the Biscuit Ford.
Aye.

❖ Cromwell

SÉAMUS Ó CEALLA ◈ *GALWAY*
SÉAMAS Ó CATHÁIN *1937*

Cromwell was a big English general and a bad man. He'd stick the bayonet in the child and hold it up in the air until one of his officers would fire a shot through it. When he came into the County Clare, he never halted until he came as far as Spancel Hill and 'twas Cromwell that started the first horse fair in Spancel Hill on June twenty-third.

Cromwell and his soldiers were marching along the road this day in some part of the County Clare and didn't he see this poor countryman coming along the road and he having a creel of turf. The creel was made of rods in them times.

He ordered the man to empty the creel on the side of the road. He did. Cromwell then put his hand in his pocket and gave him a good price for the turf. He ordered his soldiers to spill a barrelful of tar on the turf and they did as he told them. In a while's time, they saw the crowd of people coming along the road, and Cromwell waited there for a while and he told his men to be ready and if it was an army that was coming to kill every one of them.

They stood there with their swords in their hands until the crowd came closer to them and when it did, they saw that it was a funeral that was in it and four out in front and they carrying a crochar and a corpse above on it.

"Halt," says Cromwell.

They halted and the terror of the world on them.

"Leave down that corpse," says he.

They laid it down on the ground. Cromwell put his hand down in his pocket and pulled up a fistful of gold coins. He had English men and French men and Scotch men in his army. He turned to the English regiment.

"Here," says he, "is a fistful of gold for any one of ye that'll throw that corpse on the tar and set fire to it."

None of them took the offer.

"We'll fight the living," says they, "but we won't molest the dead."

Then he made the same offer to the French regiment and it was the same story. They all refused to burn the corpse.

Then he turned to the Scotch men and they said that they was soldiers as well as the other two regiments and that they would not molest the dead.

"Here," says Cromwell, turning to the friends of the dead person, "here is a handful of gold for any one of ye that'll set fire to that corpse."

No sooner was the offer made than the Irish men made one rush for the corpse to see which of them would have it first so that he could earn his fistful of gold. Cromwell drew his sword, "Stand back," he said, "and don't touch the corpse."

Then Cromwell turned to his own army. "Now," says he, "the day you see one Irish man ready to burn another for a fistful of gold, we can take Ireland that day with roasted apples!"

❖ Cromwell's Bible

TADHG Ó MURCHADA ◈ *KERRY*
SEAN O'SULLIVAN *1941*

One time Cromwell was planning to put a wall or a paling all around the coast of England. He thought that was the only way to keep an enemy out.

He had a huge, black Bible—it would take a horse to draw it!—and he had a servant always with him to take care of the Bible. One day, himself and the servant set out and they never stopped until they reached the coast. It was a very warm day, and Cromwell was exhausted when he reached the sea. Drowsiness and sleep were coming over him, and he lay down on the strand to close his eyes.

"Now," said he to the servant, "I'll stretch myself for a while, and you're to take care of the Bible until I awake. And as if your life depended on it, you're not to open it. If you do, it will be the worse for you!"

He lay down and it wasn't long till he was snoring for himself. When the servant saw that he was asleep,

"By heavens, it won't be long now till I find out what power is in this Bible!"

He opened it and, if he did, it wasn't long until a small, stout man jumped out on the strand before his eyes, and then another and another until the strand was covered with them. None of them was the size of your thumb, and they all were running around and shouting: "Give me work! Give me work! Give me work!"

The poor servant was terrified, I'd say, when he saw the huge crowd all over the strand, and his heart was full of fear that they would rouse Cromwell.

"May the Devil take the pack of ye!" he shouted. "Where would I get work for ye? Why don't ye start making ropes out of the sand?"

They started making ropes out of the sand, but, of course, if they were at it since, they couldn't make any ropes of it. They had to give up in the end, and told the servant that it was beyond their powers.

"If that's the way with ye," said the servant, "I can't help ye. Off ye go in the name of the Devil to wherever ye came from, and don't be annoying me, yourselves and your work!"

In they went, every single madman of them, into the Bible, and when the servant was rid of the last one of them, I promise you that it didn't take him long to close the Bible on them. Nor did he open it again.

When Cromwell had slept through, he sat up, took hold of the Bible and opened it, but, if he was opening it since, no help would come out of the Bible to him.

"I'm afraid that you opened this Bible, fellow, while I was asleep," said he to the servant. "And if you did, that leaves England without a paling!"

❖ Patrick Sarsfield

GALWAY
LADY GREGORY *1909*

Sarsfield was a great general the time he turned the shoes on his horse. The English it was were pursuing him, and he got off and changed the shoes the way when they saw the tracks they would think he went another road. That was a great plan.

He got to Limerick then, and he killed thousands of the English. He was a great general.

❖ Sarsfield Surrenders and Rory Takes to the Hills

DONEGAL
SEUMAS MacMANUS *1952*

My uncle Donal used to tell me how his grandfather often told him that when Limerick at last surrendered to William of Orange and there looked nothing more to fight for, and that the French flag was set on one hill and William's flag on another for choice of the Irish fighters as they marched out; and when these thronged solid to the French, with brave Patrick Sarsfield at their head, one rough fellow, Rory, who in the fighting had drawn everyone's admiration, so reckless he was—this Rory struck away on his own. A captain of Sarsfield's headed for King Louis's flag, seeing Rory strike off by himself, called, "Rory, aren't you coming with us to France?"

"No!" Rory answered, shortly.

"You're surely not going to William?"

"No, no!" said Rory.

"In the Lord's name, are you making no choice?"

"I'm choosing Ireland."

"You're mad. Ireland's lost, and there isn't a solitary soul left to fight for her."

"You're standing on Ireland," Rory said, like that. "And I'm to fight for her."

"But you haven't even a handful behind you, and England has a hundred thousand."

"I'll have behind me an army more plentiful," said Rory, "than the hairs on your head."

"What do you mean?"

"Every angel God can spare He will strap a sword on and send to my helping—and England's hundred thousand will melt like the mists before us."

"When?" asked the captain with a chuckle.

"In God's own good time. Maybe in a year, maybe five hundred years; but, be it soon or be it long, Rory wins."

And, his gun on his shoulder, Rory turned away and headed to the hills.

❖ BLACK FRANCIS

HUGH NOLAN ◈ *FERMANAGH*
HENRY GLASSIE *1972*

He was the leader of a highway gang that was in Fermanagh in days gone by.

The way it was, do ye see, after the Williamite War, there was a lot of the Irish army went away to France.

And they figured in a lot of wars that France had with other European countries.

And they were known as the *Irish Brigade.*

But then there was a section of them that didn't leave this country, but they took to the hills.

And they were called the rapparees.

And what they followed up was: they used to rob the rich, and they used to give the money to poor people, do ye know.

So that went on for a length of time.

And they were in every county in Ireland.

But this was a part of them was in Fermanagh, and whether this man was O'Brien or not, I just can't remember, but I heard it anyway.

But there was five of them.

And there was one fellow,
he was Corrigan.

And he was a terrible jump
or a terrible leap.

It was supposed that it was Lisgoole Abbey that they were going to rob this night for some ones that wasn't able to pay their rates, or meet their accounts. And they used to give the money to people like that, do ye see.

So anyway, there was one of the gang and he insulted a girl that was in this house.

And this Black Francis bid to have been clear, only for a lacerating that he gave this fellow for interfering with his girl.

He was chastising this fellow for his bad manners, and for the crime it was for to interfere with a woman-person, do ye see.

But anyway the word went to Enniskillen.

And whatever kind of a post—whether it was military or whether it was the revenue men, I can't just tell you which of the two it was—but they started out, and didn't they get the length of the place before the gang got away.

Only this Corrigan fellow.

And this Corrigan fellow leapt the Sillees River.

So Black Francis and the other ones, they were arrested.

And there was a death penalty for robbery in them days.

So anyway these ones were tried, and they were found guilty, and they were executed at Enniskillen, where the technical school is—that was the jail in them days.

So anyway, the executions took place outside in them days.

And this Corrigan fellow, he dressed himself up as a woman.

And he came along.

And when Black Francis was brought out for to be hanged, whatever way Corrigan managed it, he attracted his attention.

So he made a very long speech, Black Francis did, about seeing his sweetheart in the crowd, and that he hoped she'd be able for to protect herself.

Aw, it was a terrible speech. He was a very clever fellow, you know. And it was all on this supposed lady that was in the Gaol Square, as they called it.

And the lady was his companion: Souple Corrigan.

So anyway they were executed anyway, and Souple Corrigan made his way to America.

❖ SHAN BERNAGH

CORMIC O'HOLLAND ◈ *TYRONE*
ROSE SHAW *1930*

The Tories robbed the rich to give to the poor, and if they found that a body like ourselves had six bags of meal and McKeown's out beyond there with all them childer had none—and they crying for meat—the Tories would take from us and give them plenty, and we daren't say nothing at all.

Shan Bernagh—he was a notable Tory in this country, and 'twas said that he came of the best of quality—were ye ever at Shan's Stables? They're away far out at the back of the mountain and sure ye'd lost yourself entirely if ye went to seek them your lone, and never find them at all maybe. He would steal horses and cattle from the farmers going to the fair at Monaghan and 'twas in the Stables he kept his horses and he bid to make many a dublicate to save them from being tracked. He had his horses shod with the back of the shoe to the front of the foot so that no one would know which direction they had gone. The Stables are a deep dark hole like that that goes in under the mountain and many's the cattle that does be lost in it, falling into the Tory Holes, as some people calls them, but thanks be to God I never lost none there yet.

One Christmas Eve—it was in the bad old penal days, when the Government was hunting the priests like mad dogs—the people all gathered secretly to a midnight Mass in Barney Faddya Vhic's Glen. It is a quare lonesome place right in the heart of the mountain, but the Yeomanry—the police of them days—heard about it and they came from Clogher to stop it. The priest was standing in front of the big stone just, that was used for the altar, and it having two candles upon it. When the priest's head came before the light on the altar and darkened it they took aim and shot him dead. The priest's name was Father Milligan; he was buried a piece behind the stone with a big hob of earth to mark the grave.

Shan Bernagh swore that he would have a Yeoman's life for this and sure didn't he catch them up before they got the length of Lough More and he killed one of them and threw him in the lough.

The Browns lived away beyond at Lough Anoyd that time and they laid a trap with the Yeomen to catch Shan Bernagh. They made a great dinner and with every sort of meat and drink in it and they invited the Tories to come to it in order to betray them. Shan Bernagh and his men sat down to eat and drink their fill, with their guns and swords and belts all off them.

The servant girl that was hired at Brown's looked out over the half-door and, lo and behold ye, there was the Yeomen from Clogher marching up the street. She was afeared the Browns would kill her if she gave a sign to the Tories so she snapped up the can like as if she was going to the well and jooked out of the house. As she went past the window she looked in at the Tories and she riz the chime of a song in Irish: "God love the herring that never was catched on a bait." (By the same token, these were the very words that the servant used when he warned Saint Patrick not to eat the poisoned fish that he was offering to him.)

When Shan Bernagh heard her song he let a roar out of him and they all bounced to their feet and catched up their belts and blunderbusses and went out with their guns cocked and met the Yeomen at the door. They walked safely out and the Yeomen daren't touch them and so to their horses and away.

The Browns knew they had turned everyone against them by their falsity so they started that night and never were seen in the country since.

The servant girl was afeared to show her face so she crept into a sheuch behind a ditch, and lay there all night. Next morning she was found by a Tory and brought before Shan Bernagh, who gave her as much money as she could carry and bade her change her name and go into a strange country. Troth, she would be apt to get a severe punishment for defeating the Government.

There were hundreds of pounds offered in them days for the head of a Tory. It was Conegrah meadow thonder, right fornenst this house just, that Shan Bernagh came by his death.

The weather was hot and he went with his brother to bathe in Lough More. They put off them, and left their clothes in a heap on the broo of the lough. But a corbie lit on the clothes and joined to squally.

Said Shan's brother, "I'll not go to lodge at the widow woman's house at Conegrah the night," says he, "for there's a trap," says he, "and thon's a sure token of death, the corbie lighting on our clothes."

"Phut!" says Shan, "be sure you may trust her," says he, "for didn't I stand gossip for her child?"

So when night come Shan went his lone to the house in Conegrah meadow. The widow had lashings of whiskey in it and she made him drunk and he lay down before the fire. With that she opened the door and in came a man named McGregor. He had a hatchet in his hand and he hit Shan a great bat on the forehead—and him hearty at the time. After getting the bat Shan riz up and the two men wrastled through the house.

The great Tory would have prevailed only for the woman. She was lying on a whop of straw in the corner and while the men were fighting rings round them she jooked out of her bed and whipped the blanket about Shan's legs, the way he couldn't move at all. Then McGregor gave him another bat which knocked him senseless and he dragged him out of the house to a stone by the water below. He cut the head off him there and put it in a bag and headed off to get a big lump of money for a reward from Government.

The stead of the house in Conegrah is standing yet and ye can see the track of the hatchet in the stone thonder, where Shan Bernagh's head was cut off him.

❖ WILLIE BRENNAN

THOMAS O'RIORDAN ◈ *CORK*
SEAN O'SULLIVAN *1934*

Brennan was born in Kilmurry, near Kilworth. He listed in the army and then he deserted out of it. They were hunting him around the country day and night.

One day outside at Leary's Bridge, Brennan met the Pedlar Bawn. I never heard him called by any other name. The Pedlar was traveling for a firm in Cork, going about the country selling different kinds of things. Brennan put the blunderbuss up to him and made him hand out what he had, watch and chain and all. Then the Pedlar asked him to give him some token to show to the people of the firm in Cork that he had met him.

"Tell them that you met Brennan the Highwayman."

"Give me some token that you met me, or I'll be put to jail," said the Pedlar.

"What have I to do for you?" asked Brennan.

"Fire a shot through this side of my old coat," said the Pedlar.

He did.

"Fire another through this side now," said the Pedlar.

So he did.

"Here!" said the Pedlar. "Fire another through my old hat."

Brennan did.

"Come!" said the Pedlar. "Fire another through my old cravat."

"I have no more ammunition," said Brennan.

The Pedlar then drew a pistol, whenever he had it hid.

"Come!" said he. "Deliver!"

Brennan had to deliver, quick and lively too!

"You're a smarter man than me," said he. "All I ever went through, I robbed army, men and lords, and you beat me. Will you make a comrade for me?"

The Pedlar only flung his pack over the ditch.

"I will," said he. "I'll stand a loyal comrade until my dying day."

And so he was, a loyal comrade.

"We'll go along to County Tipperary," said Brennan. " 'Tis a wealthy county. There's agents and landlords there going around the country gathering the rent in the houses, and we'll whip them going back in the evening."

So the two of them went along to the County Tipperary. Brennan went in to a widow there one morning. The poor woman was crying and lamenting. He asked her what was the matter with her.

"What good is it for me to tell you, my good man?" said she.

She didn't know but he was a tramp.

"How do you know?" said he.

"The agent is coming here by and by, and I haven't a halfpenny to give him for the rent," said she.

"Well, what would you say to the man who'd give it to you?" said Brennan.

He asked her how much it was, and she told him—five or six pounds, I suppose. He counted it out to her.

"Tell me now," said he, "the road he goes home in the evening."

She told him the road he'd take after giving the day gathering around. He made her go down on her knees then and swear to God and to him that she would never tell anyone that she saw him, or mention that anyone gave her the money. Himself and the Pedlar met the agent going home with the money and whipped the whole lot that he had gathered that day.

Brennan is buried over in Kilcrumper near the old church wall.

❖ ❖ ❖

❖ Wicklow in the Rising of 1798

MRS. O'TOOLE ◈ *WICKLOW*
PÁDRAIG Ó TUATHAIL *1934*

The swearing in of my grandfather Larry Byrne took place at the wedding of a friend before the rebellion of Ninety-Eight broke out. Michael Dwyer swore him in, and told him to unite all the boys that might think well of it. He started in at Blackrock and Aughavanagh, Glenmalure and the Seven Churches, and united all the boys that were in Ninety-Eight from that quarter; and Michael Dwyer on the other hand through Imaal his native place and all round, and against Ninety-Eight broke out they had every man and boy in the Wicklow Mountains that was worth his salt ready for the fight.

The fourteenth night of May the rebellion broke out in the lower part of Wexford by the chapel in Boolavogue being set on fire. The priest was in bed, and he dreamed the chapel was on fire, and he jumped up, and it was really on fire, passed being quenched or put out. Then he got up and dressed himself, and he saddled his horse. He started up through Wexford, and he gathered up three farming men on horseback, and they came on through the whole County Wexford and gathered up all the help that would join them until they came to Carnew, and they was in Carnew by breakfast time in the morning, and they started from that on through the mountains to Aughavanagh and they was in Aughavanagh by evening time. When they came to Aughavanagh the news spread and the boys came in their dozens and joined them in a large army at Aughavanagh.

Then later on there did a regiment of British soldiers land called the Durham Fencibles, and they was encamped on the lands of Kiladuff joining Ballymanus, and they had a general over them, a General Skerrett, one of the best men that ever landed in Ireland, a noble gentleman, and done the most good for the opposite people—that is the Irish.

And there did another regiment come over called the Hessians and they were volunteers from England, farmer's sons, big soft fellows well-kept, well-dressed and had fine horses, a whole regiment of them. And they went up and down through the country and shot some parties, and said they would go up to Aughavanagh to clean up the rebels that were annoying the Crown.

They went on until they came to a level plain about forty or fifty acres, but it was rocks and bogs a good deal of it, so they eyed out this place and allowed they'd go up there and hunt out the rebels and shoot them down.

So Dwyer and the boys were waiting for them—they had got word of them coming on to them, and they were waiting for them. And Dwyer was the cleverest man and there was never a duck hardier on the pond than he. He planted his men at each side of this plain in hiding and told some to go out in front out of gunshot and to tempt the soldiers on; when he'd give the signal they could fire; and he had a sea-whistle that could be heard eleven miles away.

The soldiers dashed into what seemed to be a level place I told you about, but it was rocks and bogs and sloughs, and the horses stumbled and fell, and they got them up again, and they started on foot, but they wasn't as well up as the mountain fellows.

So Dwyer gave the signal for the side parties to pour in on them and to fire on them, and they did so, and they shot them to a man.

They went up to Aughavanagh, and they was set upon by the boys at Aughavanagh, the United Irishmen—the "rebels" as they called them—they set upon them and they was cleaned up to a man—there wasn't as much as one of them left to tell the tale. The horses went round the roads and the bogs and the hills, with the bridle reins dragging beside them and the saddles on them, but no rider. The people let the horses wander over the hills and never as much as took the reins or saddles off of them, but a big snow the year after killed them all.

So after two or three days the inhabitants became very uneasy to see the dead bodies of the big fat Englishmen lying there and no one to bury them, and they said to each other: "What are we going to do?" They wouldn't lay hands on them nor they wouldn't bury them. One of them came down to the corps to Kiladuff, and he made it known to the general—General Skerrett—to see if he would send up his men to bury his brother Englishmen that had been lying on the plains shot for so many days; they would give them some assistance.

So they dug a big trench, and they dragged the dead bodies into it with the horses, and covered them up, and then they expected that they would annoy them by night, but they never did. They never saw one of them.

On one occasion Dwyer and my grandfather and Hugh Byrne of Monaseed and poor McAllister—I am troubled to the heart when I think of poor McAllister; he was a true man—well, the four of them were in a cave on Lugnaquilla when the daylight came.

By and by the sun shone in through the heather which hung over the hole they crept in. They were as comfortable as the day is long lying in a big bundle of clean straw and good bedclothes that was brought from a farmer's house; and the farmer's house was my great-grandfather's. They were brought from a farmer's house near to the mountain and placed there designedly for the boys.

So the four awoke, and they began to talk, and they got up and struck their flints and steel because there was no matches. Then they lit their pipe, each of them, and they commenced to smoke and to talk as happy as the day is long, when a robin came in—and a robin is unusual so high up in the mountain, you know—a robin flew in, and she jumped around the quilt over them, and one grabbed at her, and another, and she flew out from the whole of them, and it wasn't two minutes till she came in again, and when she came in she bustled and set herself just as if she was going to jump at them, and she got wicked-looking and: "Oh!" says they, "there is something in this."

The four jumped to their feet, and one of them put his head through the hole and he pulled back excited. "Oh!" he says, "the hillsides is red with soldiers."

"Which will we lie in," says another, "or will we get out? If they have bloodhounds we're found out."

"That's right," says they, and they all jumped to their feet, and the bloodhounds came in to the bed, but they dragged on their breeches and put their hat on them, and out they went with their guns. Dwyer whipped his sea-whistle and he whistled, and he could be heard, I suppose, in Arklow, and they fired off their three shots, and the soldiers turned around and they ran for their lives, and they never got time to look back till they fell over Lugnaquilla, and they told when they got below that the hills was full of rebels.

There was a woman who used to deal in carrying bread around to the farmers herself and selling it to the women and children and otherwise, and when Ninety-Eight broke out she was a valiant heroine woman and should be good, should have been of good blood or she wouldn't have been so sound as she was, for she never divulged it, and she carried scores and maybe hundreds of back-loads of powder to the boys and a dozen of penny buns put in over the pack, and no one ever detected it that she carried back-loads of powder to the boys during the whole year of Ninety-Eight and was never detected. Her name was never made known afraid they might find out what she was at, and she would have got a horrid death, but, thanks be to God! she didn't—she was never known by anything but the "Walking Magazine."

One Sunday morning Dwyer and McAllister were at Mass in Knockananna Chapel, and they brought their guns with them and left them by the wall. The priest remonstrated with them and said that the House of God was no place to bring guns, but McAllister who was a Presbyterian but used to go to Mass with Dwyer said: "It is not always we have a rebellion, Father. Go on with the Mass!" And the priest did so.

During the Mass a neighbor came to Dwyer and said that he had been at the window and that the chapel-yard was full of soldiers, and Dwyer picked out two clever young fellows and he told them for to go away to a field a distance from the chapel-yard but in sight of it, and says he: "Take off your coats."

He told them to run along the field in their shirts as fast as they could, and he picked out two or three more young chaps of boys that were clever enough to understand him, and he told them to go down beside the soldiers and stand looking down at this field and to cry out each one in surprise and wonder: "There they go! There they go!"

And they did so, and the soldiers asked them who did they mean by there they go, and they told them—all cried out: "Dwyer and McAllister! Dwyer and McAllister!"

The soldiers started for to overtake Dwyer and McAllister, and they failed on it, for Dwyer and McAllister was hid in the chapel and when the soldiers cleared out they cleared out and went their way in peace and quietness.

The soldiers went out across the fence and they came on the two boys that ran, and they sitting with their coats on, and they smoking their pipes, and they asked them did they see two men running through the fields, and they said "No," that they were not long there. So Dwyer and McAllister walked off in safety and left the poor lads wandering about to look for them.

My great-grandfather, John Byrne, was fifty years of age and a grandfather in Ninety-Eight, and he fought in the Rising. He was captured by order of Captain Hardy and brought to Hacketstown and sentenced to be hanged.

My great-grandmother went to Captain Hardy's wife, and asked her to get him a pardon, that she had no one to work their little mountain farm at Blackrock, only herself. My great-grandmother knew Mrs. Hardy, who was a lady and a colonel's daughter, and she used sell her butter and eggs. The kind lady asked the captain to grant her one more favor—she was after getting off another rebel—and this would be the last favor she would ask, but the captain said that if he let off a man of fifty years of age and a grandfather that rebellion would never cease in Ireland. She threw herself on her knees and grasped him around the legs, and told him she would never stand up out of that until he would grant her request. So what could the captain do, and the good lady, the colonel's daughter—she was higher up than him, you know—at his feet? So my great-grandfather got his reprieve.

My grandfather, Larry Byrne, married his daughter and brought her to Rednagh. He was arrested coming home from the battle of Vinegar Hill, where he lay down on the side of Croghan Kinsella to have a sleep, along with four others of his brother-boys, only they were strangers but were brothers in the fight, don't ye know—they lay down and fell asleep, and when the soldiers sighted them at some point or other they went on and arrested them, and they brought them to Naas Gaol, and from that to Dublin before ever the widow mother of the family got to know of it.

He was in Newgate Gaol when they got to hear of it, and he was kept there for a year because they got to know that his information would be very valuable. He was out two years with Dwyer organizing the parties in the mountains, and he was Dwyer's real companion, and they knew that if they could get his information it would be very valuable, so they kept him for a year, and I may tell you that he got the height of misery—he got hunger, he got neglect, he never saw clean linen. He had, of course, nothing but the clothes on him when he was arrested; what could he have? And the shirt that he brought in he brought it out without ever seeing a drop of the world's water—wasn't that awful?—after a year, but he said it never gave any more trouble than the shirt he would be after putting on on a Sunday morning. It was God did it.

So at the end of a year they come and they took him out of prison, and they had a beautiful suit of new clothes, and they made him peel off his old clothes that he had on the hills and in prison for the year. They had to lie like the beasts—they got no bed there—they lay like beasts behind iron bars.

So they made him take off these old clothes and put on their new suit, and a few men conducted him into a closed carriage and brought him to the Castle, and put him into the tower of the Castle, and they kept him there for six weeks, and he knew what that meant—they wanted information.

So what did he meet but a rebel doctor in the castle—a rebel doctor. Would you expect that? Dr. Madden—I am not sure. He wondered at him to be so friendly to him and telling him that if he ate the kind of food he would get there hearty it would kill him. "I know," says he, "the kind you are after being kept on for the year—the worst of the worst."

So at the end of the six weeks I tell you about in the Castle one morning when he was after having his breakfast—he got a beautiful time in it, he was treated to the very best and he had a bedroom and a sitting room and he was able to read in it, and he had a lovely time in it. And one morning Major Sirr—ah! he was one of the worst of them—walked into his room with another stranger that he didn't know, and he says:

"Good morning, Byrne," very friendly, "and how are you getting on here?" And my grandfather spoke to him very coolly and said:

"It is very seldom one would get on well in prison."

"But, Byrne," says he, "you know you are not in prison. You are in the tower of the Castle."

"I know," says my grandfather, "that I am in the tower of the Castle, but I am not at my liberty."

"Well," says the stranger, "we are coming to grant you your liberty only for you to answer the few necessary questions"—that's to inform, you know —"to answer the few necessary questions we'll put you."

My grandfather told it himself—he lay back in his chair with wrath and indignation, and he says to himself. "What could I do if I had my pike and liberty!"

But he hadn't. They noticed he was not able to speak, and they said, one to the other: "Come on! We'll leave Byrne to himself, and we'll send a stranger tomorrow."

"Yes," said the other, "a perfect stranger." That would do, you know, if my grandfather would talk to a stranger.

So the next morning a perfect stranger walked into the room, and he drew a chair, and sat down at the table, and took a paper from his pocket, and laid it on the table with a unicorn stamped on it.

"And now, Byrne," says he, "I have come to take your deposition," says he, "to grant you your liberty."

He jumped to his feet—he was a six-foot man, they all were—he jumped to his feet and he asked the lad: "What did he mean?"

The fellow jumped to his feet all as quick, a bit afraid of him—and he had reason to be afraid—and he says:

"What do you mean?"

"What I mean," says my grandfather, "is not to allow you nor e'er another man on the earth for to insult my honor by forcing me to become an informer."

The fellow done nothing, but he darted to the door and he rang a bell, and he called to fellows and bid them bring the bolts. So they handcuffed him. They put the bolts on, and they might have let him walk down, but they didn't, they dragged him. But I'm forgetting to tell about the doctor. The doctor sent for him, and he went to him, and bid him a hearty good welcome, and he says: "Your face didn't deceive me." The doctor was an United Irishman himself, and he had the opinion all right that my grandfather wouldn't become the informer. "Goodbye now," says he, "and your face didn't deceive me."

So they took him back from the Castle down the winding stairs to the closed vehicle that they brought him in, and the two keepers packed him into it, and they brought him back to the Provost Gaol. The poet said that "the Provo' jail was worse than Hell," it was such a torture upon the prisoners. It was in poetry—a part of a song, don't you know—"The Provo' jail was worse than Hell." They brought him back to the Provost's, and they put him into it. They asked him no questions that night nor next, and the next day he was summoned to go to the final court-martial; they had several court-martials on him during the year, but he was never present at any of them. He never knew what passed, but this was the final, and they brought him to this, and they said everything they had to say against him for being the United Irishman, for being the rebel.

So Judge Norbury, the notorious Judge Norbury, he sentenced him to be hanged on such a day, and gave him a good many days. He gave him a great many days, I suppose to see if he would make up his mind, if he could be moved to inform still. He asked him then had he got anything to say; and my grandfather said: "No, but God save Ireland!"

And then God Almighty put this in his head—he bethought of the mother—he said that he wished to see his mother before he'd be hanged, but he did not ask them to send word to her nor to let her see him—he did not want the compliment—but he said he'd wished to see his mother before he'd die, and they didn't say that they would send her word, but they did.

There was a general over the camp that I have already told you about in Kiladuff—General Skerrett. He was the best general that ever crossed the waters to Ireland. He was the best-meaning gentleman, and the best general, and they sent to the general and told him to go and tell the widow, Mrs. Mary Byrne of Ballymanus, that her son Laurence Byrne was going to be hanged on such a date, and that she could see him if she wished; but it wasn't through kindness to her or him they did it—they thought that maybe she'd move him, don't you know, that he'd inform.

So this poor general I tell you about—Oh! she prayed for him to the day of her death—she said that he rode his horse into her yard, and went to the door, and called to know was the widow, Mrs. Mary Byrne in, and she went out, and he asked her was she the person, and she said, "Yes." And he told her—well, he beat round about, and he thought it death to tell her, but he had to tell her the news about her son going to be hanged. So she should have been a pretty stout good-nerved woman; she didn't faint or die at all, what you'd expect she ought to do.

So she stood it. Says he: "Your son is going to be hanged on such a date, and you'll be allowed to see him if you wish." He said he was very sorry for her trouble, and she the mother of eight more children. He went away—the poor gentleman went away—and he was sorry for her truly.

So she turned in, and she sent the children, little and big as they were, around to all the neighbors, and told them what was going to occur, and again nightfall that night there was as many people around the house as would wake him if he were dead. There was a crowd gathered to sympathize with her. She prepared and sent her horse to the forge to be shod, and she prepared for Dublin to go to the King, she was that stout and brave, to go to the King to get his reprieve or to look for it anyhow.

So she went to Kiladuff to the camp, and she called for General Skerrett, and he came on to her and told him her intention, and he gave her all encouragement and that relieved her heart, and he said: "If you be stout enough and brave enough to go to the King, he won't refuse you."

So her three brothers lived here and there in Ballymanus and Killamoate, farmers, and the youngest of them preferred to go to the King. "No, no," she says, "the King may refuse you," she says. "You are only his uncle, but I'll go myself, and if ever I can be let get sight of the King, he won't refuse me." And I suppose he wouldn't. He wasn't a bad king at all, King George the Third. He refused no one, I believe, of a reprieve that went to him.

So, bedad, she prepared, and she thought to go away when she was ready—I suppose up towards the middle of the night—and the people all put against her only to wait till daylight, but she couldn't have patience. She had to set out before day in the morning, and they advised her to go through the mountains, through Aughavanagh and the Military Road and not to go the lower road, fearing that she'd be robbed, because they might be expecting that a woman riding a horse—she rode her single horse, mind you!—the women in them days, farmers, used to ride a single horse—there was no spring cars—they used to ride a single horse, any of them was stout enough for it, and I suppose she was stout enough for anything.

So she rode her horse away to Dublin, and, thank goodness, no one ever interrupted her, and on her way very near Dublin, when she was going near to Tallagh, she bethought of this Mr. Ponsonby—he was a member for County Wicklow, and she bethought that her husband had voted for him; and he had either the saving of two or three from the gallows in the year, and she said she'd go to try him before she'd go to the King, and so she did.

She bid him look in his book and find her husband's name, and he was another Laurence Byrne, and he did, and he said: "I am glad, my poor woman. I am delighted," he says, "it come to my turn to save your son's life."

So he gave her the letter and told her not to let it into anyone's hands until she would see the Lord Lieutenant, no matter how difficult that would be. He ordered her to go to the Castle and said: "Hand this into his own hands, or he'll never see it." So she promised him, "never fear she would not," and she kept her word.

She fought her way to the Castle, and she had to spend three days there before she would be allowed to see the Lord Lieutenant, and only for a good gentleman that took compassion on her, I suppose she would not have got to see him at all. Well, he took compassion on her when he saw her there knocking about for three days, and he asked her in a friendly manner: "Who did she want to see, or what did she want?" He saw her knocking around, and they pushing her out—the Castle folk—for three days. So she told him her business, and she told him also if he'd get her to see the Lord Lieutenant that she'd pray for him while she lived; and he said: "If I would you'd tell on me."

So she says that she would not. "Keep your eye on me," he says, "and I'll give you a token."

So she followed him along the way, backwards and forwards, and when he come to the door of the office where he was he swung his arm—he was a thorough gentleman, whoever he was—to make sure of the right one. He says: "The Lord Lieutenant is in an armchair at the fire, and there'll be a man at a desk inside the door, and he'll put you out if you go for him, and the way you'll be certain it is he if his face is near you," he says, "he has a mark on the corner of one of his eyes." Wasn't he a very good man to do that? "He has a mark on the corner of one of his eyes," he says, "and if you see that you may be sure it is the Lord Lieutenant himself."

So he went his way, and she followed him, and he gave her the token at the door, and she rushed in, and the big fellow caught her by the shoulder, and asked her how she came to be there, and what was her business. She ran by him and never let on she heard him and went to the gentleman sitting in the armchair, and she asked him and begged his pardon and asked him if it was his Excellency she was speaking to. And he told her it was, and she dropped on her knees and handed him the letter. He opened the letter and read it. "I will," says he, "grant you your son's life through Mr. Ponsonby. Stand up." He was that kind.

Oh! she prayed for him until she died.

He told the fellow at the desk to write out so-and-so, and he did, and brought it over to the fire to him, and he signed it and he gave this document to her, and he called two fellows and they secured a car and the two went with her to the prison. They had to go to the governor of the prison and show him this document, and then the two fellows and her went on to the door of the black cell, for when he was sentenced to be hanged he was put in the black cell.

So they opened the door of the black cell and he was lying on an old plank about a foot from the ground, and she thought he was about seven foot long he was so pale and haggard and worn-looking.

So he looked at her for a great many seconds before he could believe his eyes that it was her, and when he saw it was the mother he jumped to his feet and whipped her in his arms and said: "Mother, I'll die happy now when I have seen you."

So she told him the message she had, the grand news that he wouldn't die at all, and very strange to tell you, he wasn't very much rejoiced at all. He told her that he knew his companions was all shot or hanged by that time, because, you know, he was in a year and six weeks, and never knew a word about a soul, nor was let know.

So she informed him they were not, that he was one of the worst of them himself, and there was only one or two, she said, that were gone.

So she cheered him up, and she brought him on to the friend's place they had in Dublin—a Heffernan family, there was one of them in Eccles Street and another in a street I can't remember—and he was made very happy there and would not be let away for a fortnight. A doctor told him not to face the journey home for that time after his sufferings in prison, and then he came home to Ballymanus and lived to be eighty-seven years of age. And I remember him well, although I was only eight years old, but I was, I am proud to tell you, the dear child of the family.

❖ The Famine

GALWAY
LADY GREGORY *1926*

The Famine; there's a long telling in that, it is a thing will be remembered always.

That little graveyard above, at that time it was filled up of bodies; the Union had no way to buy coffins for them. There would be a bag made, and the body put into it, that was all; and the people dying without priest, or bishop, or anything at all. But over in Connemara it was the dogs brought the bodies out of the houses, and asked no leave.

The world is better now than what it was, for I remember the time I saw men dying out of their standing with the hunger, I seen two brothers dying in a little corner of a field, and nothing around them only the wall.

I seen women watching the hen to lay an egg that they'd bring it into the market to get kitchen for the children, and they couldn't put one on the fire.

I saw three men transported for sheepstealing, and I saw twenty-eight legs of mutton taken out of the garden of one of them. To salt them they did, and to put them in a cellar in the ground. It was to New South Wales these two were sent, and they were put to work in a gold mine. And at their death there was sent back to their family four thousand pounds in money. But when it was got in no good way it did not last, it went to the bad like the froth of the stream.

There was a woman in the time of the Famine and she was dying for the want of food, and she with six or seven pounds that was in sovereigns tied about her neck, and a farthing along with them. But she would not break a sovereign to take a shilling out of it. And a rat came up and ate the thread, and brought away the sovereigns to its hole, but the farthing it left outside.

That is a true story. It is up in the mountains the woman was.

❖ VICTORY IN THE TIME OF FAMINE

MICHAEL BOYLE ◈ *FERMANAGH*
HENRY GLASSIE *1972*

There was a man named McBrien.

He lived somewhere in Rossdoney, in the Point of Rossdoney as they call it.

And he had a *wife*
  and five children,
    five young children.
And they hadn't a haet; there was no food,
  there was no food,
    and they were in a starving condition.
And he said he'd *fish*;
  he'd try and fish in the Arney River,
    that run along his land,
    that was convenient to his land.
He said he'd fish,
  try and fish to see would he get a few fish to eat
    that'd keep them from dying.
So he did; he went out this day,
  and he caught seven fish.
Well he went every day,
  well for a good many days.
And he caught seven fish every day.
And one of the children died anyway.
And he caught six then.
And he caught *six every day.*
The number went down to six.

Aye, I heard that too, about the time of the Famine. That happened in Rossdoney, the townland of Rossdoney, along the Arney River there.

Now that happened; it was told anyway.

It came down from the Famine days.

❖ Ruined by Poetry

TOMÁS Ó CRITHIN ◈ *KERRY*
ROBIN FLOWER *1945*

A good number of years ago a company set out from the capital of Ireland. They had made an arrangement to collect new poems and songs new-made throughout the land. They were a league with money put together and their intention was to start out through the country and give a reward to everyone who should come with three stanzas of a song put together by himself. There was one of them set up in County Kerry, a house like a college in the middle of the town, a great big round table on one leg, and a heap of papers and books in the middle of it, clerks sitting all round it, money scattered all over it, every kind in a box of wood, and the money was to be had by everyone who liked to draw upon it, at the rate of from half a crown to a crown for every three stanzas according to their character and value.

There were a score of tenants in this town in Kerry that they stopped in, and taken all round they had the grass of twenty cows, each one of them, and the town was quite close to the Great Lake of Killarney. Now when the business of the board was settled and everything shipshape, they set the people thinking. At first it was the children of the poor folk from beyond the limits of the town that carried off the money. Then the children of the strong farmers of the town saw how things were going, that more was to be made by putting together song stanzas and poems than to be laboring on the land as they were doing; and, thinking so, these children of the strong farmers gave up working the land and fell to making songs and poems. It didn't take long for their land to run to waste as they let it go anyhow. They didn't care, for the man that got least would have half a crown, another would get ten shillings, while any of them that had a ready wit would lift a pound every afternoon.

Now there was a gentleman living some way from this town, and, when he saw the passion driving the people of the town with the board in it, he saw at once that the town would soon go to ruin at this wild rate, and that the landlord wouldn't let them get much into arrear when they wouldn't be able to pay the rent, for the landlords were mighty hard on the people in those days. The gentleman was right enough in his conjecture, for the board and the town didn't last long, they went at it together so wildly. The old people said that, whatever trouble this board brought on the town, nobody believed that the board got anything out of it either for the people that set it up.

Not long after this the trouble came on the town, and they couldn't pay rent or rate, and the landlord was particularly enraged, for he saw that it was through their own folly and carelessness in working the land that they couldn't pay rent or rate. And the first visit he made to them was to throw them out pell-mell, leaving not a living soul of those twenty tenants in possession. Not long after their eviction, the gentleman on the other side came to the landlord with a purse of gold to pay the rent and rate, and he soon became a rich man. The others wandered off through the countryside with their children, and they were no matter of pity, for their own fault had brought about their ruin.

Fireside Tales

CEILI IN WATERFORD
Mr. and Mrs. S. C. Hall, *Ireland*, 1850

❖ THE BIRTH OF FINN MACCUMHAIL

DONEGAL

JEREMIAH CURTIN *1887*

Cumhal MacArt was a great champion in the West of Erin, and it was prophesied of him that if ever he married he would meet death in the next battle he fought.

For this reason he had no wife, and knew no woman for a long time; till one day he saw the king's daughter, who was so beautiful that he forgot all fear and married her in secret.

Next day after the marriage, news came that a battle had to be fought.

Now a Druid had told the king that his daughter's son would take the kingdom from him. So he made up his mind to look after the daughter, and not let any man come near her.

Before he went to the battle, Cumhal told his mother everything—told her of his relations with the king's daughter.

He said: "I shall be killed in battle today, according to the prophecy of the Druid, and I'm afraid if his daughter has a son the king will kill the child, for the prophecy is that he will lose the kingdom by the son of his own daughter. Now, if the king's daughter has a son do you hide and rear him, if you can. You will be his only hope and stay."

Cumhal was killed in the battle, and within that year the king's daughter had a son.

By command of his grandfather, the boy was thrown out of the castle window into a lough, to be drowned, on the day of his birth.

The boy sank from sight. But after remaining a while under the water, he rose again to the surface, and came to land holding a live salmon in his hand.

The grandmother of the boy, Cumhal's mother, stood watching on the shore, and said to herself as she saw this: "He is my grandson, the true son of my own child," and seizing the boy, she rushed away with him, and vanished, before the king's people could stop her.

When the king heard that the old woman had escaped with his daughter's son, he fell into a terrible rage, and ordered all the male children born that day in the kingdom to be put to death, hoping in this way to kill his own grandson, and save the crown for himself.

After she had disappeared from the bank of the lough, the old woman, Cumhal's mother, made her way to a thick forest, where she spent that night as best she could. Next day she came to a great oak tree. Then she hired a man to cut out a chamber in the tree.

When all was finished, and there was a nice room in the oak for herself and her grandson, and a whelp of the same age as the boy, and which she had brought with her from the castle, she said to the man: "Give me the axe which you have in your hand, there is something here that I want to fix."

The man gave the axe into her hand, and that minute she swept the head off him, saying: "You'll never tell any man about this place now."

One day the whelp ate some of the fine chippings (*bran*) left cut by the carpenter from the inside of the tree. The old woman said: "You'll be called Bran from this out."

All three lived in the tree together, and the old woman did not take her grandson out till the end of five years; and then he couldn't walk, he had been sitting so long inside.

When the old grandmother had taught the boy to walk, she brought him one day to the brow of a hill from which there was a long slope. She took a switch and said: "Now, run down this place. I will follow and strike you with this switch, and coming up I will run ahead, and you strike me as often as you can."

The first time they ran down, his grandmother struck him many times. In coming up the first time, he did not strike her at all. Every time they ran down she struck him less, and every time they ran up he struck her more.

They ran up and down for three days. And at the end of that time she could not strike him once, and he struck her at every step she took. He had now become a great runner.

When he was fifteen years of age, the old woman went with him to a hurling match between the forces of his grandfather and those of a neighboring king. Both sides were equal in skill; and neither was able to win, till the youth opposed his grandfather's people. Then, he won every game. When the ball was thrown in the air, he struck it coming down, and so again and again—never letting the ball touch the ground till he had driven it through the barrier.

The old king, who was very angry, and greatly mortified, at the defeat of his people, exclaimed, as he saw the youth, who was very fair and had white hair: "Who is that *finn cumhal* [white cap]?"

"Ah, that is it. Finn will be his name, and Finn MacCumhail he is," said the old woman.

The king ordered his people to seize and put the young man to death, on the spot. The old woman hurried to the side of her grandson. They slipped from the crowd and away they went, a hill at a leap, a glen at a step, and thirty-two miles at a running-leap. They ran a long distance, till Finn grew tired. Then the old grandmother took him on her back, putting his feet into two pockets which were in her dress, one on each side, and ran on with the same swiftness as before, a hill at a leap, a glen at a step, and thirty-two miles at a running-leap.

After a time, the old woman felt the approach of pursuit, and said to Finn: "Look behind, and tell me what you see."

"I see," said he, "a white horse with a champion on his back."

"Oh, no fear," said she. "A white horse has no endurance. He can never catch us, we are safe from him." And on they sped. A second time she felt the approach of pursuit, and again she said: "Look back, and see who is coming."

Finn looked back, and said: "I see a warrior riding on a brown horse."

"Never fear," said the old woman. "There is never a brown horse but is giddy, he cannot overtake us." She rushed on as before. A third time she said: "Look around, and see who is coming now."

Finn looked, and said: "I see a black warrior on a black horse, following fast."

"There is no horse so tough as a black horse," said the grandmother. "There is no escape from this one. My grandson, one or both of us must die. I am old, my time has nearly come. I will die, and you and Bran save yourselves. (Bran had been with them all the time.) Right here ahead is a deep bog. You jump off my back, and escape as best you can. I'll jump into the bog up to my neck. And when the king's men come, I'll say that you are in the bog before me, sunk out of sight, and I'm trying to find you. As my hair and yours are the same color, they will think my head good enough to carry back. They will cut it off, and take it in place of yours, and show it to the king. That will satisfy his anger."

Finn slipped down, took farewell of his grandmother, and hurried on with Bran. The old woman came to the bog, jumped in, and sank to her neck. The king's men were soon at the edge of the bog, and the black rider called out to the old woman: "Where is Finn?"

"He is here in the bog before me, and I'm trying can I find him."

As the horsemen could not find Finn, and thought the old woman's head would do to carry back, they cut it off, and took it with them, saying: "This will satisfy the king."

Finn and Bran went on till they came to a great cave, in which they found a herd of goats. At the further end of the cave was a smoldering fire. The two lay down to rest.

A couple of hours later, in came a giant with a salmon in his hand. This giant was of awful height, he had but one eye, and that in the middle of his forehead, as large as the sun in heaven.

When he saw Finn, he called out: "Here, take this salmon and roast it. But be careful, for if you raise a single blister on it I'll cut the head off you. I've followed this salmon for three days and three nights without stopping, and I never let it out of my sight, for it is the most wonderful salmon in the world."

The giant lay down to sleep in the middle of the cave. Finn spitted the salmon, and held it over the fire.

The minute the giant closed the one eye in his head, he began to snore. Every time he drew breath into his body, he dragged Finn, the spit, the salmon, Bran, and all the goats to his mouth. And every time he drove a breath out of himself, he threw them back to the places they were in before. Finn was drawn time after time to the mouth of the giant with such force, that he was in dread of going down his throat.

When partly cooked, a blister rose on the salmon. Finn pressed the place with his thumb, to know could he break the blister, and hide from the giant the harm that was done. But he burned his thumb, and, to ease the pain, put it between his teeth, and gnawed the skin to the flesh, the flesh to the bone, the bone to the marrow. And when he had tasted the marrow, he received the knowledge of all things. Next moment, he was drawn by the breath of the giant right up to his face, and, knowing from his thumb what to do, he plunged the hot spit into the sleeping eye of the giant and destroyed it.

That instant the giant with a single bound was at the low entrance of the cave, and, standing with his back to the wall and a foot on each side of the opening, roared out: "You'll not leave this place alive."

Now Finn killed the largest goat, skinned him as quickly as he could, then putting the skin on himself he drove the herd to where the giant stood; the goats passed out one by one between his legs. When the great goat came the giant took him by the horns. Finn slipped from the skin, and ran out.

"Oh, you've escaped," said the giant, "but before we part let me make you a present."

"I'm afraid to go near you," said Finn. "If you wish to give me a present, put it out this way, and then go back."

The giant placed a ring on the ground, then went back. Finn took up the ring and put it on the end of his little finger above the first joint. It clung so firmly that no man in the world could have taken it off.

The giant then called out, "Where are you?"

"On Finn's finger," cried the ring. That instant the giant sprang at Finn and almost came down on his head, thinking in this way to crush him to bits. Finn sprang to a distance. Again the giant asked, "Where are you?"

"On Finn's finger," answered the ring.

Again the giant made a leap, coming down just in front of Finn. Many times he called and many times almost caught Finn, who could not escape with the ring on his finger. While in this terrible struggle, not knowing how to escape, Bran ran up and asked:

"Why don't you chew your thumb?"

Finn bit his thumb to the marrow, and then knew what to do. He took the knife with which he had skinned the goat, cut off his finger at the first joint, and threw it, with the ring still on, into a deep bog near by.

Again the giant called out, "Where are you?" and the ring answered, "On Finn's finger."

Straightway the giant sprang towards the voice, sank to his shoulders in the bog, and stayed there.

Finn with Bran now went on his way, and traveled till he reached a deep and thick wood, where a thousand horses were drawing timber, and men felling and preparing it.

"What is this?" asked Finn of the overseer of the workmen.

"Oh, we are building a dun for the king. We build one every day, and every night it is burned to the ground. Our king has an only daughter. He will give her to any man who will save the dun, and he'll leave him the kingdom at his death. If any man undertakes to save the dun and fails, his life must pay for it. The king will cut his head off. The best champions in Erin have tried and failed; they are now in the king's dungeons, a whole army of them, waiting the king's pleasure. He's going to cut the heads off them all in one day."

"Why don't you chew your thumb?" asked Bran.

Finn chewed his thumb to the marrow, and then knew that on the eastern side of the world there lived an old hag with her three sons, and every evening at nightfall she sent the youngest of these to burn the king's dun.

"I will save the king's dun," said Finn.

"Well," said the overseer, "better men than you have tried and lost their lives."

"Oh," said Finn, "I'm not afraid. I'll try for the sake of the king's daughter."

Now Finn, followed by Bran, went with the overseer to the king. "I hear you will give your daughter to the man who saves your dun," said Finn.

"I will," said the king. "But if he fails I must have his head."

"Well," said Finn, "I'll risk my head for the sake of your daughter. If I fail I'm satisfied." The king gave Finn food and drink; he supped, and after supper went to the dun.

"Why don't you chew your thumb?" said Bran. "Then you'll know what to do." He did. Then Bran took her place on the roof, waiting for the old woman's son. Now the old woman in the east told her youngest son to hurry on with his torches, burn the dun, and come back without delay; for the stirabout was boiling and he must not be too late for supper.

He took the torches, and shot off through the air with a wonderful speed. Soon he was in sight of the king's dun, threw the torches upon the thatched roof to set it on fire as usual.

That moment Bran gave the torches such a push with her shoulders, that they fell into the stream which ran around the dun, and were put out. "Who is this," cried the youngest son of the old hag, "who has dared to put out my lights, and interfere with my hereditary right?"

"I," said Finn, who stood in front of him. Then began a terrible battle between Finn and the old woman's son. Bran came down from the dun to help Finn. She bit and tore his enemy's back, stripping the skin and flesh from his head to his heels.

After a terrible struggle such as had not been in the world before that night, Finn cut the head off his enemy. But for Bran, Finn could never have conquered.

The time for the return of her son had passed; supper was ready. The old woman, impatient and angry, said to the second son: "You take torches and hurry on, see why your brother loiters. I'll pay him for this when he comes home! But be careful and don't do like him, or you'll have your pay too. Hurry back, for the stirabout is boiling and ready for supper."

He started off, was met and killed exactly as his brother, except that he was stronger and the battle fiercer. But for Bran, Finn would have lost his life that night.

The old woman was raging at the delay, and said to her eldest son, who had not been out of the house for years: (It was only in case of the greatest need that she sent him. He had a cat's head, and was called Pus an Chuine, "Puss of the Corner"; he was the eldest and strongest of all the brothers.) "Now take torches, go and see what delays your brothers. I'll pay them for this when they come home."

The eldest brother shot off through the air, came to the king's dun, and threw his torches upon the roof. They had just singed the straw a little, when Bran pushed them off with such force that they fell into the stream and were quenched.

"Who is this," screamed Cat-Head, "who dares to interfere with my ancestral right?"

"I," shouted Finn. Then the struggle began fiercer than with the second brother. Bran helped from behind, tearing the flesh from his head to his heels. But at length Cat-Head fastened his teeth into Finn's breast, biting and gnawing till Finn cut the head off. The body fell to the ground, but the head lived, gnawing as terribly as before. Do what they could it was impossible to kill it. Finn hacked and cut, but could neither kill nor pull it off. When nearly exhausted, Bran said:

"Why don't you chew your thumb?"

Finn chewed his thumb, and reaching the marrow knew that the old woman in the east was ready to start with torches to find her sons, and burn the dun herself, and that she had a vial of liquid with which she could bring the sons to life; and that nothing could free him from Cat-Head but the old woman's blood.

After midnight the old hag, enraged at the delay of her sons, started and shot through the air like lightning, more swiftly than her sons. She threw her torches from afar upon the roof of the dun. But Bran as before hurled them into the stream.

Now the old woman circled around in the air looking for her sons. Finn was getting very weak from pain and loss of blood, for Cat-Head was biting at his breast all the time.

Bran called out: "Rouse yourself, O Finn. Use all your power or we are lost! If the old hag gets a drop from the vial upon the bodies of her sons, they will come to life, and then we're done for."

Thus roused, Finn with one spring reached the old woman in the air, and swept the bottle from her grasp; which falling upon the ground was emptied.

The old hag gave a scream which was heard all over the world, came to the ground, and closed with Finn. Then followed a battle greater than the world had ever known before that night, or has ever seen since. Water sprang out of gray rocks, cows cast their calves even when they had none, and hard rushes grew soft in the remotest corner of Erin, so desperate was the fighting and so awful, between Finn and the old hag. Finn would have died that night but for Bran.

Just as daylight was coming Finn swept the head off the old woman, caught some of her blood, and rubbed it around Cat-Head, who fell off dead.

He rubbed his own wounds with the blood and was cured; then rubbed some on Bran, who had been singed with the torches, and she was as well as ever. Finn, exhausted with fighting, dropped down and fell asleep.

While he was sleeping the chief steward of the king came to the dun, found it standing safe and sound, and seeing Finn lying there asleep knew that he had saved it. Bran tried to waken Finn, pulled and tugged, but could not rouse him.

The steward went to the king, and said: "I have saved the dun, and I claim the reward."

"It shall be given you," answered the king. And straightway the steward was recognized as the king's son-in-law, and orders were given to make ready for the wedding.

Bran had listened to what was going on, and when her master woke, exactly at midday, she told him of all that was taking place in the castle of the king.

Finn went to the king, and said: "I have saved your dun, and I claim the reward."

"Oh," said the king, "my steward claimed the reward, and it has been given to him."

"He had nothing to do with saving the dun. I saved it," said Finn.

"Well," answered the king, "he is the first man who told me of its safety and claimed the reward."

"Bring him here. Let me look at him," said Finn.

He was sent for, and came. "Did you save the king's dun?" asked Finn. "I did," said the steward.

"You did not, and take that for your lies," said Finn; and striking him with the edge of his open hand he swept the head off his body, dashing it against the other side of the room, flattening it like paste on the wall.

"You are the man," said the king to Finn, "who saved the dun; yours is the reward. All the champions, and there is many a man of them, who have failed to save it are in the dungeons of my fortress; their heads must be cut off before the wedding takes place."

"Will you let me see them?" asked Finn.

"I will," said the king.

Finn went down to the men, and found the first champions of Erin in the dungeons. "Will you obey me in all things if I save you from death?" said Finn. "We will," said they. Then he went back to the king and asked:

"Will you give me the lives of these champions of Erin, in place of your daughter's hand?"

"I will," said the king.

All the champions were liberated, and left the king's castle that day. Ever after they followed the orders of Finn, and these were the beginning of his forces and the first of the Fenians of Erin.

❖ ❖ ❖

❖ THE HIGH KING OF LOCHLANN AND THE FENIANS OF ERIN

KERRY

JEREMIAH CURTIN *1892*

A High King and renowned warrior named Colgán Mac Teine ruled over the four kingdoms of Lochlann. One day he summoned a meeting on the green plain before his castle. The best men and great nobles gathered around him, and the King spoke to them in a clear loud voice.

"Nobles of Lochlann," said he, "as you are now here, tell me, do you find fault with my rule?"

"We find no fault," answered they.

"It is not the same with me," said the King. "I find fault with my own rule."

"What fault is that?" asked the nobles.

"It is this: I am called King of Nations, and the nations are not all paying me tribute."

"What nation is it that pays you no tribute?"

"Green Erin, possessed by my forefathers, and it is there that Balor, the grandson of Neid, fell. Balor, High King of Lochlann, and his wife, Ceithlin, and Breac, the son of Balor, and many more whose names I do not mention at present. What I wish now is to bring Erin to obedience and to tribute to myself and my posterity."

"That is a good thought," said all the nobles, "and we are ready to help you enforce it."

With that the King gave command to meet in one place and prepare ships and provisions. Then the warriors drew out all their ships, well fastened and not easily broken. The King embarked. They raised broad and strong sails to the tops of the masts and went toward Erin with the wind till they reached the deepest sea; there waves came rolling on them, waves like hills and mountains. The wind answered the waves in the way that it put dread into the champions. When the storm was over and the sea calm they landed in Uladh. It was Cormac Mac Airt who was ruling in Erin at that time.

When Cormac heard that strong ships had come to Uladh he sent a message to Finn MacCumhail to Almhuin. Finn summoned Fenians from all parts and hurried forward to meet the High King of Lochlann. A bloody battle followed without victory for any side till Oscar, enraged at the slaughter of the Fenians, sought the High King of Lochlann on the field and found him. The King stood forth to meet Oscar, and, though strong were the spears that the two champions carried, they were soon shattered.

They drew their swords then and fought fiercely. At last Oscar got a blow on the King of Lochlann and took the head off him.

The oldest son of the King rushed against Oscar and fought wonderfully and with endurance, till Oscar, ashamed that any man should stand so long against him, got a blow on the neck of his enemy and swept the head from him. The body fell on one side and the head on other.

Now Finn and the reserve of the Fenians rushed against the men of Lochlann, and no foreigner escaped but the youngest son of the King. That boy was spared, and his name was Míogach Mac Colgáin. Finn promised to give him the two best pieces of land in Erin, and the two pieces that Míogach chose were one an island in the Shannon, and the other a piece on the mainland straight opposite.

Míogach lived with Finn fourteen years, till one day Conán spoke up and said:

"You are doing a foolish thing to keep the son of the King of Lochlann in your company. You must know well the hatred that he bears us. His father and brothers and many friends were slain by the Fenians. 'Tis better to give what you promised, and let him do for himself from this out."

"That is good counsel," said Finn and the others.

The King's son was called in.

"Go," said Finn to him, "and do for yourself from this out. Build a house, and I will give you the tribute of the two districts.

Míogach did this. In the two places which he had chosen were two fine harbors, and he had every chance to bring forces there. He had planned to bring men from other nations to destroy the Fenians and take Erin, for he was filled with hatred against Finn and his champions, and though he had spent fourteen years with them never did he offer food or drink to any man.

On a day, some years after he had sent away Míogach, Finn and the Fenians went hunting in the south, and Finn sat down at Cnoc Fírinne. He was not long sitting when he saw a man coming toward him with a sword at his side and a shield on his shoulder. He seemed a great champion, so large of limb was he and heavy. He saluted Finn kindly. Finn answered in like manner, and asked: "Have you any tale of news for me?"

"I have no tale to tell you," said the man.

"Who are you?" asked Finn.

"Do you not know him?" asked Conán.

"I do not," replied Finn.

"You ought to know him," said Conán, "because it is for you to know friends and enemies, and that man is Míogach Mac Colgáin, son of the King of Lochlann, and your greatest enemy. It is now fourteen years since he left you, and he has never offered meat or drink to you or any champion of Erin in that time."

"I am not to blame," said Míogach. "I was not any month of fourteen years without having a good dinner in my house ready to be eaten, and I have a good dinner now for you, O Finn, and unless you come to it I will put on you an injunction that a champion cannot bear. I have two houses, one on the mainland and one on the island, but do you come to the house on the mainland."

Finn was satisfied, and taking a few men, went with Míogach. He had left Oisín and the main Fenian army at Sliabh na mBan. Finn and his company found Míogach's house lined with rich silk, and every part was in the noblest colors, in the way that Conán praised it greatly. They put aside their arms, and when all were seated Míogach left them and closed the door behind him. The Fenians sat and waited long.

" 'Tis a wonder to me," said Finn, "that they keep us here all this time without food or drink."

"It is on the island they are preparing the dinner," said Goll. "When 'tis ready they will bring it."

"There is a greater wonder," said a champion from Leinster. "The fire that gave such a sweet odor when we came has the smell now of bodies in decay, and gives more smoke than we have seen in any place hitherto."

"There is a greater wonder still," said Glas Mac Aonchearda. "The house planks were of noblest colors when we entered. Now they have but one color, and are fastened with hazel twigs."

"Here is a wonder beyond all," said Faolán. "The house that had seven doors when we came has no door now but the one, and that on the north side letting in snow and wind. There is a greater wonder than that. Stuffs which we sat on are gone. There is nothing now under us but the earth, and it colder than snow at daybreak."

"We are under sentence," said Finn, "to be in the house of one door, called the Quicken Fort, and do you rise and leave the house in haste."

"We will," said Conán, and he started, but could not move from his place.

"We are tied to the earth," cried Conán.

"Finn," said Goll, "put your thumb between your teeth and grind it to know where we are."

Finn chewed his thumb and soon he was lamenting.

"Is it from pain in your thumb that you are lamenting?" asked Goll.

"It is not," said Finn. "I am lamenting because whatever time was given to me to be in this world is up now. The son of the King of Lochlann has been fourteen years preparing this house for our death. He has brought great champions in ships from all parts. The High King of the World is here with his forces. Sinnsior na gCath from Greece and twenty-six kings with him, and every king of them has twenty-six battalions and could give twenty-six battles, and there are thirty great champions in each battalion. There are also three kings from Inis Tuile, the Island of the Flood, and they are equal to three evil dragons; and three other great champions who cannot be taken in battle or in any other place. They are called Neim, Aig, Aitceas. It was the last three who put under us the enchantment that tied us to the earth where we are, and there is nothing to release us but to rub us with the blood of the three kings from the Island of the Flood, and this is most difficult to do, for we are far from our friends."

After these words all the Fenians were weeping, sighing, and lamenting for a long time.

"It is as well for us," said Finn, at last, "to have courage in time of death. We have no more to get in this world beyond what has come to us already. And do you sound the *dord-fhiann* as mournfully as you can before death."

Then they brought their mouths as near together as possible and sounded the *dord-fhiann.*

"Who will go now and bring news from the Fenians?" asked Oisín on the top of Sliabh na mBan.

"I will go," said Fia, son of Finn.

"I will go with you," said Insin Mac Suibhne.

Those two went with all their speed, and when near the house they heard the plaintive sounds inside.

"They must be treated well to be sounding the *dord-fhiann*!" said Insin.

"It is what you mean that it is very badly they are treated," said Fia. "I know the *dord-fhiann*, and it is only in time of great peril that they sound it."

When both came near Finn heard them and asked:

"Is this the voice of Fia that I hear?"

"It is, indeed."

"Do not come near us," said Finn, "for we are tied to the earth with enchantment."

Here he told Fia what had been done to them.

"Who is that with you?" asked Finn.

"Your foster son, Insin."

"My dear son," said Finn, "take my foster child away at once, do not leave him here longer exposed to the foreigners."

"It would be unseemly to treat my foster father thus and leave him bound and I free," said Insin.

"If you are unwilling to leave me," said Finn, "go with Fia and defend the ford if you are able till the Fenians come."

Then the two went to the ford.

"Guard this place well," said Fia to Insin, "and I will go to the house on the island to know what is passing there."

Fia set out, and at that very moment the Grecian champion was speaking on the island and what he said was this:

"I will go now for the head of Finn Mac Cumhail and bring it to the High King of the World."

The champion took one hundred of his own men, and they stopped not nor halted till they came to the brink of the ford, and there they saw Insin, a man of the men of Finn Mac Cumhail.

"Guide me," said the champion to Insin. "Show me where Finn is, that I may take the head off him and the heads off those who are with him and bring them to the King of the World."

"A very bad watchman indeed should I be for Finn Mac Cumhail to do that, and if you come hither it will be to find death," said Insin.

They went against Insin then and he gave them a great battle. Insin was destroying and slaying till the hundred had fallen. The Greek now fought furiously, and Insin was full of wounds and wearied, so he fell by the Greek.

"I will go for more men," said the champion to himself, "and then I will take the head of Finn Mac Cumhail to the High King."

On the way to the island he met Fia, the son of Finn.

"From what place are you coming?" asked Fia.

"I went from the island for the head of Finn Mac Cumhail, and I met a great champion in arms at the brink of the ford and he killed one hundred strong men of mine before I was able to slay him."

"I wonder greatly that yourself did not fall like the others," said Fia.

"Only strength and valor saved me, and he fell by me," said the Greek.

"If he fell by you, you have something of his to prove the deed."

"I brought his head, and think that the best token."

"Show me the head."

The Greek showed it.

"That head was beautiful this morning," said Fia, kissing it. "Do you know to whom you have given the head?"

"I do not," said the Greek, "and I care not. You are one of the High King's men, I suppose."

"I am not," answered Fia, "and you will not be his man long."

They turned at each other full of wrath and anger, and fought like two venomous wild beasts till Fia swept the head off his enemy. He went to the house, and spoke at the door.

"This is the voice of Fia," said Finn. "And who made the great noise and shouting at the ford?"

"Your foster son made most of it," replied Fia.

"How is my foster son after the combat?"

"He is dead," said Fia.

"Did you see them killing him?"

"If I had seen them I should have saved him if I could."

"And were you able to harm those who killed him?"

"I took the head off the man who slew him and brought it with me."

"I give you my blessing," said Finn. "It is a great deed that you have done. We have no one between us and death now but you, and keep the ford till the Fenians come."

Now another knight spoke up on the island, and his name was Cairbre Cathmhíle.

"My brothers went," said he, "for Finn's head, and I will go after them myself, for I am in dread that the poison of the Fenians will harm them."

He went on then and four hundred men with him. They came to the ford and saw Fia standing there.

"Who are you?" asked Cairbre.

"One of Finn Mac Cumhail's men," said Fia.

"Tell me who made the great noise at the ford a while since?" inquired Cairbre.

" 'Tis a bad question you ask, and I will not answer it."

"Cross the ford and bring me the head of that champion," said Cairbre to his men.

Fia met them boldly and furiously; he fought proudly and with great strength. The battle lasted a long time, but the end of it was that Cairbre fell, and the four hundred fell with him. Fia sat down on the brink of the ford, full of wounds and blood from that cruel battle.

"Those men did badly to go without me," said Míogach, son of the King of Lochlann. "I will go myself now with five hundred prime warriors and take food for three hundred, because among the Fenians is a man called Conán, and there is not another in the world who cares so much for his belly as that man. When people will be eating before him he will go mad at sight of food, and he not able to taste it."

Míogach took five hundred men, the best warriors. On coming to the ford they saw Fia at the brink.

"Is that Fia?" asked Míogach.

"It is, indeed," said Fia.

"It is a good man that is there," said Míogach. "I was fourteen years with Finn. You never beat a hound or a dog of mine."

"Still there is not among the Fenians a man whom you love less than me," said Fia. "You should wish well to the Fenians after what has been done for you."

"It is not sweet to me that men slew my father and two brothers. I will not let that go with the Fenians. I must have vengeance."

"Take care," said Fia, "that it is not on yourself the vengeance will turn."

"Leave the ford," said Míogach, quickly.

"It is with trouble for you that I am here," replied Fia, "if you come against me; but I am without malice to every man who will keep away from this ford. Sorry am I that I did not meet you before my body was wounded and weary."

Now Míogach moved forward like a hound full of hunger, rushing with open mouth after sheep, and his men were just like him. A fierce battle followed without gain to either side. When Fia had cut down three hundred men Míogach closed with him.

Said Oisín to those who stood with him at Sliabh na mBan: "I think it is too long that we are without an account of Finn and the men who are with him."

"I suppose it is a good dinner that is before them and they unwilling to leave it," said one of the men.

"It is not eating but defending themselves they are, as it seems to me," said Diarmuid. "I will go for tidings."

"I will go with you," said Fatha Conán.

The two went with great speed till they came near the ford and heard shouting of men.

"I hear shouting very near the house and the voice of Fia, I think. Let us hurry to help him," said Diarmuid.

The two went on swiftly to where they heard the cries, and they came up to Fia. All his weapons were gone except what he held in his two hands, and Míogach going to strike the head off him.

"Diarmuid," said Fatha Conán, "save his life for the son of Finn Mac Cumhail. Were I to wait till I cross the ford I should not find him alive, and if I cast a spear I know not which of the two I may hit. You never missed with a spear, and see what you can do now."

Then Diarmuid settled himself, and sent his spear through the middle of Míogach's side.

"A pity," said the son of the King of Lochlann, "for the man who set the cast of that spear, and it is the spear of Diarmuid that struck me."

"It is, indeed," said Diarmuid, "and to keep Fia from death."

"I will take his head from him," said Míogach, "for what he did to my people."

With that he struck the head from Fia's body.

Diarmuid rushed up then and closed with Míogach. There was a fierce battle, and fought without gain to either side, till at last Diarmuid's spirit rose, and he slew the son of the King of Lochlann. Next he went at the two hundred of the five hundred, and did not leave one without killing to give an account of the battle. Then Diarmuid and Fatha Conán brought the head of the son of the King of Lochlann, and spoke at the door of the house.

"Is that Diarmuid?" asked Finn.

"It is," said Diarmuid.

"Who made that dreadful shouting outside?" asked Finn.

"Your son made most of it, and he felled three hundred strong champions."

"How is my son now?" asked Finn.

"He is killed," replied Diarmuid. "Fatha Conán and I slew the two hundred more who were against your son."

"Did you see his enemy killing my son?"

"I did," said Diarmuid, "but he was killed before I could go to him."

"Who killed my son?"

"Míogach Mac Colgáin."

"Did you see Míogach go away after killing my son?"

"He did not go away, for I took the head off him."

"My blessing on you," said Finn. "We are here under your protection, and we have never been in peril but you released us."

"I will protect you till morning," said Diarmuid.

"Do you and Fatha Conán defend the ford till my son Oisín and the others come."

"Is it going you are, Diarmuid?" asked Conán.

"It is, indeed," said Diarmuid.

"I don't like that," said Conán, "because the clay that is under me is colder than the coldest snow in the morning. Though I think what I am suffering from hunger and thirst is far worse than the cold. The best of food and drink that Míogach had is saved for his men and the foreigners. Do you bring some of it hither."

"It is a pity to ask that of me, and the best men of the world coming to destroy us and nobody watching but Fatha Conán and myself."

"Ah, Diarmuid of the Women," said Conán. "If it was a young beauty who asked, you would bring her the food, but you do not care to bring it to me or any man here."

"Conán," said Diarmuid, "you took four women from me in your time, and you would take more if you could. Vex me no further, and I will bring you food if I find it."

The two went to the ford.

"Fatha Conán," said Diarmuid, "it was prophesied that you would bind the whole world. If you do not begin well you will do well at the end of the night. Watch the ford till I get food for Conán."

"You have never found food so easily as you will now," said Fatha Conán, "because there is food for three hundred men at the brink of the ford, and they did not eat it. They had not time."

"If I were to carry that to Conán he would dispraise it, call it the food of dead men, but I will take it to him in any case."

Diarmuid went to Conán and called through the door: "I have brought food, and know not how to give it to you."

"It was a mistake in you, Diarmuid, to bring me the food of dead men. Provoke me no further."

"If it causes my death I will go," said Diarmuid. "And, Fatha Conán, do you watch the ford while I go to the house on the island."

Diarmuid went and found Borb Mac Sinnsior with his men and they eating supper outside. Diarmuid saw the King drinking out of vessels of gold, and every man there had a beautiful vessel. Diarmuid went past Borb and seized the goblet that had been in his hand. He went next to the High King of the World, struck him in the pit of the stomach, and knocked him to the floor.

"If there were men looking on I would take your head," cried Diarmuid, seizing the dish from before the King, and it full of food.

Diarmuid departed so quickly that there was no man inside or outside who could stop him. He escaped without blood or wound, and stopped not nor halted till he went to the ford. Fatha Conán was fast asleep among the dead bodies.

When Diarmuid saw Fatha sleeping he said:

"There must be something against you to be sleeping tonight. I wish not to leave you, and if I stop to rouse you, Conán will dispraise me. I will take the food first."

Diarmuid went to the house and said: "I have food for you now, but I know not how I can place it before you."

"I am just opposite the door. You have never yet failed in making a cast," said Conán.

Diarmuid threw the dish to where Conán was, struck him between breast and mouth, so that his face was covered with the food on the plate.

"I am afraid I have soiled you!" said Diarmuid.

"That is all one to me," said Conán. "A hound never runs from a bone."

"I have a goblet of drink here. How am I to take that to you?"

"You must go to the housetop," said Conán. "There is no enchantment outside. Make a hole in the roof and pour the drink into my mouth."

Diarmuid rose with one leap to the housetop, made a hole, and spilled most of the drink on both sides of Conán's mouth.

"Ah, Diarmuid," said Conán, "if it was a young woman that was in it, in place of me, you would put the drink in her mouth, but you care not to put it in mine."

When Diarmuid heard this he grew in dread of Conán's talk, poured the rest of the drink into his mouth, sprang down, and went to guard the ford.

Now the three kings of the Island of the Flood spoke, and this is what they said: "It is bad that anyone went to Quicken Fort before us."

After that they rose up and said: "We must get liberty to go and strike their heads off the Fenians."

The kings took six hundred stout warriors and went to the ford. There they saw Diarmuid.

"Is that Diarmuid we see?"

"It is," said Diarmuid.

Then the kings spoke to one another, but in Diarmuid's hearing.

"We love Diarmuid," said they, "because we are nearly related to him, and the man is a hero. Never have we been in any place learning deeds of valor, but Diarmuid was with us."

"Give us liberty, O Diarmuid, for friendship's sake, to cross the ford."

"If you will give me liberty to go to the King of the World and bring his head with me I will let you cross the ford."

"We will not do that," replied they, "because we wish not mishap to our lord."

"Neither do I wish mishap to my lord."

"Leave the ford to us," said the kings, and they moved against Diarmuid. He fell on them furiously, and great heavy blows were exchanged, so that bodies were full of wounds and many men fell by Diarmuid in the battle, and Fatha Conán fast asleep. Then Fatha Conán rose up and was frightened at the shouting of men, the breaking of shields, and the sighing and groaning of champions and heroes who had fallen by the hand of Diarmuid. He seized his weapons, rushed forward, and thought to put his spear through Diarmuid for not waking him. Diarmuid dodged the blow and said:

"There is not a second man on earth from whom I would suffer such conduct."

Fatha Conán then met the kings' forces, and felled every man that he met. Diarmuid closed with the three kings, and he and the three fought against one another, and that was a dangerous and terrible battle for Diarmuid, he giving each king a blow and each king giving him a blow, but after a while he rose in courage in the way that he took the three heads off the kings.

The remnant of the six hundred fell by the hand of Fatha Conán.

Diarmuid and Fatha Conán took the three heads to the house then, and rubbed the blood of the kings on Finn and the men. All were freed except Conán. The blood was gone when they came to him.

"Is it here you will leave me?" asked Conán.

"It is not, indeed," said Diarmuid, giving a great pull to Conán, but he could not tear him free.

"Fatha," said Diarmuid, "help me to raise this man and take him forth."

Then Diarmuid and Fatha put their hands under Conán, and hardly were they able to take him from the ground, and if they did he left behind him the skin and the hair of his poll, the skin of his two shoulders, and the skin of the lower part of his body, and it is from that he was called "Conán, the cursed bald son of Mórna."

All the Fenians seemed near death, they looked so haggard, wretched, and weak.

"We are not fit to give battle till morning," said Finn. "Do you, Diarmuid, go to the ford with Fatha till morning, when some of our friends may come."

The two went to the ford, and by that time there were tidings from the fort on the island. The son of the King of the World, Borb Mac Sinnsior na gCath, rose up, and twenty hundred strong champions with him, and went to the ford.

"I think it too long to wait for news," said Oisín on Sliabh na mBan. "I must go myself."

And he went swiftly till he came near the ford and heard the sound of the great battle. Then he rushed on himself and met Borb, and Oisín got vexed so that his spirits rose and his strength grew in the way that he put the son of the King of the World under him and made him sigh, and then he took the head off his body.

Oisín was proud of the deed, and showed the head to his friend and the enemy. Finn and the Fenians came now from the Quicken Fort and slew those of the twenty hundred who had not fallen at the hands of Oisín, Diarmuid, and Fatha Conán.

When the people on the island discovered that all the men sent forward were slain they gave three heavy shouts of wailing. The King of the World moved and all his men with him, a great multitude, to give final battle.

When Oisín left Sliabh na mBan he commanded the Fenians to follow him to the Quicken Fort. All assembled in haste with their standards, and at the head of them Finn's standard, Scáil Gréine, Shadow of the Sun. They went forward speedily, but in good order of battle, and were nearing the ford at the same time with the High King of the World. The two forces met with spears and swords, and were slaying each other till the front half of each army was lying on the earth.

Goll, son of Mórna, and Sinnsior na gCath met then in the center of the field. Goll struck the head off his enemy and raised it aloft, boasting of the deed. The King's forces trembled at the sight and fled. The Fenians followed and hunted them. They left not a man to give account of the battle, but the man who escaped through forests or under rocks or who went by the swiftness of his feet to a ship. Those who escaped to the ships raised sails and hastened homeward, making no halt on the way. Many a strong hero was left dead on the field, and many a woman was weeping for a son, and many a woman was bewailing her husband, and many a woman lost her mind through terror and fled to the forests.

The Fenians themselves suffered greatly. Many were slain and many terribly wounded.

This is what came of the war of Colgán Mac Teine and of the revenge of Míogach his son, and of the invasion of Sinnsior na gCath, High King of the World. They thought to destroy Finn and the Fenians with slaughter and enchantments, and this was the end of their efforts.

❖ USHEEN'S RETURN TO IRELAND

GALWAY
LADY GREGORY *1926*

Usheen was the last of the Fianna and the greatest of them. It's he was brought away to Tir-Nan-Oge, that place where you'd stop for a thousand years and be as young as the first day you went.

Out hunting they were, and there was a deer came before them very often, and they would follow it with the hounds, and it would always make for the sea, and there was a rock a little way out in the water, and it would leap on to that, and they wouldn't follow it.

So one day they were going to hunt, they put Usheen out on the rock first, the way he could catch a hold of the deer and be there before it. So they found it and followed it, and when it jumped on to the rock Usheen got a hold of it. But it went down into the sea and brought him with it to some enchanted place underground that was called Tir-Nan-Oge, and there he stopped a very long time, but he thought it was only a few days he was in it.

It is in that direction, to the west he was brought, and it was to the Clare coast he came back. And in that place you wouldn't feel the time passing, and he saw the beauty of heaven and kept his youth there a thousand years.

It is a fine place, and everything that is good is in it. And if anyone is sent there with a message he will want to stop in it, and twenty years of it will seem to him like one half-hour. But as to where Tir-Nan-Oge is, it is in every place, all about us.

Well, when he thought he had been a twelvemonth there, he began to wish to see the strong men again, his brothers; and he asked whoever was in authority in that place to give him a horse and to let him go.

And they told him his brothers were all dead, but he wouldn't believe it.

So they gave him a horse, but they bade him not to get off it or to touch the ground while he would be away; and they put him back in his own country.

And when he went back to his old place, there was nothing left of the houses but broken walls, and they covered with moss; and all his friends and brothers were dead, with the length of time that had passed.

And where his own home used to be he saw the stone trough standing that used to be full of water, and where they used to be putting their hands in and washing themselves.

And when he saw it he had such a wish and such a feeling for it that he forgot what he was told and got off the horse.

And in a minute it was as if all the years came on him, and he was lying there on the ground, a very old man and all his strength gone.

❖ FAIR, BROWN, AND TREMBLING

GALWAY

JEREMIAH CURTIN *1887*

King Aedh Cúrucha lived in Tir Conal, and he had three daughters, whose names were Fair, Brown, and Trembling.

Fair and Brown had new dresses, and went to church every Sunday. Trembling was kept at home to do the cooking and work. They would not let her go out of the house at all; for she was more beautiful than the other two, and they were in dread she might marry before themselves.

They carried on in this way for seven years. At the end of seven years the son of the king of Omanya fell in love with the eldest sister.

One Sunday morning, after the other two had gone to church, the old henwife came into the kitchen to Trembling, and said: "It's at church you ought to be this day, instead of working here at home."

"How could I go?" said Trembling. "I have no clothes good enough to wear at church. And if my sisters were to see me there, they'd kill me for going out of the house."

"I'll give you," said the henwife, "a finer dress than either of them has ever seen. And now tell me what dress will you have?"

"I'll have," said Trembling, "a dress as white as snow, and green shoes for my feet."

Then the henwife put on the cloak of darkness, clipped a piece from the old clothes the young woman had on, and asked for the whitest robes in the world and the most beautiful that could be found, and a pair of green shoes.

That moment she had the robe and the shoes, and she brought them to Trembling, who put them on. When Trembling was dressed and ready, the henwife said: "I have a honey-bird here to sit on your right shoulder, and a honey-finger to put on your left. At the door stands a milk-white mare, with a golden saddle for you to sit on, and a golden bridle to hold in your hand."

Trembling sat on the golden saddle. And when she was ready to start, the henwife said: "You must not go inside the door of the church, and the minute the people rise up at the end of Mass, do you make off, and ride home as fast as the mare will carry you."

When Trembling came to the door of the church there was no one inside who could get a glimpse of her but was striving to know who she was; and when they saw her hurrying away at the end of Mass, they ran out to overtake her. But no use in their running; she was away before any man could come near her. From the minute she left the church till she got home, she overtook the wind before her, and outstripped the wind behind.

She came down at the door, went in, and found the henwife had dinner ready. She put off the white robes, and had on her old dress in a twinkling.

When the two sisters came home the henwife asked: "Have you any news today from the church?"

"We have great news," said they. "We saw a wonderful, grand lady at the church door. The like of the robes she had we have never seen on woman before. It's little that was thought of our dresses beside what she had on. And there wasn't a man at the church, from the king to the beggar, but was trying to look at her and know who she was."

The sisters would give no peace till they had two dresses like the robes of the strange lady; but honey-birds and honey-fingers were not to be found.

Next Sunday the two sisters went to church again, and left the youngest at home to cook the dinner.

After they had gone, the henwife came in and asked: "Will you go to church today?"

"I would go," said Trembling, "if I could get the going."

"What robe will you wear?" asked the henwife.

"The finest black satin that can be found, and red shoes for my feet."

"What color do you want the mare to be?"

"I want her to be so black and so glossy that I can see myself in her body."

The henwife put on the cloak of darkness, and asked for the robes and the mare. That moment she had them. When Trembling was dressed, the henwife put the honey-bird on her right shoulder and the honey-finger on her left. The saddle on the mare was silver, and so was the bridle.

When Trembling sat in the saddle and was going away, the henwife ordered her strictly not to go inside the door of the church, but to rush away as soon as the people rose at the end of Mass, and hurry home on the mare before any man could stop her.

That Sunday the people were more astonished than ever, and gazed at her more than the first time, and all they were thinking of was to know who she was. But they had no chance, for the moment the people rose at the end of Mass she slipped from the church, was in the silver saddle, and home before a man could stop her or talk to her.

The henwife had the dinner ready. Trembling took off her satin robe, and had on her old clothes before her sisters got home.

"What news have you today?" asked the henwife of the sisters when they came from the church.

"Oh, we saw the grand strange lady again! And it's little that any man could think of our dresses after looking at the robes of satin that she had on! And all at church, from high to low, had their mouths open, gazing at her, and no man was looking at us."

The two sisters gave neither rest nor peace till they got dresses as nearly like the strange lady's robes as they could find. Of course they were not so good, for the like of those robes could not be found in Erin.

When the third Sunday came, Fair and Brown went to church dressed in black satin. They left Trembling at home to work in the kitchen, and told her to be sure and have dinner ready when they came back.

After they had gone and were out of sight, the henwife came to the kitchen and said: "Well, my dear, are you for church today?"

"I would go if I had a new dress to wear."

"I'll get you any dress you ask for. What dress would you like?" asked the henwife.

"A dress red as a rose from the waist down, and white as snow from the waist up; a cape of green on my shoulders; and a hat on my head with a red, a white, and a green feather in it; and shoes for my feet with the toes red, the middle white, and the backs and heels green."

The henwife put on the cloak of darkness, wished for all these things, and had them. When Trembling was dressed, the henwife put the honey-bird on her right shoulder and the honey-finger on her left, and placing the hat on her head, clipped a few hairs from one lock and a few from another with her scissors, and that moment the most beautiful golden hair was flowing down over the girl's shoulders. Then the henwife asked what kind of a mare she would ride. She said white, with blue and gold-colored diamond-shaped spots all over her body, on her back a saddle of gold, and on her head a golden bridle.

The mare stood there before the door, and a bird sitting between her ears, which began to sing as soon as Trembling was in the saddle, and never stopped till she came home from the church.

The fame of the beautiful strange lady had gone out through the world, and all the princes and great men that were in it came to church that Sunday, each one hoping that it was himself would have her home with him after Mass.

The son of the king of Omanya forgot all about the eldest sister, and remained outside the church, so as to catch the strange lady before she could hurry away.

The church was more crowded than ever before, and there were three times as many outside. There was such a throng before the church that Trembling could only come inside the gate.

As soon as the people were rising at the end of Mass, the lady slipped out through the gate, was in the golden saddle in an instant, and sweeping away ahead of the wind. But if she was, the prince of Omanya was at her side, and, seizing her by the foot, he ran with the mare for thirty perches, and never let go of the beautiful lady till the shoe was pulled from her foot, and he was left behind with it in his hand. She came home as fast as the mare could carry her, and was thinking all the time that the henwife would kill her for losing the shoe.

Seeing her so vexed and so changed in the face, the old woman asked: "What's the trouble that's on you now?"

"Oh! I've lost one of the shoes off my feet," said Trembling.

"Don't mind that; don't be vexed," said the henwife. "Maybe it's the best thing that ever happened to you."

Then Trembling gave up all the things she had to the henwife, put on her old clothes, and went to work in the kitchen. When the sisters came home, the henwife asked: "Have you any news from the church?"

"We have indeed," said they; "for we saw the grandest sight today. The strange lady came again, in grander array than before. On herself and the horse she rode were the finest colors of the world, and between the ears of the horse was a bird which never stopped singing from the time she came till she went away. The lady herself is the most beautiful woman ever seen by man in Erin."

After Trembling had disappeared from the church, the son of the king of Omanya said to the other kings' sons: "I will have that lady for my own."

They all said: "You didn't win her just by taking the shoe off her foot, you'll have to win her by the point of the sword. You'll have to fight for her with us before you can call her your own."

"Well," said the son of the king of Omanya, "when I find the lady that shoe will fit, I'll fight for her, never fear, before I leave her to any of you."

Then all the kings' sons were uneasy, and anxious to know who was she that lost the shoe; and they began to travel all over Erin to know could they find her. The prince of Omanya and all the others went in a great company together, and made the round of Erin. They went everywhere—north, south, east, and west. They visited every place where a woman was to be found, and left not a house in the kingdom they did not search, to know could they find the woman the shoe would fit, not caring whether she was rich or poor, of high or low degree.

The prince of Omanya always kept the shoe. And when the young women saw it, they had great hopes, for it was of proper size, neither large nor small, and it would beat any man to know of what material it was made. One thought it would fit her if she cut a little from her great toe; and another, with too short a foot, put something in the tip of her stocking. But no use, they only spoiled their feet, and were curing them for months afterwards.

The two sisters, Fair and Brown, heard that the princes of the world were looking all over Erin for the woman that could wear the shoe, and every day they were talking of trying it on. And one day Trembling spoke up and said: "Maybe it's my foot that the shoe will fit."

"Oh, the breaking of the dog's foot on you! Why say so when you were at home every Sunday?"

They were that way waiting, and scolding the younger sister, till the princes were near the place. The day they were to come, the sisters put Trembling in a closet, and locked the door on her. When the company came to the house, the prince of Omanya gave the shoe to the sisters. But though they tried and tried, it would fit neither of them.

"Is there any other young woman in the house?" asked the prince.

"There is," said Trembling, speaking up in the closet. "I'm here."

"Oh! we have her for nothing but to put out the ashes," said the sisters.

But the prince and the others wouldn't leave the house till they had seen her. So the two sisters had to open the door. When Trembling came out, the shoe was given to her, and it fitted exactly.

The prince of Omanya looked at her and said: "You are the woman the shoe fits, and you are the woman I took the shoe from."

Then Trembling spoke up, and said: "Do you stay here till I return."

Then she went to the henwife's house. The old woman put on the cloak of darkness, got everything for her she had the first Sunday at church, and put her on the white mare in the same fashion. Then Trembling rode along the highway to the front of the house. All who saw her the first time said: "This is the lady we saw at church."

Then she went away a second time, and a second time came back on the black mare in the second dress which the henwife gave her. All who saw her the second Sunday said: "That is the lady we saw at church."

A third time she asked for a short absence, and soon came back on the third mare and in the third dress. All who saw her the third time said: "That is the lady we saw at church." Every man was satisfied, and knew that she was the woman.

Then all the princes and great men spoke up, and said to the son of the king of Omanya: "You'll have to fight now for her before we let her go with you."

"I'm here before you, ready for combat," answered the prince.

Then the son of the king of Lochlin stepped forth. The struggle began, and a terrible struggle it was. They fought for nine hours. And then the son of the king of Lochlin stopped, gave up his claim, and left the field. Next day the son of the king of Spain fought six hours, and yielded his claim. On the third day the son of the king of Nyerfói fought eight hours, and stopped. The fourth day the son of the king of Greece fought six hours, and stopped. On the fifth day no more strange princes wanted to fight. And all the sons of kings in Erin said they would not fight with a man of their own land, that the strangers had had their chance, and as no others came to claim the woman, she belonged of right to the son of the king of Omanya.

The marriage-day was fixed, and the invitations were sent out. The wedding lasted for a year and a day. When the wedding was over, the king's son brought home the bride, and when the time came a son was born. The young woman sent for her eldest sister, Fair, to be with her and care for her. One day, when Trembling was well, and when her husband was away hunting, the two sisters went out to walk. And when they came to the seaside, the eldest pushed the youngest sister in. A great whale came and swallowed her.

The eldest sister came home alone, and the husband asked, "Where is your sister?"

"She has gone home to her father in Ballyshannon. Now that I am well, I don't need her."

"Well," said the husband, looking at her, "I'm in dread it's my wife that has gone."

"Oh! no," said she. "It's my sister Fair that's gone."

Since the sisters were very much alike, the prince was in doubt. That night he put his sword between them, and said: "If you are my wife, this sword will get warm; if not, it will stay cold."

In the morning when he rose up, the sword was as cold as when he put it there.

It happened when the two sisters were walking by the seashore that a little cowboy was down by the water minding cattle, and saw Fair push Trembling into the sea; and next day, when the tide came in, he saw the whale swim up and throw her out on the sand. When she was on the sand she said to the cowboy: "When you go home in the evening with the cows, tell the master that my sister Fair pushed me into the sea yesterday; that a whale swallowed me, and then threw me out, but will come again and swallow me with the coming of the next tide; then he'll go out with the tide, and come again with tomorrow's tide, and throw me again on the strand. The whale will cast me out three times. I'm under the enchantment of this whale, and cannot leave the beach or escape myself. Unless my husband saves me before I'm swallowed the fourth time, I shall be lost. He must come and shoot the whale with a silver bullet when he turns on the broad of his back. Under the breast-fin of the whale is a reddish-brown spot. My husband must hit him in that spot, for it is the only place in which he can be killed."

When the cowboy got home, the eldest sister gave him a draught of oblivion, and he did not tell.

Next day he went again to the sea. The whale came and cast Trembling on shore again. She asked the boy: "Did you tell the master what I told you to tell him?"

"I did not," said he. "I forgot."

"How did you forget?" asked she.

"The woman of the house gave me a drink that made me forget."

"Well, don't forget telling him this night. And if she gives you a drink, don't take it from her."

As soon as the cowboy came home, the eldest sister offered him a drink. He refused to take it till he had delivered his message and told all to the master. The third day the prince went down with his gun and a silver bullet in it. He was not long down when the whale came and threw Trembling upon the beach as the two days before. She had no power to speak to her husband till he had killed the whale. Then the whale went out, turned over once on the broad of his back, and showed the spot for a moment only. That moment the prince fired. He had but the one chance, and a short one at that. But he took it, and hit the spot,and the whale, mad with pain, made the sea all around red with blood, and died.

That minute Trembling was able to speak, and went home with her husband, who sent word to her father what the eldest sister had done. The father came, and told him any death he chose to give her to give it. The prince told the father he would leave her life and death with himself. The father had her put out then on the sea in a barrel, with provisions in it for seven years.

In time Trembling had a second child, a daughter. The prince and she sent the cowboy to school, and trained him up as one of their own children, and said: "If the little girl that is born to us now lives, no other man in the world will get her but him."

The cowboy and the prince's daughter lived on till they were married. The mother said to her husband: "You could not have saved me from the whale but for the little cowboy. On that account I don't grudge him my daughter."

The son of the king of Omanya and Trembling had fourteen children, and they lived happily till the two died of old age.

❖ THE CORPSE WATCHERS

WEXFORD
PATRICK KENNEDY *1866*

There was once a poor woman that had three daughters, and one day the eldest said, "Mother, bake my cake and kill my cock, till I go seek my fortune." So she did, and when all was ready, says her mother to her, "Which will you have—half of these with my blessing, or the whole with my curse?" "Curse or no curse," says she, "the whole is little enough." So away she set, and if the mother didn't give her her curse, she didn't give her her blessing.

She walked and she walked till she was tired and hungry, and then she sat down to take her dinner. While she was eating it, a poor woman came up, and asked for a bit. "The dickens a bit you'll get from me," says she. "It's all too little for myself." And the poor woman walked away very sorrowful.

At nightfall she got lodging at a farmer's, and the woman of the house told her that she'd give her a spadeful of gold and a shovelful of silver if she'd only sit up and watch her son's corpse that was waking in the next room. She said she'd do that. And so, when the family were in their bed, she sat by the fire, and cast an eye from time to time on the corpse that was lying under the table.

All at once the dead man got up in his shroud, and stood before her, and said. "All alone, fair maid!" she gave him no answer, and when he said it the third time, he struck her with a switch, and she became a gray flag.

About a week after, the second daughter went to seek her fortune, and she didn't care for her mother's blessing no more nor her sister, and the very same thing happened to her. She was left a gray flag by the side of the other.

At last the youngest went off in search of the other two, and she took care to carry her mother's blessing with her. She shared her dinner with the poor woman on the road, and *she* told her that she would watch over her.

Well, she got lodging in the same place as the others, and agreed to mind the corpse. She sat up by the fire with the dog and cat, and amused herself with some apples and nuts the mistress gave her. She thought it a pity that the man under the table was a corpse, he was so handsome.

But at last he got up, and says he, "All alone, fair maid!" And she wasn't long about an answer:

"All alone I am not.
I've little dog Douse and Pussy, my cat;
I've apples to roast, and nuts to crack,
And all alone I am not."

"Ho, ho!" says he, "you're a girl of courage, though you wouldn't have enough to follow me. I am now going to cross the quaking bog, and go through the burning forest. I must then enter the cave of terror, and climb the hill of glass, and drop from the top of it into the Dead Sea."

"I'll follow you," says she, "for I engaged to mind you." He thought to prevent her, but she was as stiff as he was stout.

Out he sprang through the window, and she followed him till they came to the Green Hills, and then says he:

"Open, open, Green Hills, and let the Light of the Green Hills through."
"Aye," says the girl, "and let the fair maid, too."

They opened, and the man and woman passed through, and there they were, on the edge of a bog.

He trod lightly over the shaky bits of moss and sod. And while she was thinking of how she'd get across, the old beggar appeared to her, but much nicer dressed, touched her shoes with her stick, and the soles spread a foot on each side. So she easily got over the shaky marsh.

The burning wood was at the edge of the bog, and there the good fairy flung a damp, thick cloak over her, and through the flames she went, and a hair of her head was not singed.

Then they passed through the dark cavern of horrors, where she'd have heard the most horrible yells, only that the fairy stopped her ears with wax. She saw frightful things, with blue vapors round them, and felt the sharp rocks, and the slimy backs of frogs and snakes.

When they got out of the cavern, they were at the mountain of glass. And then the fairy made her slippers so sticky with a tap of her rod, that she followed the young corpse easily to the top. There was the deep sea a quarter of a mile under them, and so the corpse said to her, "Go home to my mother, and tell her how far you came to do her bidding. Farewell." He sprung head foremost down into the sea, and after him she plunged, without stopping a moment to think about it.

She was stupefied at first, but when they reached the waters she recovered her thoughts. After piercing down a great depth, they saw a green light towards the bottom. At last they were below the sea, that seemed a green sky above them; and sitting in a beautiful meadow, she half asleep, and her head resting against his side. She couldn't keep her eyes open, and she couldn't tell how long she slept. But when she woke, she was in bed at his house, and he and his mother sitting by her bedside, and watching her.

It was a witch that had a spite to the young man, because he wouldn't marry her, and so she got power to keep him in a state between life and death till a young woman would rescue him by doing what she had just done.

So at her request her sisters got their own shape again, and were sent back to their mother, with their spades of gold and shovels of silver. Maybe they were better after that, but I doubt it much.

The youngest got the young gentleman for her husband. I'm sure she deserved him, and, if they didn't live happy, *that we may*!

❖ A WIDOW'S SON

PAT DIRANE ◈ *GALWAY*
JOHN MILLINGTON SYNGE *1898*

There was once a widow living among the woods, and her only son living along with her. He went out every morning through the trees to get sticks, and one day as he was lying on the ground he saw a swarm of flies flying over what the cow leaves behind her. He took up his sickle and hit one blow at them, and hit that hard he left no single one of them living.

That evening he said to his mother that it was time he was going out into the world to seek his fortune, for he was able to destroy a whole swarm of flies at one blow, and he asked her to make him three cakes the way he might take them with him in the morning.

He started the next day a while after the dawn, with his three cakes in his wallet, and he ate one of them near ten o'clock.

He got hungry again by midday and ate the second, and when night was coming on him he ate the third. After that he met a man on the road who asked him where he was going.

"I'm looking for some place where I can work for my living," said the young man.

"Come with me," said the other man, "and sleep tonight in the barn, and I'll give you work tomorrow to see what you're able for."

The next morning the farmer brought him out and showed him his cows and told him to take them out to graze on the hills, and to keep good watch that no one should come near them to milk them. The young man drove out the cows into the fields, and when the heat of the day came on he lay down on his back and looked up into the sky. A while after he saw a black spot in the northwest, and it grew larger and nearer till he saw a great giant coming towards him.

He got up on to his feet and he caught the giant round the legs with his two arms, and he drove him down into the hard ground above his ankles, the way he was not able to free himself. Then the giant told him to do him no hurt, and gave him his magic rod, and told him to strike on the rock, and he would find his beautiful black horse, and his sword and his fine suit.

The young man struck the rock and it opened before him, and he found the beautiful black horse, and the giant's sword and the suit lying before him. He took out the sword alone, and he struck one blow with it and struck off the giant's head. Then he put back the sword into the rock, and went out again to his cattle, till it was time to drive them home to the farmer.

When they came to milk the cows they found a power of milk in them, and the farmer asked the young man if he had seen nothing out on the hills, for the other cowboys had been bringing home the cows with no drop of milk in them. And the young man said he had seen nothing.

The next day he went out again with the cows. He lay down on his back in the heat of the day, and after a while he saw a black spot in the northwest, and it grew larger and nearer, till he saw it was a great giant coming to attack him.

"You killed my brother," said the giant; "come here, till I make a garter of your body."

The young man went to him and caught him by the legs and drove him down into the hard ground up to his ankles.

Then he hit the rod against the rock, and took out the sword and struck off the giant's head.

That evening the farmer found twice as much milk in the cows as the evening before, and he asked the young man if he had seen anything. The young man said that he had seen nothing.

The third day the third giant came to him and said, "You have killed my two brothers; come here, till I make a garter of your body."

And he did with this giant as he had done with the other two, and that evening there was so much milk in the cows it was dropping out of their udders on the pathway.

The next day the farmer called him and told him he might leave the cows in the stalls that day, for there was a great curiosity to be seen, namely, a beautiful king's daughter that was to be eaten by a great fish, if there was no one in it that could save her. But the young man said such a sight was all one to him, and he went out with the cows on to the hills. When he came to the rock he hit it with his rod and brought out the suit and put it on him, and brought out the sword and strapped it on his side, like an officer, and he got on the black horse and rode faster than the wind till he came to where the beautiful king's daughter was sitting on the shore in a golden chair, waiting for the great fish.

When the great fish came in on the sea, bigger than a whale, with two wings on the back of it, the young man went down into the surf and struck at it with his sword and cut off one of its wings. All the sea turned red with the bleeding out of it, till it swam away and left the young man on the shore.

Then he turned his horse and rode faster than the wind till he came to the rock, and he took the suit off him and put it back in the rock, with the giant's sword and the black horse, and drove the cows down to the farm.

The man came out before him and said he had missed the greatest wonder ever was, and that a noble person was after coming down with a fine suit on him and cutting off one of the wings from the great fish.

"And there'll be the same necessity on her for two mornings more," said the farmer, "and you'd do right to come and look on it."

But the young man said he would not come.

The next morning he went out with his cows, and he took the sword and the suit and the black horse out of the rock, and he rode faster than the wind till he came where the king's daughter was sitting on the shore. When the people saw him coming there was great wonder on them to know if it was the same man they had seen the day before. The king's daughter called out to him to come and kneel before her, and when he kneeled down she took her scissors and cut off a lock of hair from the back of his head and hid it in her clothes.

Then the great fish came in from the sea, and he went down into the surf and cut the other wing off from it. All the sea turned red with the bleeding out of it, till it swam away and left them.

That evening the farmer came out before him and told him of the great wonder he had missed, and asked him would he go the next day and look on it. The young man said he would not go.

The third day he came again on the black horse to where the king's daughter was sitting on a golden chair waiting for the great fish. When it came in from the sea the young man went down before it, and every time it opened its mouth to eat him, he struck into its mouth, till his sword went out through its neck, and it rolled back and died.

Then he rode off faster than the wind, and he put the suit and the sword and the black horse into the rock, and drove home the cows.

The farmer was there before him and he told him that there was to be a great marriage feast held for three days, and on the third day the king's daughter would be married to the man that killed the great fish, if they were able to find him.

A great feast was held, and men of great strength came and said it was themselves were after killing the great fish.

But on the third day the young man put on the suit, and strapped the sword to his side like an officer, and got on the black horse and rode faster than the wind, till he came to the palace.

The king's daughter saw him, and she brought him in and made him kneel down before her. Then she looked at the back of his head and she saw the place where she had cut off the lock with her own hand. She led him in to the king, and they were married, and the young man was given all the estate.

That is my story.

❖ JACK AND BILL

AN OLD MAN ◈ *GALWAY*
WILLIAM BUTLER YEATS *1902*

There was a king one time who was very much put out because he had no son, and he went at last to consult his chief adviser. And the chief adviser said, "It's easy enough managed if you do as I tell you. Let you send someone," says he, "to such a place to catch a fish. And when the fish is brought in, give it to the queen, your wife, to eat."

So the king sent as he was told, and the fish was caught and brought in, and he gave it to the cook, and bade her put it before the fire, but to be careful with it, and not to let any blob or blister rise on it. But it is impossible to cook a fish before the fire without the skin of it rising in some place or other, and so there came a blob on the skin, and the cook put her finger on it to smooth it down, and then she put her finger into her mouth to cool it, and so she got a taste of the fish. And then it was sent up to the queen, and she ate it, and what was left of it was thrown out into the yard, and there was a mare in the yard and a greyhound, and they ate the bits that were thrown out.

And before the year was out, the queen had a young son, and the cook had a young son, and the mare had two foals, and the greyhound had two pups.

And the two young sons were sent out for a while to some place to be cared, and when they came back they were so much like one another no person could know which was the queen's son and which was the cook's. And the queen was vexed at that, and she went to the chief adviser and said, "Tell me some way that I can know which is my own son, for I don't like to be giving the same eating and drinking to the cook's son as to my own." "It is easy to know that," said the chief adviser, "if you will do as I tell you. Go you outside, and stand at the door they will be coming in by, and when they see you, your own son will bow his head, but the cook's son will only laugh."

So she did that, and when her own son bowed his head, her servants put a mark on him that she would know him again. And when they were all sitting at their dinner after that, she said to Jack, that was the cook's son, "It is time for you to go away out of this, for you are not my son." And her own son, that we will call Bill, said, "Do not send him away, are we not brothers?" But Jack said, "I would have been long ago out of this house if I knew it was not my own father and mother owned it." And for all Bill could say to him, he would not stop. But before he went, they were by the well that was in the garden, and he said to Bill, "If harm ever happens to me, that water on the top of the well will be blood, and the water below will be honey."

Then he took one of the pups, and one of the two horses, that was foaled after the mare eating the fish, and the wind that was after him could not catch him, and he caught the wind that was before him. And he went on till he came to a weaver's house, and he asked him for a lodging, and he gave it to him. And then he went on till he came to a king's house, and he sent in at the door to ask, "Did he want a servant?" "All I want," said the king, "is a boy that will drive out the cows to the field every morning, and bring them in at night to be milked." "I will do that for you," said Jack; so the king engaged him.

In the morning Jack was sent out with the four-and-twenty cows, and the place he was told to drive them to had not a blade of grass in it for them, but was full of stones. So Jack looked about for some place where there would be better grass, and after a while he saw a field with good green grass in it, and it belonging to a giant. So he knocked down a bit of the wall and drove them in, and he went up himself into an apple tree and began to eat the apples. Then the giant came into the field. "Fee-faw-fum," says he, "I smell the blood of an Irishman. I see you where you are, up in the tree," he said; "you are too big for one mouthful, and too small for two mouthfuls, and I don't know what I'll do with you if I don't grind you up and make snuff for my nose." "As you are strong, be merciful," says Jack up in the tree. "Come down out of that, you little dwarf," said the giant, "or I'll tear you and the tree asunder." So Jack came down. "Would you sooner be driving red-hot knives into one another's hearts," said the giant, "or would you sooner be fighting one another on red-hot flags?" "Fighting on red-hot flags is what I'm used to at home," said Jack, "and your dirty feet will be sinking in them and my feet will be rising." So then they began the fight. The ground that was hard they made soft, and the ground that was soft they made hard, and they made spring wells come up through the green flags. They were like that all through the day, no one getting the upper hand of the other, and at last a little bird came and sat on the bush and said to Jack, "If you don't make an end of him by sunset he'll make an end of you." Then Jack put out his strength, and he brought the giant down on his knees. "Give me my life," says the giant, "and I'll give you the three best gifts." "What are those?" said Jack. "A sword that nothing can stand against, and a suit that when you put it on, you will see everybody, and nobody will see you, and a pair of shoes that will make you run faster than the wind blows." "Where are they to be found?" said Jack. "In that red door you see there in the hill." So Jack went and got them out. "Where will I try the sword?" says he. "Try it on that ugly black stump of a tree," says the giant. "I see nothing blacker or uglier than your own head," says Jack.

And with that he made one stroke, and cut off the giant's head that it went into the air, and he caught it on the sword as it was coming down, and made two halves of it. "It is well for you I did not join the body again," said the head, "or you would have never been able to strike it off again." "I did not give you the chance of that," said Jack. And he brought away the great suit with him.

So he brought the cows home at evening, and everyone wondered at all the milk they gave that night. And when the king was sitting at dinner with the princess, his daughter, and the rest, he said, "I think I only hear two roars from beyond tonight in place of three."

The next morning Jack went out again with the cows, and he saw another field full of grass, and he knocked down the wall and let the cows in. All happened the same as the day before, but the giant that came this time had two heads, and they fought together, and the little bird came and spoke to Jack as before. And when Jack had brought the giant down, he said, "Give me my life, and I'll give you the best thing I have." "What is that?" says Jack. "It's a suit that you can put on, and you will see every one but no one can see you." "Where is it?" said Jack. "It's inside that little red door at the side of the hill." So Jack went and brought out the suit. And then he cut off the giant's two heads, and caught them coming down and made four halves of them. And they said it was well for him he had not given them time to join the body.

That night when the cows came home they gave so much milk that all the vessels that could be found were filled up.

The next morning Jack went out again, and all happened as before, and the giant this time had four heads, and Jack made eight halves of them. And the giant had told him to go to a little blue door in the side of the hill, and there he got a pair of shoes that when you put them on would go faster than the wind.

That night the cows gave so much milk that there were not vessels enough to hold it, and it was given to tenants and to poor people passing the road, and the rest was thrown out at the windows. I was passing that way myself, and I got a drink of it.

That night the king said to Jack, "Why is it the cows are giving so much milk these days? Are you bringing them to any other grass?" "I am not," said Jack "but I have a good stick, and whenever they would stop still or lie down, I give them blows of it, that they jump and leap over walls and stones and ditches; that's the way to make cows give plenty of milk."

And that night at the dinner, the king said, "I hear no roars at all."

The next morning, the king and the princess were watching at the window to see what would Jack do when he got to the field. And Jack knew they were there, and he got a stick, and began to batter the cows, that they went leaping and jumping over stones, and walls, and ditches. "There is no lie in what Jack said," said the king then.

Now there was a great serpent at that time used to come every seven years, and he had to get a king's daughter to eat, unless she would have some good man to fight for her. And it was the princess at the place Jack was had to be given to it that time, and the king had been feeding a bully underground for seven years, and you may believe he got the best of everything, to be ready to fight it.

And when the time came, the princess went out, and the bully with her down to the shore, and when they got there what did he do, but to tie the princess to a tree, the way the serpent would be able to swallow her easy with no delay, and he himself went and hid up in an ivy tree. And Jack knew what was going on, for the princess had told him about it, and had asked would he help her, but he said he would not. But he came out now, and he put on the suit he had taken from the first giant, and he came by the place the princess was, but she didn't know him. "Is that right for a princess to be tied to a tree?" said Jack. "It is not, indeed," said she, and she told him what had happened, and how the serpent was coming to take her. "If you will let me sleep for a while with my head in your lap," said Jack, "you could wake me when it is coming." So he did that, and she awakened him when she saw the serpent coming, and Jack got up and fought with it, and drove it back into the sea. And then he cut the rope that fastened her, and he went away. The bully came down then out of the tree, and he brought the princess to where the king was, and he said, "I got a friend of mine to come and fight the serpent today, where I was a little timorous after being so long shut up underground, but I'll do the fighting myself tomorrow."

The next day they went out again, and the same thing happened, the bully tied up the princess where the serpent could come at her fair and easy, and went up himself to hide in the ivy tree. Then Jack put on the suit he had taken from the second giant, and he walked out, and the princess did not know him, but she told him all that had happened yesterday, and how some young gentleman she did not know had come and saved her. So Jack asked might he lie down and take a sleep with his head in her lap, the way she could awake him. And all happened the same way as the day before. And the bully gave her up to the king, and said he had brought another of his friends to fight for her that day.

The next day she was brought down to the shore as before, and a great many people gathered to see the serpent that was coming to bring the king's daughter away. And Jack brought out the suit of clothes he had brought away from the third giant, and she did not know him, and they talked as before. But when he was asleep this time, she thought she would make sure of being able to find him again, and she took out her scissors and cut off a piece of his hair, and made a little packet of it and put it away. And she did another thing, she took off one of the shoes that was on his feet.

And when she saw the serpent coming she woke him, and he said, "This time I will put the serpent in a way that he will eat no more king's daughters." So he took out the sword he had got from the giant, and he put it in at the back of the serpent's neck, the way blood and water came spouting out that went for fifty miles inland, and made an end of him. And then he made off, and no one saw what way he went, and the bully brought the princess to the king, and claimed to have saved her, and it is he who was made much of, and was the right-hand man after that.

But when the feast was made ready for the wedding, the princess took out the bit of hair she had, and she said she would marry no one but the man whose hair could match that, and she showed the shoe and said that she would marry no one whose foot would not fit that shoe as well. And the bully tried to put on the shoe, but so much as his toe would not go into it, and as to his hair, it didn't match at all to the bit of hair she had cut from the man that saved her.

So then the king gave a great ball, to bring all the chief men of the country together to try would the shoe fit any of them. And they were all going to carpenters and joiners getting bits of their feet cut off to try could they wear the shoe, but it was no use, not one of them could get it on.

Then the king went to his chief adviser and asked what could he do. And the chief adviser bade him to give another ball, and this time he said, "Give it to poor as well as rich."

So the ball was given, and many came flocking to it, but the shoe would not fit any one of them. And the chief adviser said, "Is everyone here that belongs to the house?" "They are all here," said the king, "except the boy that minds the cows, and I would not like him to be coming up here."

Jack was below in the yard at the time, and he heard what the king said, and he was very angry, and he went and got his sword and came running up the stairs to strike off the king's head, but the man that kept the gate met him on the stairs before he could get to the king, and quieted him down, and when he got to the top of the stairs and the princess saw him, she gave a cry and ran into his arms. And they tried the shoe and it fitted him, and his hair matched to the piece that had been cut off. So then they were married, and a great feast was given for three days and three nights.

And at the end of that time, one morning there came a deer outside the window, with bells on it, and they ringing. And it called out, "Here is the hunt, where is the huntsman and the hound?" So when Jack heard that he got up and took his horse and his hound and went hunting the deer. When it was in the hollow he was on the hill, and when it was on the hill he was in the hollow, and that went on all through the day, and when night fell it went into a wood. And Jack went into the wood after it, and all he could see was a mud-wall cabin, and he went in, and there he saw an old woman, about two hundred years old, and she sitting over the fire. "Did you see a deer pass this way?" says Jack. "I did not," says she, "but it's too late now for you to be following a deer, let you stop the night here." "What will I do with my horse and my hound?" said Jack. "Here are two ribs of hair," says she, "and let you tie them up with them." So Jack went out and tied up the horse and the hound, and when he came in again the old woman said, "You killed my three sons, and I'm going to kill you now," and she put on a pair of boxing-gloves, each one of them nine stone weight, and the nails in them fifteen inches long. Then they began to fight, and Jack was getting the worst of it. "Help, hound!" he cried out, then "Squeeze, hair," cried out the old woman, and the rib of hair that was about the hound's neck squeezed him to death. "Help, horse!" Jack called out, then "Squeeze, hair," called out the old woman, and the rib of hair that was about the horse's neck began to tighten and squeeze him to death. Then the old woman made an end of Jack and threw him outside the door.

To go back now to Bill. He was out in the garden one day, and he took a look at the well, and what did he see but the water at the top was blood, and what was underneath was honey. So he went into the house again, and he said to his mother, "I will never eat a second meal at the same table, or sleep a second night in the same bed, till I know what is happening to Jack."

So he took the other horse and hound then, and set off, over hills where cock never crows and horn never sounds, and the Devil never blows his bugle. And at last he came to the weaver's house, and when he went in, the weaver says, "You are welcome, and I can give you better treatment than I did the last time you came in to me," for she thought it was Jack who was there, they were so much like one another. "That is good," said Bill to himself, "my brother has been here." And he gave the weaver the full of a basin of gold in the morning before he left.

Then he went on till he came to the king's house, and when he was at the door the princess came running down the stairs, and said, "Welcome to you back again." And all the people said, "It is a wonder you have gone hunting three days after your marriage, and to stop so long away." So he stopped that night with the princess, and she thought it was her own husband all the time.

And in the morning the deer came, and bells ringing on her, under the windows, and called out, "The hunt is here, where are the huntsmen and the hounds?" Then Bill got up and got his horse and his hound, and followed her over hills and hollows till they came to the wood, and there he saw nothing but the mud-wall cabin and the old woman sitting by the fire, and she bade him stop the night there, and gave him two ribs of hair to tie his horse and his hound with. But Bill was wittier than Jack was, and before he went out, he threw the ribs of hair into the fire secretly. When he came in the old woman said, "Your brother killed my three sons, and I killed him, and I'll kill you along with him." And she put her gloves on, and they began the fight, and then Bill called out, "Help, horse." "Squeeze, hair," called the old woman; "I can't squeeze, I'm in the fire," said the hair. And the horse came in and gave her a blow of his hoof. "Help, hound," said Bill then. "Squeeze, hair," said the old woman; "I can't, I'm in the fire," said the second hair. Then the hound put his teeth in her, and Bill brought her down, and she cried for mercy. "Give me my life," she said, "and I'll tell you where you'll get your brother again, and his hound and horse." "Where's that?" said Bill. "Do you see that rod over the fire?" said she; "take it down and go outside the door where you'll see three green stones, and strike them with the rod, for they are your brother, and his horse and hound, and they'll come to life again." "I will, but I'll make a green stone of you first," said Bill, and he cut off her head with his sword.

Then he went out and struck the stones, and sure enough there were Jack, and his horse and hound, alive and well. And they began striking other stones around, and men came from them, that had been turned to stones, hundreds and thousands of them.

Then they set out for home, but on the way they had some dispute or some argument together, for Jack was not well pleased to hear he had spent the night with his wife, and Bill got angry, and he struck Jack with the rod, and turned him to a green stone. And he went home, but the princess saw he had something on his mind, and he said then, "I have killed my brother." And he went back then and brought him to life, and they lived happy ever after, and they had children by the basketful, and threw them out by the shovelful. I was passing one time myself, and they called me in and gave me a cup of tea.

❖ THE MULE

AN OLD MAN ◈ *GALWAY*
LADY GREGORY *1910*

Well, I will tell you the story of a Mule was in the world one time.

There were three sons of a King that had died, and they were living together, and there was a stable and a bird, and one of the sons was a bit simple. The bird used to be coming to the stable every morning and to be singing sweetly, and they all three fell in love with it and used to be trying to take it, but they could not. But one day the one that was a bit simple, that they called the Fool, took the tail off it. The bird said to him then: "You must follow me now until you find me." And it went away, and he went following after it. And when he was on the height it was in the hollow, and when he was in the hollow it was on the height, and he never could come up with it; and at last it went out of his sight.

He came then to a wall, and he made a leap over it, and where did he come down but spread-legs on the back of a Mule that was in the field. "Are you a good jock?" says the Mule.

"I am middling good," says he.

"Hold on so," says the Mule, "and I will bring you to the place where the bird is."

There was a wall in front of them—a double wall—and the Mule faced it, and went over it with one leap, and the Fool on his back. "You are the best jock ever I saw," says the Mule.

"You are the best Mule ever I saw," says the Fool.

They went on then as far as they could through the course of the day, till the Mule said: "I'm hungry now; go get me a few grains of oats."

"How can I do that," says the Fool, "when I have no money?"

"Go in there to that inn and get it for me, as I told you," says the Mule.

"How much will do you?" says he.

"Seven stone," says the Mule.

So they stopped at the inn, and the Fool put him into the stable and bade the innkeeper to give him seven stone of oats. "Go in now and get your own dinner," says the Mule. So he went in and he got his dinner; and when he was ready to go, the innkeeper asked for the money. "I have none," says he.

"Well, I will keep the Mule in the stable till such time as you can pay me," says the innkeeper, and he went out and was going to lock the stable door, and the Mule gave a kick that broke his leg, and there he was lying on the ground.

"Come on now," says the Mule; and the Fool got up on his back, and away with them again, and they came to a wall that was five miles in height. "At it now," says the Fool, and the Mule faced at it and crossed it with one leap.

"You are a jock that can't be beat," says the Mule.

"You are a Mule that can't be beat," says the Fool.

There was before them a lake that was five miles in length and five miles in breadth. "I am thirsty now," says the Mule, "after that feed I had. And I'll stop now till I'll take a drink," he says.

"Do not," says the Fool, "or you will be heavy and not able to go."

"Wait till you see that," says the Mule.

So he stopped and he began to drink, and he never stopped till he had drunk up the whole of the lake that was five miles in length and five miles in breadth. They went on again till they came to a mountain that was before them, and the whole of the mountain was in one blaze, and there was a high wall before it, fifteen feet high.

"Hold on now," says the Mule.

"Here, at it," says the Fool, and the Mule crossed it with one leap; and when he came where the blaze was, he let out of his mouth all the water of the lake he had swallowed, and it quenched the blaze, and there they saw before them the bird. But if they did it went under ground, and the Mule followed it under ground into the enchanted place where it lived; and when they got there, it was not a bird, but the finest young lady that could be seen, and a King's daughter. The Fool asked her then to come along with him till he would marry her. "I will not," she said, "until such time as you will find my father, that I have hidden away from you."

So he brought the Mule out to the stable, and he didn't know where to go look for the King. And when they were in the stable the Mule said: "The young lady has a hen clutching, and the place where it is clutching is in her own room, under her bed. And under it you will find eleven eggs," he said, "and one of them is yellow and spotted. And take that one in your hand, and be going to smash it against the floor, and the King that is inside of it will cry out and will ask you to spare his life."

So he went looking for the hen, and all happened as the Mule had said.

"Will you marry me now?" says he to the young lady.

"I will not," says she, "till you find my father that I have hidden a second time."

So the place where she hid her father that time was in a duck's bill, and she put the duck out swimming in the middle of a pond.

The young man went then to the stable and asked the Mule did he know where the King was hidden, and the Mule told him it was in the duck's bill. "And look at my tail," he said, "and see is there e'er a gray rib in it."

So he looked, and there was a gray rib.

"Pull it out," says the Mule, "and bring it to the pond where the duck is, and throw it out over the water, and however far the duck is, that rib will bring it back to the land. And catch a hold of it then, and threaten to cut the neck of it, and the King will cry out from its bill and ask you to spare him."

So he did all that, and he spared the King, and then he went to the King's daughter.

"Will you marry me this time?" says he.

"I will not," says she, "till you find my father the third time."

The place she hid him the third time was in a block of wood, and the Mule said to the young man: "Take a nail out from my shoe and drive it into the block of wood till you will split it."

So he drew the nail, and he put it on the block of wood, and was going to split it, and the King called out for mercy, and he spared him.

After that he married the young lady, and himself and herself and the old King lived together, and there never were three people happier.

And the Mule said: "Where will I go now?"

"Go back," says the Fool, "to your own place, for you know the way well to it. But come back here at the end of seven years," he said, "till you'll see how I am getting on."

So at the end of the seven years the Mule came back, and he asked to be taken into service.

"I will never make a servant of you," says the Fool, "when I remember all the things you did for me, and all you helped me."

"If that is so," says the Mule, "go and root up that little bush you see beyond, and give me three blows with the stump of it."

So he did that, and with the three blows of the bush the enchantment went from the Mule, and who was he but the young man's own father, the King that was thought to be dead.

So they all four lived together then and ever since, and the time I saw them myself they were well and happy and having great riches.

❖ THE KING OF IRELAND'S SON

JOE ◈ *GALWAY*
BRENDAN BEHAN *1962*

Once upon a time, and a very good time it was too, when the streets were paved with penny loaves and houses were whitewashed with buttermilk and the pigs ran round with knives and forks in their snouts shouting: "Eat me, eat me!" there lived a King of Ireland and he had three sons named Art, Neart and Ceart. Art is a man's name simply, Neart means strength and Ceart means right or justice. Well, Art was his father's favorite and the other two boys were very jealous of him. At one particular time, you could hear, all around the country, heavenly music coming from somewhere, and the King wanted to know where it was coming from. So he said to his three sons: "Go out and whichever of you finds out where the heavenly music is coming from, can have half my kingdom."

So the three of them set off out until they came to a big hole and from this big hole they could hear the sound of the music coming. Neart and Ceart said to Art: "Will you go down? You're the lightest and the youngest and we'll let you down into this hole on a rope. You can see where the music is coming from and then we'll pull you up again," hoping never to see him again.

Art said: "Certainly, I will. I think that's a good idea."

Down on the end of a rope he was lowered and he went along a cave like a long tunnel, along and along and along until it got very dark. He walked for hours until it must have been night-time, for in the tunnel he couldn't tell night from day. In the end and when his feet were falling off him, he saw a light. Over to the light he went and he met an old man and he said to the old man that was there: "Could you tell me where the heavenly music is coming from?"

"No, then," said the old man, "I can't. But I tell you what you can do. You can stop the night and tomorrow you can walk—it's a day's journey—on to my father's place and he might be able to tell you."

So the old man put him up for the night and gave him the best of food. They had rashers and eggs with black pudding and white pudding and a Cork drisheen, three Hafner's sausages each, the best of homemade wholemeal bread, all washed down with lashings of strong tea, and after that they both went to bed, as well they might after such a feed.

The next morning Art woke up and started on his journey for another day's traveling along the tunnel, until he came to another light and he went in and met an old, old man and he said to him: "Are you the father of the other old man that I saw back along there?"

"That's not an old man," said the second old man, "he's only a hundred."

"Well," said Art, "I'd like to know where the heavenly music is coming from and he said you might be able to help me."

"Well," said the second old man, "that I can't help you. But my father that lives further up might be able to. Come in anyway and I'll feed you for the night and you can get up in the morning and go up and ask my father."

So Art went in and the old, old man gave him a great meal. They had bowls of stirabout, followed by huge plates of the best Limerick ham with spring cabbage and lovely potatoes, that were like balls of flour melting in your mouth, and with all this they drank three pints each of the freshest buttermilk Art had ever tasted. I can tell you he slept soundly that night.

And the next morning he got up and after saying goodbye to the old, old man, he walked for another whole day along the tunnel until he came to another light and there was an old, old, old man. So Art said to him: "Are you the father of the old, old man back there along the tunnel?"

"Well, I am," said the old, old, old man, "but that fellow's not as old as he makes out; he's only a hundred and fifty and he eats all them new-fangled foods, as you probably found out."

"Well," said Art, "he did me very well. But what I wanted to know was if you can tell me where the heavenly music comes from?"

"Well, now," said the old, old, old man, "we'll talk about that in the morning. Come on in now and have a bit to eat and rest yourself. You must be famished after that day's walking."

So in Art went and the old, old, old man got some food ready. They started off with two great bowls of yellow buck porridge each and after that, they had four crubeens apiece with fresh soda bread and homemade butter and they had three pints of the creamiest porter Art had ever drunk to go with it all.

The next morning, he got up and he said to the old man: "Now can you tell me where the heavenly music is coming from?"

"Well, no," said the old, old, old man, "but I know that there's nobody else living at the end of this tunnel except a terrible fierce man, a giant, and," he said, "I wouldn't go near him if I were you. But if you do decide to go up to him, he lives a terrible far distance away at the very end. You'll find, however," he said, "a little stallion when you go a couple of miles up the road there and, if you get up on him, he'll carry you to where the heavenly music comes from. But," he said, "you'll want to be very wary of that giant."

Art went along and he came up to where, sure enough, there was a stallion and there was light with more light further on. So the stallion said to him: "Do you want a lift?"

"I do," said Art, "but I'm going up to where the heavenly music is."

"Well, that's all right," said the stallion, "no offense given and no offense taken. Jump up there on me back and I'll take you."

So up on the stallion's back he jumped and the stallion galloped away for nearly a whole day, until he came to one of the most beautiful gardens Art had ever seen. "This," said the stallion, "is the nearest I can take you to where the heavenly music comes from."

Art went up through the garden, wondering at every more marvelous thing that he saw. Nearer and nearer came the heavenly music and at last Art came to a house and the music was coming from there. Into the house Art went and there was the most beautiful girl he had ever seen. And she was singing and making the heavenly music.

"Good morning," said Art and then he said quickly, "don't let me interrupt your song which is the loveliest I've ever heard."

"Oh!" she answered him, "I'm glad you've interrupted it. I have to make music here for an old giant that captured me. I'm the King of Greece's daughter," she said, "and I've been here for a year and a day and I can't get away from this old fellow until someone comes to rescue me. But," she said, "I'd sooner you went away for he's a very big man and very very fierce."

"I'm not afraid of him," said Art, "what can he do?"

"Well," she said, "he'll ask you a number of riddles. He has to hide for three nights and you have to hide for three nights . . ."

Before she could finish, or before Art could say whether he was going to stay or go, he heard a deep voice saying: "Who is this I see in here?" In comes this huge giant and caught poor Art by the throat. "What are you doing here?" he roared.

"I came to find the heavenly music," said Art.

"Well, now you've found it," said the giant, "and much good may it do you. And I'll tell you something," he said, "I'm going to hide for three days and, if you don't find me before the three days are up, I'll cut your head off, skin you, cook you and eat you. And after that," he roared, "if you have found me, you'll hide for three days and if I find you, I'll still kill, skin, cook and eat you."

So poor Art didn't know what to say but, "Well, I'd like to go back and see to my little stallion."

"Right," said the giant, "but we'll start in the morning."

"This is an awful thing," said Art to the stallion when he got back, "what am I going to do—how do I know where he's going to hide?"

"That's all right," said the stallion, "it's getting late at night so we'll want to eat something for, honest to God, my belly thinks my throat is cut. Sit down there now," said the stallion, "and put your left hand into my right ear and you'll find a tablecloth. Spread out the tablecloth," he said, and Art did as he was told. "Now," said the stallion, "put your right hand into my left ear and take out what you'll find there." Art did that and took out the best of fine food and the finest of old drink. "Now," said the stallion, "you take that for yourself and stick your right hand into my left ear again." So Art did that and pulled out a bucket of water and a truss of hay. And Art ate the best of fine food and the finest of old drink and the stallion had the hay and the water. "Now," said the stallion when they were finshed, "spread yourself out under my legs and we'll go to sleep for the night." So they went to sleep for the night.

The next morning when they woke up, they could hear the giant shouting: "Now come and find me if you can."

"I can tell you where he is," the little stallion said to Art, "he's at the top of the tree." So Art climbed to the top of the tree and there, right enough, was the giant who comes down very highly annoyed. "Aah!" he roared, "you found me today, but you won't find me tomorrow."

After this, Art had great confidence in the stallion; and that night, he again had a feed of the best of fine food and the finest of old drink, and the stallion had a truss of hay and a bucket of clear water, and they carried on a learned discussion until it was time to go to bed.

Next morning when they got up, the stallion said: "Now go on in through the house and out into the back garden and there you'll see a football. Give the football a good kick."

"All right," said Art and off he went and, in the back garden, he gave the football a terrific kick and out spun the giant.

"Well," said the giant very nastily, "you got me this time, but you won't get me tomorrow for I've got a trick up my sleeve yet."

Art went back to the stallion and told him what had happened and said: "What will we do now?"

"Well," said the stallion, "first of all, we'll have a feed." They ate again all kinds of lovely foods and talked until it was time to go to sleep.

In the morning, Art said: "What will I do now? Where is he hiding?"

"I'll tell you what to do," said the stallion. "When you go inside, ask the girl where he is. But," he said, "without the giant understanding you. Just signal to her, where is he?"

So Art goes and sees the daughter of the King of Greece and she is singing away there and he makes signs to ask where is the giant. The girl pointed to a ring on her finger and, at first, Art didn't understand. But she motioned him to take the ring off, which he did. He looked at it and made signs to show that he didn't believe that the giant could fit in such a small ring. But the girl kept singing away and pointed to him to throw it in the fire. So he did that and there was an enormous screech: "Oh! I'm burnt! I'm burnt!" and out jumped the giant. "Now," he roared, "you caught me the three times, but now it's your turn."

"All right," said Art, "I'll hide tomorrow."

"Well, now," said Art to the stallion when he went back, "we're in a right fix now. Where am I going to hide? Sure I'm a stranger here and don't know the place at all."

"That's all right," said the stallion, "I'll tell you in the morning. In the meantime, put your hands into my two ears and take out the grub." So they had a feed and then Art got under the stallion's legs and slept there for the night.

When he woke up: "Now," said the stallion, "the first thing you do is to take a hair out of my tail and, the hole it leaves, get up into that." So Art took the hair out of the stallion's tale, got up into the hole and stopped there. And the giant searched all round and couldn't find Art all day and nearly went tearing mad. Art came out that night and the giant said: "I didn't find you today but I'll find you tomorrow and eat you."

So that night Art said to the stallion: "Where am I going to hide tomorrow?"

"That's all right," said the stallion, "put your hands into my two ears and take out the food and we'll have a feed first. Then you can stretch out under my legs and have a sleep and we'll talk about the matter in the morning."

In the morning Art said: "Now, where am I going to hide?"

"Take a nail out of my hoof," said the stallion, "get up into the hole and draw the nail up after you." So Art did that and stayed there all day, while the giant went round roaring and swearing.

At night, the giant went back to his house and Art came out of the hole and said: "So you didn't find me."

"No," said the giant, "but I will tomorrow and then I'll kill, skin, cook, and eat you."

Then Art said to the stallion: "Where will I hide tomorrow?" and the stallion said: "One thing at a time. Get out the grub there and we'll have a feed and we'll see about the other matter in the morning."

"Now," said the stallion in the morning, when they woke up fresh and early, "pull out one of my teeth, get up into the hole and draw the tooth up after you." The giant came rampaging around the place and couldn't find Art and, to cut a long story short, he nearly went demented.

In the evening, Art came out and went into the house and there was the King of Greece's daughter. The music was stopped but she looked happier than ever and she said: "You have broken the spell. I had to wait for a stranger to come and beat the giant six times."

"We've done that," said Art, "now I'll take you away from here."

"All right," she said, "although I'm the daughter of the King of Greece."

"Well," said Art, "that's nothing. I'm the King of Ireland's son." So she jumped up on the back of the stallion behind Art and they rode out of the tunnel and back to his father's palace. The King of Greece's daughter then sang some of the heavenly music for the King of Ireland and the King gave Art half his kingdom. The two brothers were banished and Art and the King of Greece's daughter got married and they had a wedding and everybody ate and drank, and wasn't I at the wedding as well as everybody else and I got a present of a pair of paper boots and a pair of stockings made of buttermilk; and that's the end of my story and all I'm going to tell you.

❖ HUDDON AND DUDDON AND DONALD O'LEARY

HUGH NOLAN ◈ *FERMANAGH*
HENRY GLASSIE *1972*

Huddon and Duddon and Donald O'Leary was three neighbors that lived in this country a long time ago, when the people wasn't very well off, and they had different little ways of making their living.

So these three men, what they made their living by was: each man had a bullock. And in the part of the country where they lived, hauling and drawing, what would be done in other parts by horses, was done be bullocks.

So anyway, one man would be trying to get all of the work that he could to knock the other man out, and that was the way they carried on. But they were still getting a little that was keeping them going.

But Donald O'Leary was the favorite of the people of the locality. He was a pleasant sort of a man, and he wasn't too hard to pay, and he was very obliging. And the other two men was different from him in many ways.

So anyway, the way it was with the people of the locality, if two or three wanted him on the one day, well, some two would wait till next day before they'd employ either of the other two men.

So that left the other two that they got very jealous with Donald. And they came to the conclusion that the proper way of dealing with him was to kill his bullock. And he wouldn't be able to get another.

So anyway, there was one morning Donald got up very early; he had a big day's work. And when he went out to the field, his bullock was dead.

So he came back to the house and there was no one there, only the mother, and he came back with the sad news. And it wasn't very long till the report went out all over the locality about Donald O'Leary getting his bull dead that morning. Everybody was very sorry for him. So there gathered a great crowd of men to his place. And in them days anything in the line of a beast that died, they were skinned and then buried in the field where they died.

So. These men joined to work and they skinned his bullock, and there was another few men started and they dug a grave for him. The bullock was skinned and he was lowered into the grave; the grave was covered up.

So there was a couple of men prepared for to roll up the skin, and as a general rule when a skin used to be a-rolling up, the fleshy part was kept to the inside. But when these men started, Donald told them for to keep the hairy side in, and keep the fleshy side out before they'd tie it on the rope.

So these men done as Donald told them, and when all was finished up, they all went away home, and Donald went in and got some refreshment and started away to the skin store that was a good many miles from where he lived.

So he trudged on anyway and there came a terrible heavy steep rain. And Donald paid no attention to it. He wasn't much uneasy about what kind the weather was; it was his future he was thinking of, the loss he had come to, and all to this.

So before this rain was over didn't there light a magpie on the bundle that he had on his back and started to pick at a little flesh that was left.

So he put up his hand very cautiously and he got ahold of the magpie. And he had an overcoat on him, and he opened the overcoat and he put the magpie in between the overcoat and his tag coat and buttoned the coat again. Trudged on.

Finally he landed at this town where the skins used to be sold and went into the skin store, sold the skin, and all it brought was ten shillings.

So anyway he come out anyway. He hadn't much inclination for remaining any longer in the town and he just considered that the proper thing for him to do was to go into the public house and take a half-one of whiskey and head back for home.

So he went into this particular pub and there was a young lady at the bar. So he was a very nice class of a fellow. He could talk to girls very nicely; he had a great flow of speech. He had a *gift* in that line.

So anyway, he hold her that he wanted a half-one of good whiskey.

So she had been instructed by her employer that when a stranger came in that she didn't know, or that wasn't in the habit of calling, for to not be exact about the kind of whiskey that she give him. The second class would do him all right.

So of course, she was doing as she was told by the *boss.*

And she was putting up her hand for to take down the bottle.

And he put his hand inside of the coat and he gave the magpie a *nip.*

And the magpie gave a *screech.*

So the girl jumped; she says, "What's that?"

"Oh," he says, "miss," he says, "it's a bird that I do carry along with me. And it's able for to tell everything that's going to happen.

"And it's after telling me that you're going to give me bad whiskey."

So, damn it, she nearly dropped.

And she pushed back the bottle that she was taking down, and she pushed it back onto the shelf again, and she went away and, oh, she gave him a powerful fine half-one: the *best* of whiskey.

So anyway, when he was drinking it, she says to him, "Would you sell that bird?"

"Oh," he says, "I wouldn't like to do that. I have this bird a long time," he says, "and it has been very useful to me, traveling. And I don't know," he says, "whether I'd sell him or not."

"Well," she says, "if you got a good price for it now, would you not sell it?"

"Well now, of course," he says, "there's a lot in that question. It would want to be good before I'd part with it."

"Well, we'll say," she says, "that you got forty pound for it: would you not part with it?"

So he considered for a while, you know, either way.

"Och," he says, "if ye fancy it," he says, "I'll take your bid," he says.

So anyway, she went away and she counted the forty pound.

So he took the magpie from under the coat.

And she put him into a box in under the counter.

And he started off with his forty pound.

So, oh now, he went home in better humor than he came.

Anyway, when he got the length of his own locality, Huddon and Duddon was waiting to see how did he do with the skin.

"Och," he says, "I think we have been fools," he says, "to be killing ourselves, before day and after night, hauling and dragging and pulling.

"Look," he says, "what I got for the skin. And when would we make that?" he says. "Not till the day of our death, struggling with bullocks."

So he took and he counted out the forty pound.

So they said nothing; turned away.

So. The next morning at daybreak the two boys was seen leaving the locality with two bundles on their backs. They'd killed the two bullocks and skinned them and started away.

Landed at this skin store where Donald peddled his skin. All they could get was ten bob.

Aw, they tramped here and they tramped there, and there was *nobody* wanting anything of the kind, only these ones that was running the skin store. So they had to do with the ten bob apiece.

So, they started for home in terrible vengeance, vowing for to take Donald's life that night.

So anyway, they were coming on near home and they met some person and the news that they had for them: Donald O'Leary's mother had died sudden during the day.

So they intended that when he'd go to bed, for to go in through the side wall and take him out, and kill him. But then, when the mother was dead, the game was up for that night, for they knew that there would be people there during the night and that they couldn't do it.

So. The next day followed, and on the second day Donald started away for to get the mother buried. He got her rolled up very nicely and got her on his back and started away to a cemetery—aw, it was a good many mile from where he lived.

So. It was a nice day, a nice sunshiny day, and he got dry, and he was coming forward to a well that was on the roadside. And there was a paling around this well for to keep cattle from going into it, and to keep youngsters from being drownded or playing about it.

And he took the parcel down off his back.

And he left her standing up, leaned against the paling.

And he went in and he took a drink.

So, he came back out on the road, and he looked in both ways, and meeting him he seen a figure. He didn't know what it was, whether it was man or woman. The stretch of the road was that long.

So, he stood and he watched it for a long time, and he seen that it was a woman.

So he started on, meeting her.

And he met her. He bid her, oh, a very nice time of the day. He started to chat with her about the locality, and all to this. He was a terrible nice-talking fellow, and she took a wonderful interest in him, just at once, you know.

He was in no hurry parting with her, but in the long run, he started moving one foot and then moving another, do you see, as people does when they be parting with people that they're talking to.

So anyway, before he got properly into a walking mood, he says, "Miss, when you go the length of that well," he says, "will you stop for to have a drink. Me mother's there. And she leaned against the paling, and I suppose maybe she's fell asleep. And when you go the length of her, would you tell her that I'm in a hurry and for her to come on? And she's very deaf, and you'll have to give her a shake or she'll not hear you."

Oh, the girl was only too glad.

On she went anyway, and on Donald went, and he still kept peeping, looking behind him. So finally she landed at the well. She says in a loud voice, "Your son told you for to follow him: he's in a hurry."

No answer.

She said it again. There was no answer, so she went forward, she gave the woman a shake that way that the woman went over her head and went down into the well.

Aw. She started to scream. Donald cut round on the road, you know, in a terrible unease to discover what the screams was about. So she came running the length of him and she told him what happened, and he took a-crying then, roaring and crying.

The *whole* people of the locality all came out. They could hear the cries. They didn't know what was wrong. There was no time until there was a large number of people on the road, and around the well.

Ah, it was a sad case. The woman was taken out of the well. She was brought to some house, and there was a wake in there for a while.

The next day then the whole people of the locality, they got a way of bringing her to the cemetery and she was buried.

So then, Donald was going about all the time crying.

So the people of the locality thought a pity of him.

So some of them suggested that they'd rise a testimonial; that'd be a *collection.*

So anyway, it was agreed to. And a collector went out into the whole locality.

And he kept knocking about that locality, crying betimes and lamenting about the mother being dead, and all to this.

They gathered him fifty pound.

So he got the fifty pound anyway and he started back for home.

Now, Huddon and Duddon had been watching for him from the day before.

So finally, they came to meet him, made wonderful inquiries how did he get the mother buried.

"Oh," he says, "I hadn't to bury her atall."

"Then what'd you do with her?" says some of them.

"Oh," he says, "as soon as I went into the town, when it was found out," he says, "what I had in the bundle, there was a party in the town, had arrived in the town, and they were buying all kinds of bones to make gunpowder.

"So," he says, "they started me," he says, "and they never quit with me till—" pulling out the fifty pound and showing it to them.

So they parted anyway.

The next morning the two boys was seen leaving the locality with two parcels on their backs. Two *dead women*.

So they trudged on anyway to this town. There was no signs of anyone about the street looking for bones.

So they came to the conclusion that they'd have to do like the old hawkers, you see: they'd have to call out what they had. So they started on up and down the street:

"*Bones to make gunpowder.*

"*Bones to make gunpowder.*

"*Bones to make gunpowder.*"

No time till the police came along and examined what they had in the bundles. Took the two away to the police station. And there was a special court on them.

They got away—there was no other charges against them. They got away—they got off on the condition that they'd bury these two corpses in the nearest burying ground. Had to do it or else they were going to jail.

So now, it was a hard day on them.

So anyhow, they got through with it anyway. And they started for home, *vowing* again and again that Donald O'Leary would never see the light of the next day. They'd kill him that night.

So anyway, they waited on and waited on till it got late at night. Donald had went to bed. They come the length of his wee hut, and they tore down the side wall and they took him out of bed. They had a big long sack with them. And they put him into the sack.

And they had to go through fields for to get to the county road. And they had two greyhounds; the greyhounds found them out after they come home, and weren't they running along with them down the field. And just as they arrived at the roadside, didn't the greyhounds rise a hare. And it was breaking day at the time.

So they were terrible fond of a slip, these two, Huddon and Duddon, so didn't they drop the bag and away after the hounds.

So Donald was lying in the sack on the roadside.

In the distance, he heard a man shouting.

And he knew the voice.

He was a cattle drover; he was more of a cattle dealer than a cattle drover.

And Donald knew that he knew *him*, do you see.

So anyway, he started the song.

And he was singing at a terrible rate.

And this man came along with his cattle, and you know the way cattle will scare at a thing that's on the road, shying and jumping.

Finally he got them by anyway, and when he came the length of the bag, Donald was singing away.

So. He says, "In the name of God, Donald O'Leary, is this you?"

"It is indeed," says Donald.

"And what has ye here," he says, "at this hour of the morning, tied up in a sack, and you singing?"

"Well," he says, "if you were in my position," he says, "you would be singing too."

"Why?" says this fellow.

"Well," he says, "I'm going away to Heaven. And that's what has me singing."

"Going away to Heaven?" says the fellow.

"Aye, indeed."

"I wish," he says, "it was there I was going instead of after these cattle."

"Well," says Donald, "if you like, open the mouth of that sack and I'll get out and let you get in. I wouldn't do it for everyone. But I know *you*," he says, "for a long *time*."

So anyway, the lad opened the sack. And Donald got out. And he got in.

And Donald tied up the sack.

He away after the cattle, and he got them all rounded up, and he turned them away on a road that he knew that Huddon and Duddon wouldn't be on.

And he started away the leaving the whole day. Aw, he drove to different places. He got plenty of money that day with them. He could get what he wanted.

So finally, coming on to night, he gathered the cattle up again and he started back for his own locality.

So he waited till everybody would be in bed before he just come close to where Huddon and Duddon lived.

So anyway, he started shouting at an awful rate, using the language, you know, that you use for cattle, calling cattle.

So now, didn't they hear him, and them in bed.

And they knew it was Donald's voice.

So they jumped out. Their two houses was beside other.

So they both was sure it was Donald's voice. Donald kept shouting away, down at the road. So they made for the road anyway.

So anyway they come the length of Donald and the whole big drove of cattle.

So they questioned him. How did he come along with the cattle? Was he not threw in the river?

He said, "I was," he says. "But where yez threw me in," he says, "I just landed in the middle of a stock farm. The greatest-looking cattle," he says, "that ever I beamed an eye on.

"So," he says, "I seen that a lock of them would be useful to us all," he says, "and I picked as many of the best of them as I could round up," he says, "got them out," he says, "and I got them here."

So, Huddon says to him, "Would you show us where them cattle is in the river?"

"Oh, indeed I would," says he. "You're welcome. You're as well entitled to them as I am."

Huddon says, "Will you come, Duddon?"

"Oh aye, surely," says he. "I want a lock of beasts as well as you."

"All right," says Donald. "Come on."

Three of them marched down to the river anyway, and Donald says, "Just let some one of yez lep in there."

So, *aw*, Huddon took a race and he leapt in.

No time till the water joined to go down his throat, and he joined to *balder* and *roar*.

"*Go on to him quick*," says Donald. "Go on to him quick now, Duddon," he says, "because he'll get in trouble with the cattle. Ye'd want to be there."

Duddon took a jump and he leapt in too.

And that was the last of Huddon and Duddon.

Donald O'Leary lived a happy man from that till the day he died.

❖ THE THREE WISHES

TYRONE

WILLIAM CARLETON *1846*

In ancient times there lived a man called Billy Duffy, and he was known to be a great rogue. They say he was descended from the family of the Duffys, which was the reason, I suppose, of his carrying their name upon him.

Billy, in his youthful days, was the best hand at doing nothing in all Europe. Devil a mortal could come next or near him at idleness; and, in consequence of his great practice that way, you may be sure that if any man could make a fortune by it, he would have done it.

Billy was the only son of his father, barring two daughters. But they have nothing to do with the story I'm telling you. Indeed it was kind father and grandfather for Billy to be handy at the knavery as well as at the idleness, for it was well known that not one of their blood ever did an honest act, except with a roguish intention. In short, they were altogether a decent connection, and a credit to the name. As for Billy, all the villainy of the family, both plain and ornamental, came down to him by way of legacy, for it so happened that the father, in spite of all his cleverness, had nothing but his roguery to leave him.

Billy, to do him justice, improved the fortune he got. Every day advanced him farther into dishonesty and poverty, until, at the long run, he was acknowledged on all hands to be the completest swindler and the poorest vagabond in the whole parish.

Billy's father, in his young days, had often been forced to acknowledge the inconvenience of not having a trade, in consequence of some nice point in law, called the Vagrant Act, that sometimes troubled him. On this account he made up his mind to give Bill an occupation, and he accordingly bound him to a blacksmith. But whether Bill was to live or die by forgery was a puzzle to his father, though the neighbors said that *both* was most likely. At all events, he was put apprentice to a smith for seven years, and a hard card his master had to play in managing him. He took the proper method, however, for Bill was so lazy and roguish that it would vex a saint to keep him in order.

"Bill," says his master to him one day that he had been sunning himself about the ditches, instead of minding his business, "Bill, my boy, I'm vexed to the heart to see you in such a bad state of health. You're very ill with that complaint called an all-overness. However," says he, "I think I can cure you. Nothing will bring you about but three or four sound doses, every day, of a medicine called 'the oil of the hazel.' Take the first dose now," says he. And he immediately banged him with a hazel cudgel until Bill's bones ached for a week afterwards.

"If you were my son," said his master, "I tell you that, as long as I could get a piece of advice growing convenient in the hedges, I'd have you a different youth from what you are. If working was a sin, Bill, devil an innocenter boy ever broke bread than you would be. Good people's scarce you think, but however that may be, I throw it out as a hint, that you must take your medicine till you're cured, whenever you happen to get unwell in the same way."

From this out he kept Bill's nose to the grinding-stone, and whenever his complaint returned, he never failed to give him a hearty dose for his improvement.

In the course of time, however, Bill was his own man and his own master, but it would puzzle a saint to know whether the master or the man was the more precious youth in the eyes of the world.

He immediately married a wife, and devil a doubt of it, but if he kept her in whiskey and sugar, she kept him in hot water. Bill drank and she drank. Bill fought and she fought. Bill was idle and she was idle. Bill whacked her and she whacked Bill. If Bill gave her one black eye, she gave him another, just to keep herself in countenance. Never was there a blessed pair so well met, and a beautiful sight it was to see them both at breakfast time blinking at each other across the potato basket, Bill with his right eye black, and she with her left.

In short, they were the talk of the whole town; and to see Bill of a morning staggering home drunk, his shirt-sleeves rolled upon his smutted arms, his breast open, and an old tattered leather apron, with one corner tucked up under his belt, singing one minute, and fighting with his wife the next—she reeling beside him, with a discolored eye, as aforesaid, a dirty ragged cap on one side of her head, a pair of Bill's old slippers on her feet, a squalling brat on her arm—now cuffiing and dragging Bill, and again kissing and hugging him! Yes, it was a pleasant picture to see this loving pair in such a state.

This might do for a while, but it could not last. They were idle, drunken, and ill-conducted. And it was not to be supposed that they would get a farthing candle on their words. They were of course driven to great straits; and faith, they soon found that their fighting, and drinking, and idleness made them the laughing-sport of the neighbors, but neither brought food to their children, put a coat upon their backs, nor satisfied their landlord when he came to look for his own. Still the never a one of Bill but was a funny fellow with strangers, though, as we said, the greatest rogue unhanged.

One day he was standing against his own anvil, completely in a brown study, being brought to his wit's end how to make out a breakfast for the family. The wife was scolding and cursing in the house, and the naked creatures of children squalling about her knees for food. Bill was fairly at an amplush, and knew not where or how to turn himself, when a poor withered old beggar came into the forge, tottering on his staff. A long white beard fell from his chin, and he looked so thin and hungry that you might blow him, one would think, over the house. Bill at this moment had been brought to his senses by distress, and his heart had a touch of pity towards the old man; for, on looking at him a second time, he clearly saw starvation and sorrow in his face.

"God save you, honest man!" said Bill.

The old man gave a sigh, and raising himself, with great pain, on his staff, he looked at Bill in a very beseeching way.

"Musha, God save you kindly," says he, "maybe you could give a poor, hungry, helpless old man a mouthful of something to eat? You see yourself I'm not able to work; if I was, I'd scorn to be beholding to any one."

"Faith, honest man," said Bill, "if you knew who you're speaking to, you'd as soon ask a monkey for a churn-staff as me for either meat or money. There's not a blackguard in the three kingdoms so fairly on the shaughran as I am for both the one and the other. The wife within is sending the curses thick and heavy on me, and the childer's playing the cat's melody to keep her in comfort. Take my word of it, poor man, if I had either meat or money, I'd help you, for I know particularly well what it is to want them at the present speaking. An empty sack won't stand, neighbor."

So far Bill told him truth. The good thought was in his heart, because he found himself on a footing with the beggar, and nothing brings down pride, or softens the heart, like feeling what it is to want.

"Why, you are in a worse state than I am," said the old man. "You have a family to provide for, and I have only myself to support."

"You may kiss the book on that, my old worthy," replied Bill. "But come, what I can do for you I will. Plant yourself up here beside the fire, and I'll give it a blast or two of my bellows that will warm the old blood in your body. It's a cold, miserable, snowy day, and a good heat will be of service."

"Thank you kindly," said the old man. "I *am* cold, and a warming at your fire will do me good, sure enough. Oh, it *is* a bitter, bitter day, God bless it!"

He then sat down, and Bill blew a rousing blast that soon made the stranger edge back from the heat. In a short time he felt quite comfortable, and when the numbness was taken out of his joints, he buttoned himself up and prepared to depart.

"Now," says he to Bill, "you hadn't the food to give me, but what you could you did. Ask any three wishes you choose, and be they what they may, take my word for it, they shall be granted."

Now, the truth is, that Bill, though he believed himself a great man in point of cuteness, wanted, after all, a full quarter of being square; for there is always a great difference between a wise man and a knave. Bill was so much of a rogue that he could not, for the blood of him, ask an honest wish, but stood scratching his head in a puzzle.

"Three wishes," said he. "Why, let me see—did you say *three?*"

"Aye," replied the stranger, "three wishes—that was what I said."

"Well," said Bill, "here goes—aha!—let me alone, my old worthy! Faith I'll overreach the parish, if what you say is true. I'll cheat them in dozens, rich and poor, old and young; let me alone, man—I have it here," and he tapped his forehead with great glee. "Faith, you're the sort to meet of a frosty morning, when a man wants his breakfast. And I'm sorry that I have neither money nor credit to get a bottle of whiskey, that we might take our morning together."

"Well, but let us hear the wishes," said the old man. "My time is short, and I cannot stay much longer."

"Do you see this sledge hammer?" said Bill. "I wish, in the first place, that whoever takes it up in their hands may never be able to lay it down till I give them leave. And that whoever begins to sledge with it may never stop sledging till it's my pleasure to release him.

"Secondly—I have an armchair, and I wish that whoever sits down in it may never rise out of it till they have my consent.

"And thirdly—that whatever money I put into my purse, nobody may have power to take it out of it but myself."

"You devil's rip!" says the old man in a passion, shaking his staff across Bill's nose. "Why did you not ask something that would serve you both here and hereafter? Sure it's as common as the market cross, that there's not a vagabone in his Majesty's dominions stands more in need of both."

"Oh! by the elevens," said Bill. "I forgot that altogether! Maybe you'd be civil enough to let me change one of them? The sorra a prettier wish ever was made than I'll make, if you'll give me another chance."

"Get out, you reprobate," said the old fellow, still in a passion. "Your day of grace is past. Little you know who was speaking to you all this time. I'm Saint Moroky, you blackguard, and I gave you an opportunity of doing something for yourself and your family. But you neglected it, and now your fate is cast, you dirty, bog-trotting profligate. Sure it's well known what you are. Aren't you a byword in everybody's mouth, you and your scold of a wife? By this and by that, if ever you happen to come across me again, I'll send you to where you won't freeze, you villain!"

He then gave Bill a rap of his cudgel over the head, and laid him at his length beside the bellows, kicked a broken coal scuttle out of his way, and left the forge in a fury.

When Billy recovered himself from the effects of the blow, and began to think on what had happened, he could have quartered himself with vexation for not asking great wealth as one of the wishes at least. But now the die was cast on him, and he could only make the most of the three he pitched upon.

He now bethought him how he might turn them to the best account, and here his cunning came to his aid. He began by sending for his wealthiest neighbors on pretense of business, and when he got them under his roof, he offered them the armchair to sit down in. He now had them safe, nor could all the art of man relieve them except worthy Bill was willing. Bill's plan was to make the best bargain he could before he released his prisoners, and let him alone for knowing how to make their purses bleed. There wasn't a wealthy man in the country he did not fleece. The parson of the parish bled heavily, so did the lawyer. And a rich attorney, who had retired from practice, swore that the court of chancery itself was paradise compared to Bill's chair.

This was all very good for a time. The fame of his chair, however, soon spread; so did that of his sledge. In a short time neither man, woman, nor child would darken his door. All avoided him and his fixtures as they would a spring-gun or man-trap. Bill, so long as he fleeced his neighbors, never wrought a hand's turn, so that when his money was out, he found himself as badly off as ever. In addition to this, his character was fifty times worse than before, for it was the general belief that he had dealings with the Devil. Nothing now could exceed his misery, distress, and ill-temper. The wife and he and their children all fought among one another like devils. Everybody hated them, cursed them, and avoided them. The people thought they were acquainted with more than Christian people ought to know, for the family, they said, was very like one that the Devil drove. All this, of course, came to Bill's ears, and it vexed him very much.

One day he was walking about the fields, thinking of how he could raise the wind once more. The day was dark, and he found himself, before he stopped, in the bottom of a lonely glen covered by great bushes that grew on each side.

"Well," thought he, when every other means of raising money failed him, "it's reported that I'm in league with the Devil, and as it's a folly to have the name of the connection without the profit. I'm ready to make a bargain with him any day. So," said he, raising his voice, "Nick, you sinner, if you be convenient and willing, why, stand out here, show your best leg. Here's your man."

The words were hardly out of his mouth, when a dark sober-looking old gentleman, not unlike a lawyer, walked up to him. Bill looked at the foot and saw the hoof.

"Morrow, Nick," says Bill.

"Morrow, Bill," says Nick. "Well, Bill, what's the news?"

"Devil a much myself hears of late," says Bill. "Is there any thing fresh below?"

"I can't exactly say, Bill. I spend little of my time down now. The Whigs are in office, and my hands are consequently too full of business here to pay much attention to anything else."

"A fine place this, sir," says Bill, "to take a constitutional walk in. When *I* want an appetite I often come this way myself—hem! High feeding is very bad without exercise."

"High feeding! Come, come, Bill, you know you didn't taste a morsel these four-and-twenty hours."

"You know that's a bounce, Nick. I eat a breakfast this morning that would put a stone of flesh on you, if you only smelt at it."

"No matter. This is not to the purpose. What's that you were muttering to yourself a while ago? If you want to come to the brunt, here I'm for you."

"Nick," said Bill, "you're complete. You want nothing barring a pair of Brian O'Lynn's breeches."

Bill, in fact, was bent on making his companion open the bargain, because he had often heard that in that case, with proper care on his own part, he might defeat him in the long run. The other, however, was his match.

"What was the nature of Brian's garment?" inquired Nick.

"Why, you know the song," said Bill:

"Brian O'Lynn had no breeches to wear,
So he got a sheep's skin for to make him a pair;
With the fleshy side out, and the woolly side in,
They'll be pleasant and *cool*, says Brian O'Lynn.

A *cool* pair would serve you, Nick."

"You're mighty waggish today, Mr. Duffy."

"And good right I have," said Bill. "I'm a man snug and well-to-do in the world; have lots of money, plenty of good eating and drinking, and what more need a man wish for?"

"True," said the other. "In the meantime it's rather odd that so respectable a man should not have six inches of unbroken cloth in his apparel. You are as naked a tatterdemallion as I ever laid my eyes on. In full dress for a party of scarecrows, William?"

"That's my own fancy, Nick. I don't work at my trade like a gentleman. This is my forge dress, you know."

"Well, but what did you summon me here for?" said the other. "You may as well speak out, I tell you, for, my good friend, unless *you* do *I* shan't. Smell that."

"I smell more than that," said Bill, "and by the way, I'll thank you to give me the windy side of you—curse all sulphur, I say. There, that's what I call an improvement in my condition. But as you are so stiff," says Bill, "why, the short and the long of it is—that—hem—you see I'm—tut—sure you know I have a thriving trade of my own, and that if I like I needn't be at a loss, but in the meantime I'm rather in a kind of a so—so—don't you *take?*"

And Bill winked knowingly, hoping to trick him into the first proposal.

"You must speak aboveboard, my friend," says the other. "I'm a man of few words, blunt and honest. If you have any thing to say, be plain. Don't think I can be losing my time with such a pitiful rascal as you are."

"Well," says Bill, "I want money, then, and am ready to come into terms. What have you to say to that, Nick?"

"Let me see—let me look at you," says his companion, turning him about. "Now, Bill, in the first place, are you not as finished a scarecrow as ever stood upon two legs?"

"I play second fiddle to you there again," says Bill.

"There you stand with the blackguard's coat of arms quartered under your eye, and—"

"Don't make little of blackguards," says Bill, "nor speak disparagingly of your own crest."

"Why, what would you bring, you brazen rascal, if you were fairly put up at auction?"

"Faith, I'd bring more bidders than you would," said Bill, "if you were to go off at auction tomorrow. I tell you they should bid *downwards* to come to your value, Nicholas. We have no coin small enough to purchase you."

"Well, no matter," said Nick. "If you are willing to be mine at the expiration of seven years, I will give you more money than ever the rascally breed of you was worth."

"Done!" said Bill. "But no disparagement to my family, in the meantime. So down with the hard cash, and don't be a nagur."

The money was accordingly paid down. But as nobody was present, except the giver and receiver, the amount of what Bill got was never known.

"Won't you give me a luck penny?" said the old gentleman.

"Tut," said Billy. "So prosperous an old fellow as you cannot want it; however, the Devil's luck to you, with all my heart, and it's rubbing grease to a fat pig to say so. Be off now, or I'll commit suicide on you. Your absence is a cordial to most people, you infernal old profligate. You have injured my morals even for the short time you have been with me, for I don't find myself so virtuous as I was."

"Is that your gratitude, Billy?"

"Is it gratitude *you* speak of, man? I wonder you don't blush when you name it. However, when you come again, if you bring a third eye in your head, you will see what I mean, Nicholas, ahagur."

The old gentleman, as Bill spoke, hopped across the ditch, on his way to Downing Street, where of late 'tis thought he possesses much influence.

Bill now began by degrees to show off, but still wrought a little at his trade to blindfold the neighbors. In a very short time, however, he became a great man. So long indeed as he was a poor rascal, no decent person would speak to him. Even the proud serving men at the Big House would turn up their noses at him. And he well deserved to be made little of by others, because he was mean enough to make little of himself. But when it was seen and known that he had oceans of money, it was wonderful to think, although he was now a greater blackguard than ever, how those who despised him before, began to come round him and court his company. Bill, however, had neither sense nor spirit to make those sunshiny friends know their distance—not he. Instead of that, he was proud to be seen in decent company, and so long as the money lasted, it was "hail fellow well met" between himself and every fair-faced sponger who had a horse under him, a decent coat to his back, and a good appetite to eat his dinners. With riches and all, Bill was the same man still, but, somehow or other, there is a great difference between a rich profligate and a poor one, and Bill found it so to his cost in both cases.

Before half the seven years was passed, Bill had his carriage and his equipages; was hand and glove with my Lord This, and my Lord That; kept hounds and hunters; was the first sportsman at the Curragh; patronized every boxing ruffian he could pick up; and betted night and day on cards, dice, and horses. Bill, in short, should be a blood, and except he did all this, he could not presume to mingle with the fashionable bloods of his time.

It's an old proverb, however, that "what is got over the Devil's back is sure to go off under it," and in Bill's case this proved true. In short, the Devil himself could not supply him with money so fast as he made it fly. It was "come easy, go easy" with Bill, and so sign was on it, before he came within two years of his time he found his purse empty.

And now came the value of his summer friends to be known. When it was discovered that the cash was no longer flush with him—that stud, and carriage, and hounds were going to the hammer—whish! off they went, friends, relations, pot-companions, dinner-eaters, blacklegs and all, like a flock of crows that had smelt gunpowder. Down Bill soon went, week after week, and day after day, until at last, he was obliged to put on the leather apron, and take to the hammer again. And not only that, for as no experience could make him wise, he once more began his taproom brawls, his quarrels with Judy, and took to his "high feeding" at the dry potatoes and salt. Now, too, came the cutting tongues of all who knew him, like razors upon him. Those that he scorned because they were poor and himself rich, now paid him back his own with interest. And those that he measured himself with, because they were rich, and who only countenanced him in consequence of his wealth, gave him the hardest word in their cheeks. The Devil mend him! He deserved it, and more if he got it.

Bill, however, who was a hardened sinner, never fretted himself down an ounce of flesh by what was said to him, or of him. Not he. He cursed, and fought, and swore, and schemed away as usual, taking in everyone he could; and surely none could match him at villainy of all sorts and sizes.

At last the seven years became expired, and Bill was one morning sitting in his forge, sober and hungry, the wife cursing him, and the children squalling as before. He was thinking how he might defraud some honest neighbors out of a breakfast to stop their mouths and his own too, when who walks into him but Old Nick, to demand his bargain.

"Morrow, Bill," says he with a sneer.

"The Devil welcome you!" says Bill. "But you have a fresh memory."

"A bargain's a bargain between two honest men, any day," says Satan. "When I speak of *honest* men, I mean yourself and me, Bill." And he put his tongue in his cheek to make game of the unfortunate rogue he came for.

"Nick, my worthy fellow," said Bill, "have bowels. You wouldn't do a shabby thing. You wouldn't disgrace your own character by putting more weight upon a falling man. You know what it is to get a come-down yourself, my worthy. So just keep your toe in your pump, and walk off with yourself somewhere else. A cool walk will serve you better than my company, Nicholas."

"Bill, it's no use in shirking," said his friend. "Your swindling tricks may enable you to cheat others, but you won't cheat *me*, I guess. You want nothing to make you perfect in your way but to travel. And travel you shall under my guidance, Billy. No, no—*I'm* not to be swindled, my good fellow. I have rather a—a—better opinion of myself, Mr. D., than to think that you could outwit one Nicholas Clutie, Esquire—ehem!"

"You may sneer, you sinner," replied Bill, "but I tell you for your comfort, that I have outwitted men who could buy and sell you to your face. Despair, you villain, when I tell you that no attorney could stand before me."

Satan's countenance got blank when he heard this. He wriggled and fidgeted about, and appeared to be not quite comfortable.

"In that case, then," says he, "the sooner I deceive you the better, so turn out for the Low Countries."

"Is it come to that in earnest?" said Bill, "and are you going to act the rascal at the long run?"

" 'Pon honor, Bill."

"Have patience, then, you sinner, till I finish this horseshoe—it's the last of a set I'm finishing for one of your friend the attorney's horses. And here, Nick, I hate idleness, you know it's the mother of mischief, take this sledge hammer, and give a dozen strokes or so, till I get it out of hands, and then, here's with you, since it must be so."

He then gave the bellows a puff that blew half a peck of dust in Club-foot's face, whipped out the red-hot iron, and set Satan sledging away for the bare life.

"Faith," says Bill to him, when the shoe was finished, "it's a thousand pities ever the sledge should be out of your hand; the great Parra Gow was a child to you at sledging, you're such an able tyke. Now just exercise yourself till I bid the wife and childer goodbye, and then I'm off."

Out went Bill, of course without the slightest notion of coming back; no more than Nick had that he could not give up the sledging, and indeed neither could he, but he was forced to work away as if he was sledging for a wager. This was just what Bill wanted. He was now compelled to sledge away until it was Bill's pleasure to release him. And so we leave him very industriously employed, while we look after the worthy who outwitted him.

In the meantime, Bill broke cover, and took to the country at large; wrought a little journeywork wherever he could get it, and in this way went from one place to another, till in the course of a month, he walked back very coolly into his own forge, to see how things went on in his absence. There he found Satan in a rage, the perspiration pouring from him in torrents, hammering with might and main upon the naked anvil. Bill calmly leaned his back against the wall, placed his hat upon the side of his head, put his hands into his breeches pockets, and began to whistle Shawn Gow's hornpipe. At length he says in a very quiet and good-humored way:

"Morrow, Nick."

"Oh!" says Nick, still hammering away. "Oh! you double-distilled villain (hech!), may the most refined, ornamental (hech!), double-rectified, super-extra, and original (hech!) collection of curses that ever was gathered (hech!) into a single nosegay of ill fortune (hech!) shine in the buttonhole of your conscience (hech!) while your name is Bill Duffy! I denounce you (hech!) as a double-milled villain, a finished, hot-pressed knave (hech!), in comparison of whom all the other knaves I ever knew (hech!), attorneys included, are honest men. I brand you (hech!) as the pearl of cheats, a tiptop take-in (hech!). I denounce you, I say again, for the villainous treatment (hech!) I have received at your hands in this most untoward (hech!) and unfortunate transaction between us; for (hech!) unfortunate in every sense, is he that has any thing to do with (hech!) such a prime and finished imposter."

"You're very warm, Nicky," says Bill. "What puts you into a passion, you old sinner? Sure if it's your own will and pleasure to take exercise at my anvil, *I'm* not to be abused for it. Upon my credit, Nicky, you ought to blush for using such blackguard language, so unbecoming your grave character. You cannot say that it was I set you a-hammering at the empty anvil, you profligate. However, as you are so industrious, I simply say it would be a thousand pities to take you from it. Nick, I love industry in my heart, and I always encourage it; so, work away. It's not often you spend your time so creditably. I'm afraid if you weren't at that you'd be worse employed."

"Bill, have bowels," said the operative. "You wouldn't go to lay more weight on a falling man, you know. You wouldn't disgrace your character by such a piece of iniquity as keeping an inoffensive gentleman, advanced in years, at such an unbecoming and rascally job as this. Generosity's your top virtue, Bill; not but that you have many other excellent ones, as well as that, among which, as you say yourself, I reckon industry. But still it is in generosity you *shine*. Come, Bill, honor bright, and release me."

"Name the terms, you profligate."

"You're above terms, William. A generous fellow like you never thinks of terms."

"Goodbye, old gentleman," said Bill, very coolly. "I'll drop in to see you once a month."

"No, no, Bill, you infern—a—a—you excellent, worthy, delightful fellow, not so fast. Not so fast. Come, name your terms, you sland—my dear Bill, name your terms."

"Seven years more."

"I agree, but—"

"And the same supply of cash as before, down on the nail here."

"Very good; very good. You're rather simple, Bill, rather soft, I must confess. Well, no matter. I shall yet turn the tab—a—hem? You are an exceedingly simple fellow, Bill. Still, there will come a day, my *dear* Bill—there will come—"

"Do you grumble, you vagrant? Another word, and I double the terms."

"Mum, William—mum; *tace* is Latin for a candle."

"Seven years more of grace, and the same measure of the needful that I got before. Aye or no?"

"Of grace, Bill! Aye! aye! aye! There's the cash. I accept the terms. O blood! The rascal—of grace! Bill!"

"Well, now drop the hammer, and vanish," says Billy. "But what would you think to take this sledge, while you stay, and give me a—eh, why in such a hurry?" he added, seeing that Satan withdrew in double-quick time.

"Hollo, Nicholas!" he shouted, "come back. You forgot something." And when the old gentleman looked behind him, Billy shook the hammer at him, on which he vanished altogether.

Billy now got into his old courses. And what shows the kind of people the world is made of, he also took up with his old company. When they saw that he had the money once more, and was sowing it about him in all directions, they immediately began to find excuses for his former extravagance.

"Say what you will," said one, "Bill Duffy's a spirited fellow, and bleeds like a prince."

"He's as hospitable a man in his own house, or out of it, as ever lived," said another.

"His only fault is," observed a third, "that he is, if anything, too generous, and doesn't know the value of money. His fault's on the right side, however."

"He has the spunk in him," said a fourth, "keeps a capital table, prime wines, and a standing welcome for his friends."

"Why," said a fifth, "if he doesn't enjoy his money while he lives, he won't when he's dead. So more power to him, and a wider throat to his purse."

Indeed, the very persons who were cramming themselves at his expense despised him at heart. They knew very well, however, how to take him on the weak side. Praise his generosity, and he would do anything. Call him a man of spirit, and you might fleece him to his face. Sometimes he would toss a purse of guineas to this knave, another to that flatterer, a third to a bully, and a fourth to some broken-down rake—and all to convince them that he was a sterling friend—a man of mettle and liberality. But never was he known to help a virtuous and struggling family—to assist the widow or the fatherless, or to do any other act that was truly useful. It is to be supposed the reason of this was, that as he spent it, as most of the world do, in the service of the Devil, by whose aid he got it, he was prevented from turning it to a good account. Between you and me, dear reader, there are more persons acting after Bill's fashion in the same world than you dream about.

When his money was out again, his friends served him the same rascally game once more. No sooner did his poverty become plain, than the knaves began to be troubled with small fits of modesty, such as an unwillingness to come to his place when there was no longer anything to be got there. A kind of virgin bashfulness prevented them from speaking to him when they saw him getting out on the wrong side of his clothes. Many of them would turn away from him in the prettiest and most delicate manner when they thought he wanted to borrow money from them—all for fear of putting him to the blush by asking it. Others again, when they saw him coming towards their houses about dinner hour, would become so confused, from mere gratitude, as to think themselves in another place, and their servants, seized, as it were, with the same feeling, would tell Bill that their masters were "not at home."

At length, after traveling the same villainous round as before, Bill was forced to betake himself, as a last remedy, to the forge. In other words, he found that there is, after all, nothing in this world that a man can rely on so firmly and surely as his own industry. Bill, however, wanted the organ of common sense, for his experience—and it was sharp enough to leave an impression—ran off him like water off a duck.

He took to his employment sorely against his grain. But he had now no choice. He must either work or starve, and starvation is like a great doctor, nobody tries it till every other remedy fails them. Bill had been twice rich, twice a gentleman among blackguards, but always a blackguard among gentlemen; for no wealth or acquaintance with decent society could rub the rust of his native vulgarity off him. He was now a common blinking sot in his forge; a drunken bully in the taproom, cursing and browbeating everyone as well as his wife; boasting of how much money he had spent in his day; swaggering about the high doings he carried on; telling stories about himself and Lord This at the Curragh; the dinners he gave—how much they cost him, and attempting to extort credit upon the strength of his former wealth. He was too ignorant, however, to know that he was publishing his own disgrace, and that it was a mean-spirited thing to be proud of what ought to make him blush through a deal board nine inches thick.

He was one morning industriously engaged in a quarrel with his wife, who, with a three-legged stool in her hand, appeared to mistake his head for his own anvil. He, in the meantime, paid his addresses to her with his leather apron, when who steps in to jog his memory about the little agreement that was between them, but Old Nick. The wife, it seems, in spite of all her exertions to the contrary, was getting the worst of it, and Sir Nicholas, willing to appear a gentleman of great gallantry, thought he could not do less than take up the lady's quarrel, particularly as Bill had laid her in a sleeping posture. Now Satan thought this too bad, and as he felt himself under many obligations to the sex, he determined to defend one of them on the present occasion. So as Judy rose, he turned upon the husband, and floored him by a clever facer.

"You unmanly villain," said he, "is this the way you treat your wife? 'Pon honor, Bill, I'll chastise you on the spot, I could not stand by a spectator of such ungentlemanly conduct without giving up all claim to gallant—"

Whack. The word was divided in his mouth by the blow of a churnstaff from Judy, who no sooner saw Bill struck, than she nailed Satan, who "fell" once more.

"What, you villain! That's for striking my husband like a murderer behind his back," said Judy, and she suited the action to the word. "That's for interfering between man and wife. Would you murder the poor man before my face? eh? If *he* beats me, you shabby dog you, who has a better right? I'm sure it's nothing out of your pocket. Must you have your finger in every pie?"

This was anything but idle talk; for at every word she gave him a remembrance hot and heavy. Nicholas backed, danced, and hopped. She advanced, still drubbing him with great perseverance, till at length he fell into the redoubtable armchair, which stood exactly behind him. Bill, who had been putting in two blows for Judy's one, seeing that his enemy was safe, now got between the Devil and his wife, a situation that few will be disposed to envy him.

"Tenderness, Judy," said the husband. "I hate cruelty. Go put the tongs in the fire, and make them red-hot. Nicholas, you have a nose," said he.

Satan began to rise, but was rather surprised to find that he could not budge.

"Nicholas," says Bill, "how is your pulse? you don't look well; that is to say, you look worse than usual."

The other attempted to rise, but found it a mistake.

"I'll thank you to come along," said Bill. "I have a fancy to travel under your guidance, and we'll take the Low Countries in our way, won't we? Get to your legs, you sinner; you know a bargain's a bargain between two *honest men*, Nicholas; meaning *yourself* and *me*. Judy, are the tongs hot?"

Satan's face was worth looking at, as he turned his eyes from the husband to the wife, and then fastened them on the tongs, now nearly at a furnace heat in the fire, conscious at the same time that he could not move out of the chair.

"Billy," said he, "you won't forget that I rewarded your generosity the last time I saw you in the way of business."

"Faith, Nicholas, it fails me to remember any generosity I ever showed you. Don't be womanish. I simply want to see what kind of stuff your nose is made of, and whether it will stretch like a rogue's conscience. If it does, we will flatter it up the chimley with the red-hot tongs, and when this old hat is fixed on the top of it, let us alone for a weathercock."

"Have a fellow-feeling, Mr. Duffy. You know *we* ought not to dispute. Drop the matter, and I give you the next seven years."

"We know all that," says Billy, opening the red-hot tongs very coolly.

"Mr. Duffy," said Satan, "if you cannot remember my friendship to yourself, don't forget how often I stood your father's friend, your grandfather's friend, and the friend of all your relations up to the tenth generation. I intended also to stand by your children after you, so long as the name of Duffy, and a respectable one it is, might last."

"Don't be blushing, Nick," says Bill, "you're too modest; that was ever your failing. Hold up your head, there's money bid for you. I'll give you such a nose, my good friend, that you will have to keep an outrider before you, to carry the end of it on his shoulder."

"Mr. Duffy, I pledge my honor to raise your children in the world as high as they can go; no matter whether they desire it or not."

"That's very kind of you," says the other, "and I'll do as much for your nose."

He gripped it as he spoke, and the old boy immediately sung out. Bill pulled, and the nose went with him like a piece of warm wax. He then transferred the tongs to Judy, got a ladder, resumed the tongs, ascended the chimney, and tugged stoutly at the nose until he got it five feet above the roof. He then fixed the hat upon the top of it, and came down.

"There's a weathercock," said Billy. "I defy Ireland to show such a beauty. Faith, Nick, it would make the prettiest steeple for a church in all Europe, and the old hat fits it to a shaving."

In this state, with his nose twisted up the chimney, Satan sat for some time, experiencing the novelty of what might be termed a peculiar sensation. At last the worthy husband and wife began to relent.

"I think," said Bill, "that we have made the most of the nose, as well as the joke. I believe, Judy, it's long enough."

"What is?" said Judy.

"Why, the joke," said the husband.

"Faith, and I think so is the nose," said Judy.

"What do you say yourself, Satan?" said Bill.

"Nothing at all, William," said the other. "But that—ha! ha!—it's a good joke—an excellent joke, and a goodly nose, too, as it *stands*. You were always a gentlemanly man, Bill, and did things with a grace; still, if I might give an opinion on such a trifle—"

"It's no trifle at all," says Bill, "if you speak of the nose."

"Very well, it is not," says the other. "Still, I am decidedly of opinion, that if you could shorten both the joke and the nose without further violence, you would lay me under very heavy obligations, which I shall be ready to acknowledge and repay as I ought."

"Come," said Bill, "shell out once more, and be off for seven years. As much as you came down with the last time, and vanish."

The words were scarcely spoken, when the money was at his feet, and Satan invisible. Nothing could surpass the mirth of Bill and his wife, at the result of this adventure. They laughed till they fell down on the floor.

It is useless to go over the same ground again. Bill was still incorrigible. The money went as the Devil's money always goes. Bill caroused and squandered, but could never turn a penny of it to a good purpose. In this way, year after year went, till the seventh was closed, and Bill's hour come. He was now, and had been for some time past, as miserable a knave as ever. Not a shilling had he, nor a shilling's worth, with the exception of his forge, his cabin, and a few articles of crazy furniture. In this state he was standing in his forge as before, straining his ingenuity how to make out a breakfast, when Satan came to look after him.

The old gentleman was sorely puzzled how to get at him. He kept skulking and sneaking about the forge for some time, till he saw that Bill hadn't a cross to bless himself with. He immediately changed himself into a guinea, and lay in an open place where he knew Bill would see him.

"If," said he, "I get once into his possession, I can manage him."

The honest smith took the bait, for it was well gilded. He clutched the guinea, put it into his purse, and closed it up.

"Ho! ho!" shouted the Devil out of the purse. "You're caught, Bill. I've secured you at last, you knave you. Why don't you despair, you villain, when you think of what's before you?"

"Why you unlucky old dog," said Bill. "Is it there you are? Will you always drive your head into every loophole that's set for you? Faith, Nick achora, I never had you bagged till now."

Satan then began to swell and tug and struggle with a view of getting out of the purse, but in vain. He found himself fast, and perceived that he was once more in Bill's power.

"Mr. Duffy," said he, "we understand each other. I'll give the seven years additional, and the cash on the nail."

"Be easy, Nicholas. You know the weight of the hammer, that's enough. It's not a whipping with feathers you're going to get, anyhow. Just be easy."

"Mr. Duffy, I grant I'm not your match. Release me, and I double the cash. I was merely trying your temper when I took the shape of a guinea."

"Faith and I'll try yours before you leave it, I've a notion."

He immediately commenced with the sledge, and Satan sang out with a considerable want of firmness.

"Am I heavy enough?" said Bill.

"Lighter, lighter, William, if you love me. I haven't been well, latterly, Mr. Duffy. I have been delicate. My health, in short, is in a very precarious state, Mr. Duffy."

"I can believe *that*," said Bill, "and it will be more so before I have done with you. Am I doing it right?"

"Beautifully, William. But a little of the heaviest; strike me light, Bill, my head's tender. Oh!"

"Heads or tails, my old boy," exclaimed the other. "I don't care which. It's all the same to me what side of you is up—but here goes to help the impression—hech!"

"Bill," said Nicholas, "is this gentlemanly treatment in your own respectable shop? Do you think, if you dropped into my little place, that I'd act this rascally part towards you? Have you no compunction?"

"I know," replied Bill, sledging away with vehemence, "that you're notorious for giving your friends a *warm* welcome. Divil an old youth more so. But you must be dealing in bad coin, must you? However, good or bad, you're in for a sweat now, you sinner. Am I doing it pretty?"

"Lovely, William—but, if possible, a little more delicate."

"Oh, how delicate you are! Maybe a cup of tea would serve you, or a little small gruel to compose your stomach."

"Mr. Duffy," said the gentleman in the purse, "hold your hand, and let us understand one another. I have a proposal to make."

"Hear the sinner, anyhow," said the wife.

"Name your own sum," said Satan, "only set me free."

"No, the sorra may take the toe you'll budge till you let Bill off," said the wife. "Hold him hard, Bill, barring he sets you clear of your engagement."

"There it is, my poesy," said Bill. "That's the condition. If you don't give me up, here's at you once more—and you must double the cash you gave the last time, too. So if you're of that opinion, say aye, leave the cash, and be off."

"Oh, murder," groaned the old one. "Am I to be done by an Irish spalpeen! I who was never done before."

"Keep a mannerly tongue in your head, Nick," said Bill. "If you're not *done* by this time you must be the Devil's tough morsel, for I'm sure you're long enough *at the fire*, you villain. Do you agree to the terms?"

"Aye, aye," replied the other. "Let me out. And I hope I have done with you."

The money again immediately appeared in a glittering heap before Bill, upon which he exclaimed:

"The aye has it, you dog. Take to your pumps now, and fair weather after you, you vagrant. But Nicholas—Nick—here—here."

The other looked back, and saw Bill, with a broad grin upon him, shaking the purse at him. "Nicholas, come back," said he, "I'm short a guinea."

The other shook his fist in return, and shouted out, looking over his shoulder as he spoke, but not stopping:

"Oh, you superlative villain, keep from me. I wish to have done with you. And all I hope is, that I'll never meet you either here or hereafter." So saying, he disappeared.

It would be useless to stop now, merely to inform our readers that Bill was beyond improvement. In short, he once more took to his old habits, and lived on exactly in the same manner as before. He had two sons, one as great a blackguard as himself, and who was also named after him. The other was a well-conducted, virtuous young man, called James, who left his father, and having relied upon his own industry and honest perseverance in life, arrived afterwards to great wealth, and built the town called Bally James Duff, which is so called from its founder until this day.

Bill, at length, in spite of all his wealth, was obliged, as he himself said, "to travel." In other words, he fell asleep one day, and forgot to awaken; or, in still plainer terms, he died.

Now, it is usual, when a man dies, to close the history of his life and adventures at once. But with our hero this cannot be the case. The moment Bill departed, he very naturally bent his steps towards the residence of Saint

Moroky, as being, in his opinion, likely to lead him towards the snuggest berth he could readily make out. On arriving he gave a very humble kind of a knock, and Saint Moroky appeared.

"God save your Reverence!" said Bill, very submissively.

"Be off. There's no admittance here for so pure a youth as you are," said Saint Moroky.

He was now so cold and fatigued that he cared little where he went, provided only, as he said himself, "he could rest his bones, and get an air of the fire." Accordingly, after arriving at a large black gate, he knocked, as before, and was told he would get instant admittance the moment he gave his name, in order that they might find out his berth from the registry, taking it for granted that he had been booked for them, as is usual in such cases.

"I think your master is acquainted with me," said Billy.

"If he were not, you'd not come here," said the porter. "There are no friendly visits made to us. What's your name?"

"Billy Duffy," he replied.

The porter and several of his companions gave a yell of terror, such as Bill had never heard before, and immediately every bolt was bolted, every chain drawn tight across the gate, and every available weight and bar placed against it, as if those who were inside dreaded a siege.

"Off, instantly," said the porter, "and let his Majesty know that the rascal he dreads so much is here at the gate."

In fact, such a racket and tumult were never heard as the very mention of Billy Duffy created among them.

"Oh," said Bill, with his eye to the bar of the gate, "I doubt I have got a bad name," and he shook his head like an innocent man who did not deserve it.

In the meantime, his old acquaintance came running towards the gate, with such haste and consternation that his tail was several times nearly tripping up his heels.

"Don't admit that rascal," he shouted. "Bar the gate. Make every chain and lock and bolt fast. I won't be safe. None of us will be safe. And I won't stay here, nor none of us need stay here, if he gets in. My bones are sore yet after him. No, no. Begone, you villain. You'll get no entrance here. I know you too well."

Bill could not help giving a broad, malicious grin at Satan, and, putting his nose through the bars, he exclaimed:

"Ha! you old dog, I have you afraid of me at last, have I?"

He had scarcely uttered the words, when his foe, who stood inside, instantly tweaked him by the nose, and Bill felt as if he had been gripped by the same red-hot tongs with which he himself had formerly tweaked the nose of Nicholas.

"Well," said he, "that's not the way *I* treated *you* once upon a time. Troth you're undecent. But you know what it is to get tinker's reckoning —to be paid in advance—so I owe you nothing for *that*, Nicholas."

Bill then departed, but soon found that in consequence of the inflammable materials which strong drink had thrown into his nose, that organ immediately took fire, and, indeed, to tell the truth, kept burning night and day, winter and summer, without ever once going out, from that hour to this.

Such was the sad fate of Billy Duffy, who has been walking without stop or stay, from place to place, ever since. And in consequence of the flame on his nose, and his beard being tangled like a wisp of hay, he has been christened by the country folk Will-o'-the-Wisp, while, as it were to show the mischief of his disposition, the circulating knave, knowing that he must seek the coldest bogs and quagmires in order to cool his nose, seizes upon that opportunity of misleading the unthinking and tipsy night travelers from their way, just that he may have the satisfaction of still taking in as many as possible.

❖ Willy the Wisp

MYLES DOLAN ◈ *CAVAN*
MICHAEL J. MURPHY *1974*

This man he was a blacksmith and he was a very heavy drinker, and no matter how much money he could make he could never get enough to do him. So someone told him that if he'd go out to such'n a place, in the middle of the night, and call Old Nick three times, Nick'd appear to him, and give him as much money as he'd want.

So begod he'd do anything for money; so he went out to this place in the middle of the night and called three times to Old Nick, and the Divil appeared to him: and he give him as much money as he'd spend for seven years; but he'd have to come and take him when the time would be up.

Well begod anyway, he was a blacksmith, and he had piles of money: he had so much money he was drinking away, and he was building a town; he joined to build a town in the County Meath, and the town he built was Trim.

He was building this town and he still had the forge; and this saint appeared to him; and he helped him; and he says to the blacksmith:

"I'll give you three wishes, and whatever you wish for you'll get it."

"Well," he says, "the first wish I want, any man that takes my hammer in his hand he cannot get rid of it till I take it from him.

"And the second wish is," he says, "that anyone that sits in my armchair he'll never get out of it till I take him out of it.

"And the third wish," he says, "any money that goes into my purse will never come out till I take it out of it."

"Ah . . . if only you had wished for Heaven and you'd get it," says the saint.

But anyway, he was working away at the town, and in the forge, and he was shoeing a horse, and the seven years was up and the Divil come for him. And Willy—that was his name—was in the forge, working in the forge, when the Divil come.

"Come . . ."

"Right," says Willy. "Take that hammer and time this shoe with a few taps."

The Divil took the hammer.

"When I shoe this mare I'll be with you," says Willy.

The Divil took the hammer, and Willy left him and went up to his house and left him there hammering in the forge for three days, and when Willy came back the Divil was hammering away. And the Divil begged him for all sakes and as much more money to release him for another seven years.

"Right," says Willy. "Give me that hammer."

And away with the Divil.

So Willy had piles of money for another seven years.

Still working away in his forge, and the seven more years was up and the Divil come for him. And Willy was working in the forge again.

"Are you ready for to come the day? You must come the day," says the Divil.

"Right," says Willy. "I'll be with you when I get a cup of tea. Come up to the house," he says, "and when I have a cup of tea I'll be with you. Sit down in that chair."

Got the cup of tea. The Divil sat down. So Willy left him in the armchair, and Willy went down to the forge and reddened an iron, and come up and started to persecute the Divil.

The Divil begged him for all sakes to let him free and he'd give him as much more money for another seven years; but he'd surely have to come then.

"Right," says Willy. "Come on, get out."

And the Divil went; and Willy carried on for another seven years more.

And the Divil come in the latter end and Willy was once more working in the forge.

"Are you coming? ... You have to come."

"Right," says Willy. "I'll be with you."

Of course all his money was gone and the time was up, seven years, he would get no more. So Willy threw his coat on his shoulder and walked off with the Divil and was just going by a public house.

"I'm very dry," says Willy, "I'd like a drink. I have no money," he says. "You could turn yourself into a half-crown," he says, "and put it in my purse, and you'd be out of the public house as soon as me."

So, all right, the Divil did it. Willy put the half-crown into his purse and went back to the forge. He lit the fire, and he put the purse into the fire and reddened the purse and the half-crown in it, and he put it on the anvil and joined to hammer it with the sledge.

The Divil yelled to be let go. He says:

"Let me go," he says, "and I'll give you as much more money and never ask you to come with me."

"Right," says Willy.

So he did, and the Divil was free; and Willie worked away. And when Willy died he went to Heaven. He was met at the gates.

"Aw, you can't come in here. You sold yourself to the Divil. You'll have to go below."

He went down below to Hell and the Divil wouldn't let him in there either: he was afraid if Willy got in he'd lay Hell waste. So he lit a wisp in the fire and he gave it to Willy and sent him back. And he's going from Heaven to Hell to this day, and that's what they call "Willy The Wisp."

❖ THE BUIDEACH, THE TINKER, AND THE BLACK DONKEY

PETER SREHANE ◈ *MAYO*
DOUGLAS HYDE *1895*

In times long ago there was a poor widow living near Castlebar, in the County Mayo. She had an only son, and he never grew one inch from the time he was five years old, and the people called him Buideach as a nickname.

One day when the Buideach was about fifteen years of age his mother went to Castlebar. She was not gone more than an hour when there came a big Tinker, and a Black Donkey with him, to the door, and "Are you in, woman of the house?" said the Tinker.

"She is not," said the Buideach, "and she told me not to let anyone in until she'd come home herself."

The Tinker walked in, and when he looked at the Buideach he said, "Indeed you're a nice boy to keep anyone at all out, you could not keep out a turkey cock."

The Buideach rose of a leap and gave the big Tinker a fist between the two eyes and pitched him out on the top of his head, under the feet of the Black Donkey.

The Tinker rose up in a rage and made an attempt to get hold of the Buideach, but he gave him another fist at the butt of the ear and threw him out again under the feet of the Black Donkey.

The donkey began to bray pitifully, and when the Buideach went out to see why, the Tinker was dead. "You have killed my master," said the Black Donkey, "and indeed I am not sorry for it, he often gave me a heavy beating without cause."

The Buideach was astonished when he heard the Black Donkey speaking, and he said, "You are not a proper donkey."

"Indeed, I have only been an ass for seven years. My story is a pitiful one. I was the son of a gentleman."

"Musha, then, I would like to hear your story," said the Buideach.

"Come in, then, to the end of the house. Cover up the Tinker in the dunghill, and I will tell you my story."

The Buideach drew the dead man over to the dunghill and covered him up. The Black Donkey walked into the house and said, "I was the son of a gentleman, but I was a bad son, and I died under a heavy load of deadly sins on my poor soul; and I would be burning in Hell now were it not for the Virgin Mary. I used to say a little prayer in honor of her every night, and when I went into the presence of the Great Judge I was sentenced to Hell until His mother spoke to the Judge and He changed his sentence, and there was made of me a Black Donkey, and I was given to the Tinker for the space of seven years, until he should die a worldly death. The Tinker was a limb of the Devil, and it was I who gave you strength to kill him. But you are not done with him yet. He will come to life again at the end of seven days, and if you are there before him he will kill you as sure as you are alive."

"I never left this townland since I was born," said the Buideach, "and I would not like to desert my mother."

"Would it not be better for you to leave your mother than to lose your life in a state of mortal sin and be forever burning in Hell?"

"I don't know any place where I could go into hiding," said the Buideach. "But since it has turned out that it was you who put strength into my hand to kill the Tinker, perhaps you would direct me to some place where I could be safe from him."

"Did you ever hear talk of Lough Derg?"

"Indeed, I did," said the Buideach. "My grandmother was once on a pilgrimage there, but I don't know where it is."

"I will bring you there tomorrow night. There is a monastery underground on the island, and an old friar in it who sees the Virgin Mary every Saturday. Tell him your case and take his advice in every single thing. He will put you to penance, but penance on this world is better than the pains of Hell forever. You know where the little dun is, which is at the back of the old castle. If you are in the dun about three hours after nightfall I shall be there before you and bring you to Lough Derg."

"I shall be there if I'm alive," said the Buideach. "But is there any fear of me that the Tinker will get up before that time?"

"There is no fear," said the Black Donkey, "unless you tell somebody that you killed him. If you tell anything about him he will get up and he will slay yourself and your mother."

"By my soul, then, I'll be silent about him," said the Buideach.

That evening when the Buideach's mother came home she asked him did anybody come to the house since she went away.

"I did not see anyone," said he, "but an old pedlar with a bag, and he got nothing from me."

"I see the track of the shoe of a horse or a donkey outside the door, and it was not there in the morning when I was going out," said she.

"It was Páidin Éamoinn the fool, who was riding Big Mary O'Brien's ass," said the Buideach.

The Buideach never slept a wink all that night but thinking of the Tinker and the Black Donkey. The next day he was in great anxiety. His mother observed that and asked him what was on him.

"There's not a feather on me," says he.

That night when the mother was asleep the Buideach stole out and never stopped until he came to the little dun. The Black Donkey was there before him and said, "Are you ready?"

"I am," said the Buideach, "but I am grieved that I did not get my mother's blessing. She will be very anxious until I come back again."

"Indeed she will not be anxious at all, because there is another Buideach at your mother's side at home, so like you that she won't know that it is not yourself that's in it; but I'll bring him away with me before you come back."

"I am very much obliged to you and I am ready to go with you now," said he.

"Leap up on my back. There is a long journey before us," said the Donkey.

The Buideach leapt on his back, and the moment he did so he heard thunder and saw great lightning. There came down a big cloud which closed around the black ass and its rider. The Buideach lost the sight of his eyes, and a heavy sleep fell upon him, and when he awoke he was on an island in Lough Derg, standing in the presence of the ancient friar.

The friar began to talk to him, and said, "What brought you here, my son?"

"Well, then, indeed, I don't rightly know," said the Buideach.

"I will know soon," said the friar. "Come with me."

He followed the old friar down under the earth, until they came to a little chamber that was cut in the rock. "Now," said the friar, "go down on your knees and make your confession and do not conceal any crime."

The Buideach went down on his knees and told everything that happened to him concerning the Tinker and the Black Donkey.

The friar then put him under penance for seven days and seven nights, without food or drink, walking on his bare knees amongst the rocks and sharp stones. He went through the penance, and by the seventh day there was not a morsel of skin or flesh on his knees, and he was like a shadow with the hunger. When he had the penance finished the old friar came and said, "It's time for you to be going home."

"I have no knowledge of the way or of how to go back," said the Buideach.

"Your friend the Black Donkey will bring you back," said the friar. "He will be here tonight; and when you go home spend your life piously and do not tell to anyone except to your father confessor that you were here."

"Tell me, Father, is there any danger of me from the Tinker?"

"There is not," said the friar; "he is an ass himself now with a tinker from the province of Munster, and he will be in that shape for one-and-twenty years, and after that he will go to eternal rest. Depart now to your chamber. You will hear a little bell after the darkness of night, and as soon as you shall hear it, go up onto the island, and the Black Donkey will be there before you, and he will bring you home; my blessing with you."

The Buideach went to his room, and as soon as he heard the bell he went up to the island and his friend the Black Donkey was waiting for him.

"Jump up on my back, Buideach, I have not a moment to lose," said the donkey.

He did so, and on the spot he heard the thunder and saw the lightning. A great cloud came down and enveloped the Black Donkey and its rider. Heavy sleep fell upon the Buideach, and when he awoke he found himself in the little dun at home, standing in the presence of the Black Donkey.

"Go home now to your mother. The other Buideach is gone from her side. She is in deep sleep and she won't feel you going in."

"Is there any fear of me from the Tinker?" said he.

"Did not the blessed friar tell you that there is not," said the Black Donkey. "I will protect you. Put your hand in my left ear, and you will get there a purse which will never be empty during your life. Be good to poor people and to widows and to orphans, and you will have a long life and a happy death, and Heaven at the end."

The Buideach went home and went to sleep, and the mother never had had a notion that the other Buideach was not her own son.

At the end of a week after this the Buideach said to his mother, "Is not this a fair day in Castlebar?"

"Yes, indeed," said she.

"Well then, you ought to go there and buy a cow," says he.

"Don't be humbugging your mother or you'll have no luck," says she.

"Upon my word I am not humbugging," said he. "God sent a purse my way, and there is more than the price of a cow in it."

"Perhaps you did not get it honestly. Tell me, where did you find it?"

"I'll tell you nothing about it, except that I found it honestly, and if you have any doubt about my word, let the thing be."

Women are nearly always given to covetousness, and she was not free from it.

"Give me the price of the cow."

He handed her twenty pieces of gold. "You'll get a good cow for all that money," said he.

"I will," said she, "but I'd like to have the price of a pig."

"Do not be greedy, Mother," said he. "You won't get any more this time."

The mother went to the fair and she bought a milch cow, and some clothes for the Buideach, and when he got her gone he went to the parish priest and said that he would like to make confession. He told the priest then everything that happened to him from the time he met the Tinker and the Black Donkey.

"Indeed, you are a good boy," said the priest. "Give me some of the gold."

The Buideach gave him twenty pieces, but he was not satisfied with that, and he asked for the price of a horse.

"I did not think that a priest would be covetous," said he, "but I see now that they are as covetous as women. Here are twenty more pieces for you. Are you satisfied now?"

"I am, and I am not," said the priest. "Since you have a purse which will never be empty as long as you live, you should be able to give me as much as would set up a fine church in place of the miserable one which we have in the parish now."

"Get workmen and masons, and begin the church, and I'll give you the workmen's wages from week to week," said the Buideach.

"I'd sooner have it now," said the priest. "A thousand pieces will do the work, and if you give them to me now I'll put up the church."

The Buideach gave him one thousand pieces of gold out of the purse, and the purse was none the lighter for it.

The Buideach came home and his mother was there before him, with a fine milch cow and new clothes for himself. "Indeed, that's a good cow," said he. "We can give the poor people some milk every morning."

"Indeed they must wait until I churn, and I'll give them the buttermilk —until I buy a pig."

"It's the new milk you'll give the poor people," said the Buideach. "We can buy butter."

"I think you have lost your senses," says the mother. "You'll want the little share of riches which God sent you before I'm a year in the grave."

"How do you know but that I might not be in the grave before you?" said he. "But at all events God will send me my enough."

When they were talking there came a poor woman, and three children to the door and asked for alms in the honor of God and Mary.

"I have nothing for ye this time," said the widow.

"Don't say that, Mother," said the Buideach. "I have alms to give in the name of God and His mother Mary." With that he went out and gave a gold piece to the poor woman, and said to his mother, "Milk the cow and give those poor children a drink."

"I will not," said the mother.

"Then I'll do it myself," said he.

He got the vessel, milked the cow, and gave lots of new milk to the poor children and to the woman. When they were gone away the mother said to him, "Your purse will be soon empty."

"I have no fear of that," said he. "It's God who sent it to me, and I'll make a good use of it," says he.

"Have your own way," said she. "But you'll be sorry for it yet."

The next day lots of people came to the Buideach asking for alms, and he never let them go away from him empty-handed. The name and fame of the Buideach went through the country like lightning, and men said that he was in partnership with the Good People. But others said that it was the Devil who was giving him the gold, and they made a complaint against him to the parish priest. But the priest said that the Buideach was a decent good boy, and that it was God who gave him the means, and that he was making good use of them.

The Buideach went on well now, and he began growing until he was almost six feet high.

His mother died and he fell in love with a pretty girl, and he was not long until they were married.

He had not a day's luck from that time forward. His wife got to know that he had a wonderful purse and nothing could satisfy her but she must get it. He refused her often, but she was giving him no rest, day or night, until she got the purse from him at last. Then, when she got it, she had no respect for it. She went to Castlebar to buy silks and satins, but when she opened the purse, in place of gold pieces being in it there was nothing but pieces of pebbles. She came back and great anger on her, and said, "Isn't it a nice fool you made of me giving me a purse filled with little stones instead of the purse with the gold in it."

"I gave you the right purse," said he. "I have no second one."

He seized the purse and opened it, and as sure as I'm telling it to you, there was nothing in it but little bits of pebbles.

There was an awful grief upon the Buideach, and it was not long until he was mad, tearing his hair, and beating his head against the wall.

The priest was sent for but he could get neither sense nor reason out of the Buideach. He tore off his clothes and went naked and mad through the country.

About a week after that the neighbors found the poor Buideach dead at the foot of a bush in the little dun.

That old bush is growing in the dun yet, and the people call it the "Buideach's Bush," but as for himself it is certain that he went to Heaven.

❖ THE MAN WHO HAD NO STORY

MICHAEL JAMES TIMONEY ◈ *DONEGAL*
SÉAMAS Ó CATHÁIN *1965*

Well, there was a man down here in Barr an Ghaoith a long time ago and his name was Brian Ó Braonacháin. The trade that he had was cutting rods, making baskets of them, and selling them in Glenties and in Dunloe and in Fintown and everywhere he could get them sold.

But one year he was down here and there wasn't a single rod in the whole of Barr an Ghaoith that he hadn't cut, made baskets of, sold, and then spent the money.

Those were bad times—the English were in power and they wouldn't let the Irish earn a single penny in any way. And Brian didn't know what to do.

But in those days there was a little glen outside of Barr an Ghaoith that they called Alt an Torr and there were remarkably fine rods growing there. But nobody dared cut any rods there, for everyone made out that it was a fairy glen.

But one morning Brian said to his wife that if she made him up a little lunch he would go out and cut the makings of a couple of baskets and perhaps no harm would come to him.

The wife got up and made up a lunch for him. He put it in his pocket and he took a hook and a rope under his arm.

He went out to the glen and he wasn't long in the glen until he had cut two fine bundles of rods.

When he was tying them together so that he could carry them with the rope on his back, a terrible fog started to gather around him. He decided that he would sit down and eat his lunch and perhaps that the fog would clear. He sat down and he ate the lunch he had with him and when he had finished eating it was so dark that he could not see his finger in front of him.

He stood up and he got terribly scared. He looked to the east and he looked to the west and he saw a light. Where there is light there must be people, he thought, and he headed for the light. And he tripped and fell the whole time, but in the end he came up to the light. There was a big long house there. The door was open and there was a fine light coming out of the window and the door.

He put his head in the door and an old woman was sitting in the corner and an old man on the other side of the fire. Both of them saluted Brian Ó Braonacháin from Barr an Ghaoith and wished him welcome, and they asked him to come up and sit in at the fire.

Brian came up and he sat in at the fire between the pair of them. They talked for a while. But he had not been sitting there long when the old man asked him to tell a fairy tale.

"That is something that I never did in all my life," said Brian, "tell a story of any kind. I can't tell Fenian tales or fairy tales of any kind."

"Well," said the old woman, said she, "take that bucket and go down to the well below the house and fetch a bucket of water and do something for your keep."

"I'll do anything," said Brian, "except tell a story."

He took the bucket, went down to the well and filled it with water from the well. He left it standing on the flagstone beside the well, so that the water would run off it, before he brought it in. But a big blast of wind came and he was swept off up into the sky. He was blown east and he was blown west and when he fell to the ground he could see neither the bucket nor the well nor anything at all.

He looked around and he saw a light and he made out that where there was light there must be people and he headed for the light. He tripped and fell the whole time, it was so dark. But at last he came to the light. There was a big long house there, far bigger than the first house, two lights in it and a fine light out of the door.

He put his head in the door, and what was it but a wake-house. There was a row of men sitting by the back wall of the house and a row of men sitting by the front wall of the house and up at the fire there was a girl with curly black hair sitting on a chair. She saluted and welcomed Brian Ó Braonacháin from Barr an Ghaoith and she asked him to come up and sit beside her on the chair.

Brian came up and he sat beside her on the chair and very shy he was, too. But he had not been sitting long when a big man who was in the company stood up.

"It is a very lonely wake we are having here tonight," said he, "a couple of us must go to get a fiddler, so that we can start dancing."

"Oh," said the girl with the curly black hair, "you don't need to go for any fiddler tonight," said she, "you have the best fiddler in Ireland among you here tonight," said she, "Brian Ó Braonacháin from Barr an Ghaoith."

"Oh, that is something I never did in my life," said Brian, "play a tune on a fiddle, and there is no music or singing or fiddling of any kind in my head."

"Oh," said she, "don't make me a liar, you are the very man who can fiddle."

Before Brian knew he had the bow and the fiddle in his hand and he played away and they danced away, and they all said that they had never heard any fiddler playing a tune on a fiddle better than Brian Ó Braonacháin from Barr an Ghaoith.

The big man who was in the company stood up and said that the dancing must stop now. "A couple of us must go for the priest, so that we can say Mass," said he, "for this corpse must go out of here before daybreak."

"Oh," said the girl with the curly dark hair, "there is no need to go for any priest tonight, the best priest in Ireland is sitting here beside me on the chair, Brian Ó Braonacháin from Barr an Ghaoith."

"Oh, I have nothing of a priest's power or holiness," said Brian, "and I do not know anything about a priest's work in any way."

"Come, come," said she, "you will do that just as well as you did the rest."

Before Brian knew he was standing at the altar with two clerks and with the vestments on him.

He started to say Mass and he gave out the prayers after Mass. And the whole congregation that was listening said that they never heard any priest in Ireland giving out prayers better than Brian Ó Braonacháin.

Then the corpse was placed in a coffin outside the door and four men put the coffin on their shoulders. They were three fairly short men and one big tall man and the coffin was terribly shaky.

"One or two of us," said the big man who was in the company, said he, "must go for a doctor so that we can cut a piece off the legs of that big man to make him level with the other three."

"Oh," said the girl with the curly black hair, "you don't need to go for any doctor tonight, the best doctor in Ireland is here among you tonight, Brian Ó Braonacháin from Barr an Ghaoith."

"Oh, that is something I never did in my life," said Brian, "doctoring of any sort. I never got any doctor's schooling at all."

"You'll do that just as well as you did the rest," said she.

The lances were given to Brian and he cut a piece off the big man's legs, under his knees, and he stuck the legs back on, and he made him level with the other three men.

Then they put the coffin on their shoulders and they walked gently and carefully west, until they came to the graveyard. There was a big stone wall around the graveyard, ten feet high, or maybe twelve. And they had to lift one man up on the wall first and they were going up one by one and going down into the graveyard on the other side. And the last man on top of the wall ready to go down into the graveyard was Brian Ó Braonacháin.

But a big blast of wind came and he was swept off up into the sky. He was blown to the east and he was blown to the west. When he fell down to the ground, he could see neither the graveyard nor the coffin nor the funeral. But where did he fall? He fell down on the flagstone beside the well where he had been at the beginning of the night. He looked at the bucket and the water was hardly dry on the outside of it.

He took the bucket and up he went into the house. And the old man and the old woman were sitting where he had left them at nightfall. He left the bucket by the dresser and he came up and sat in between the pair of them again.

"Now, Brian," said the old man, "can you tell a fairy tale?"

"I can," said he, "I am the man who has got a story to tell."

He began to tell the old woman and the old man what he had gone through since nightfall.

"Well, Brian," said the old man, "wherever you are from now on," said he, "and whenever anybody asks you to tell a story, tell them that story, and you are the man who will have a story to tell."

The old woman got up and made Brian a good supper. And when he had had his supper she made up a feather bed for him and he went to bed. And he wasn't in bed long before he fell asleep, for he was tired after all he had gone through since nightfall.

But when he woke in the morning, where was he? He was lying in Alt an Torr outside Barr an Ghaoith with his head on the two bundles of rods. He got up and went home and he never cut a rod from that day to this.

BIBLIOGRAPHY AND NOTES

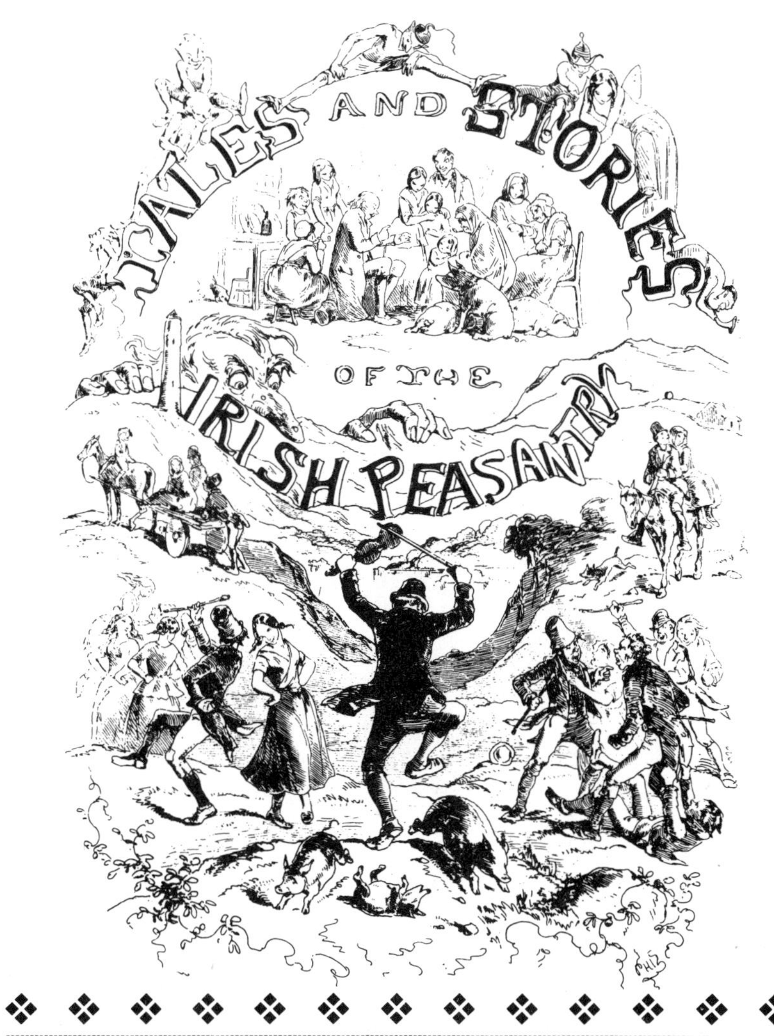

TITLE PAGE
William Carleton, *Tales and Stories of the Irish Peasantry*, 1846

❖ Bibliography

This list includes the books and articles from which I drew this book's tales. Specific sources for each of the tales follow. The list also contains works I found especially helpful in constructing the Preface and Introduction. Then I added a few more works so that this list can serve you as an introductory bibliography of the Irish tradition.

Aalen, F. H. A. *Man and the Landscape in Ireland.* London: Academic Press, 1978.

Aarne, Antti, and Stith Thompson. *The Types of the Folktale: A Classification and Bibliography.* Folklore Fellows' Communications 184. Helsinki: Suomalainen Tiedeakatemia, 1961.

Anderson, Alan Orr, and Marjorie Ogilvie Anderson. *Adomnan's Life of Columba.* London: Thomas Nelson, 1961.

Arensberg, Conrad. *The Irish Countryman.* Garden City, N.Y.: Natural History Press, 1968; first pub. 1937.

Bayne, Samuel G. *On an Irish Jaunting-Car Through Donegal and Connemara.* New York: Harper & Brothers, 1902.

Beckett, J. C. *The Making of Modern Ireland, 1603–1923.* New York: Alfred A. Knopf, 1973.

Behan, Brendan. *Brendan Behan's Island: An Irish Sketch-book.* New York: Bernard Geis Associates (Random House), 1962.

Bell, Sam Hanna. *Erin's Orange Lily.* London: Dennis Dobson, 1956.

Bourke, Éamon. *Eochair, A King's Son in Ireland.* Recorded by Liam Costello; edited by Kevin O'Nolan. Dublin: Comhairle Bhéaloideas Éireann, 1982.

Boylan, Henry. *A Dictionary of Irish Biography.* Dublin: Gill & Macmillan, 1978.

Breathnach, Breandán. *Folk Music and Dances of Ireland.* Dublin: Talbot Press, 1971.

Buchanan, Ronald H. "The Folklore of an Irish Townland." *Ulster Folklife* 2 (1956): 43–55.

Bullock, Shan F. *After Sixty Years.* London: Simpson, Low, & Marston, [1931].

Bullock, Shan F. *Irish Pastorals.* New York: McClure, Phillips, 1901.

Byrne, Donn. *Ireland: The Rock Whence I Was Hewn.* Boston: Little, Brown, 1929.

Carbery, Mary. *The Farm by Lough Gur: The Story of Mary Fogarty (Sissy O'Brien).* London: Longmans, Green, 1937.

Carleton, William. *Tales and Stories of the Irish Peasantry. (Tales and Sketches Illustrating the Character, Usages, Traditions, Sports and Pastimes of the Irish Peasantry.)* Dublin: James Duffy, 1846.

Carleton, William, *Traits and Stories of the Irish Peasantry.* London: William Tegg, 1869; first pub. 1842.

Carney, James. *The Problem of St. Patrick.* Dublin: Dublin Institute for Advanced Studies, 1973.

Carpenter, Andrew, ed. *My Uncle John: Edward Stephens's Life of J. M. Synge.* London: Oxford University Press, 1974.

Casey, Daniel J., and Robert E. Rhodes, eds. *Views of the Irish Peasantry.* Hamden, Conn.: Archon Books, 1977.

Christiansen, Reidar Th. *The Migratory Legends: A Proposed List of Types with a Systematic Catalogue of the Norwegian Variants.* Folklore Fellows' Communications 175. Helsinki: Suomalainen Tiedeakatemia, 1958.

Colum, Padraic. *Story Telling New and Old.* New York: Macmillan, 1968; first pub. 1927.

Corkery, Daniel. *Synge and Anglo-Irish Literature.* Cork: Mercier Press, 1966.

Coxhead, Elizabeth. *Lady Gregory: A Literary Portrait.* London: Secker & Warburg, 1966; first pub. 1961.

Croker, T. Crofton. *Fairy Legends and Traditions of the South of Ireland.* London: John Murray, 1825.

Croker, T. Crofton. *Fairy Legends and Traditions of the South of Ireland: The New Series: Two Volumes in One.* London: John Murray, 1828.

Croker, T. Crofton. *Fairy Legends and Traditions of the South of Ireland.* Family Library 47. London: John Murray, 1834.

Croker, T. Crofton. *Fairy Legends and Traditions of the South of Ireland.* Edited by Thomas Wright. London: William Tegg, 1862.

Croker, T. Crofton. *Popular Songs of Ireland.* London: Henry Colburn, 1839.

Croker, T. Crofton. *Researches in the South of Ireland, Illustrative of the Scenery, Architectural Remains, and the Manners and Superstitions of the Peasantry.* London: John Murray, 1824.

Cross, Eric. *The Tailor and Ansty.* New York: Devin-Adair, 1964; first pub. 1942.

Cross, Tom Peete, and Clark Harris Slover. *Ancient Irish Tales.* New York: Henry Holt, 1936.

Curtin, Jeremiah. *Irish Folk-Tales.* Edited by Séamus Ó Duilearga (James Delargy). Dublin: Educational Company of Ireland, 1943.

Curtin, Jeremiah. *Myths and Folk-Lore of Ireland.* Boston: Little, Brown, 1906; first pub. 1890.

Curtin, Jeremiah. *Tales of the Fairies and of the Ghost World Collected from Oral Tradition in South-West Munster.* Boston: Little, Brown, 1895.

Curtis, Edmund. *A History of Ireland.* London: Methuen, 1961; first pub. 1936.

Daly, Dominic. *The Young Douglas Hyde: The Dawn of the Irish Revolution and Renaissance, 1874–1893.* Dublin: Irish University Press, 1974.

Danaher, Kevin (Caoimhín Ó Danachair). *Folktales of the Irish Countryside.* Cork: Mercier Press, 1967.

Danaher, Kevin (Caoimhín Ó Danachair). *Gentle Places and Simple Things.* Cork: Mercier Press, 1964.

Danaher, Kevin (Caoimhín Ó Danachair). *In Ireland Long Ago.* Cork: Mercier Press, 1962.

Danaher, Kevin (Caoimhín Ó Danachair). *Irish Country People.* Cork: Mercier Press, 1966.

Danaher, Kevin (Caoimhín Ó Danachair). *The Pleasant Land of Ireland.* Cork: Mercier Press, 1970.

Danaher, Kevin (Caoimhín Ó Danachair). *The Year in Ireland.* Cork: Mercier Press, 1972.

Deeney, Daniel. *Peasant Lore from Gaelic Ireland.* London: David Nutt, 1900.

Delargy, James H. (Séamus Ó Duilearga). "Clare Folk Tales." *Béaloideas* 5, no. 1 (1935): 24–27.

Delargy, James H. (Séamus Ó Duilearga). "Folklore." In *Saorstát Eireann: Irish Free State Official Handbook,* pp. 264–266. Dublin: Talbot Press, 1932.

Delargy, James H. (Séamus Ó Duilearga). "Four Clare Folktales." *Béaloideas* 32 (1964): 43–70.

Delargy, James H. (Séamus Ó Duilearga). "The Gaelic Story-Teller. With Some Notes on Gaelic Folk-Tales." *Proceedings of the British Academy* (1945): 177–221.

de Paor, Máire and Liam. *Early Christian Ireland.* London: Thames & Hudson, 1978; first pub. 1958.

Dillon, Myles, and Nora K. Chadwick. *The Celtic Realms.* New York: New American Library, 1967.

Donoghue, Denis, ed. *W. B. Yeats: Memoirs.* New York: Macmillan, 1972.

Dorson, Richard M. *The British Folklorists: A History.* Chicago: University of Chicago Press, 1968.

Doyle, Lynn. *An Ulster Childhood.* London: Duckworth, 1926.

Dunleavy, Gareth W. *Douglas Hyde.* Irish Writers Series. Lewisburg, Pa.: Bucknell University Press, 1974.

Ellmann, Richard. *James Joyce.* New York: Oxford University Press, 1959.

Evans, E. Estyn, ed. *Harvest Home: The Last Sheaf: A Selection from the Writings of T. G. F. Paterson.* Dundalk: Dundalgan Press for the Armagh County Museum, 1975.

Evans, E. Estyn. *Irish Folk Ways.* New York: Devin-Adair, 1957.

Evans, E. Estyn. *Irish Heritage: The Landscape, the People, and Their Work.* Dundalk: W. Tempest, Dundalgan Press, 1942.

Evans, E. Estyn. *Mourne Country: Landscape and Life in South Down.* Dundalk: W. Tempest, Dundalgan Press, 1967; first pub. 1951.

Evans, E. Estyn. *The Personality of Ireland: Habitat, Heritage, and History.* Cambridge: Cambridge University Press, 1973.

Evans, E. Estyn, and Bryan S. Turner. *Ireland's Eye: The Photographs of Robert John Welch.* Belfast: Blackstaff Press, 1977.

Flower, Robin. *The Irish Tradition.* Oxford: Oxford University Press, 1978; first pub. 1947.

Flower, Robin. *The Western Island: Or, The Great Blasket.* New York: Oxford University Press, 1945.

Foster, Jeanne Cooper. *Ulster Folklore*. Belfast: H. R. Carter, 1951.

Fox, Robin. *The Tory Islanders: A People of the Celtic Fringe*. Cambridge: Cambridge University Press, 1978.

Gailey, Alan. *Irish Folk Drama*. Cork: Mercier Press, 1969.

Gibbings, Robert. *Lovely Is the Lee*. New York: E. P. Dutton, 1945.

Glassie, Henry. *All Silver and No Brass: An Irish Christmas Mumming*. Bloomington: Indiana University Press; Dublin: Dolmen Press, 1976. Philadelphia: University of Pennsylvania Press; Dingle: Brandon Books, 1983.

Glassie, Henry. *Irish Folk History: Texts from the North*. Philadelphia: University of Pennsylvania Press; Dublin: O'Brien Press, 1982.

Glassie, Henry. *Passing the Time in Ballymenone: Culture and History of an Ulster Community*. Philadelphia: University of Pennsylvania Press; Dublin: O'Brien Press, 1982.

Green, Alice Stopford. *Irish Nationality*. New York: Henry Holt, 1911.

Gregory, Lady Augusta. *A Book of Saints and Wonders*. Dundrum: Dun Emer Press, 1906; London: John Murray, 1907.

Gregory, Lady Augusta. *Cuchulain of Muirthemne: The Story of the Men of the Red Branch of Ulster*. London: John Murray, 1902.

Gregory, Lady Augusta. *Gods and Fighting Men: The Story of the Tuatha De Danaan and the Fianna of Ireland*. London: John Murray, 1904.

Gregory, Lady Augusta. *The Kiltartan History Book*. Dublin: Maunsel, 1909; London: T. Fisher Unwin, 1926.

Gregory, Lady Augusta. *The Kiltartan Wonder Book*. Dublin: Maunsel, [1910].

Gregory, Lady Augusta. *Poets and Dreamers: Studies and Translations from the Irish*. Dublin: Hodges, Figgis, 1903.

Gregory, Lady Augusta. *Visions and Beliefs in the West of Ireland*. Coole Edition. New York: Oxford University Press, 1970; first pub. 1920.

Hall, Mr. and Mrs. S. C. *Ireland: Its Scenery, Character, &c.* 3 vols. London: Hall, Virtue, [1850]; first pub. 1841–1843.

Hall, Mrs. S. C. *Sketches of Irish Character*. New York: E. Ferrett, 1845.

Harbinson, Robert. *Song of Erne*. London: Faber & Faber, 1960.

Heaney, Seamus. *Door into the Dark*. London: Faber & Faber, 1969.

Hone, Joseph. *W. B. Yeats: 1865–1939*. New York: Macmillan, 1943.

Hyde, Douglas. *Beside the Fire: A Collection of Irish Gaelic Folk Stories*. London: David Nutt, 1890.

Hyde, Douglas. *Legends of Saints and Sinners*. London: Gresham, [1915].

Hyde, Douglas. *A Literary History of Ireland from Earliest Times to the Present Day*. London: Ernest Benn, 1967; first pub. 1899.

Hyde, Douglas. *Mayo Stories Told by Thomas Casey*. Irish Texts Society 36. Dublin: Educational Company of Ireland, 1939.

Hyde, Douglas. *The Story of Early Gaelic Literature*. London: T. Fisher Unwin, 1905.

Hymes, Dell. "Discovering Oral Performance and Measured Verse in American Indian Narrative." *New Literary History* 8 (1976–1977): 431–457.

Jarrell, Mackie L. " 'Jack and the Dane': Swift Traditions in Ireland." *Journal of American Folklore* 77, no. 304 (1964): 99–117.

Johnson, Clifton. *The Isle of the Shamrock.* New York: Macmillan, 1901.

Joyce, P. W. *Old Celtic Romances: Translated from the Gaelic.* London: C. Kegan Paul, 1879.

Joyce, Stanislaus. *My Brother's Keeper: James Joyce's Early Years.* Edited by Richard Ellmann. New York: Viking Press, 1958.

Kavanagh, Patrick, ed. *The Autobiography of William Carleton.* London: MacGibbon & Kee, 1968; first ed. 1898.

Kavanagh, Patrick. *The Green Fool.* London: Martin Brian & O'Keefe, 1971; first pub. 1938.

Kavanagh, Peter, ed. *The Complete Poems of Patrick Kavanagh.* New York: Peter Kavanagh Hand Press, 1972.

Kavanagh, Peter. *Irish Mythology: A Dictionary.* New York: Peter Kavanagh Hand Press, 1958–1959.

Keating, Geoffrey. *General History of Ireland.* Translated by Dermod O'Connor. Dublin: James Duffy, 1861; first pub. 1724.

Kee, Robert. *The Green Flag: A History of Irish Nationalism.* London: Weidenfeld & Nicholson, 1972.

Keightley, Thomas. *The Fairy Mythology, Illustrative of the Romance and Superstition of Various Countries.* London: H. G. Bohn, 1850; first ed. 1828.

Kennedy, Patrick. *The Fireside Stories of Ireland.* Dublin: McGlashan & Gill, 1870.

Kennedy, Patrick. *Legendary Fictions of the Irish Celts.* London: Macmillan, 1866.

Kiely, Benedict. *Poor Scholar: A Study of the Works and Days of William Carleton (1794–1869).* Dublin: Talbot Press, 1972; first pub. 1947.

Kinsella, Thomas. *The Tain.* Dolmen Editions 9. Dublin: Dolmen Press, 1969.

Le Fanu, W. R. *Seventy Years of Irish Life: Being Anecdotes and Reminiscences.* New York: Macmillan, 1894.

Little, George A. *Malachi Horan Remembers.* Dublin: M. H. Gill, 1944.

Logan, Patrick. *Irish Country Cures.* Belfast: Appletree Press, 1981.

Lover, Samuel. *Legends and Stories of Ireland.* Dublin: W. F. Wakeman, 1834; first pub. 1831.

Lover, Samuel. *Legends and Stories of Ireland: Second Series.* London: Baldwin & Cradock, 1834.

Lover, Samuel. *Legends and Stories of Ireland.* Plymouth: Popham, Radford, [1875].

Lover, Samuel. *The Songs of Ireland.* New York: Dick & Fitzgerald, 1860.

Lynd, Robert. *Home Life in Ireland.* London: Mills & Boon, 1909.

Maher, James, ed. *Romantic Slievenamon in History, Folklore and Song: A Tipperary Anthology.* Mullinahone: privately published, 1955.

McAnally, D. R. *Irish Wonders: Popular Tales as Told by the People.* Boston: Houghton Mifflin, 1888.

MacDonagh, Thomas. *Literature in Ireland: Studies Irish and Anglo-Irish.* Dublin. Talbot Press [1916].

MacManus, Diarmuid. *Irish Earth Folk.* New York: Devin-Adair, 1959.

MacManus, Seumas. *The Bold Heroes of Hungry Hill, and Other Irish Folk Tales.* London: J. M. Dent, 1952.

MacManus, Seumas. *Heavy Hangs the Golden Grain.* New York: Macmillan, 1952.

MacManus, Seumas. *The Rocky Road to Dublin.* New York: Devin-Adair, 1947.

MacManus, Seumas. *Through the Turf Smoke: The Love, Lore, and Laughter of Old Ireland.* New York: Doubleday & McClure, 1899.

MacManus, Seumas. *Yourself and the Neighbours.* New York: Devin-Adair, 1945; first pub. 1914.

MacNeice, Louis. *The Poetry of W. B. Yeats.* London: Oxford University Press, 1941.

MacNeill, Máire. *The Festival of Lughnasa: A Study of the Survival of the Celtic Festival of the Begnning of Harvest.* London: Oxford University Press, 1962.

Mercier, Vivian. *The Irish Comic Tradition.* Oxford: Oxford University Press, 1962.

Millman, Lawrence. *Our Like Will Not Be There Again: Notes from the West of Ireland.* Boston: Little, Brown, 1977.

Mogey, John M. *Rural Life in Northern Ireland: Five Regional Studies Made for the Northern Ireland Council of Social Service.* London: Oxford University Press, 1947.

Montague, John. *The Rough Field.* Dublin: Dolmen Press, 1972.

Morton, Robin. *Come Day, Go Day, God Send Sunday: The Songs and Life Story, Told in His Own Words, of John Maguire, Traditional Singer and Farmer from Co. Fermanagh.* London: Routledge & Kegan Paul, 1973.

Murphy, Gerard. *Glimpses of Gaelic Ireland: Two Lectures.* Dublin: C. J. Fallon, 1948.

Murphy, Gerard. *Tales from Ireland.* Dublin: Browne & Nolan, 1947.

Murphy, Michael J. *At Slieve Gullion's Foot.* Dundalk: W. Tempest, Dundalgan Press, 1941.

Murphy, Michael J. "The Folk Stories of Dan Rooney of Lurgancanty." *Ulster Folklife* 11 (1965): 80–86.

Murphy, Michael J. "Folktales and Traditions from County Cavan and South Armagh." *Ulster Folklife* 19 (1973): 30–37.

Murphy, Michael J. "Four Folktales About Woman." *Ulster Folklife* 13 (1967): 1–8.

Murphy, Michael J. *Mountainy Crack: Tales of Slieve Gullioners.* Belfast: Blackstaff Press, 1976.

Murphy, Michael J. *Now You're Talking . . . Folk Tales from the North of Ireland.* Belfast: Blackstaff Press, 1975.

Murphy, Michael J. *Tyrone Folk Quest.* Belfast: Blackstaff Press, 1973.

Murphy, Michael J. *Ulster Folk of Field and Fireside.* Dundalk: W. Tempest, Dundalgan Press, 1983.

Murphy, Richard. *The Battle of Aughrim and the God Who Eats Corn.* London: Faber & Faber, 1968.

O'Brien, Flann. *At Swim-Two-Birds.* New York: Pantheon Books, 1939.

Ó Catháin, Séamas. "An Fear nach rabh Scéal ar bith aige." *Béaloideas* 37–38 (1969–1970): 51–64.

Ó Catháin, Séamas. *The Bedside Book of Irish Folklore.* Cork: Mercier Press, 1980.
Ó Catháin, Séamas. *Irish Life and Lore.* Cork: Mercier Press, 1982.
Ó Catháin, Séamas, and Patrick O'Flanagan. *The Living Landscape: Kilgalligan, Erris, County Mayo.* Dublin: Comhairle Bhéaloideas Éireann, 1975.
Ó Crohan, Tomás. *The Islandman.* Translated by Robin Flower. New York: Charles Scribner's Sons, 1935.
O'Donoghue, John, *In a Quiet Land.* London: Country Book Club, 1959.
O'Donoghue, John, *In Kerry Long Ago.* London: B. T. Batsford, 1960.
O'Donovan, John, trans, and ed. *Annals of the Kingdom of Ireland by the Four Masters from the Earliest Period to the Year 1616.* 7 vols. Dublin: Hodges, Smith, 1854.
O'Faolain, Sean. *An Irish Journey.* London: Longmans, Green, 1940.
Ó hEochaidh, Seán. *Fairy Legends from Donegal.* Translated by Máire MacNeill; edited by Séamus Ó Catháin. Dublin: Comhairle Bhéaloideas Éireann, 1977.
O'Neill, Timothy P. *Life and Tradition in Rural Ireland.* London: J. M. Dent, 1977.
O'Rahilly, Thomas F. *Early Irish History and Mythology.* Dublin: Dublin Institute for Advanced Studies, 1976; first pub. 1946.
O'Sullivan, Maurice. *Twenty Years A-Growing.* Translated by Moya Llewelyn Davies and George Thomson. New York: Viking Press 1933.
O'Sullivan, Sean (Seán Ó Súilleabháin). "The Devil in Irish Folk Narrative." In Fritz Harkort, Karel C. Peeters, and Robert Wildhaber, eds., *Volksüberlieferung: Festschrift für Kurt Ranke zur Vollendung des 60. Lebensjahres,* pp. 275–286. Göttingen: Otto Schwartz, 1968.
O'Sullivan, Sean (Seán Ó Súilleabháin). *The Folklore of Ireland.* New York: Hastings House, 1974.
O'Sullivan, Sean (Seán Ó Súilleabháin). *Folktales of Ireland.* Chicago: University of Chicago Press, 1966.
O'Sullivan, Sean (Seán Ó Súilleabháin). *A Handbook of Irish Folklore.* Hatboro, Pa.: Folklore Associates, 1963; first pub. 1942.
O'Sullivan, Sean (Seán Ó Súilleabháin). *Irish Folk Custom and Belief.* Dublin: Cultural Relations Committee of Ireland, [1972].
O'Sullivan, Sean (Seán Ó Súilleabháin). *Legends from Ireland.* London: B. T. Batsford, 1977.
O'Sullivan, Sean (Seán Ó Súilleabháin). "Oliver Cromwell in Irish Oral Tradition." In Linda Dégh, Henry Glassie, and Felix Oinas, eds., *Folklore Today: A Festschrift for Richard M. Dorson,* pp. 473–483. Bloomington: Indiana University, 1976.
O'Sullivan, Sean (Seán Ó Súilleabháin). "Scéalta Cráibhtheacha." *Béaloideas* 21 (1951–1952): 1–337.
O'Sullivan, Sean (Seán Ó Súilleabháin). *Storytelling in Irish Tradition.* Cork: Mercier Press for Cultural Relations Committee of Ireland, 1973.
O'Sullivan, Sean (Seán Ó Súilleabháin), and Reidar Th. Christiansen. *The*

Types of the Irish Folktale. Folklore Fellows' Communications 188. Helsinki: Suomalainen Tiedeakatemia, 1967.

Ó Tuathail, Pádraig. "Wicklow Traditions of 1798." *Béaloideas* 5, no. 2 (1935): 154–188.

Paterson, T. G. F. *Country Cracks: Old Tales from the County of Armagh.* Dundalk: W. Tempest, Dundalgan Press, 1945.

Rees, Alwyn, and Brinley Rees. *Celtic Heritage: Ancient Tradition in Ireland and Wales.* London: Thames & Hudson, 1978; first pub. 1961.

Robinson, Lennox, ed. *Lady Gregory's Journals, 1916–1930.* New York: Macmillan, 1947.

Rolleston, T. W. *The High Deeds of Finn, and Other Bardic Romances.* New York: Thomas Y. Crowell, 1910.

Sayers, Peig. *An Old Woman's Reflections.* Translated by Seamus Ennis. London: Oxford University Press, 1962; first pub. 1939.

Sayers, Peig. *Peig: The Autobiography of Peig Sayers of the Great Blasket Island.* Translated by Bryan MacMahon. Syracuse, N.Y.: Syracuse University Press, 1974; written 1935.

Seymour, St. John. *Irish Witchcraft and Demonology.* New York: Causeway, 1973; first pub. 1913.

Shaw, Rose. *Carleton's Country.* Dublin: Talbot Press, 1930.

Sheehy, Jeanne. *The Rediscovery of Ireland's Past: The Celtic Revival, 1830–1930.* London: Thames & Hudson, 1980.

Skelton, Robin. *The Writings of J. M. Synge.* Indianapolis: Bobbs-Merrill, 1971.

Smythe, Colin, ed. *Seventy Years: Being the Autobiography of Lady Gregory.* New York: Macmillan, 1974.

Stephens, James. *The Crock of Gold.* New York: Macmillan, 1926; first pub. 1913.

Stephens, James. *Irish Fairy Tales.* New York: Macmillan, 1923.

Stephens, Lilo, ed. *My Wallet of Photographs: The Collected Photographs of J. M. Synge.* Dolmen Editions 13. Dublin: Dolmen Press, 1971.

Synge, John Millington. *The Aran Islands.* Boston: John W. Luce, 1911; first pub. 1906.

Tunney, Paddy. *The Stone Fiddle: My Way to Traditional Song.* Dublin: Gilbert Dalton, 1979.

Wilde, Lady Jane. *Ancient Cures, Charms, and Usages of Ireland: Contributions to Irish Lore.* London: Ward & Downey, 1890.

Wilde, Lady Jane. *Ancient Legends, Mystic Charms and Superstitions of Ireland: With Sketches of the Irish Past.* London: Chatto & Windus, 1902; first ed. 1887.

Wilde, Sir William R. *Irish Popular Superstitions.* Dublin: McGlashan, [1852].

Yeats, William Butler. *The Autobiography of William Butler Yeats: Consisting of Reveries over Childhood and Youth, The Trembling of the Veil, and Dramatis Personae.* New York: Macmillan, 1953.

Yeats, William Butler. *The Celtic Twilight.* Dublin: Maunsel; London: A. H. Bullen, 1902; first ed. 1893.

Yeats, William Butler. *Fairy and Folk Tales of Ireland.* New York: Macmillan, 1973. (Reprint of *Fairy and Folk Tales of the Irish Peasantry,* 1888, and *Irish Fairy Tales,* 1892.)

Yeats, William Butler. *Stories from Carleton: With an Introduction.* London: Walter Scott, [1889].

❖ NOTES

PREFACE

The story of Saint Patrick was built out of tales described by Douglas Hyde, *A Literary History of Ireland* (1967), pp. 116, 383. The scribe's characterization of the *Tain* as a deception and figment comes as a coda to the text Cecile O'Rahilly provides in *Táin Bó Cúalnge from the Book of Leinster* (Dublin: Dublin Institute for Advanced Studies, 1970), p. 272. John O'Donovan edited the *Annals of the Kingdom of Ireland by the Four Masters* in seven volumes (1854). It was written in Donegal between 1632 and 1636. Geoffrey Keating's *General History of Ireland,* written between 1620 and 1634, was translated in the eighteenth century by Dermod O'Connor, and in the twentieth century for the Irish Texts Society (1902–1914) by David Comyn and Patrick S. Dinneen.

INTRODUCTION

AT THE END OF A SHORT WINTER'S DAY This is the night of November 22, 1972. I recorded the stories George Armstrong told the rector on August 14, 1978, and December 18, 1979. John Brodison's story of the Big Wind can be found in *Passing the Time in Ballymenone* (1982), pp. 45–47. The story of George Armstrong's return is tale 42 in this collection.

CONNECTIONS At the heart of this brief discussion is the idea in the currently dominant American definition of folklore, propounded by Dan Ben-Amos, "Toward a Definition of Folklore in Context," in Américo Paredes and Richard Bauman, eds., *Toward New Perspectives in Folklore* (Austin: University of Texas Press, 1972), pp. 3–15.

TRADITION For T. Crofton Croker I relied primarily on the memoir written by his son, T. F. Dillon Croker, published in Thomas Wright's edition of Croker's *Fairy Legends* (1862), pp. iv–xix. Kevin Danaher added a biographical introduction to the reprint of *Researches in the South of Ireland* (Dublin: Irish Academic Press, 1981), pp. v–viii. Richard M. Dorson treats Croker in *The British Folklorists* (1968), pp. 44–52, and he treats Thomas Keightley on pp. 52–57. Croker's descriptions of his fieldwork come from a letter he wrote in 1825, quoted in T. F. D. Croker's memoir, *Fairy Legends* (1862), pp. vi–vii. Croker's account of fairy habitations come from *Researches in the South of Ireland*, p. 80. Keightley's "Leprechaun in the Garden" is in *The Fairy Mythology* (1850), pp. 376–378. Croker's "Seeing Is Believing" is in *Fairy Legends* (1862), pp. 85–88. Samuel Lover tells of telling his sketches orally in *Legends and Stories of Ireland* (1834 [1831]), pp. viii–ix. His description of Paddy the Sport comes from the same book, pp. 205, and 212. Paddy's tale appears as tale 37 in this collection. Croker's stories "The Crookened Back" and "The Capture of Bridget Pursell" both appear in this collection: tales 87 and 58.

William Carleton is excellently introduced by Benedict Kiely, *Poor Scholar* (1972). I also used Patrick Kavanagh's edition of *The Autobiography of William Carleton* (1968) and Carleton's autobiographical introduction to *Traits and Stories of the Irish Peasantry* (1869), 1: i–xxiv, during which, p. iv, he praises Samuel Lover. Carleton as a writer of sketches is represented by tale 70 in this collection, and Carleton as a storyteller is represented by his tale of the blacksmith and the Devil, tale 119 in this collection. W. B. Yeats describes Carleton in his *Stories from Carleton* (1889), pp. xvi–xvii.

William Butler Yeats' great manifesto for folk art comes from *The Celtic Twilight* (1902), pp. 232–233. Joseph Hone tells of Yeats in the period of the Nobel Prize in *W. B. Yeats* (1943), pp. 366–390. Yeats' statement that Lady Gregory and Synge should have accompanied him is found at p. 381 in Hone's biography. For John Millington Synge, I found these books especially helpful: Edward Stephens' *My Uncle John* (1974), edited by Andrew Carpenter; Robin Skelton's *The Writings of J. M. Synge* (1971); and Daniel Corkery's *Synge and Anglo-Irish Literature* (1966). Corkery quotes Yeats' advice to Synge on p. 62, and on p. 66 quotes Synge on the collaborative nature of art. The folktale from which Synge wrote *In the Shadow of the Glen* is tale 25 in this collection.

Douglas Hyde is presented by Dominic Daly in *The Young Douglas Hyde* (1974) and Gareth W. Dunleavy in *Douglas Hyde* (1974). W. B. Yeats describes Hyde in the introduction to *Fairy and Folk Tales of the Irish Peasantry* (1888); reprinted in *Fairy and Folk Tales of Ireland* (1973), p. 7. Douglas Hyde characterizes nineteenth-century work on Irish folktales in *Beside the Fire* (1890), p. x.

The encounter of W. B. Yeats and James Joyce is described and analyzed by Richard Ellmann in *James Joyce* (1959), pp. 102–114. Stanislaus Joyce tells of Joyce's review of *Poets and Dreamers* in *My Brother's Keeper* (1958), pp. 220–224. Joyce's benefactor, Lady Gregory, is rudely mentioned in *Ulysses* (Paris: Shakespeare & Company, 1922), p. 208.

The founding and development of the Irish Folklore Commission is described by Richard M. Dorson in his foreword, pp. xxvi–xxxii, and Sean O'Sullivan in his introduction, pp. xxxiii–xxxix, to O'Sullivan's *Folktales of Ireland* (1966), and by Séamas Ó Catháin in *The Bedside Book of Irish Folklore* (1980), pp. 32–34. James H. Delargy's argument can be found in his paper in the *Irish Free State Official Handbook* (1932), pp. 264–266.

Dell Hymes describes the poetic nature of American Indian narrative in his paper in *New Literary History* (1976–1977), pp. 431–457, gathered into his important book, *"In Vain I Tried to Tell You": Essays in Native American Ethnopoetics* (Philadelphia: University of Pennsylvania Press. 1981), pp. 309–341. See also Dennis Tedlock, *The Spoken Word and the Work of Interpretation* (Philadelphia: University of Pennsylvania Press, 1983). I describe my treatment of stories in *Passing the Time in Ballymenone* (1982), pp. 36–49.

COMMUNICATION Thomas Wright evaluates Crofton Croker's work in the editor's preface to *Fairy Legends* (1862), p. ii. Croker's observation on the similarity of legends comes in that volume, p. 21, and his linking of an Irish tale to the East comes on p. 50. Samuel Lover's warning to scholars appears in the introduction to *Legends and Stories of Ireland* (1834 [1831]), p. xviii. Lover's comment on the German analogue to "The Devil's Mill" is in the same volume, p. 156. A version of the tale Lover sketched appears as tale 43 in this collection. Croker states his purpose in *Fairy Legends* (1828), p. vii.

Folklore's historic-geographic method is presented by Kaarle Krohn, *Folklore Methodology: Formulated by Julius Krohn and Expanded by Nordic Researchers,* trans. Roger L. Welsch (Austin: University of Texas Press, 1971; first pub. 1926). Douglas Hyde classifies the stories of Ireland in *Beside the Fire* (1890), pp. xxxiv–xli. In this collection, "Finn and His Men Bewitched" and tales 109, 110, and 111 are Fenian tales, and Aarne-Thompson international tale type 300 is represented by tales 114 and 115.

Lady Gregory is excellently introduced by Elizabeth Coxhead in *Lady Gregory* (1966). I also found helpful Lennox Robinson's edition of *Lady Gregory's Journals* (1947) and Colin Smythe's edition of her autobiography, *Seventy Years* (1974). Lady Gregory tells of her interest in the stories' beautiful sentences in *Visions and Beliefs in the West of Ireland* (1970), p. 15. W. B. Yeats praised her language in his preface to her *Cuchulain of Muirthemne* (1902). She asserted the scientific responsibility of the folklorist in *The Kiltartan Wonder Book* (1910), p. 105. In *The Kiltartan History Book* (1909), p. 49, (1926), p. 152, she wrote that she might have named it "Myths in the Making."

Jeremiah Curtin is sketched in James H. Delargy's introduction to *Irish Folk-Tales* (1943). Douglas Hyde's opinion of Curtin comes in *Beside the Fire,* p. xv.

THE TALES

THE OLD STORY

THE LEGEND OF KNOCKFIERNA T. Crofton Croker, *Fairy Legends* (1862), pp. 6–9.

FINN AND HIS MEN BEWITCHED Patrick Kennedy, *Legendary Fictions of the Irish Celts* (1866), pp. 206–208. This story blends numbers 2, 29, and 10 from Sean O'Sullivan's typology of Fenian tales in his *Handbook of Irish Folklore* (1963), pp. 590–595. See tale 110 in this collection.

THE KING OF IRELAND'S SON Douglas Hyde, *Beside the Fire* (1890), pp. 19–47. This is Aarne-Thompson international tale type 513A, with type 507A added.

Type 513A, Six Go Through the World, is one of the most common *Märchen* in Europe and in Ireland. For a sense of the flexibility of folk themes and structures, compare this tale with numbers 116, 117, and 121 in this collection.

FAITH

SAINTS

1 THE BAPTISM OF CONOR MAC NESSA Sean O'Sullivan, *Legends from Ireland* (1977), pp. 104–105. Recorded for the Irish Folklore Commission by Seán Ó hEochaidh. Published in Irish in *Béaloideas* (1951–1952), pp. 26–27. Conor was the king of Ulster in the time of the epic *Táin Bó Cúailnge,* of which Thomas Kinsella has prepared a superb translation for modern readers, *The Tain* (1969).

2 SAINT PATRICK Lady Gregory,*The Kiltartan History Book* (1926), p. 24. Not in the first edition (1909). The traditional date for Patrick's arrival in Ireland is 432. The traditional date of his death is March 17, 493. James Carney adroitly weighs the historical evidence in *The Problem of St. Patrick* (1973).

3 SAINT PATRICK ON INISHMORE Henry Glassie, *Passing the Time in Ballymenone* (1982), p. 170; *Irish Folk History* (1982), pp. 21–22. Mr. Nolan's account of Saint Patrick's company accords with the description provided by the Four Masters in the seventeenth century. See John O'Donovan, ed., *Annals of the Kingdom of Ireland* (1854), 1: 134–141. Inishmore is an island in Upper Lough Erne.

4 SAINT PATRICK AND CROM DUBH Douglas Hyde, *Legends of Saints and Sinners* (1915), pp. 3–11. Another tale of the encounter of Saint Patrick and Crom Dubh appears in Sean O'Sullivan, *Legends from Ireland* (1977), pp. 109–112. Saint Patrick's battle seems to be a memory of the saint's destruction of a ring of stone idols, Cromm Cruiach, at Magh Sleacht in County Cavan. See Douglas Hyde, *A Literary History of Ireland* (1967), pp. 84–88.

5 SAINT BRIGIT These are stories 1, 2, 3, 8, 18, and 19 from the twenty in the first edition (1906), pp. 1–14, and the twenty-two in the first commercial edition (1907), pp. 1–16, of Lady Gregory's *Book of Saints and Wonders.* The fourth in this sequence is a version of O'Sullivan-Christiansen Irish folktale type 2400, known widely in Ireland.

6 SAINT COLUMCILLE Henry Glassie, *Passing the Time in Ballymenone* (1982), pp. 176–178; *Irish Folk History* (1982), pp. 29–32. Adamnan's seventh-century biography, edited by Alan Orr Anderson and Marjorie Ogilvie Anderson (1961), tells of the battle of Cúl Dreimne in 561, which led to Columcille's exile, and the Council of Druim Ceat in 575, but it does not include the tale of the dispute over the book. That is found in A. O'Kelleher and G. Schoepperle, eds., *Life of Columcille Compiled by Manus O'Donnell in 1532* (Urbana: University of Illinois Press, 1918), pp. 176–201. Sean O'Sullivan, *Legends from Ireland* (1977), pp. 106–108, offers another folk text.

7 COLUMCILLE'S COFFIN Séamas Ó Catháin, *The Bedside Book of Irish Folklore* (1980), pp. 77–78. Columcille died at Iona in June 597.

8 SAINT KEVIN These three tales were gathered from those included in Mr. and Mrs. S. C. Hall, *Ireland* (1850), 1: 221–223. The third of the stories, the only one in this book to which I made an addition (the word "O'Toole" in the first sentence), is a popular one, appearing, for instance, as the first sketch in Samuel Lover's first series of *Legends and Stories of Ireland* (1834 [1831]), pp. 1–16.

9 SAINT FINBAR Sean O'Sullivan, *Legends from Ireland* (1977), p. 152. Recorded for the Irish Folklore Commission by Nora Ní Chróinín.

THE PRIEST AND HIS PEOPLE

10 JAMES MURRAY AND SAINT MARTIN Jeremiah Curtin, *Tales of the Fairies and of the Ghost World* (1895), pp. 118–121. Three comparable tales in Irish can be found in Sean O'Sullivan's important collection of religious stories, "Scéalta Cráibtheacha," *Béaloideas* (1951–1952), pp. 202–207. Two of them are translated in O'Sullivan's *Legends from Ireland* (1977), pp. 114–116.

11 THE BEST ROAD TO HEAVEN Lady Gregory, *Poets and Dreamers* (1903), pp. 106–107.

12 THE MAN FROM KILMACOLIVER Rose Springfield, "Folklore of Slievenamon: The Legend of the Seven Bishops," in James Maher, ed., *Romantic Slievenamon in History, Folklore, and Song* (1955), p. 94. The richly carved Ahenny Cross dates to the eighth century.

13 THE PIOUS MAN Kevin Danaher, *Folktales of the Irish Countryside* (1967), pp. 38–39. This is O'Sullivan-Christiansen Irish folktale type 1848*, known especially in the South and West of Ireland, and related to Aarne-Thompson international tale type 1848, distributed lightly through western Europe.

14 AN ACTUAL SAINT Lawrence Millman, *Our Like Will Not Be There Again* (1977), pp. 50–51. This story, related to Aarne-Thompson international type 759B, is especially common in the West of Ireland. A comparable story in Irish appears in Sean O'Sullivan's "Scéalta Cráibtheacha," *Béaloideas* (1951–1952), pp. 233–235.

15 OLD THORNS AND OLD PRIESTS Michael J. Murphy, *Now You're Talking* (1975), pp. 11–12.

16 PRIESTS AND FARMING MEN Unpublished. Tape-recorded from Peter Flanagan, November 12, 1972. This pair of "bids" comes as a set. Mr. Flanagan also told them to me on January 2, 1974, and December 12, 1983.

17 SAVED BY THE PRIEST Séamas Ó Catháin, *Irish Life and Lore* (1982), pp. 70–72.

18 THE DOOM Lady Wilde, *Ancient Legends, Mystic Charms and Superstitions of Ireland* (1902), pp. 67–69. Assuming "Innismore" to be one of the Arans, I attribute the tale to Galway.

19 THE RIGHT CURE George A. Little, *Malachi Horan Remembers* (1944), pp. 88–91. Peter Flanagan similarly describes the significance of the curing power of holy wells in *Passing the Time in Ballymenone* (1982), pp. 171–174, 307–310.

20 HELL AND HEAVEN W. B. Yeats, *The Celtic Twilight* (1902), pp. 77–78. This text, lacking the last paragraph, also appears in Lady Gregory's *Visions and Beliefs in the West of Ireland* (1970), pp. 200–201.

21 THE WOLF'S PROPHECY Lady Gregory, *A Book of Saints and Wonders* (1907), pp. 131–133.

WIT

THE WISE AND THE FOOLISH

22 THE THREE QUESTIONS Michael J. Murphy, *Now You're Talking* (1975), pp. 16–17. Murphy presents a slightly different version of this tale (Aarne-Thompson international type 922), which he remembered from his father, in "Folktales and Traditions from County Cavan and South Armagh," *Ulster Folklife* (1973), pp. 34–35.

23 THE FARMER'S ANSWERS Lady Gregory, *Poets and Dreamers* (1903), pp. 183–184. Aarne-Thompson international tale type 922 is found commonly and widely in Ireland. See O'Sullivan and Christiansen's *Types of the Irish Folktale,* pp. 181–182. And it is known in India, throughout Europe from Turkey to Sweden, and in North and South America.

24 HALF A BLANKET Michael J. Murphy, *Now You're Talking* (1975), p. 42. This is Aarne-Thompson international tale type 980A, known in China, Japan, and widely in Europe.

25 THE SHADOW OF THE GLEN John M. Synge, *The Aran Islands* (1911), pp. 57–60. Out of this tale (Aarne-Thompson international tale type 1350, known throughout Ireland), Synge wrote his play *In the Shadow of the Glen* in 1902.

26 A HUNGRY HIRED BOY Michael J. Murphy, *Now You're Talking* (1975), pp. 19–21.

27 THE FIRST MIRROR Séamas Ó Catháin, *The Bedside Book of Irish Folklore* (1980), pp. 8–10. Ireland shares this tale, Aarne-Thompson international type 1336A, with Finland, Greece, Turkey, China, and the southern United States.

28 ROBIN'S ESCAPE Lady Gregory, *Poets and Dreamers* (1903), pp. 150–153. Aarne-Thompson international tale type 1641 is known throughout Ireland, the rest of Europe, the Orient, and North and South America.

WITS AND POETS

29 JONATHAN SWIFT, DEAN OF SAINT PATRICK'S CATHEDRAL Lady Gregory, *The Kiltartan History Book* (1926), pp. 56–58. Swift does not appear in the first edition (1909). The popularity of Jonathan Swift (1667–1745) as a folktale character

in Ireland is described by Mackie L. Jarrell, " 'Jack and the Dane,' " *Journal of American Folklore* (1964), pp. 99–117.

30 DANIEL O'CONNELL Seumas MacManus, *Through the Turf Smoke* (1899); two of the three stories on pp. 171–188. Tales of the wit of Daniel O'Connell (1775–1847), the Liberator, are common in Ireland. Other versions of the first of these tales can be found in Sean O'Sullivan's books *Folktales of Ireland* (1966), pp. 231–232, and *Legends from Ireland* (1977), pp. 128–131.

31 OWEN ROE O'SULLIVAN Eric Cross, *The Tailor and Ansty* (1964), pp. 204–208. The first of these stories about the Kerry poet O'Sullivan (1748–1784) is found told about Daniel O'Connell in Michael J. Murphy's *Now You're Talking* (1975), p. 54.

32 ROBERT BURNS Unpublished. Tape-recorded from Peter Flanagan, November 12, 1972. He told the first and second of these tales, which he learned from two sisters named Farmer in South Fermanagh, on December 29, 1973. A 1979 telling of the first of Mr. Flanagan's Burns stories appears in *Passing the Time in Ballymenone* (1982), pp. 709–710. On December 12, 1983, he told the second story again and added a new one in which a boy climbs a tree and sits eating a bun while watching Burns make love to a woman behind a bush. Burns tells him: "Go on, my son, and eat your bun./Nature's work must be done."

33 TERRY THE GRUNTER Séamas Ó Catháin, *Irish Life and Lore* (1982), p. 78. Recorded for the Irish Folklore Commission by Bríd Ní Ghamhnáin. The first of Terry's poems, which Peter Flanagan attributes to Robert Burns, is also attributed to Jonathan Swift in Ireland. See Michael J. Murphy, *Now You're Talking* (1975), p. 60.

34 THOMAS MOORE AND THE TRAMP Unpublished. Tape-recorded from Peter Flanagan, November 12, 1972. The tramp's poem is attributed in Cork to a specific local poet. See D. K. Wilgus, "Irish Traditional Narrative Songs in English: 1800–1916," in Daniel J. Casey and Robert E. Rhodes, eds., *Views of the Irish Peasantry* (1977), pp. 114–115.

TALL TALES

35 JOHN BRODISON AND THE POLICEMAN Unpublished. Tape-recorded from Michael Boyle, November 25, 1972. This tale, conceivably related to Aarne-Thompson international type 1529, which is not listed in O'Sullivan and Christiansen's *Types of the Irish Folktale,* was also told by Mr. Buckley of Cork. See Eric Cross, *The Tailor and Ansty* (1964), p. 98.

36 A BIG POTATO Unpublished. Tape-recorded from Hugh Nolan, November 28, 1972. This tale, which would be classed as Aarne-Thompson international type 1960D, was also told by Mr. Nolan on November 22, 1972, and August 14, 1978, and I recorded it from Michael Boyle, who also attributed it to John Brodison, on November 25, 1972. Mr. Nolan and Mr. Boyle are gone, but Joe Murphy learned their tale and, crediting it to Brodison, told it to me on December 13, 1983.

37 THE FOX AND THE RANGER Samuel Lover, *Legends and Stories of Ireland* (first series, 1834 [1831]), pp. 229–234; (complete edition, 1875), pp. 142–146. I guessed Wicklow from the mention of Blessington and Lover's home in Dublin. A good version of this tale—Aarne-Thompson international type 67**, found widely in Ireland—appears in George A. Little, *Malachi Horan Remembers* (1944), pp. 109–110.

38 THE HORSE'S LAST DRUNK Eric Cross, *The Tailor and Ansty* (1964), pp. 79–80. I recorded this story—Aarne-Thompson international tale type 1911A—from Hugh Nolan, November 8, 1972, and June 16, 1977. The story, as O'Sullivan and Christiansen demonstrate in *Types of the Irish Folktale,* pp. 326–327, is common in Ireland. Other interesting texts can be found in Sean O'Sullivan, *Folktales of Ireland* (1966), pp. 249–252; Séamas Ó Catháin, *The Bedside Book of Irish Folklore* (1980), pp. 40–41.

39 HARE AND HOUND Michael J. Murphy, "Folk Stories of Dan Rooney," *Ulster Folklife* (1965), p. 85. This is connected to number 110 in Sean O'Sullivan's catalogue of humorous tales in *A Handbook of Irish Folklore* (1963), p. 648.

40 SLEEPY PENDOODLE Unpublished. Tape-recorded from Michael Boyle, October 26, 1972. Hugh Nolan also learned this tale from his neighbor Hugh McGiveney, and I recorded it from him on November 8, 1972, June 11, 1977, and June 22, 1977.

41 A MEDICAL EXPERT FROM LISNASKEA Paddy Tunney, *The Stone Fiddle* (1979), pp. 102–103. This is Aarne-Thompson international tale type 660 remade into a tall tale, as in America. See William Hugh Jansen, *Abraham "Oregon" Smith* (New York: Arno Press, 1977), pp. 236–243.

42 GEORGE ARMSTRONG'S RETURN Unpublished. Tape-recorded from Hugh Nolan, June 16, 1977. An earlier telling of this tale by Mr. Nolan appears in *Passing the Time in Ballymenone* (1982), pp. 51–54, and in *Irish Folk History* (1982), pp. 117–121. Tall tales are called "pants" in Ballymenone.

OUTWITTING THE DEVIL

43 THE LAWYER AND THE DEVIL Michael J. Murphy, *Now You're Talking* (1975), pp. 116–117. Aarne-Thompson international tale type 1187, famous from its appearance in Greek myth, is found across Europe and is particularly common in Ireland. Samuel Lover built a sketch out of this tale, *Legends and Stories of Ireland* (first series, 1834 [1831]), pp. 141–156, which William Butler Yeats edited for inclusion in his *Irish Fairy Tales* of 1892. See W. B. Yeats, *Fairy and Folk Tales of Ireland* (1973), pp. 335–340.

44 COALS ON THE DEVIL'S HEARTH Unpublished. Tape-recorded from Hugh Nolan, December 18, 1979. An earlier telling of this tale, which Mr. Nolan learned from James Quigley and which plays on the idea in Aarne-Thompson international tale type 1187, can be found in *Passing the Time in Ballymenone* (1982), pp. 538–540, and in *Irish Folk History* (1982), pp. 121–125.

MYSTERY

DEATH AND TOKENS

45 NO MAN GOES BEYOND HIS DAY Robin Flower, *The Western Island* (1945), pp. 120–121. Ó Crithin is the same man as Tomás Ó Crohan (1856–1937), whose life unfolds through his grand autobiography, *The Islandman* (1935).

46 A LIGHT TOKENS THE DEATH OF MR. CORRIGAN Unpublished. Tape-recorded from Hugh Nolan, November 15, 1972.

47 A CLOCK TOKEN Lady Gregory, *Visions and Beliefs in the West of Ireland* (1970), p. 174.

48 THE BANSHEE CRIES FOR THE O'BRIENS Lady Gregory, *Visions and Beliefs in the West of Ireland* (1970), pp. 266–267.

49 THE BANSHEE CRIES FOR THE BOYLES T. G. F. Paterson, *County Cracks* (1945), p. 75.

50 EXPERIENCE OF THE BANSHEE Unpublished. Tape-recorded from Joseph and Peter Flanagan, June 12, 1977.

GHOSTS

51 GRANDFATHER'S GHOST Ronald Buchanan, "Folklore of an Irish Townland," *Ulster Folklife* (1956), p. 47. Ronald Buchanan generously supplied me with the name of the storyteller in a letter dated October 15, 1984.

52 TERRIBLE GHOSTS Unpublished. Tape-recorded from Peter Flanagan, July 30, 1972. I recorded the second of these stories from Mr. Flanagan again on June 12, 1977.

53 THE SOLDIER IN THE HAUNTED HOUSE James H. Delargy, "Clare Folk Tales," *Béaloideas* (1935), pp. 25–27. Delargy comments that the tale is popular in Ireland. It seems related to Aarne-Thompson international tale type 326A*.

54 DANIEL CROWLEY AND THE GHOSTS Jeremiah Curtin, *Tales of the Fairies and of the Ghost World* (1895), pp. 46–53.

55 GHOSTS ALONG THE ARNEY Unpublished. Tape-recorded from Hugh Nolan, August 30, 1972. The last story in the sequence appears in *Passing the Time in Ballymenone* (1982), pp. 68–69. I first heard about the headless ghost of Arney from Hugh Patrick Owens, and recorded the story from Mr. Nolan again on Novembers 8, 1972.

56 THE GRAVE OF HIS FATHERS Robin Flower, *The Western Island* (1945), pp. 55–57. Peig Sayers (1873–1958) has left us two autobiographical books: *An Old Woman's Reflections* (1962), and *Peig* (1974).

AWAY

57 THE COFFIN Kevin Danaher, *Folktales of the Irish Countryside* (1967), pp. 70–72. This one among the stories of women who are away has received the number 990* in O'Sullivan and Christiansen's *Types of the Irish Folktale.*

58 THE CAPTURE OF BRIDGET PURCELL T. Crofton Croker, *Fairy Legends* (1862), pp. 39–41.

59 TAKEN Robin Flower, *The Western Island* (1945), pp. 135–137. Ó Crithin is Tomás Ó Crohan, author of *The Islandman* (1935).

60 HOW THE SHOEMAKER SAVED HIS WIFE Seán Ó hEochaidh, *Fairy Legends from Donegal* (1977), pp. 57–61.

ENCOUNTERS WITH FAIRIES

61 THE MOUNTAIN ELF Unpublished. Tape-recorded from Peter Flanagan, July 30, 1972. You will learn about Peter Flanagan, the mummer, in *All Silver and No Brass* (1976).

62 INISHKEEN'S ON FIRE Unpublished. Tape-recorded from Ellen Cutler, August 7, 1972. Inishkeen is an island in Upper Lough Erne. Mrs. Cutler said that steel tongs placed across the cradle would have protected the baby from the fairies. Irish tales repetitively display iron and steel as defense against supernatural forces. Mrs. Cutler's story is O'Sullivan-Christiansen Irish folktale type 501*, found throughout Ireland. Another recent version of the tale appears in Linda-May Ballard, "Ulster Oral Narrative: The Stress on Authenticity," *Ulster Folklife* 26 (1980): 35–37: See tale 79 in this collection for a parallel conclusion, tale 72 for a reversal of the conclusion.

63 THE BLOOD OF ADAM Kevin Danaher, *Folktales of the Irish Countryside* (1967), pp. 41–42. This story, known widely in Ireland, is founded on the general belief that fairies are fallen angels. It is Christiansen migratory legend type 5050, common in Norway.

64 WE HAD ONE OF THEM IN THE HOUSE FOR A WHILE Lady Gregory, *Visions and Beliefs in the West of Ireland* (1970), pp. 219–220. Mr. Kelleher's story of "Geoffrey-a-wee" is structured like Aarne-Thompson international tale type 113A. See also tale 83.

65 FAIRY PROPERTY Robert Gibbings, *Lovely Is the Lee* (1945), pp. 64–67. See also tale 92.

66 THE BLACKSMITH OF BEDLAM AND THE FAIRY HOST Seán Ó hEochaidh, *Fairy Legends from Donegal* (1977), pp. 307–311.

FAIRY TRAITS AND TREASURE

67 FAIRY FORTHS Henry Glassie, *Passing the Time in Ballymenone* (1982), pp. 543–545.

68 GORTDONAGHY FORTH Unpublished. Tape-recorded from Ellen Cutler, August 7, 1972. She told the first and last of these stories, dealing with the forth that stands next to her home atop Gortdonaghy Hill, again on June 22, 1977.

69 THE FAIRIES RIDE FROM GORTDONAGHY TO DRUMANE Unpublished. Tape-recorded from Hugh Nolan, August 30, 1972.

70 LANTY'S NEW HOUSE William Carleton, *Tales and Stories of the Irish Peasantry* (1846), pp. 76–77. This is Christiansen migratory legend type 5075.

71 JACK AND THE CLURICAUNE Mr. and Mrs. S. C. Hall, *Ireland* (1850), 3: 35–37. The classic text of this popular story is Crofton Croker's "The Field of Boliauns," *Fairy Legends* (1862), pp. 102–105.

72 BRIDGET AND THE LURIKEEN Patrick Kennedy, *Legendary Fictions of the Irish Celts* (1866), pp, 130–131. After he presents this tale, Kennedy compares it with a Wexford version of a story like tale 71.

73 FAIRY TALES Unpublished. Tape-recorded from Peter Flanagan, June 12, 1977. An earlier telling of the last in this sequence by Mr. Flanagan (which relates intriguingly to tale 111), can be found in *Passing the Time in Ballymenone* (1982), pp. 545–546. His brother, Joseph, also told me that tale on June 9, 1977.

74 THE FAIRY SHILLING Seán Ó hEochaidh, *Fairy Legends from Donegal* (1977), pp. 138–143. This is connected to O'Sullivan-Christiansen Irish folktale type 580*. A comparable Donegal story of the rejection of fairy wealth appears in Sean O'Sullivan's *Folktales of Ireland* (1966), pp. 174–175. There, p. 272, O'Sullivan notes parallels from Israel and Norway.

75 THE BREAKING OF THE FORTH T. G. F. Paterson, *Country Cracks* (1945), pp. 74–75.

76 DREAMS OF GOLD Lady Gregory, *Visions and Beliefs in the West of Ireland* (1970), p. 166. The second story is Aarne-Thompson international tale type 1645, known from Sweden to Turkey and as far east as Japan.

77 THE CASTLE'S TREASURE William Wilde, *Irish Popular Superstitions* (1852), pp. 96–98.

ENCHANTED NATURE

78 THE AIR IS FULL OF THEM Lady Gregory, *Visions and Beliefs in the West of Ireland* (1970), pp. 211–212.

79 THE FEET WATER Kevin Danaher, *Folktales of the Irish Countryside* (1967), pp. 127–129.

80 THE FAIRY RABBIT AND THE BLESSED EARTH OF TORY Seán Ó hEochaidh, *Fairy Legends from Donegal* (1977), pp. 247–249.

81 THE CATS' JUDGMENT Robert Gibbings, *Lovely Is the Lee* (1945), pp. 72–73.

82 NEVER ASK A CAT A QUESTION George A. Little, *Malachi Horan Remembers* (1944), pp. 143–145.

83 CATS ARE QUEER ARTICLES Eric Cross, *The Tailor and Ansty* (1964), pp. 48–51. Especially common in Germany and Ireland, this is Aarne-Thompson international tale type 113A. I recorded it from Hugh Nolan on October 27, 1972, and June 11, 1977.

84 TOM MOORE AND THE SEAL WOMAN Jeremiah Curtin, *Tales of the Fairies and of the Ghost World* (1895), pp. 151–154. This is Christiansen migratory legend type 4080, known in Norway and common in Ireland. Here are some other versions: Lady Gregory, *The Kiltartan Wonder Book* (1910), pp. 52–55; John O'Donoghue, *In Kerry Long Ago* (1960), pp. 124–126; Seán Ó hEochaidh, *Fairy Legends from Donegal* (1977), pp. 222–225.

85 THE SWINE OF THE GODS W. B. Yeats, *The Celtic Twilight* (1902), pp. 113–114.

ILLNESS AND WITCHCRAFT

86 A PIG ON THE ROAD FROM GORT Lady Gregory, *Visions and Beliefs in the West of Ireland* (1970), p. 89.

87 THE CROOKENED BACK T. Crofton Croker, *Fairy Legends* (1862), pp. 149–152. When the tale ended, the narrator's grandson asked, "Granny, what was it?" She answered, "It was the Phooka."

88 MAURICE GRIFFIN THE FAIRY DOCTOR Jeremiah Curtin, *Tales of the Fairies and of the Ghost World* (1895), pp. 81–87.

89 BIDDY EARLY Lady Gregory, *Visions and Beliefs in the West of Ireland* (1970), pp. 45–47.

90 THE BLACK ART Henry Glassie, *Passing the Time in Ballymenone* (1982), pp. 535–536. In his notes to Lady Gregory's *Visions and Beliefs in the West of Ireland* (1970), p. 302, W. B. Yeats remarks that the story of the witch who changes into a hare is "the best remembered of all witch stories" in Ireland.

91 MAGICAL THEFT Séamas Ó Catháin, *Irish Life and Lore* (1982), pp. 25–27.

92 PAUDYEEN O'KELLY AND THE WEASEL Douglas Hyde, *Beside The Fire* (1890), pp. 72–91.

STRANGE SOUNDS AND VISIONS OF WAR

93 ONE QUEER EXPERIENCE Clifton Johnson, *The Isle of the Shamrock* (1901), pp. 202–204. Johnson does not name the narrator. I gathered it out of a book by another American traveler: Samuel Bayne, *On an Irish Jaunting-Car* (1902), p. 78.

94 MANY A ONE SAW WHAT WE SAW George A. Little, *Malachi Horan Remembers* (1944), pp. 30–32.

HISTORY

ANCIENT DAYS

95 THE OLD TIMES IN IRELAND Lady Gregory, *The Kiltartan History Book* (1926), pp. 13–14. The text in the first edition (1909) contains a different middle section. The opening, shared in both editions, derives from the *Book of Invasions of Ireland,* for which see Douglas Hyde, *A Literary History of Ireland* (1967),

pp. 281-292, and Thomas O'Rahilly, *Early Irish History and Mythology* (1976), pp. 75–170, 193–208.

96 THE BATH OF THE WHITE COWS Patrick Kennedy, *Legendary Fictions of the Irish Celts* (1866), pp. 304–307. The story seems to derive from Geoffrey Keating's *General History of Ireland.*

WAR

97 THE BATTLE OF THE FORD OF BISCUITS Henry Glassie, *Passing the Time in Ballymenone* (1982), pp. 213–215. Contemporary accounts of the battle, which took place in 1594, agree basically with Mr. Nolan's telling. See *Ballymenone,* pp. 630–633. A later telling of this story by Mr. Nolan appears in *Ballymenone,* pp. 656–659, and *Irish Folk History* (1982), pp. 41–44.

98 CROMWELL Séamas Ó Catháin, *The Bedside Book of Irish Folklore* (1980), pp. 57–58. Recorded for the Irish Folktale Commission by Seán Ó Flanagáin. Oliver Cromwell's violent Irish campaign of 1649–1650 engendered a great body of Irish legend.

99 CROMWELL'S BIBLE Sean O'Sullivan, "Cromwell in Oral Tradition," in Linda Dégh, Henry Glassie, and Felix Oinas, eds., *Folklore Today* (1976), pp. 479–480. While other versions of tale 98 have been found in Ireland (O'Sullivan provides one, pp. 477–478, and refers to others), this tale, though it incorporates international types (Aarne-Thompson type 1174, Christiansen migratory legend type 3020), has been recorded but once. Sean O'Sullivan supplies a pair of tales of Cromwell in *Folktales of Ireland* (1966), pp. 236–242. In letters of October 30 and November 19, 1984, Séamas Ó Catháin kindly supplied me with the name of the teller of this tale and the recording dates for tales of his own that he has allowed me to reprint in this anthology.

100 PATRICK SARSFIELD Lady Gregory, *The Kiltartan History Book* (1909), p. 18; (1926), pp. 46–47. Sarsfield was second in command at the defense of Limerick in 1690. Peter Flanagan sings a song commemorating his major success then: *Passing the Time in Ballymenone* (1982), pp. 694–695. The next year Sarsfield surrendered to the Williamite forces and left for France. Soon he was dead on the battlefield.

101 SARSFIELD SURRENDERS AND RORY TAKES TO THE HILLS Seumas MacManus, *Heavy Hangs the Golden Grain* (1952), pp. 158–159.

RAPPAREES

102 BLACK FRANCIS Henry Glassie, *Passing the Time in Ballymenone* (1982), pp. 47–49. Black Francis was hanged at Enniskillen in 1782.

103 SHAN BERNAGH Rose Shaw, *Carleton's Country* (1930), pp. 69–74. The Irish outlaw displayed his nobility in his gifts to the poor, his deference to women, his defense of the priest. Black Francis (tale 102) comparably fights for the priest in *Passing the Time in Ballymenone* (1982), pp. 132–136.

104 WILLIE BRENNAN Sean O'Sullivan, *Legends from Ireland* (1977), pp. 139–141. Recorded for the Irish Folklore Commission by Tomás Ó Ciardha. The first story is Aarne-Thompson international tale type 1527A; the second has attached itself to noble outlaws from Robin Hood to Jesse James, including Black Francis (tale 102): Peadar Livingstone, *The Fermanagh Story* (Enniskillen: Cumann Seanchais Chlochair, 1969), p. 131. Brennan has survived in memory from his time in the early nineteenth century to our own largely because of the folksong "Brennan on the Moor," for which see Colm O Lochlainn, *More Irish Street Ballads* (Dublin: Three Candles, 1965), pp. 144–145, 147.

LATER DAYS

105 WICKLOW IN THE RISING OF 1798 Pádraig Ó Tuathail, "Wicklow Traditions of 1798," *Béaloideas* (1935), pp. 155–187. The three extracts I lifted from Mrs. O'Toole's narrative are found on pp. 155–157, 174–176, 168–174. Séamas Ó Catháin includes a different excerpt from her account in *The Bedside Book of Irish Folklore* (1980), pp. 29–31.

106 THE FAMINE Lady Gregory, *The Kiltartan History Book* (1926), pp. 77–80. The first of these two statements also appears in the first edition (1909), pp. 34–35. The dreadful tale of the Famine of 1846–1848 is told by Cecil Woodham-Smith in *The Great Hunger* (London: Hamish Hamilton, 1962).

107 VICTORY IN THE TIME OF FAMINE Henry Glassie, *Passing the Time in Ballymenone* (1982), p. 518; *Irish Folk History* (1982), pp. 95–96. This tale is possibly a transformation of Aarne-Thompson international type 832. The late Alex McConnell, father of the great musician Cathal, recorded a version of this legend from Michael Boyle's uncle for the Irish Folklore Commission. It is found in manuscript book 1403 (1955), pp. 26–27, in the archive at the Department of Irish Folklore of the University of Dublin College at Belfield.

108 RUINED BY POETRY Robin Flower, *The Western Island* (1945), pp. 19–21. Ó Crithin is Tomás Ó Crohan, author of *The Islandman* (1935).

FIRESIDE TALES

FENIAN TALES

109 THE BIRTH OF FINN MAC CUMHAIL Jeremiah Curtin, *Myths and Folk-Lore of Ireland* (1906), pp. 204–220. In 1887, Curtin collected mainly in Limerick, Donegal, and Galway; my ascription to Donegal is but a guess. This tale begins as number 1 of Sean O'Sullivan's catalogue of Tales of the Fianna in *A Handbook of Irish Folklore* (1963), pp. 589–590, then it swings out to embrace Aarne-Thompson international tale types 1137, famous from the *Odyssey,* and 300 (see tales 114 and 115 in this collection). Curtin's tale brings Finn into the world. A good selection of tales of Finn at his peak awaits you within part 2 of Sean

O'Sullivan's *Folktales of Ireland* (1966). Finn at the end is amusingly, sadly portrayed in Flann O'Brien's wonderful novel *At Swim-Two-Birds* (1939).

110 THE HIGH KING OF LOCHLANN AND THE FENIANS OF ERIN Jeremiah Curtin, *Irish Folk-Tales* (1943), pp. 113–124. First published in the *New York Sun*, November 6, 1892. Much of Curtin's work in 1892 was conducted in Kerry, but my attribution to Kerry is only a guess. In his notes to the tale (p. 163), James H. Delargy says this is a folk version of a literary tale, the earliest text of which dates to 1603. It has been found in oral tradition in Scotland and in Donegal.

111 USHEEN'S RETURN TO IRELAND Lady Gregory, *The Kiltartan History Book* (1926), pp. 20–22. This sequence of two tales does not appear in the first edition (1909). This is number 18 in Sean O'Sullivan's typology of Fenian tales in *A Handbook of Irish Folklore* (1963), p. 593, and is O'Sullivan-Christiansen Irish folktale type 470*, known especially in Connacht and Munster and related to Aarne-Thompson international tale type 470*, most usual in northern and eastern Europe.

MATURITY

112 FAIR, BROWN, AND TREMBLING Jeremiah Curtin, *Myths and Folk-Lore of Ireland* (1906), pp. 78–92. In 1887, Curtin collected mainly in Limerick, Donegal, and Galway; my ascription to Galway is but a guess. This is Aarne-Thompson international tale type 510, Cinderella, common throughout Europe, with type 403 as an appendage.

113 THE CORPSE WATCHERS Patrick Kennedy, *Legendary Fictions of the Irish Celts* (1866), pp. 54–57. Versions of Aarne-Thompson international tale type 480, The Kind and the Unkind Girls, are common throughout Europe. Kennedy wrote of this tale that it was the "one which was repeated oftenest in our hearing during our country experience. It probably owed its popularity to the bit of a rhyme, and the repetition of the adventures of the three sisters, nearly in the same words. It may seem strange that this circumstance, which would have brought *ennui* and discomfort on our readers, should have recommended it to the fireside audiences. Let it be considered that they expected to sit up to a certain hour, and that listening to a story was the pleasantest occupation they could fancy for the time. Length, then, in a tale was a recommendation, and these repetitions contributed to that desirable end."

114 A WIDOW'S SON John Millington Synge, *The Aran Islands* (1911), pp. 78–84. After opening with a suggestion of Aarne-Thompson international tale type 1640, this settles into the usual Irish version of Aarne-Thompson type 300, the most common *Märchen* in Ireland. See Sean O'Sullivan, *Storytelling in Irish Tradition* (1973), p. 16. The distribution of this tale type is global. It is known in Africa and America, and it is particularly common in India, Greece, Russia, Hungary, Germany, France, Denmark, and Norway, though Ireland has yielded the largest number of versions.

115 JACK AND BILL W. B. Yeats, *The Celtic Twilight* (1902), pp. 209–230. This story, combining Aarne-Thompson international tale types 303 and 300, came from the fieldwork Lady Gregory reported in *Poets and Dreamers* (1903). Her version of the tale appears in *The Kiltartan Wonder Book* (1910), pp. 31–51.

116 THE MULE Lady Gregory, *The Kiltartan Wonder Book* (1910), pp. 1–7. This story seems to gather Aarne-Thompson international tale types 550, 531, and 329 into a distinctly Irish form.

117 THE KING OF IRELAND'S SON Brendan Behan, *Brendan Behan's Island* (1962), pp. 136–141. As can be seen from O'Sullivan and Christiansen's *Types of the Irish Folktale,* pp. 116–117, the incorporation of Aarne-Thompson international tale type 329 into type 550 is frequent in Ireland.

WIT AND FAITH

118 HUDDON AND DUDDON AND DONALD O'LEARY Unpublished. Tape-recorded from Hugh Nolan, November 28, 1972. I also recorded this tale from Mr. Nolan on June 11, 1977. The history of this story provides us a good means for examining the creativity of the storyteller who must, Mr. Nolan said, repeat the tale accurately while using words of his own. Mr. Nolan learned the story from a Christmas number of the *Fermanagh Herald,* published in Enniskillen. Although the paper's editor, Mr. P. J. O'Hare, could not find it when he generously searched his files for me, the story was surely reprinted from W. B. Yeats' "Donald and his Neighbours," in *Fairy and Folk Tales of the Irish Peasantry* (1888), reprinted in *Fairy and Folk Tales of Ireland* (1973), pp. 270–273. Yeats got the story from a chapbook, *Royal Hibernian Tales,* published in 1825. Before that it had been in oral circulation in County Antrim, and it is Aarne-Thompson international tale type 1535, which is especially common in India and Germany, and which I have heard in the southern United States and once published: "Three Southern Mountain Jack Tales," *Tennessee Folklore Society Bulletin* 30, no. 3 (1964): 88–102 (which also includes a version of type 300, Ireland's most usual *Märchen*). Michael Boyle learned the story from Hugh Nolan, and their tellings made it the most popular "fireside tale" of the next generation in Ballymenone. Mr. Nolan's story is longer and richer than his source. Here, for comparison, is the opening of the tale as Mr. Nolan would have read it: "Hudden and Dudden and Donald O'Nery were near neighbours in the barony of Balinconlig, and ploughed with three bullocks; but the two former, envying the present prosperity of the latter, determined to kill his bullock, to prevent his farm being properly cultivated and laboured, that going into the world he might be induced to sell his lands, which they meant to get possession of." The whole text of the original is not only in Yeats' anthology; it is in *Béaloideas* 10 (1940), pp. 184–186, and Séamas Ó Catháin, *The Bedside Book of Irish Folklore* (1980), pp. 51–55. You would find it fascinating to read Mr. Nolan's oral performance against the entire written text from which he learned the tale.

119 THE THREE WISHES William Carleton, *Tales and Stories of the Irish Peasantry* (1846), pp. 330–357. Here Carleton retells one of Ireland's most popular stories, Aarne-Thompson international tale type 330, known throughout Europe.

120 WILLY THE WISP Michael J. Murphy, *Now You're Talking* (1975), pp. 120–123 Hugh Nolan and Peter Flanagan both remembered this tale—Aarne-Thompson international type 330—as being the most popular story of their youth. Hugh McGiveney named one of his cats Willy the Wisp: see tale 40 in this collection.

121 THE BUIDEACH, THE TINKER, AND THE BLACK DONKEY Douglas Hyde, *Legends of Saints and Sinners* (1915), pp. 247–257. Structured like a *Märchen,* incorporating memories of Aarne-Thompson international tale types 531 and 580*, this story centers upon the supernatural to become something peculiarly Irish.

122 THE MAN WHO HAD NO STORY Séamas Ó Catháin, "An Fear nach rabh Scéal ar bith aige," *Béaloideas* (1969–1970), pp. 55–59. Ó Catháin's paper includes the text in Irish, and he reprinted the English text in *The Bedside Book of Irish Folktale* (1980), pp. 81–86. This is O'Sullivan-Christiansen Irish folktale type 2412B. Sean O'Sullivan's *Folktales of Ireland* (1966), pp. 182–184, contains another version of this characteristically Irish story.

PERMISSIONS ACKNOWLEDGMENTS

Grateful acknowledgment is made to the authors, publishers, and other copyright holders for permission to reprint the following previously published material:

"Owen Roe O'Sullivan," "The Horse's Last Drunk," and "Cats Are Queer Articles" from *The Tailor and Ansty* by Eric Cross. Reprinted by permission of Devin-Adair Publishers.

"The King of Ireland's Son" from *Brendan Behan's Island* by Brendan Behan. Copyright © 1962 by Brendan Behan and Paul Hogarth. Reprinted by permission of Hope, Leresche & Sayle.

"An Actual Saint" from *Our Like Will Not Be There Again* by Lawrence Millman. Copyright © 1977 by Lawrence Millman. Reprinted by permission of Little, Brown & Company.

"Sarsfield Surrenders and Rory Takes to the Hills" from *Heavy Hangs the Golden Grain* by Seumas MacManus. Copyright 1950 by Seumas MacManus. Copyright renewed 1977. Reprinted by permission of Patricia MacManus.

"The Pious Man," "The Coffin," "The Blood of Adam," and "The Feet Water" from *Folktales of the Irish Countryside* by Kevin Danaher; "Saved by the Priest," "Terry the Grunter," and "Magical Theft" from *Irish Life and Love* by Séamas Ó Catháin; "Columcille's Coffin," "The First Mirror," and "Cromwell" from *The Bedside Book of Irish Folklore* by Séamas Ó Catháin. Reprinted by permission of The Mercier Press Ltd. "Terry the Grunter " and "Cromwell" also by permission of the Head of the Department of Irish Folklore, University College, Belfield, Dublin.

"Old Thorns and Old Priests," "The Three Questions," "Half a Blanket," "A Hungry Hired Boy," "The Lawyer and the Devil," and "Willy the Wisp" from *Now You're Talking* by Michael J. Murphy. Reprinted by permission of Michael J. Murphy and Blackstaff Press, Belfast.

"Hare and Hound," collected by Michael J. Murphy, and "Grandfather's Ghost," collected by Ronald H. Buchanan, *Ulster Folklife Magazine.* Reprinted by permission of the collectors, and the Ulster Folklife Society. "Hare and Hound" also by permission of Prof. Bo Almqvist, Department of Irish Folklore, University College, Belfield, Dublin.

"How the Shoemaker Saved His Wife," "The Blacksmith of Bedlam and the Fairy Host," "The Fairy Shilling," and "The Fairy Rabbit and the Blessed Earth of Tory" from *Fairy Legends from Donegal* by Sean Ó hEochaidh. Reprinted by permission of the Department of Irish Folklore, University College, Belfield, Dublin.

"The Baptism of Conor MacNessa," "Saint Finbar," and "Willie Brennan" from *Legends from Ireland* by Sean O'Sullivan. Reprinted by permission of Sean O'Sullivan.

"No Man Goes Beyond His Day," "The Grave of His Father," "Taken," and "Ruined by Poetry" from *The Western Island* by Robin Flower. Reprinted by permission of Oxford University Press.

"Fairy Property," and "The Cats' Judgment" from *Lovely Is the Lee* by Robert Gibbings. Reprinted by permission of Laurence Pollinger Limited, and the Estate of Robert Gibbings.

"The Soldier in the Haunted House," "Wicklow in the Rising of 1798," and "The Man Who Had No Story" reprinted from *Béaloideas* by permission of the Folklore of Ireland Society, Department of Modern Irish, University College, Galway.

"A Clock Token," "The Banshee Cries for the O'Briens," "We Had One of Them in